Citizen Politics

Public Opinion and Political Parties in Advanced Industrial Democracies

FOURTH EDITION

RUSSELL J. DALTON

UNIVERSITY OF CALIFORNIA, IRVINE

CQ PRESS

A DIVISION OF CONGRESSIONAL QUARTERLY INC.
WASHINGTON, DC

CQ Press
1255 22nd Street, NW, Suite 400
Washington, DC 20037

Phone, 202-729-1900; toll-free, 1-866-427-7737 (1-866-4CQ-PRESS)

Web: www.cqpress.com

Cover design: Circle Graphics

☉ The paper used in this publication exceeds the requirements of the American National Standard for Information Sciences—Permanence of Paper for Printed Library Materials, ANSI Z39.48-1992.

Printed and bound in the United States of America

09   08   07   06   05   1   2   3   4   5

Library of Congress Cataloging-in-Publication Data

Dalton, Russell J.
  Citizen politics : public opinion and political parties in advanced industrial democracies / Russell J. Dalton.—4th ed.
     p. cm.
Includes bibliographical references and index.
  ISBN 1-56802-999-3 (softcover : alk. paper)
  1. Political parties. 2. Political participation. 3. Democracy. 4. Public opinion. 5. Comparative government.   I. Title.

  JF2011.D34 2006
  323'.042—dc22

                                                                            2005016096

To my three sons,
Penn, Mac, and Snickers

Contents

Tables and Figures

FIGURES

Preface

When I began work on the first edition of this book in the 1980s, many political scientists were openly expressing reservations about the viability of modern democracy. President Jimmy Carter lamented that the gap between American citizens and their government had never been so wide. Prognostications about a future crisis of democracy were commonplace.

Against this backdrop, the first edition of *Citizen Politics* (1988) argued that democracy was alive and well in the advanced industrial democracies, whose citizens believed in the democratic creed and wanted their governments to meet these expectations. The first edition presented evidence of contemporary publics becoming more active in the political process, more likely to participate in elite-challenging activities, more likely to vote on issues and other policy criteria, and more demanding of their representatives. If democracy was in crisis, it was one of institutions, not of the democratic spirit among citizens.

Events ultimately overtook this contrarian perspective in support of democracy. The toppling of the Berlin Wall, the collapse of communism in the Soviet Union and Eastern Europe, and the spread of democracy in the 1990s created a euphoria surrounding the democratic process. Even those who had proclaimed the limits of democracy a few years earlier now trumpeted this new wave of democratization. Suddenly it seemed apparent to everyone that democracy represented the start of a new era.

Many rushed to join the new parade, but I remained skeptical of fads—even those reinforcing my own views. My approach to academic trends instead continued to follow the advice of Will Rogers, who compared politics to keeping your balance onboard a ship: when the ship leans left, you should lean right; when the ship leans right, you should lean left. Thus, in revising subsequent editions of *Citizen Politics,* I highlighted the strengths of democratic processes, but also the problems confronting democracy in meeting contemporary challenges.

Before celebrating the inevitability of democracy, we should acknowledge that advanced industrial societies are today addressing new issues, new styles of participation, the inclusion of new groups, and new expectations for democracy—profound changes transforming the nature of the democratic process. These shifts in citizen politics represent opportunities for expanding the process as well as risks. The individual societies must respond to these challenges if democratization is to continue. Indeed, I would argue that the ability to adapt provides democracy its strength.

This book introduces students to what is known about citizens' political behavior, questions about it that remain unanswered, and the implications of findings thus far. The analyses focus on citizen politics in the United States, Great Britain, Germany, and France, and with this new edition expands comparative coverage to examine these four nations in a larger, cross-national context. Students of comparative politics can examine the rich variety of public opinion in different democracies, and those interested in only one nation will nonetheless benefit from comparisons that highlight the similarities and dissimilarities among these nations.

I hope this book is of value to several audiences, but it was primarily written for classroom use in courses on comparative political parties, public opinion, and European politics. The first half (chapters 1–6) introduces the principles of public opinion and the broad contours of citizen action and citizen beliefs. The second half (chapters 7–11) covers party alignments and can be combined, in the second part of the school term, with other texts on political parties. The volume concludes with a discussion of citizen attitudes toward democratic institutions and the political process and the choices that face the various polities.

A new feature of this fourth edition is a data supplement from the 1999–2002 World Values Survey/European Values Survey. These data are used throughout the book, and a subset of items is available to instructors. Appendix B details the list of variables, and matching SPSS files are available online at http://www.cqpress.com/cs/dalton. I find that computer-based research projects on public opinion enrich the subject matter of the course for students and provide them with a firsthand opportunity to understand the process of public opinion research.

At the graduate level, this book is a useful core text for courses on West European politics or comparative political behavior. It summarizes the existing knowledge in the field and introduces the controversies that at present divide researchers. I hope instructors find that this introductory analysis facilitates discussion of readings from primary research materials. Even senior scholars may find familiar data interpreted in new and thought-provoking ways.

ACKNOWLEDGMENTS

For four editions, my research has benefited from the advice and criticism of colleagues, comments of students who have used this text, and insights I have gained from working with other scholars. I am deeply indebted to Kendall Baker and Kai Hildebrandt for their collaboration on *Germany Transformed*. Many of the themes we first explored in that book appear in more comparative terms in these pages. I am also fortunate to have worked with an exceptional group of scholars on the Political Action project, which shaped my understanding of political participation. More important, many of these individuals have become career-long colleagues and friends: Samuel Barnes, Max Kaase, Hans-Dieter Klingemann, and M. Kent Jennings. Most recently, Martin Wattenberg and I collaborated on *Parties without Partisans,* an edited study of party change from which I borrowed several ideas. I have benefited greatly from Marty's advice.

During the writing of this book, many others helped with advice, survey data, or moral support. Paul Abramson, Paul Beck, Scott Flanagan, Dieter Fuchs, Manfred Kuechler, Michael Lewis-Beck, Mary MacIntosh, Lamont Rodgers, Robert Rohrschneider, and Martin Wattenberg commented on the manuscript throughout the various editions. I also appreciate the reviewers for this new edition: Hans-Dieter Klingemann, Wissenschaftszentrum Berlin; Geoffrey Evans, Oxford University; Neal G. Jesse, Bowling Green State University; and Hubert Tworzecki, Emory University. An equal debt is due to the students in my Citizen Politics course at the University of California, Irvine, who have used this book and shared their reactions.

This is the first edition of the book published by CQ Press. It has been a great pleasure to work with such a quality publisher. As Rick said in Casablanca, "I think this is the start of a beautiful friendship." I want to thank the editors who worked on the project: Katharine Miller, Charisse Kiino, Colleen Ganey, and Sally Ryman.

I also want to acknowledge a special debt to Ronald Inglehart. Ron was my mentor at the University of Michigan, and his provocative views about citizen politics have deeply influenced my own thinking. He has developed the World Values Survey into a global resource for social science research; many of the analyses in this book are based upon World Values Survey data. I have always admired Ron's enthusiasm for social research and his creativity as a scholar. In innumerable ways, I am in his debt.

This book has a bold objective: to provide an overview of the nature of citizen politics in advanced industrial democracies. The task is clearly beyond the means of one individual, but with a little help from these friends, the resulting product begins to outline the political changes and choices that today face the citizenry in these established democracies.

CHAPTER 1

Introduction

THIS IS a book about you and me—as citizens, voters, protesters, campaign workers, community activists, party members, and political spectators—we are the driving force of the democratic process. Within the established democracies, the spectacle of an American party convention, the intensity of a French farmers' protest, the community spirit of a New England town meeting, or the dedication of an English environmental group creates an equally impressive image of the amazing democratic process.

Granting power to the people, even if that process is incomplete, is a radical development in the course of human history. A generation ago, scholars worried that democracy was limited to a small set of Western nations. Other analysts were concerned about the viability of democracy even in these nations. Then, the world changed: we watched in awe as the force of "people power" tore down the Berlin Wall, led to freedom in South Africa, brought democracy back to the Philippines, and created a democratization wave on a global scale. Many of the nations of Eastern Europe that were once part of the Soviet empire are now members of the European Union and offer new freedoms and liberties to their citizens. New democracies have been established in East Asia and in Africa. Still, despite the recent spread of democratization, barely half of the world's nations have real democratic institutions and procedures.

While it is intriguing to look at these new democracies and their people (and we will do so at times), our inquiry here focuses on citizen politics in the established democracies of the West. These established democratic systems provide models of success for the new democracies, and yet, because the process of democratization itself is open-ended, we shall argue that the expansion of citizen influence is a continuing challenge even for the established democracies.

As the democratization wave swept across the world in the 1990s, it created a temporary euphoria about the democratic process among Western publics. Some claimed that liberal democracy represented the "end of history" and that eventually all nations would become democratic (Fukuyama 1992). Soon, however, new concerns emerged about the potential political problems facing the established democracies. Some scholars argue that social and civic engagement is weakening, which threatens the vitality of the democratic process, while others point to growing popular skepticism about the politicians, parties, and political institutions that are the essential elements of the democratic process. Ironically, democracy's success in winning

1

the Cold War is accompanied by new questions about the vitality of its own process.

This book presents a populist view of democracy, emphasizing the attitudes and behaviors of the average citizen. Our analyses are therefore incomplete; we do not study the role of elites, interest groups, and other political actors. We also do not presume that the public is all-knowing or all-powerful. Indeed, there are many examples of the public's ignorance or error on policy issues (as there are examples of elite errors), as well as many instances in which policymakers disregard the public's preferences. The democratic process, like all human activities, is imperfect—but its strength lies in the premise that people are the best judges of their own destiny. The success of democracy is largely measured by the public's participation in the process, the respect for citizen rights, and the responsiveness of the system to popular demands. As Adlai Stevenson once said, in a democracy the people get the kind of government they deserve (for better or worse).

Before proceeding, we should acknowledge the complexity of the topic of the citizen's role in democracy. It is difficult to make simple generalizations about public opinion because the public is not homogeneous. There is not a single public. The public in any nation consists of millions of individuals, each with his or her own view of the world and of the citizen's role in politics. Some people are liberal, some moderate, some conservative; others are socialist, reactionary, communist, or none of the above. Opinions are often divided on contemporary political issues—this is why the issues are controversial and require a political decision. Some people favor strict environmental laws; some see environmental standards as excessive. Some favor international trade; some are skeptical of its claimed benefits. The study of public opinion underscores the diversity of the public.

People also differ in the extent of their political interest and in the experiences they bring to politics. Although a few individuals are full-time political activists, most people have modest political interests and ambitions. On some issues a broad spectrum of society may be involved; other issues are greeted with apathy. Public opinion generally defines the acceptable bounds of politics, within which political elites resolve the remaining controversies. When elites exceed these bounds, or when the issues immediately affect people's lives, the potential for political action is great. The difficulty is to understand and predict which course of action the public will choose.

In short, as social scientists we deal with the most complex problem in nature: to understand and predict human behavior. Yet this is not a hopeless task. The development of scientific public opinion surveys provides a valuable tool for researchers. From a sample of a few thousand precisely selected individuals, we can make reliable statements about the distribution of attitudes and opinions (Weisberg et al. 1996). The survey interview allows us not only to observe behavior but also to study the motivations and expectations guiding behavior. Furthermore, researchers can divide a survey into subgroups to examine the diversity in individual opinions.

Readers will find that this is book relies heavily on public opinion surveys. I do not claim that all we know about the public is found in the statistics and percentages of public opinion surveys. Some of the most insightful writings about political behavior are qualitative studies of the topic. And yet, even insightful political analysts may make contradictory claims about the public. The value of the empirical method is that it provides a specific reference standard against which we can measure contrasting descriptions of public opinion or behavior. Surveys enable people to describe their political views in their own words, and thus survey research offers a tremendously valuable research tool for social scientists.

Drawing on an extensive collection of opinion surveys, this book examines the nature of public opinion in several advanced industrial democracies.[1] We describe how individuals view politics, how they participate in the process, what opinions they hold, and how they choose their leaders through competitive elections. These findings should further our understanding of citizen politics and thereby of the working of the political process in contemporary democracies.

THE COMPARATIVE STUDY OF PUBLIC OPINION

This is an explicitly comparative study, exploring public opinion and political behavior in several democracies. Our goal is to strike a balance between attention to national detail and the general characteristics of citizens that transcend national boundaries.

There are several advantages to the comparative study of political behavior in Western democracies. A common historical and cultural tradition unites Europe and North America. Although these nations differ in the specifics of their government and party systems, they share broad similarities in the functioning of the democratic process and the role of the citizen in the process. A comparative approach thus provides a basis for studying those aspects of political behavior that should be valid across nations. General theories of why people participate in democratic politics should apply to citizens regardless of their nationality. Theories to explain party preferences should hold for Americans and Europeans if they represent basic features of human nature. And yet, most of the major studies of public opinion focus only on one nation.

In most instances we expect to find similar patterns of behavior in different democracies. If our theories do not function similarly across nations, however, then we have learned something new and important. Science often progresses by finding exceptions to general theory, which necessitate further theoretical work. The same applies to social science.

Comparative analysis also allows us to examine the effects of political structures on citizens' political behavior. For example, does the nature of a nation's electoral system affect the public's voting behavior? Or, does the structure of political institutions affect the patterns of political participation?

Each nation represents a "natural experiment" wherein general theories of political behavior can be tested in a different political context.

Finally, even if we are interested only in a single nation, comparative research is still very valuable. An old Hebrew riddle expresses this idea: "*Question*: Who first discovered water? *Answer:* I don't know, but it wasn't a fish." Immersing oneself in a single environment makes the defining characteristics of that environment unobtrusive and unnoticed. It is difficult to understand what is unique and distinctive about American political behavior, for example, by studying only American politics. Indeed, many students of American politics may be surprised to learn that the United States is often the atypical case in cross-national comparisons. American public opinion and political processes are unique in many ways, but we perceive this only by rising above the waters.

THE CHOICE OF NATIONS

To balance our needs for comparison and attention to national differences, we focus on citizen politics in four nations: the United States, Great Britain, the Federal Republic of Germany (FRG), and France.[2] The choice of these nations was based on several criteria. By many standards, these are the major powers among the Western democracies. Their population, size, economy, military strength, and political influence earn them leadership positions in international circles. The actions of any of these nations can have significant consequences for all the others.

These nations also were chosen because they highlight many of the significant variations in the structure of democratic politics. Table 1.1 summarizes some of the most important differences. For example, Great Britain has a pure parliamentary system of government. The popularly elected House of Commons selects the prime minister to head the executive branch. This produces a fusion of legislative and executive power, because the same party and the same group of elites direct both branches of government. In contrast, American government has a presidential system, with extensive checks and balances to maintain a separation of legislative and executive power. French politics functions within a modified presidential system. The public directly elects both the president and the National Assembly, which selects the premier to head the administration of government. Germany has a parliamentary system, with the popularly elected Bundestag selecting the chancellor as head of the executive branch. The German system, however, also includes a strong federal structure and a separation of powers that is uncommon for a parliamentary government. Perceptive analyses of these contrasting institutional forms and their implications for the nature of democratic politics are found in the research of Arend Lijphart (1999).

Electoral systems are equally diverse. Great Britain and the United States select the members of their national legislatures from single-member districts, where a plurality is sufficient for election. Germany uses a hybrid system for Bundestag elections; half the deputies are elected from single-member dis-

TABLE 1.1 A Comparison of Political Systems

National Characteristic	United States	Great Britain	Germany	France
Population (in millions)	290.3	60.1	82.4	60.1
Gross domestic product/capita	$36,300	$25,500	$26,200	$26,000
Political regime established	1789	Seventeenth century	1949	1958
State form	Republic	Constitutional monarchy	Republic	Republic
Government structure	Presidential	Parliamentary	Modified parliamentary	Modified presidential
Chief executive	President	Prime minister	Chancellor	President
Method of selection	Direct election	Elected by parliament	Elected by parliament	Direct election
Legislature	Bicameral	Bicameral	Bicameral	Bicameral
Lower house	House of Representatives	House of Commons	Bundestag	National Assembly
Upper house	Senate	House of Lords	Bundesrat	Senate
Power of upper house	Equal	Weaker	Equal on state issues	Weaker
Electoral system				
Lower house	Single-member districts	Single-member districts	Proportional representation & single-member districts	Single-member districts
Upper house	Statewide elections	Inheritance & appointment	Appointed by states	Appointed by communes
Major Parties	Democrats Republicans	Labour Liberal Democrats Conservatives	Democratic Socialist (PDS) Greens Social Democrats Free Democrats Christian Democrats (CDU/CSU)	Communists Socialists Greens UDF Gaullists (UPM) National Front

SOURCE: Compiled by the author; population and GNP statistics are 2002 data from CIA *World Factbook*.

tricts and half are selected from party lists. The French electoral system is based on deputies winning a majority in single-member districts, with a second ballot (*tour*) if no candidate receives a majority on the first ballot. Rein Taagepera and Matthew Shugart (1989) and G. Bingham Powell (2000) have presented excellent studies of how such institutional arrangements can affect electoral outcomes.

The party systems of these four nations are also varied. Party competition in the United States is usually limited to the Democratic and Republican parties. Both are broad "catchall" parties that combine diverse political groups into weakly structured electoral coalitions. In contrast, most European political parties are hierarchically organized and firmly controlled by the party leadership. Candidates are elected primarily because of their party label and not because of their personal attributes; in the legislature most party members vote as a bloc. Party options are also more diverse in Europe. British voters can select from at least three major party groups; Germans have five major parties in the Bundestag. French party politics is synonymous with diversity and political polarization. Jacques Fauvet described French politics in the following terms:

> France contains two fundamental temperaments—that of the left and right; three principal tendencies, if one adds the center; six spiritual families; ten parties, large or small, traversed by multiple currents; fourteen parliamentary groups without much discipline; and forty million opinions. (quoted in Ehrmann and Schain 1992, 231)

Although Fauvet was describing French politics in the late 1950s, much of his description still applies today. France, a nation of perpetual political effervescence, provides the spice of comparative politics.

The contrasts across nations take on an added dimension as a consequence of German unification. Western Germans have developed the characteristics of a stable, advanced industrial democracy; the former East Germany, like most of the rest of Eastern Europe, is only beginning this process. Democracy is a relatively new experience for eastern Germans, whose understanding of the democratic process and commitment to democratic norms are uncertain. Furthermore, when possible, we broaden the scope of our cross-national comparisons to place our four nations in the context of other advanced industrial democracies.

A NEW STYLE OF CITIZEN POLITICS

The reader will quickly realize that this volume emphasizes the changing nature of citizen political behavior. I maintain that these changes derive from the socioeconomic transformation of the Western societies over the past fifty years. These nations are developing a set of characteristics that collectively represent a new form of *advanced industrial* or *postindustrial* society (Bell 1973; Inglehart 1977, 1990).

The most dramatic changes involve economic conditions. An unprecedented expansion of economic well-being occurred in the second half of the twentieth century. The economies of Western Europe and North America grew at phenomenal rates in the post–World War II decades. For example, analysts describe the astonishing expansion of the West German economy as the *Wirtschaftswunder* (Economic Miracle). Average income levels in our four nations are several times greater than at any time in prewar history. By most economic standards, the four nations of this study rank among the most affluent nations of the world.

A restructured labor force is another major change in society. The size of the agricultural workforce has decreased dramatically in most Western nations, and industrial employment has remained stable or declined; employment in the service sector has increased markedly. In addition, because of the expansion of national and local governments, public employment now constitutes a significant share of the labor force. All four of the core nations in this volume have passed Daniel Bell's (1973) threshold for postindustrialism: half of the labor force employed in the service or governmental sector.

Advanced industrialism is also associated with changes in the context of the workplace and the residential neighborhood. The continuing decline of rural populations and the expanding size of metropolitan centers stimulate changes in life expectations and lifestyles. Urbanization brings an increasing separation of the home from the workplace, a greater diversity of occupations and interests, an expanded range of career opportunities, and more geographic and social mobility. With these trends come changes in the forms of social interaction, as communal forms of organization are replaced by voluntary associations, which in turn become less institutionalized and more spontaneous in organization. Communities are becoming less bounded; individuals are involved in increasingly complex and competing social networks that divide their loyalties; and institutional ties are becoming more fluid.

Educational opportunities also have expanded rapidly over the past several decades. European governments historically restricted university education to a privileged few, while the vast majority of their citizens received minimal education (often only four years). In the late 1930s the proportion of university students among 20–24 year olds was only 1 percent in England, 1 percent in Germany, and 3 percent in France. Access to education broadened after World War II, however, as minimal education standards were raised and university enrollments skyrocketed. By 1997 about half of college-age European youth were enrolled in some form of tertiary schooling, as were over three-quarters of American youth (World Bank 2000). This expansion of academic opportunities has fundamentally changed the educational composition of contemporary mass publics.

These increases in education have been accompanied by parallel increases in information resources. The electronic media, especially television, have experienced exceptional growth, and access to other information sources, such as books and magazines, has increased. Even more revolutionary has been the rapid development of electronic information processing: computers, the Internet, and related technologies. Information is no longer a scarce commodity. Indeed, the contemporary information problem is how to adapt to life in cyberspace, managing an ever-growing volume of sophisticated knowledge.

Western democracies have also changed the extent of government involvement in society. Two world wars and the Great Depression expanded the government's role in economic and social activities, and Western publics now hold government responsible for protecting and managing society. Many European societies have developed extensive welfare programs, where a network of generous social programs protect the individual against economic or medical hardship. Unemployment, illness, and similar problems still occur, but under the welfare state, their consequences are less dire than during earlier periods. In addition, government is now seen as responsible for protecting the environment, ensuring social rights, enabling lifestyle choices, and a host of other new obligations.

Despite these trends, there has been mounting public concern in Europe, North America, and Japan about whether this developmental trend can continue. Everywhere, it seems, there has been a retrenchment in government social programs. Increased international economic competition has created new economic strains within these nations. Elation about the end of the Cold War and the democratization of Eastern Europe has been tempered by worries about growing nationalism, international terrorism, ethnic conflict, and new financial burdens. In some established democracies, there are real worries that economic problems will revive reactionary political groups.

Admittedly, the miraculous economic growth rates of the post–World War II period can seem like distant history. And yet the transformation of Western democracies involves more than simply the politics of affluence. Changes in occupational and social structures are continuing, and with them an alteration in life conditions and lifestyles. Expanded educational opportunities represent an enduring trait of modern societies. The information revolution is continuing—in fact it is growing at an amazing rate. Advanced industrial societies are dramatically different from their pre-1950s predecessors.

This book maintains that one result of these social changes is the development of a new style of citizen politics. Our premise is that as the socioeconomic characteristics of these nations have changed, so too have the characteristics of the public. More educational opportunities mean a growth in political skills and resources, producing the most sophisticated publics in the history of democracies. Changing economic conditions redefine citizens' issue interests. The weakening of social networks and institutional loyalties is associated with the decline of traditional political alignments and voting patterns. Contemporary publics and contemporary democratic politics have been dramatically transformed over the past several decades.

The elements of this new style of citizen politics are not always, or necessarily, linked together. Some elements may be transitory; others may be coincidental. Nevertheless, several traits coexist for the present, defining a new pattern of citizen political behavior. The goal of this volume is to systematically describe this new pattern of political thought and action.

One aspect of the new citizen politics is political participation (chapters 2–4). Greater participation in political and economic decision making is an important social goal. Participation in elections is the most common form of political action—but this form is declining in most nations. At the same time, protest, citizen action groups, and unconventional political participation are increasing. Citizens are less likely to be passive subjects and more likely to demand a say in the decisions affecting their lives. The new style of citizen politics reflects a more active participation in the democratic process.

Another broad area of change involves the values and attitudes of the public (chapters 5–6). Industrial societies aimed at providing affluence and economic security. The success of advanced industrialism fulfills many basic economic needs for a sizable sector of society. Thus the concerns of some people are shifting to new political goals (Inglehart 1990, 1997). Several of these new issues are common to advanced industrial democracies: social equality, environmental protection, the dangers of nuclear energy, sexual equality, and human rights. In some instances, historic conditions have focused these general concerns on specific national problems—for example, racial equality in the United States, regional conflicts in Britain, or center-periphery differences in France. Many of these issues are now loosely integrated into an alternative political agenda that is another element of the new style of citizen politics.

Partisan politics is also changing (chapters 7–11). Until recently, comparative party research emphasized the stability of democratic party systems. This situation has changed. Stable party alignments are weakening, producing increased fragmentation and volatility in most Western party systems. Declining class differences in voting behavior reflect the general erosion in the social bases of voting. Studies in most of these nations document a decline in the public's identification with political parties and growing disenchantment with parties in general. These patterns have produced a *dealignment* of contemporary party systems (Dalton and Wattenberg 2000).

These trends are at least partially the result of the addition of new issues to the political agenda and the difficulties the established parties have had in responding to these issues. New parties have arisen across the face of Europe—ranging from green parties on the New Left to New Right parties at the opposite end of the political spectrum—while new political movements seek access to the Democratic and Republican parties in the United States. Increased party volatility is also caused by the changing characteristics of contemporary publics. Unsophisticated voters once relied on social-group cues and partisan cues to make their political decisions. Because of the dramatic spread of education and information sources, however, more people can now deal with the complexities of politics and make their own political decisions.

Consequently, issues and other short-term factors are becoming a more important basis of voting behavior as the influence of traditional group and party allegiances wanes. The new style of citizen politics features a more issue-oriented and candidate-oriented electorate.

Finally, public orientations toward government represent a new paradox for democracy (chapter 12). New issues have been added to the agenda; the democratic process has become more inclusive; and the government has generally improved the quality of life—but at the same time people have become more critical of government. The conflict over new issues and new participation patterns may offer a partial explanation of these trends. In addition, emerging value priorities that stress individualism and political participation produce skepticism of elite-controlled hierarchical organizations (such as bureaucracies, political parties, and large interest groups).

One thing you quickly learn about political science is that serious researchers can reach different conclusions based on similar evidence. This book's basic premise of political change has been questioned by many others. In reviewing European public opinion trends, for example, Dieter Fuchs and Hans-Dieter Klingemann conclude: "The hypotheses we tested are based on the premise that a fundamental change had taken place in the relationship between citizens and the state, provoking a challenge to representative democracy. . . [but] the postulated fundamental change in the citizens' relationship with the state largely did *not* occur" (1995, 429). Others have claimed that the evidence of increasing electoral change is a myth (Mair 1993; Bartolini and Mair 1990). Begin your reading from this skeptical position, and then see if the evidence supports it.

My own sense is that this is an exciting time to study public opinion because so much is changing, and that the puzzle for researchers, students and the citizens is to understand how democracy functions in its new context. The development of this new style of citizen politics creates new strains for the political systems of advanced industrial democracies. Protests, social movements, partisan volatility, and political skepticism are disrupting the traditional political order. Adjustment to new issue concerns and new patterns of citizen participation may be a difficult process. More people now take democratic ideals seriously, and they expect political systems to live up to those ideals. I believe that democracy is not an end state, but an evolutionary process. Thus, the new style of citizen politics is a sign of vitality and an opportunity for these societies to make further progress toward their democratic goals.

SUGGESTED READINGS

Franklin, Mark, and Christopher Wlezien, eds. *The Future of Election Studies*. Amsterdam: Elsevier, 2002.

Geer, John, ed. *Public Opinion and Polling around the World*. 2 vols. Santa Barbara, Calif.: ABC-CLIO, 2005.

NOTES

1. Most of the data in this volume come from the Inter-university Consortium for Political and Social Research at the University of Michigan, Ann Arbor (www.icpsr.umich.edu). Additional data were made available by the Zentralarchiv für empirische Sozialforschung, University of Cologne, Germany, and the ESRC Archive, University of Essex, England. See appendix A for additional information on the major data sources. Neither these archives nor the original collectors of the data bear responsibility for the analyses presented here.

2. For a brief review of these nations, see Almond, Dalton, Powell, and Strom (2005). More detailed national studies are found in Norton (2000) for Britain, Conradt (2004) for Germany, and Safran (2002) for France.

PART ONE

POLITICS AND THE PUBLIC

CHAPTER 2

The Nature of Mass Beliefs

Any discussion of citizen politics is ultimately based on assumptions about the political abilities of the electorate—the public's level of knowledge, understanding, and interest in political matters. For voters to make meaningful decisions, they must understand the options on which they are deciding. Citizens also need sufficient knowledge of the workings of the political system if they intend to influence and control the actions of their representatives. In short, for citizen politics to be purposeful, the electorate must have at least a basic level of political skills.

Examining the sophistication of voters also improves our understanding of the public opinion data presented in this book. With what depth of knowledge and conviction are opinions held? Do survey responses represent reasoned assessments of the issues or the snap judgments of individuals faced by an interviewer on their doorstep? It is common to see the public labeled as uninformed (especially when public opinion conflicts with the speaker's own views). Conversely, the electorate cannot be wiser than when it supports one's own position. Can we judge the merits of either position based on the empirical evidence from public opinion surveys?

Debates about the public's political abilities are one of the major controversies in political behavior research. This controversy involves normative assumptions about what level of sophistication is required for democracies to fulfill their political ideals, as well as differences in evaluating the empirical evidence.

THE SUPERCITIZEN

Political theorists have long maintained that democracy is workable only when the public has a high degree of political information and sophistication. Mill, Locke, Tocqueville, and other writers saw these public traits as requirements for a successful democratic system. Most theorists have further claimed that the citizenry should support the political system and share a deep commitment to democratic ideals such as pluralism, free expression, and minority rights (see chapter 12). Otherwise, an uninformed and unsophisticated electorate might be manipulated by misguided or unscrupulous elites. In a sense, these theorists posited a supercitizen model: in order for democracy to survive, the public must be a paragon of civic virtue.

This ideal of the democratic supercitizen was often illustrated by examples from American politics, drawn from a popular lore about the sophistication of Americans.[1] Alexis de Tocqueville (1966) praised the social and community

Internet Resource

Visit the Virtual Library on Democracy for links to various sources on public opinion, political parties, and democracy:

http://www.democ.uci.edu/resource.htm

involvement of Americans when he described the United States in the nineteenth century. Voters in early America supposedly yearned for the stimulating political debates of election campaigns and flocked to political rallies in great numbers. New England town hall meetings became a legendary example of the American political spirit. Even on the frontier, it was claimed, conversations around the general store's cracker barrel displayed a deep interest in political matters.

While these democratic norms were initially of European origin, history painted a less positive picture of the citizenry in many European nations. The right to vote came much later to most Europeans, often delayed until the beginning of the twentieth century. The aristocratic institutions and deferential traditions of British politics limited public participation beyond the act of voting and severely restricted the size of the eligible electorate. In France, the excesses of the French Revolution raised doubts about the principle of mass participation. In addition, the instability of the political system supposedly produced a sense of "incivism" (lack of civic engagement), and people avoided political discussions and political involvement.

Germany presented the most graphic example of what might follow when democratic norms are lacking among the public. Under the authoritarian governments that ruled during the Wilhelmine Empire (1871–1918), people were taught to be seen and not heard. The democratic Weimar Republic (1919–1933) provided a brief and turbulent interlude in Germany's nondemocratic history, but the frailty of democratic norms contributed to that system's demise and the rise of Hitler's Third Reich. However, these historical experiences strengthened the belief that a sophisticated, involved, and democratic public is a requirement for democracy to succeed. And since a strong democratic culture eventually developed in the postwar Federal Republic, German democracy has flourished.

THE UNSOPHISTICATED CITIZEN

The start of scientific public opinion surveying in the 1950s and 1960s provided the first opportunity to move beyond the insights of theorists and social commentators, finally making it possible to test the lofty images of the democratic citizen against reality. The public itself was directly consulted.

In contrast to the classic images celebrated in democratic theory, early surveys painted an unflattering picture of the American public, whose political sophistication seemed to fall far short of the supercitizen model. Most people's political interest and involvement barely extended beyond casting an occasional vote in elections. Furthermore, Americans apparently brought little understanding to their participation in politics. It was not clear that people based their voting decisions on rational evaluations of candidates and their issue positions. Instead, voting was conditioned by group loyalties and personalistic considerations. The seminal work in the area summarized these findings as follows:

> Our data reveal that certain requirements commonly assumed for the successful operation of democracy are not met by the behavior of the "average" citizen. . . . Many vote without real involvement in the election. . . . The citizen is not highly informed on the details of the campaign. . . . In any rigorous or narrow sense the voters are not highly rational. (Berelson, Lazarsfeld, and McPhee 1954, 307–310)

The landmark study, *The American Voter*, supported these early findings, as Angus Campbell and his colleagues (1960) documented a lack of political sophistication and ideological understanding by the American electorate.

In an influential essay on mass belief systems, Philip Converse (1964) spelled out the criteria for measuring political sophistication. As modeled in figure 2.1, Converse maintained that there should be a basic *structure* at the core of individual political beliefs. An ideological framework such as liberalism or conservatism presumably provides this structure, at least at higher

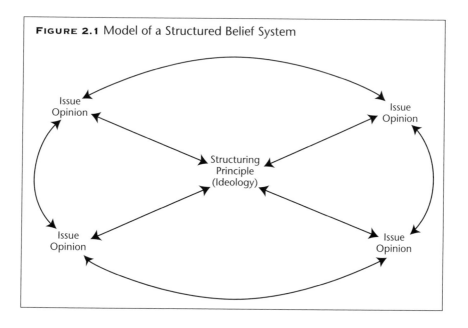

FIGURE 2.1 Model of a Structured Belief System

levels of sophistication. In addition, there should be *constraint* between individual issue positions. Constraint is measured by the strength of the linkage between specific issue positions and core beliefs and by the interrelationship among issues. A person who is liberal on one issue is expected to be liberal on others, and opinions on one issue should be ideologically (or at least logically) consistent with other beliefs. Finally, Converse said, issue opinions should be relatively *stable* over time so that voters held beliefs that consistently guided their behavior. The overall result should be a tightly structured system of beliefs like that depicted in the figure.

In testing this model, Converse maintained that most Americans were deficient on these criteria. First, public opinion apparently lacked a general ideological structure. Most individuals did not judge political phenomena in ideological terms, such as liberalism/conservatism or capitalism/socialism. Converse reckoned that barely a tenth of the American public used ideological concepts to structure their belief system. Second, there was seemingly only a weak relationship between issues that presumably are connected. For example, voters who felt taxes were too high nevertheless favored increases in spending for many specific government programs. Third, issue beliefs were not very stable over time. An analysis of the same group of individuals interviewed across three elections found that the opinions of many people seemed to vary randomly. The lack of structure, constraint, and stability led Converse (1970) to conclude that public opinion researchers are often studying "nonattitudes"—that is, on many issues of long-standing political concern, many voters apparently do not have informed opinions or any opinions. Similarly, *The American Voter* declared that the electorate "is almost completely unable to judge the rationality of government actions; knowing little of the particular policies and what has led to them, the mass electorate is not able either to appraise its goals or the appropriateness of the means chosen to secure these goals" (Campbell et al. 1960, 543). This research was soon followed by a series of surveys showing that many people could not name their elected representatives, were unfamiliar with the institutions of government, and did not understand the mechanics of the political process. The image of the American voter had fallen to a new low. (Moreover, more recent research indicates that little has changed in the past generation [Delli Carpini and Keeter 1996].)

This image of the unsophisticated citizen also seemed to apply to Western Europeans. Once one moved beyond election turnout, political involvement in Europe was frequently even lower than that in the United States (Almond and Verba 1963; Verba, Nie, and Kim 1978). European voters also lacked well-formed opinions on the pressing issues of the day (Converse and Pierce 1986, ch. 7; Butler and Stokes 1969). For instance, 60 percent of the British did not recognize the terms *Left* and *Right* as they applied to politics. There were, again, the telltale signs of nonattitudes—weak linkages between opinions on related issues and excessive opinion instability over time.

Other research raised doubts about the public's commitment to political tolerance and other values underlying the democratic process. The general public displayed support for democratic ideals in the abstract, but not when applied to real political groups and movements, such as communists, Nazis, atheists, and political nonconformists (Prothro and Grigg 1960; McClosky 1964; McClosky and Brill 1983). Again, the empirical reality apparently fell short of the democratic ideal.

ELITIST THEORY OF DEMOCRACY

Having found that most citizens apparently fail to meet the requirements of classic democratic theory, political scientists faced a paradox: most individuals are not "good" democratic citizens, and yet democracies such as the United States and Great Britain have existed for generations. Gradually, scholars developed an *elitist theory of democracy* to interpret these survey findings in a positive light (Berelson, Lazarsfeld, and McPhee 1954, 313–323; Almond and Verba 1963, chap. 15). The new theory contended that democratic politics might prove unworkable if every person were active on every issue at all times. Images of the centrifugal forces destroying the Weimar Republic were fresh in many minds, generating concerns about the possible effects of excessive participation. Suggesting that the model citizen "is not the active citizen; he is the potentially active citizen" (Almond and Verba 1963, 347), these researchers argued that people must believe that they can influence the government and must be willing to make an effort if the issue is sufficiently important. Few will realize this potential, however. The balance between action and potential presumably assures that political elites have enough freedom to make necessary decisions, while keeping the public interest in mind.

Another element of this elitist theory stresses the heterogeneity of the public. "Some people are and should be highly interested in politics, but not everyone is or needs to be" (Berelson, Lazarsfeld, and McPhee 1954, 315). From this perspective, the responsiveness of the political system is secured by a small core of active citizens and political elites, leaving the rest of the public blissfully uninformed and uninvolved. The mix between involved and indifferent voters supposedly assures the stability and flexibility of democratic systems.

The elitist theory of democracy is drawn from the realities of political life—or at least from the hard evidence of survey research. It is, however, a very undemocratic theory of democracy. The theory maintains that "the democratic citizen . . . must be active, yet passive; involved, yet not too involved; influential, yet deferential" (Almond and Verba 1963, 478–479). The values and goals of democracy are at least partially obscured by a mountain of survey data.

Accepting this new creed, some analysts used the evidence to justify an extreme elitist model of the democratic process, implying that citizen activism is undemocratic and politically destabilizing (Dye and Ziegler 1970; Crozier,

Huntington, and Watanuki 1975). As Thomas Dye and Harmon Ziegler (1970, 328) bluntly claimed,

> The survival of democracy depends upon the commitment of elites to democratic ideals rather than upon broad support for democracy by the masses. Political apathy and nonparticipation among the masses contribute to the survival of democracy. Fortunately for democracy, the antidemocratic masses are generally more apathetic than elites.

If a supportive and quiescent public ensures a smoothly functioning political system, then it is virtually the duty of the individual to remain uninvolved. When the public began to challenge political elites during the turbulent 1960s and 1970s, these political scientists cautioned that democracy required a public of followers who would not question political elites too extensively. They argued that too much democracy could threaten the democratic process.

I believe that the elitist theory overlooks the complexities of the democratic process and takes an unsophisticated view of the evidence. For instance, this theory ignores the inconsistencies that exist among political elites. Members of the U.S. Congress routinely endorse formal budget limits and then act to circumvent these same limits in the next piece of legislation; in one vote they endorse strict measures to limit control crime, in the next they refuse to ban assault weapons.[2] Such inconsistencies in elite behavior are treated as examples of the complexity of politics; in the public these same patterns are signs of a lack of sophistication. In addition, the elitist critique of the public's abilities has been challenged on both normative and empirical grounds in recent years.[3] The picture of the public's abilities is not nearly as bleak as that painted by the elitist theory of democracy. As our scientific knowledge has increased, so, too, has our image of the electorate and its abilities.

POLITICAL SOPHISTICATION RECONSIDERED

Our challenge to prior descriptions of an unsophisticated electorate is based on several points. Profound social and political changes in the advanced industrial democracies have increased the public's political abilities. In addition, research has enriched our understanding of how voters actually think about political matters. Each point deserves detailed attention.[4]

A Process of Cognitive Mobilization

The public's political skills and resources—traits such as education, media exposure, and political awareness—have vastly expanded since the mid-twentieth century. These trends contributed to a growth in the public's overall level of political sophistication through what is described as a process of "cognitive mobilization" (Inglehart 1990; Dalton 1984). This process involves two separate developments. First, the cost of acquiring information about politics has decreased. Second, the public's ability to process political information has increased. Cognitive mobilization thus means that more citizens now have the political resources and skills to deal with the complexities of politics and to reach their own political decisions.

The public's access to political information has increased in many ways. The average citizen once might have suffered from a lack of information. In the past, one could read newspapers or magazines, but this is a time-consuming task, especially for an electorate with limited education. Particularly in Europe, the printed press was of uneven quality, and many mass newspapers were little more than scandal sheets. Today, there is a nearly unlimited supply and variety of political news, but it should be remembered that this is a relatively recent development.

The expansion of the mass media, especially television, is the clearest example of this change (Norris 2000). In the early 1950s, television was still a novelty for most Americans and a luxury for most Europeans. Television sets were in only half of American homes, in less than 10 percent of homes in Great Britain and France, and in less than 5 percent of those in West Germany. The expansion of television ownership over the next two decades was closely paralleled by the public's increasing reliance on television as a source of political information (figure 2.2). In the 1952 American election, 51 percent of the electorate used television news as an information source. By 1960, this statistic had risen to a plateau of about 90 percent. In 1961 only 50 percent of the West German public depended on television for political information; by 1974, the Germans had also reached the 90 percent plateau. British and French trends presented similar patterns.

As television viewership increased, so also did the amount of political information provided by the medium. The now-standard American nightly half-hour national news program began only in 1963. Since then, technology and viewer interest have increased the proportion of television programming devoted to news and political affairs. Today, news reporting is instantaneous and done on a worldwide scale. Most Americans have access to news on a twenty-four-hour-a-day basis; CNN, C-SPAN, and other cable channels create a rich media environment.

The educational content of the electronic media is even greater in Europe, where government-supervised television and radio networks devote more time to news, politics, and current events (Humphreys 1996). Moreover, new information technologies and the competition from cable and satellite channels is transforming the media environment in Europe. Most European households receive cable or satellite channels ranging from the national networks, to those of neighboring nations, to a host of news and government information channels. Government restrictions on television coverage of elections has also weakened, expanding the media's political role. For example, until the 1964 election the British government prohibited the BBC from carrying election news during the campaign period. Now television coverage is a central part of British campaigns as well as German and French elections (Norris et al. 1999; Semetko and Schoenbach 1994). And in several European nations, political parties receive free

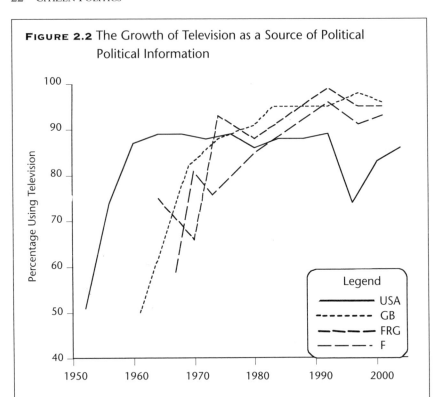

FIGURE 2.2 The Growth of Television as a Source of Political Political Information

SOURCES: United States, 1952–2004, American National Election Studies; Great Britain, 1963–1974, British Election Studies; Germany, 1961–1969, German Election Studies; France, 1965–1974, Gallup (1976b); Great Britain, France, and Germany, 1980–2001, Eurobarometer 15 (1980), 37 (1992), 47 (1997), and 55 (2001).

NOTE: Figure entries are the percentages who use television as a source of political information.

television airtime during campaigns. So just as people are watching more television, this medium provides them with a large amount of political content in most European nations.

As a result of these trends, television is now the primary information source for Western publics. People typically cite television as their most frequently used source of political information (table 2.1).[5] Political scientists are divided on whether the expansion of television as a news source is a boon or a curse for the democratic process. Some scholars argue that the medium tends to trivialize information, emphasizing entertainment and drama over substance, and creating a negative climate of opinion (e.g., Patterson 1993; Swanson and Mancini 1996). These concerns are well-founded, because television does have limits. However, television also can

TABLE 2.1 Most Important Source of Political Information (in percentages)

	United States	Great Britain	France	Germany
Television	70	54	66	75
Newspapers	39	44	40	59
Magazines, other print	4	16	23	24
Personal discussion	—	18	25	20
Radio	15	28	36	38
Internet	11	18	15	14
Other	1	33	29	14
Total	140	211	234	244

SOURCES: United States, Pew Center for People and the Press, November 10–12, 2000, survey, in which only two responses were possible; other nations, Eurobarometer 60 (spring 2003), in which multiple responses were possible.

create a better sense of the political process by allowing us all to watch legislative deliberations, to see candidates as they campaign, and to experience history firsthand. Observing an important parliamentary debate on television or watching the presidential inauguration live puts citizens in direct contact with their government and gives them a better understanding of how democracy works. Television has great positive and negative potential, and the objective of democratic polities should be to maximize the positive benefits (Norris 2000).

The high ranking for television does not mean that other media are not used. Large proportions of the public read newspapers and magazines, hear news on the radio, use the Internet, or learn about politics from their friends. People thus have access to an array of media sources that would have been unimaginable a generation ago. These increases in the quantity and quality of political information provided by the media should improve public awareness of political affairs.

In addition to the media, a lot of politically relevant information is available from a citizen's daily life experiences (Fiorina 1990; Popkin 1991). Governments now exercise a large role in society, and their performance of this role offers important political information. For instance, contemporary governments can strongly influence economic conditions. Thus, the performance of the economy is a meaningful measure of how to judge the incumbents. Similarly, government runs most schools, sets health standards, administers family and social programs, protects the environment, and provides for our transportation needs. When a commuter notes that highways are deteriorating (or being improved) or parents note improvements (or deterioration) in their children's schools, these are significant political facts. Political information is virtually unavoidable.

Expanded access to political information provides an opportunity to the citizenry, but this abundance of news may produce only a noisy cacophony unless one can process the information. Thus it is important that the public's political skills also increase.

The most visible change in political skills involves educational levels. Advanced industrial societies require a more educated and technically sophisticated electorate, and modern affluence has expanded educational opportunities (see chapter 1). University enrollments grew dramatically during the latter half of the twentieth century. By the 1990s, graduate degrees were almost as common as bachelor's degrees had been at mid-century. These trends have steadily raised the educational level of contemporary electorates. For instance, almost half of the 1948 American electorate had a primary education or less, and only a tenth had some college education. By 2004, the portion of the electorate with some college education outnumbered voters with only primary education by a ten-to-one ratio, and those with some college-education made up almost two-thirds of the electorate. Parallel changes are transforming European publics. In postwar West Germany, for example, the number of citizens with only primary schooling exceeded those with a secondary school diploma (*Mittlere Reife*) by about five to one. Today, the number of better-educated Germans is twice as large as the lesser educated.

There is not a direct one-to-one relationship between years of schooling and political sophistication. Nevertheless, survey research broadly shows that education is linked to a citizen's level of political knowledge, interest, and sophistication (Nie, Junn, and Stehlik-Barry 1996). Paul Sniderman, Richard Brody, and Philip Tetlock (1991) presented persuasive evidence that educational levels are related to the modes of political decision making that citizens use. Samuel Popkin (1991, 36) suggested that rising educational levels increase the breadth of citizens' political interests, even if they do not raise overall levels of political knowledge or issue constraint by the same amount. A doubling of the public's educational level may not double the level of political sophistication, but some increase should occur. Thus, contemporary electorates are clearly the most educated in the long history of democracies, and this should contribute toward making a more sophisticated electorate and a new style of citizen politics.

Philip Converse (1972, 1990) maintained that political attention is an even more important indicator of the public's political skills. Reflecting and reinforcing the general development of cognitive mobilization, political interest has increased in our four core nations (see figure 2.3).[6] Interest in specific elections may vary from campaign to campaign, but these data suggest a trend of increasing politicization. Political interest has grown most steadily in the Federal Republic of Germany, partially for the reasons already cited and partially because of the nation's resocialization to democracy. Yet there are similar trends of expanding interest in Great Britain and France. Americans' interest in campaigns has varied over time with little secular trend, although interest spiked sharply in reaction to the contentious Bush-Kerry

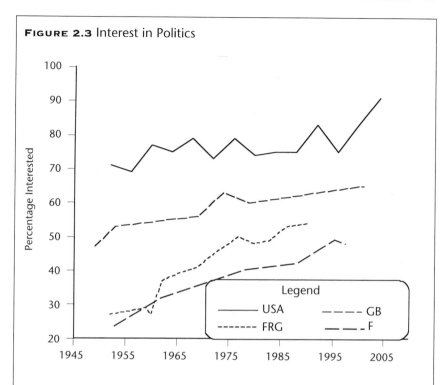

FIGURE 2.3 Interest in Politics

SOURCES: United States, 1952–2004, American National Election Studies; Great Britain, 1949–1953, Gallup (1976a); 1963–1979, 2001 British Election Studies; Germany, Institut für Demoskopie surveys; France, 1953 and 1978, Charlot (1980), 1962, Gallup (1976b), 1978–1997, French Election Studies.

campaign in 2004. Most Western democracies display a pattern of generally increasing political interest (Dalton and Wattenberg 2000, chap. 3). In sum, the trend of increasing political interest in advanced industrial democracies is unmistakable.

This debate on the sophistication of mass publics is not finished. For instance, Michael Delli Carpini and Scott Keeter (1996) claim that political information is limited and not increasing among Americans. In contrast, Morris Fiorina (1990, 335) makes the provocative argument that the more surprising fact is that citizens have as much information as they do, since the acquisition of political knowledge cannot be justified by narrow rationalist calculations of the value of that knowledge in influencing government policy. In part, it is a debate about expectations—what do we expect of citizens in democracies?—and, in part, it is a debate over empirical evidence—what levels of political sophistication do voters actually possess?[7] When these factors are intermixed, it is easy to draw contrasting conclusions from the same empirical evidence.

I think the best evidence will come from the actual impact of cognitive mobilization on various aspects of citizen politics. More people seem to be shedding their reliance on social group and partisan cues as a basis of voting (see chapters 8 and 9). The present level of issue voting is generally higher than during earlier periods (see chapter 10). Cognitive mobilization also expands political participation to include more demanding forms of political activity (see chapters 3 and 4). We examine many of these specific trends more closely in the following chapters, and we argue that the stereotype of an unsophisticated voter is clearly much less applicable today than during the 1950s.

Sophistication versus Satisficing

It probably was inevitable that early empirical studies would reach negative conclusions about the public's political sophistication. Analysts judged citizens against the lofty ideals of classic democratic theory, and reality fell short of the theoretical ideals. When this occurred, analysts stressed the shortfall.

I agree that the rational citizen cannot afford to keep informed on all political issues—few political elites or political scientists attempt this task. To the surprise of some political science professors, politics is only one part of people's lives. Because of the pressing needs of family and career, people can devote only a limited amount of time to politics. For instance, when the 1999 World Values Survey asked Americans what was very important in their lives, politics came at the end of the list:

- Family (95 percent)
- Friends (64 percent)
- Religion (58 percent)
- Work (54 percent)
- Leisure (43 percent)
- Politics (16 percent)

The pattern was quite similar in Great Britain, France, Germany, and most other advanced industrial democracies. Citing such evidence, the elitist theorists argue that many (or most) citizens are overwhelmed and so become political dropouts—and that democracy is better for it.

We need a more balanced view of the topic, stripping away the idealized standards of classic democratic theory and the rationalizations of elitist democratic theory, and instead looking at politics from the perspective of the citizen. People make political decisions on a regular basis, whether those decisions involve voting in an election, donating funds to a political group, or participating in a political discussion. Rather than asking whether citizens meet the expectations of democratic theorists, we should recognize that people are making these political choices and examine how these choices are actually made.

Following politics is demanding, but politics does have important effects on citizens' lives. Most citizens therefore do not drop out but, instead, find a means of balancing the costs and benefits of political activity. One way of managing is by using "shortcuts" to simplify the complexities of politics. Samuel Popkin writes (1991, 218) that "the use of information shortcuts is . . . an inescapable fact of life, and will occur no matter how educated we are, how much information we have, and how much thinking we do." In other words, rather than insisting that the public measure up to the abstract ideals of democratic theory, we should focus on how people make satisfactory, or *satisficing,* decisions.

The political science literature identifies three methods that citizens may use as information shortcuts. One approach suggests that people have specialized interests. Instead of following all issues, citizens concentrate their attention on a few topics of direct personal relevance or interest. The total electorate thus is divided into several partially overlapping *issue publics* (Converse 1964). Being part of an issue public implies that citizens have devoted prior attention to the issue and have firm beliefs. Many farmers, for example, closely monitor government agricultural policy while paying scant attention to urban renewal programs. Parents of school-age children may display considerable interest in educational policy, while the elderly are interested in Social Security. The largest issue publics generally exist for topics of broad concern, such as economic policy, taxes, and basic social programs. At the other extreme, only a few voters regularly follow issues of foreign aid, agriculture, or international trade. Very few citizens are interested in every issue, but most citizens are members of at least one issue public. To paraphrase Will Rogers, "Everybody is sophisticated, only on different subjects."

The concept of issue publics influences how we think about political sophistication. When citizens are allowed to define politics according to their own interests, a surprising level of political sophistication often appears. David RePass (1971) documented a high level of rational issue voting when citizens identified their own issue interests. Similarly, research demonstrates that members of an issue public are more likely to follow media coverage of the issue, gather information on the issue, hold stable preferences, and use these preferences as a basis of voting choice (Hutchings 2003; Krosnick 1990; Price and Zaller 1993; Feldman 1989). Furthermore, membership in an issue public appears to be based more on an individual's self-interest and values, rather than on a generalized attention to politics. Thus low issue constraint and stability in public opinion surveys do not mean that the electorate is unsophisticated; the alternative explanation is that not all citizens are interested in all issues.

Some political scientists view issue publics as a negative aspect of politics because a proliferation of issue groups works against policymaking based on a broad, coherent ideological framework. We should be concerned about such policy fragmentation, but such criticism may be overstated. If citizens limit their issue interests, it does not mean that they fail to judge these issues using a broad political framework; different clusters of issue interests still may emanate from a common underlying set of values. In addition, Robert Lane (1973, 1962) pointed out the potential negative consequences of an overly structured belief system—for example, dogmatism and intolerance. In a slightly different context, Robert Dahl (1971) restated the Madisonian principle that the existence of many competing political groups, with overlapping and cross-cutting memberships and shifting political alignments, is an essential characteristic of pluralist democracy. In some instances, therefore, issue publics may be a positive feature of citizen politics.

A second model of satisficing behavior generalizes the idea of issue publics into a broader framework of *schema theory* (Conover and Feldman 1984; Peffley and Hurwitz 1985). Instead of viewing belief systems as interconnecting a diverse range of political attitudes, as originally proposed by Converse, schema theorists maintain there is a vertical structure (or network) of beliefs within specific political domains, as illustrated in figure 2.4. A broad organizing structure is linked to general political orientations; specific issue opinions are derived from one or more of these general orientations. For instance, attitudes toward government programs assisting minorities might reflect both orientations toward the role of government and attitudes toward minorities (Sniderman, Brody, and Tetlock 1991). At the same time, even if opinions on specific issues are strongly linked to broader political orientations, the relationships between specific issue opinions can be weak because issues may not be directly linked together. Thus this model lacks the direct linkage between opinions on different issues that is posited in the *American Voter* model (see figure 2.1).

Furthermore, the specific political attitudes included within a schema, and the structures used to organize information, may vary across individuals. Some voters' beliefs will include only one part of the structure of figure 2.4,

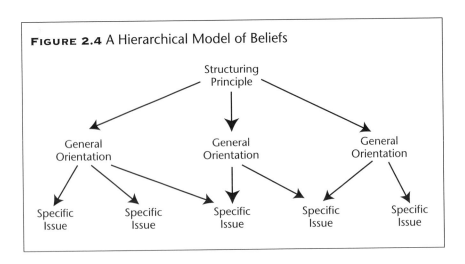

FIGURE 2.4 A Hierarchical Model of Beliefs

such as the issues on the left of the figure. Other people's schematic structure might include another subset of issues and general orientations. Thus the literature on schema theory tries to identify specific cognitive structures (or schema) that are relevant for subsets of issues, such as a foreign policy schema, a racial schema, or a schema for judging political candidates.[8]

In short, a complex belief system may exist within an issue public, linking issue positions to a structuring principle such as Left/Right position—even if schema are not linked across issue publics. Such belief structures provide voters with a method of managing information and making political judgments. Thus even if citizens are not sophisticated on all political topics, they may have logical and structured beliefs within specific domains that enable them to manage political decision making.

A third model of satisficing involves the use of reference standards to simplify decisions. Instead of having to develop a complex schema, people can use political cues, or *heuristics,* to orient themselves to politics (Lupia and McCubbins 1998; Sniderman, Brody, and Tetlock 1991; Ferejohn and Kuklinski 1990). The cue provides a shortcut to collecting and processing information; one relies on the political directions of the cue-giver.

Social groups are one common source of political cues. Many policy issues can be cast as conflicts between class, religious, ethnic, or other social groupings. Membership in a social group, either formally or through psychological ties, can act as a guidepost in dealing with policy questions. French steelworkers, for example, might prefer larger social welfare programs because the labor union suggests it will benefit workers like themselves, while avowed Bavarian Catholics might follow their pastor's advice to support government aid for religious schools. These voters may not explain their policy preferences with sophisticated ideological arguments or reference to specific legislative proposals, but on the whole they still are making reasonable political choices.

Early voting studies emphasized social groups as a source of voting cues. Paul Lazarsfeld, Bernard Berelson, and Hazel Gaudet (1948) constructed an "index of political predisposition" based on social class, religion, and rural/urban residence that was a potent predictor of voting behavior. The highly stratified nature of West European societies produced even stronger group cues—and large group differences in European voting patterns (see chapter 8). Thus, when the French steelworker sees that other people of the same social class and the same secular orientation favor a leftist party, he may also support a leftist party because it represents people like him (and presumably his interests).

Group references are a common basis of party evaluation (Converse 1964; Klingemann 1979). For many less educated citizens, group references may reflect political orientations that they have difficulty explaining in the terminology that would classify them as sophisticated ideologues. When social conflicts are salient, and the parties take clear positions on these conflicts, then social characteristics can provide effective cues for orienting oneself to politics.

An even more powerful source of political cues is partisanship. Many citizens develop a psychological bond to a specific political party that may persist through an entire lifetime (see chapter 9). This *party identification* sometimes is based on nonpolitical criteria, such as inheritance of parental partisanship, and it may serve as a surrogate for social-group cues. As a standing sum of the individual's political history, partisanship provides a useful guide to political behavior.

The usefulness of social-group cues is limited to topics directly related to group interests, but party identification has broader applications (see chapter 9). Parties are central participants in democratic politics, so most political phenomena can be judged within a partisan framework. Party attachments obviously can simplify voting choices, since most elections involve a choice between parties. In Western Europe, where parties act as cohesive units, party voting is an effective and efficient method of decision making. The heterogeneity of American parties lessens the policy value of party voting, but the complexity of American elections makes party a valuable voting cue when one must decide on a long list of federal, state, and local candidates. Partisanship can also shape evaluations of political leaders and new political issues. If voters are unsure about an issue, party cues can suggest where their interests lie. An issue supported by one's party is more likely to benefit oneself, while the policies of the opposition are suspect. In sum, because of its heuristic value, party identification frequently is viewed as the central thread connecting the citizen and the political process.

Left/Right (or liberal/conservative) orientations are another potential source of political cues. Most voters do not express sophisticated ideological views, but they still can locate themselves within a broad ideological family, or *tendance* (Fuchs and Klingemann 1989; Westholm and Niemi 1992; Jacoby 1991). A Left/Right orientation provides a reference structure for evaluating political objects. When an individual complains that a candidate is too liberal, or another is too conservative, this is a shortcut to learning about the candidates' views on specific issues and evaluating them on this basis.

In most nations partisanship and ideological orientations exist side by side and have reinforcing effects. But Left/Right orientations hold special importance in political systems where party cues are weak or fluid, as in France. The French party system is notoriously volatile, which undercuts the continuity and value of partisanship. Ideological leanings thus play a larger role in guiding the political behavior of the French and can bring some order to an ever-changing political landscape (Fleury and Lewis-Beck 1993; Michelat 1993).

Table 2.2 summarizes the diverse criteria that people use in making political judgments. People in several nations were asked to describe the good and bad points of two major political parties in their nation. Only a small percentage actively employ ideological concepts in judging the parties. This does not mean, however, that the remaining individuals are devoid of

TABLE 2.2 Bases of Party Evaluations (in percentages)

Criteria based on	United States	Great Britain	West Germany
Ideological concepts	21	21	34
Social groups	40	41	45
Party organizations and competence	49	35	66
Policy concepts	45	46	53
Nature of the times	64	59	86
Political figures	40	18	38
Intrinsic values	46	65	49
No content	14	18	6
Total	319	303	377

SOURCE: Political Action Study, 1974–75.

NOTE: Totals exceed 100 percent because multiple responses were possible.

political judgments. About 40 percent of the American, British, and German electorates evaluated the parties according to social-group alignments. Even more people judged the parties by their organization and political competence. Nearly half of the survey responses mentioned outright policy criteria. Even the broadest and most frequently used criteria—judging parties by the nature of the times—can provide a meaningful basis of evaluation. These data are a quarter-century old; we expect new evidence would find that cognitive mobilization is shifting the criteria that citizens use toward more information-based factors (Wattenberg 1998). In short, far from suggesting that citizens are uninformed and unsophisticated, these data display a diversity and complexity of public opinion that often is overlooked.

POLITICS AND THE PUBLIC

This chapter has described trends that are affecting all advanced industrial democracies: the rise of political interest, cognitive skills, and information resources. There are, of course, important differences in these traits across nations. Generalized political interest and involvement apparently are more extensive in the United States than in Great Britain, France, or Germany. Conversely, politics and public opinion generally are more ideological in Europe than in the United States.

The evidence presented here yields a generally positive view of social change, describing the increasing political sophistication or cognitive mobilization of contemporary publics. But let me also offer a caveat. While political engagement may be increasing, these trends are not as apparent among younger generations, who are the very individuals who should benefit most from these trends (Milner 2002; Franklin 2004). Subsequent chapters discuss the decreasing electoral participation of the young, and the growing skepticism about politics among these same cohorts. American and European youth are typically interested in society and in participating in the decisions affecting their lives—but they are often disaffected from conventional politics. The current challenge is to engage these youth, who possess the skills and resources to be sophisticated citizens, to become involved in the political process.

Furthermore, although political sophistication has increased, democratic electorates will never match the political sophistication posited by classic democratic theory and displayed by political elites, such as members of Congress or Parliament. It makes little sense to debate this point. Instead, survey research can be more useful in describing how citizens actually perceive and evaluate politics and reach political decisions—how people deal with the decision-making tasks they face. Despite the criticisms of the naysayers, citizens regularly make political choices on the basis of diverse criteria. How are these choices made?

This chapter describes a pattern of public opinion that Donald Kinder and David Sears (1985) described as the "pluralistic roots of political beliefs." People rely on various methods to manage the complexities of politics. Many voters focus their attention on a few issues of particular interest, rather than devoting equal attention to all issues. Thus the electorate is composed of overlapping issue publics, each judging government action on different policies. The bases of evaluation also vary within the electorate. Some citizens judge politics by a broad ideological framework, but this is only a minority of the public. Many more people use political cues, such as social-reference groups or party attachments, to guide their behavior. By limiting their issue interests and relying on other decision-making shortcuts, the average voter can balance the costs and benefits of political involvement and still make reasonable political decisions.[9] Perhaps the best description comes from Jon Krosnick (1990, 82), who cites social psychological research to argue that people are inevitably "cognitive misers" who find shortcuts or heuristics to make satisficing political choices, rather than seeking a complete array of relevant information.

Several studies provide evidence on the diversity of decision-making processes within the public. Sniderman, Brody, and Tetlock (1991; also Moon 1990), for example, demonstrated that better-educated individuals are more likely to use ideological criteria in making political choices; the lesser-educated are more likely to use group references or other political cues to make their decisions; in both cases the decisions may broadly reflect individuals' interests. Similarly, Arthur Lupia's (1994) research on voting on insurance initiatives in California found that a small attentive public was well informed on the initiatives and made choices appropriate for their expressed interests. In addition, a larger group of voters used group cues—such as which proposals were supported by Ralph Nader and which by the insurance industry—that also led to rational voting choices. This is pluralistic decision making in practice.

This pluralistic model has several implications for our study of public opinion in later chapters. We should not interpret unstable or inconsistent issue opinions as evidence that voters lack any attitudes. Survey questions are imprecise; the public's issue interests are specialized; and a complex mix of beliefs may be related to a single issue. In addition, we must be sensitive to the diversity and complexity of mass politics. Simple models of political behavior that assume a homogeneous electorate may be theoretically elegant and empirically parsimonious, yet unrealistic. Recognizing that people function on the basis of diverse criteria and motivations, we should try to model this diversity, instead of adopting overly generalized theories of citizen politics. Finally, we must not underestimate the potential for change. As this chapter documents, the publics of these nations have undergone a major transformation during the postwar period. Public opinion reflects a dynamic process, and we should avoid static views of an unchanging (or unchangeable) public.

We should not, of course, be guilty of overestimating the sophistication of the citizenry. There will always be instances in which the public holds ill-advised or ill-informed opinions; some citizens will remain ignorant of all political matters. Such is the imperfect nature of human behavior. A few individuals deserve the rating of full ideologues, and a small number are devoid of all bases for making meaningful political choices. The important lesson is not to ignore or belittle the varied criteria citizens actually use in dealing with politics.

The ultimate question, then, is not whether the public meets the maximum ideological standards of classic democratic theory, but whether the public has a sufficient basis for rational political action. Phrased in these terms, and based on the evidence presented in this chapter, we can be more optimistic about the political abilities of contemporary publics.

SUGGESTED READINGS

Converse, Philip. "The Nature of Belief Systems in Mass Publics." In *Ideology and Discontent*, edited by David Apter. New York: Free Press, 1964.

Delli Carpini, Michael, and Scott Keeter. *What Americans Know about Politics and Why It Matters*. New Haven, Conn.: Yale University Press, 1996.

Hutchings, Vincent. *Public Opinion and Democratic Accountability*. Princeton, N.J.: Princeton University Press, 2003.

Kaase, Max, and Ken Newton. *Beliefs in Government*. Oxford: Oxford University Press, 1995.

Lupia, Arthur, and Mathew McCubbins. *The Democratic Dilemma: Can Citizens Learn What They Need to Know?* Cambridge: Cambridge University Press, 1998.

Norris, Pippa. *Virtuous Circle: Political Communications in Postindustrial Societies*. Cambridge: Cambridge University Press, 2000.

Popkin, Samuel. *The Reasoning Voter,* 2nd ed. Chicago: University of Chicago Press, 1994.

Sniderman, Paul, Richard Brody, and Philip Tetlock. *Reasoning and Choice.* New York: Cambridge University Press, 1991.

NOTES

1. There were, of course, dissenting voices. Walter Bagehot (1978), Joseph Schumpeter (1943), Graham Wallas (1908), and Walter Lippmann (1922) were highly critical of a participatory view of democracy. For a review of this literature, see Eckstein (1984).

2. For other examples of such inconsistencies, see Arnold (1990). Furthermore, the elitist theory overlooks the problem of democratic accountability if its assumptions were true, and it ignores the evidence on abuses of power among democratically elected elites.

3. For example, other research has questioned the evidence that elites are more politically tolerant than the general public (Jackman 1972; Sniderman et al. 1991).

4. Another source of debate has been methodological, focusing on how sophistication is measured. For a discussion of these points, see Dalton (1996, 27–31) and Zaller and Feldman (1992).

5. The differences between the U.S. and Europe are partially a function of different question texts and the response options provided to respondents. The European nations asked about sources of information on the European Union. The question in the United States asked about the use of information sources for news about what is going on in the world today.

6. The British, German, and French questions measure general interest in politics, and the questions differ across nations. The American question asked about interest in campaigns. Because of the differences in question wordings, the absolute levels of political interest should not be compared across nations; for such comparisons, see Jennings and van Deth (1989). For trends in political interest in additional nations, see Dalton and Wattenberg (2000), ch. 3.

7. Critics of the public's level of knowledge often ignore parallel findings among elite groups. For instance, Michael Zimmerman (1990, 1991) found that newspaper editors and elected politicians displayed surprisingly low levels of knowledge about historical and scientific facts.

8. This literature is quite diverse in its applications (see Hurwitz and Peffley 1987; Sniderman, Brody, and Kuklinski 1984; Graber 1988; Miller, Wattenberg, and Malanchuk 1986; Rohrschneider 1993a). For a critique of schema theory, see Kuklinski, Luskin, and Bolland (1991).

9. The public's reliance on various decision-making shortcuts—satisficing behavior— is common to decision makers in business and government (Cyert and March 1963). Nevertheless, democratic elitists denigrate the public when they adopt this model for political choices.

CHAPTER 3

Political Participation

Democracy should be a celebration by an involved public. An active citizenry is required because it is through discussion, popular interest, and involvement in politics that societal goals should be defined and carried out. Without public involvement in the process, democracy loses both its legitimacy and its guiding force. Thomas Jefferson said that a well-informed electorate is the most important constraint on government. Thus, when Germans take the time to cast informed votes, British electors canvass their neighbors, or Americans write their president, the democratic process is at work. The recent global spread of democratization has brought these democratic freedoms to millions of people. The jubilation that accompanied the first democratic elections in Eastern Europe, the open elections in South Africa, and the return of democracy in Indonesia all attest to the value that citizens place on these freedoms.

Although it seems we should all be celebrating the triumph of democracy by participating in the democratic process, there is great controversy about whether citizens of established democracies are instead becoming apathetic about their democratic rights The socioeconomic development of advanced industrial democracies and the process of cognitive mobilization should spur increases in political participation. Yet turnout in elections is trending downward in the United States and many other democracies. Moreover, Robert Putnam (1995, 2000) has warned that civic engagement is decreasing to dangerously low levels in America. A recent bipartisan report on the state of American democracy echoed the perception that fewer citizens are politically engaged; too many are becoming spectators instead of participants in the democratic process—and democracy will suffer as a result (Bennet and Nunn 1998; Patterson 2003). Are we celebrating the success of democracy by staying home?

In order to study these questions, this chapter examines participation in several types of "conventional" citizen action: voting, campaigns, group activities, and other methods normally associated with conventional politics. More contentious forms of political engagement (protests, demonstrations, and so on) are examined in the next chapter because the sources and motivations of contentious participation deserve separate attention.

THE MODES OF PARTICIPATION

Think for a moment about what you would do if you wanted to influence the government on a policy that was important to you. We often equate political participation with the act of voting. If you think of political influence from

35

the citizen's perspective, however, participation is not limited to voting, nor is voting necessarily the most effective means of affecting the political process. Instead of waiting several years until the next election to vote for a candidate who supports your position (if there is one), you might immediately try to contact political elites directly, or you might work with others who share your interests, or you might find other ways to advocate your cause now. In short, democratic participation can take many forms.

Sidney Verba, Norman Nie, and Jae-on Kim (1971, 1978) identified four general types of political action that citizens engage in: voting, campaign activity, communal activity (working with a group in the community), and directly contacting officials (see table 3.1). They found that people do not use these activities interchangeably, as many early analysts assumed. Instead, people tend to specialize in activities that match their motivations and goals. Specific kinds of activities frequently cluster together; a person who performs one act from a particular cluster is likely to perform other acts from the same cluster but not necessarily activities from another cluster. They labeled these clusters of activities as *modes of democratic participation.*

These participation modes differ in the requirements they place on participants and in the nature of the actions involved. Verba, Nie, and Kim (1978) classified the differences between modes in terms of several criteria: (1) whether the act conveys information about the individual's political preferences and/or applies pressure for compliance; (2) whether the act is directed toward a broad social outcome or a particular interest; (3) the potential degree of conflict involved in the activity; (4) the amount of effort required; and (5) the amount of cooperation with others required by the act.

Voting, for example, is a high-pressure activity because it selects government officials, but its policy focus is uncertain because an election involves many issues. Voting also is a reasonably simple act that requires little initiative or cooperation with others. Involvement in political campaigns makes much greater demands on the time and motivation of individuals. Although campaign work occurs within an electoral setting, it can be more policy-focused than the simple act of voting. Participation in community groups, or communal activity, may require even more effort by the individual, and it produces a qualitatively different form of citizen input. Citizen groups can control both the methods of action and the policy focus of their activities.

TABLE 3.1 Dimensions of Political Activity and Modes of Activity

Mode of activity	Type of influence	Scope of outcome	Conflict	Initiative required	Cooperate with others
Voting	High pressure / low information	Collective	Conflictual	Little	Little
Campaign activity	High pressure / low to high information	Collective	Conflictual	Some	Some or much
Communal activity	Low to high pressure / high information	Collective	Maybe yes / maybe no	Some or much	Some or much
Contacting officials on personal matters	Low pressure / high information	Particular	Nonconflictual	Much	Little
Protest	High pressure / high information	Collective	Very conflictual	Some or much	Some or much

SOURCE: Verba, Nie, and Kim (1978, 55) with modifications

Finally, an individual may choose to contact the government directly by writing a letter, speaking with a government official, or sending an email. Sometimes this activity is for a particular reason—to have a pothole fixed or request other government services—and other times it can concern broad policy questions. The important point is that different forms of political participation are not equal: they involve different groups of individuals and wield different influence on the political process.

It is instructive to see what Americans say they would do to influence policy. A typical survey question asks what the individual would do if an unjust or unfair law were being passed by Congress and he or she wanted to do something to stop it (Jennings and van Deth 1979). Nearly four-fifths say that they would contact their representatives directly, more than three-quarters would work with a group of like-minded others to influence the government, and about a sixth mention voting or protest. People try to influence politics through multiple means.

Using different modes of action seems to be a common feature of democratic politics. Studies of political participation in Britain (Parry, Moyser, and Day 1992; Pattie, Seyd, and Whiteley 2004) and Germany (Koch, Wasmer, and Schmidt 2001; Ühlinger 1989) yielded basic findings that are very similar to the Verba et al. studies of American participation.[1] Our discussion of citizen action focuses on the three most common modes of conventional participation: voting, campaign activity, and communal activity.[2]

Voting

The history of modern democracies has followed a pattern of almost ever-expanding citizen eligibility to participate in elections. The voting franchise in most nations initially was restricted to property owners, with long residency requirements. The United States was one of the first nations to begin liberalizing suffrage laws; by 1850, virtually the entire white adult male population in the United States was enfranchised. Voting rights expanded more slowly in Western European societies, which lacked the populist tradition of the United States. In addition, social cleavages were more sharply polarized there; many European conservatives were hesitant to enfranchise a working class that might vote them out of office. A socialist movement that was emerging throughout the nineteenth century pressed for the political equality of the working class, but mass suffrage often was delayed until war or revolution disrupted the conservative political order. French adult males gained voting rights with the formation of the Third Republic in 1870. Great Britain limited its election rolls until early in the twentieth century by placing significant residency and financial restrictions on voting and by allowing multiple votes by business owners and university graduates. Electoral reforms following World War I granted voting rights to virtually all British males. Germany, too, limited the franchise and allowed multiple votes during the Wilhelmine Empire; true democratic elections with universal mass suffrage began with the creation of the Weimar Republic in 1919.

During the twentieth century, governments gradually extended suffrage to the rest of the adult population. Women's right to vote was acknowledged first in Britain (1918); Germany (1919) and the United States (1920) quickly followed. France lagged behind most of Western Europe in this instance, en-franchising women only in 1944. The Voting Rights Act of 1965 removed most of the remaining formal restrictions on the voting participation of American blacks. Finally, in the 1970s all four nations lowered the voting age to eighteen.

The right to vote now extends to virtually the entire adult population in contemporary democracies. There are, however, distinct national differences in the rate at which citizens actually turn out to vote. Table 3.2 presents the rates of voting turnout for twenty-three industrialized democracies from the 1950s to the end of the 1990s. Turnout is calculated as a percentage of the voting age public, rather than of registered voters, to compensate for differ-ent registration rules across nations. These data display large cross-national differences in participation levels across democratic nations. In the United States and Switzerland, for instance, national elections involve half of the vot-ing age population (or less). Voting rates are consistently higher in most Eu-ropean nations, especially in Germany, where typically close to 80 percent of the public cast a ballot in Bundestag elections. Turnout ranges between 60 percent and 80 percent in most British House of Commons elections and French National Assembly elections.

The other significant pattern in table 3.2 is the trend in participation rates over time. Comparing the two end points for the twenty nations with a com-plete time series, fifteen have experienced turnout declines of more than 2 percent (including Britain, France, Germany, and the United States), two have stable turnout levels (plus or minus 2 percent), and three saw a turnout in-crease of more than 2 percent. More refined analyses indicate that voting rates peaked in the 1960s and have since declined, especially in the 1990s (Franklin 2004; Wattenberg 2002; Bromley and Curtice 2002). The first elec-tions of the twenty-first century have generated a mixed pattern. Turnout in Britain plummeted from 69 percent of the voting age public in 1997 to 58 percent in 2001; and turnout in the 2002 French National Assembly elections was down 8 percent. Turnout was up slightly in the 2002 German elections, and turnout in the 2004 U.S. elections increased by about 5 percent. Thus, voting participation remains below levels of earlier decades.

Several factors have apparently contributed to the long-term trend. Mark Franklin's (2004) recent study emphasizes the role of generational change in decreasing turnout. Younger generations seem disengaged from electoral pol-itics, and the lowering of the voting age has diminished participation rates. The erosion of both trust in government and attachment to political parties has undoubtedly contributed to these trends as well (see chapter 9 and figure 3.2, p. 53). Furthermore, it is ironic that as the number of voting opportuni-ties has increased in most nations, the average turnout in elections has de-creased (Dalton and Gray 2003). More and more, citizens complain about

TABLE 3.2 Levels of Turnout from the 1950s to the 1990s (in percentages)

	1950s	1960s	1970s	1980s	1990s
Australia	83	84	85	83	82
Austria	89	90	88	87	80
Belgium	88	87	88	89	84
Canada	70	72	68	67	60
Denmark	78	87	86	85	82
Finland	76	85	82	79	70
FRANCE	71	67	67	64	61
GERMANY (WEST)	84	83	86	79	74
GREAT BRITAIN	79	74	74	73	72
Greece	—	—	83	86	85
Iceland	91	89	89	90	87
Ireland	74	74	82	76	70
Israel	79	82	81	81	85
Italy	93	94	94	93	90
Japan	74	71	72	71	67
Netherlands	88	90	85	81	73
New Zealand	91	84	83	86	79
Norway	78	83	80	83	76
Portugal	—	—	87	81	75
Spain	—	—	76	76	79
Sweden	77	83	87	86	81
Switzerland	61	53	61	40	36
UNITED STATES	59	62	54	52	53
20-nation average	79	80	80	77	73

SOURCE: Institute for Democracy and Electoral Assistance, http://www.idea.int/.

NOTE: Turnout figures are based on voting-age public (not registered voters) in parliamentary elections; for the United States, we used presidential election turnout. Australia and Belgium have strict enforcement of compulsory voting.

"voter fatigue," even though the number of actual opportunities to vote remains quite limited in most nations.

Another set of factors explain cross-national differences in turnout levels. Election turnout in the United States is significantly lower than in most other nations, and the decrease in U.S. turnout over the past forty years has worsened this situation. Some analysts cite these statistics as evidence of the American electorate's limited political involvement (and, by implication, limited political abilities). A more complex set of factors—including voter registration systems and other electoral procedures—is at work, however, strongly influencing transatlantic differences in turnout (Wattenberg 2002; Franklin 2004; Blais 2000). Most Europeans are automatically enrolled on the roster of registered voters, which are updated by the government. Thus, a much larger percentage of the European public is registered to participate in elections. In contrast, most Americans must take the initiative to register themselves, and many eligible voters fail to do so. By many estimates, participation in American elections would increase by several percentage points if the United States adopted the European system of registration (Blais 2000). The scheduling of most European elections on weekends also encourages turnout, because more voters can find the time to visit the polls. In addition, most European electoral systems are based on proportional representation (PR) rather than on plurality-based single-member districts, as in the United States. Proportional representation stimulates turnout because any party, large or small, can receive representation in the legislature as a direct function of its share of the popular vote. (In plurality systems such as those of the United States and Britain, the margin of victory in a district does not matter.) Some nations, including Australia and Belgium, even require that citizens vote or face fines imposed by the government.

Other research demonstrates that political competition is another strong influence on turnout rates (Powell 1986; Crepaz 1990). Sharp social or ideological cleavages between parties stimulate turnout. When European voters go to the polls, they are deciding whether their country will be run by parties with socialist, green, conservative, ethnic, or even religious programs, and these sharp party differences encourage higher voting rates. The number of party choices, the competitiveness of elections, and the structure of legislative power in a system are also predictors of turnout (Jackman 1987; Franklin 2004).

The United States also differs from most other democracies in that its government asks citizens to vote on a very large number of choices. The typical European voter may cast three or four ballots in a four-year period, but many Americans face a dozen or more separate elections in the space of four years. Furthermore, Americans are expected to vote for a much wider range of political offices. Only one house of the bicameral national legislature is directly elected in Britain, Germany, and France; the French president is one of the few directly elected European heads of state. Local, regional, and even national elections in Europe normally consist of casting a single ballot for a single office. The extensive list of elected offices and long ballots common to American elections are unknown in West Europe. Finally, direct democracy techniques such as the referendum and initiative are used only sparingly in France and Britain and not at all in German national politics.

Thus the American political system places unusual demands on the voters to decide on an array of political offices, government bond and tax proposals, and other policy initiatives. Voting in low-information contests, such as those for local nonpartisan offices, poses a real challenge for American voters. It is no coincidence that the one European country that has a comparable turnout level to the United States—Switzerland—also presents its citizens with extensive voting opportunities.

Rather than counting only the number of people who vote in national elections, an alternative measure of participation focuses on the *amount of electing* being done by the public. When the context of American elections is considered, that the amount of electing is actually quite high:

> No country can approach the United States in the frequency and variety of elections, and thus in the amount of electing. No other country elects its lower house as often as every two years, or its president as frequently as every four years. No other country popularly elects its state governors and town mayors, or has as wide a variety of nonrepresentative offices (judges, sheriffs, attorneys general, city treasurers, and so on) subject to election. Only one other country (Switzerland) can compete in the number and variety of local referendums, and only two (Belgium and Turkey) hold party "primaries" in most parts of the country. Even if differences in turnout rates are taken into account, American citizens do not necessarily vote less often than other nationalities; most probably, they do more voting. (Crewe 1981, 262)

A simple comparison of the electoral experiences of a typical European and American voter highlights this difference in the amount of voting: between 1999 and 2004, a resident of Oxford, England, could have voted four times, while a resident of Irvine, California, could have cast about forty votes in the single year of 2004.[3]

Turnout rates in national elections thus provide a poor indicator of the overall political involvement of the public. In addition, the simple quantity of voting is less important than the quality of this participation mode. Verba, Nie, and Kim (1978, ch. 3) describe voting as a high-pressure activity because government officials are being chosen, but there is limited specific policy information or influence because elections involve a diverse range of issues. Therefore, the infrequent opportunity of most Europeans to cast a single vote for a prepackaged party is a limited tool of political influence. Such influence may increase when elections extend to a wide range of political offices and include referendums, as in the United States. Still, it is difficult to treat elections as mandates on specific policies because they assess relative support for broad programs and not specific policies. Even a sophisticated policy-oriented electorate cannot be assured that important policy options are represented in an election or that the government will follow the promised policies in the period between elections. Consequently, research shows that many people vote because of a sense of civic duty, involvement in a campaign, or as an expression of partisan support, rather than as a major means to influence policy.

The limited effects of voting have led some critics to claim that by focusing mass participation on voting alone, parties and political elites are actually trying to limit citizen influence in order to protect their privileged position in the policy process (Piven and Cloward 2000). Even if this skepticism is deserved, voting will remain an important aspect of democratic politics, as much for its symbolic value as for its instrumental influence on policy. Voting is the one activity that binds the individual to the political system and legitimizes the rest of the democratic process. And the decline in voting turnout seems to confirm the popular impression that democratic participation is now waning.

Campaign Activity

Participation in campaigns represents an extension of electoral participation beyond the act of voting. This mode includes working for a party or candidate, attending campaign meetings, persuading others how to vote, membership in a party or political organization, and other forms of party activity during and between elections. Fewer people are routinely active in campaigns because this mode is more demanding than merely casting a vote. Campaign work requires more initiative, and there is greater need to coordinate participation with others (see table 3.1, p. 37). Along with the additional effort, however, campaign activity can offer more political influence to the individual citizen and convey more information than voting. Campaign work is important to parties and candidates, and candidates generally are more sensitive to, and aware of, the policy interests of their activists (Verba and Nie 1972, chs. 17–19).

Campaign activities can take many forms, depending on the context of electioneering in the nation. For example, in the United States, where campaigns are now largely media events, popular involvement in organized campaign activities is limited (see table 3.3). The 2004 election was an exception, because the unusual politicization of the campaign stimulated participation to rise above previous levels. But on the whole, few Americans attend party meetings, work for a party or candidate, or belong to a party or political club. Additional poll data indicate a decreased attendance at political meetings and party work since the early 1970s (Verba, Schlozman, and Brady 1995, 72; Putnam 2000, ch. 2). The most frequent campaign activities instead involve individualistic forms of participation: giving money to a campaign or trying to persuade others how to vote. Personal involvement in campaign discussions has held steady or even increased slightly over the past several decades, with a clear spike upward in 2004.

British campaigns differ in several ways from American elections. British elections do not follow a regular time schedule; the prime minister may dissolve Parliament and call for new elections at almost any time during a legislative term. Therefore, elections are often quickly organized and brief, averaging little more than a month. In addition, British parties depend, for much of their campaign work, on a pool of formal party members who attend political rallies, canvass the constituency during the campaign, and go door-to-door contacting potential voters on election day. Beyond the core of party members, there is limited participation in most campaign activities (see table 3.4). Moreover, with declines in the percentage of party members has come a general decrease in organized campaign activities.

Germany's development of a democratic political system during the later twentieth century increased citizen involvement in campaigns and most other aspects of the politics (Ühlinger 1989). Membership in the political parties

TABLE 3.3 Trends in American Campaign Activity (in percentages)

	1952	1956	1960	1964	1968	1972	1976	1980	1984	1988	1992	1996	2000	2004
Work for a party or candidate	3	3	6	5	6	5	4	4	4	3	3	2	3	3
Go to a meeting	7	7	8	8	9	9	6	8	8	7	8	5	5	8
Give money	4	10	12	11	9	10	16	8	8	9	7	7	6	10
Wear a button or have a bumper sticker	—	16	21	17	15	14	8	7	9	9	11	10	10	21
Persuade others how to vote	28	28	34	31	33	32	37	36	32	29	38	27	34	49

SOURCE: American National Election Study, 1952–2004.

TABLE 3.4 Trends in British Campaign Activity (in percentages)

	1964	1966	1970	1974	1975	1979	1983	1987	1997	2001
Canvass	3	2	1	2	2	2	2	2	2	—
Work for party or candidate	8	2	2	2	3	2	2	2	—	3
Attend meeting (indoors)	8	7	5	5	6	4	3	4	4	1
Attend meeting (outdoors)	8	3	6	4	3	2	—	—	7	
Display poster	—	—	10	9	11	8	12	10	9	—
Party member	14	—	10	—	8	—	7	9	4	4
Read electoral address	46	49	53	51	43	56	49	49	62	69

SOURCES: 1964–1975, 1983–1997, British Gallup Poll; participation data for 1979; and party membership data for all years, British Election Studies; 2001, MORI poll.

grew from the 1950s until the 1980s, and participation in campaigns also grew. For example, 11 percent of the public attended a campaign meeting in the 1961 election; by 1976 this figure had nearly doubled (20 percent). Beginning in the 1970s, popular displays of party support also became a visible aspect of campaigns. But since the 1980s, participation in campaigns has dropped off, much as it has in the rest of Europe (Dalton and Wattenberg 2000, ch. 3; Koch, Wasmer, and Schmidt 2001). Formal party membership has also decreased (Scarrow 2000).

Still, relative to other Europeans, the German public is still politically engaged.[4] In the 1999 European Parliament (EP) election, for instance, German voters closely followed the campaign in the media and nearly one in ten was contacted by a party worker during the campaign—although the EP elections generally attract much less attention than do Bundestag elections (see table 3.5).

The available evidence on party and campaign activity in France is less extensive. Formal party membership increased during the Fifth Republic until the 1980s, and then decreased during the 1990s. There are ongoing discussions about the general depoliticization of French politics (Boy and Mayer 1993). Attendance at campaign meetings, public displays of party support, and other campaign activities probably have decreased during the past two decades, although published empirical evidence is limited. Data from the 1999 EP election show that many French voters followed the

TABLE 3.5 Participation in Various Activities for European Parliament Election (in percentages)

	Great Britain	France	Germany
Followed EP campaign			
Interested in EP election	55	65	76
Watched TV program on election	48	54	85
Read newspaper report on election	54	57	73
Active in EP campaign			
Talked to friends about election	47	60	74
Attended a meeting	3	6	5
Looked up a web site	5	2	6
Active in national campaign			
Tried to persuade others	—	28	29
Participated in campaign	—	7	7
Contacted by party/candidate	—	13	7

SOURCES: 1999 European Election Study; last three items, Comparative Study of Electoral Systems, Module 2.

campaign at levels roughly comparable to the British and Germans (see table 3.5).

Although national histories differ, campaign activity has generally decreased across these four nations. Evidence from a larger set of nations suggests that this pattern is common to most advanced industrial democracies (Dalton and Wattenberg 2000, chap. 3). Fewer citizens now attend political rallies, work for a party or candidate, or actively participate in election campaigns (giving money to U.S. campaigns seems to be a notable exception). The expanding electoral role of the mass media may be one factor behind these trends, because it lessens the importance of party-organized activities designed to inform the public. The media's role has also encouraged the spread of American-style electioneering to Western Europe. British candidates orchestrate "walkabouts" to generate stories for the evening television news, campaigns focus more attention on candidate personalities than in the past, and televised preelection debates are becoming the norm.

These data seem to provide further evidence of the disengagement of contemporary publics. Although many individuals are still drawn to the excitement and competition of elections, campaign participation now is more often individualistic, involving activities such as a display of party support or discussing the elections with friends. Meanwhile, the collective activities that once marked election campaigns are now less frequent. Thus the *level* of campaign activity may be changing as well as the *nature* of the public's involvement.

Communal Activity

The essence of grassroots democracy is represented in communal activity, which can take a wide variety of forms. Communal activity often involves group efforts to deal with social or community problems, ranging from issues of schools or roads to protecting the local environment. From the PTA to local neighborhood committees, this is democracy in action. The existence of such autonomous groups and independent action defines the characteristics of the civil society that theorists from Jefferson to the present have considered a foundation of the democratic process. Tocqueville, for example, saw such group activity as a distinctive feature of American democracy:

> The political activity that pervades the United States must be seen to be understood. No sooner do you set foot upon American ground than you are stunned by a kind of tumult; . . . here the people of one quarter of a town are meeting to decide upon the building of a church; there the election of a representative is going on; a little farther, the delegates of a district are hastening to the town in order to consult upon some local improvements; in another place, the laborers of a village quit their plows to deliberate upon a project of a road or a public school. . . . To take a hand in the regulation of society and to discuss it is (the) biggest concern and, so to speak, the only pleasure an American knows. (Tocqueville 1966, 249–250)

Today, participation in citizen groups can include involvement in public interest groups with broad policy concerns, such as environmental advocacy, women's issues, or consumer protection.

This mode is distinct from campaigns because communal participation takes place largely outside the regularized, institutional setting and lacks a partisan focus. Because such participation is not structured by an election, a relatively high level of political sophistication and initiative is required of communal activists (see table 3.1, p. 37). Citizens define their own issue interests, the methods of influencing policymakers, and the timing of influence. The issue may be as broad as nuclear disarmament or as narrow as the policies of the local school district—and citizens, not elites, decide. Control over the framework of participation means that communal activities can convey more information and exert more political pressure than the public's restricted participation in campaigns. In short, the communal mode shifts control of participation to the public and thereby increases the citizenry's political influence.

Political scientists are now intensely debating whether communal activity and participation in citizen groups is following the same downward spiral as election turnout. In a provocative series of analyses, Robert Putnam (1995, 2000) claims that we are now "bowling alone." Tracking the decline of traditional American social and civic associations across the second half of the twentieth century, he finds that participation in groups ranging from the Elks and the Moose, to the PTA, to bowling leagues has dropped off markedly over the past four decades. Putnam notes that such groups taught skills and norms that spurred democratic political involvement, and argues that with the decline of such associations, involvement has stagnated. He documents a secular decline in the number of Americans who attended a public meeting on town or school affairs, who belonged to a "better government" group, or who served on a committee for a local organization. Instead, too many of us are sitting at home in front of our television sets or computer monitors.

Putnam's critics maintain that he is studying the "old" forms of group activity—that contemporary publics are not engaged in Elks and Moose lodges but in self-help groups, neighborhood associations, and issue-oriented organizations such as environmental groups and the women's movement (Skocpol and Fiorina 1999). In fact, Putnam gives examples of these new forms of action when he lists the range of social activities held in one California church:

> In January 1991 the weekly calendar of the Crystal Cathedral . . . included sessions devoted to Women in the Marketplace, Conquering Compulsive Behaviors, Career Builders' Workshop, Stretch and Walk Time for Women, Cancer Conquerors, Positive Christian Singles, Gamblers Anonymous, Women Who Love Too Much, Overeaters Anonymous, and Friday Night Live. (Putnam 2000, 66)

These are examples of the new forms of social organization that are not tapped by membership in the traditional social institutions. Skocpol (2003) also suggests that the changes in group membership reflect the diminished needs for political groups to mobilize a membership as a basis of funding and public legitimacy, rather than a diminished interest in politics.

The unstructured nature of communal activities makes it difficult to measure participation levels accurately or to compare levels across nations. Still, citizens in all four nations in our study are engaged in communal activities to a significant degree. Group-based participation has long been a distinctive aspect of the American political culture, where membership in social groups often exceeds that in other democracies. Verba, Schlozman, and Brady (1995, 72) found that American participation in community groups increased from 30 percent in 1967 to 34 percent in 1987, and when Putnam replicated this question in 2000, participation on a community project had increased further to 38 percent of the public.[5] The World Values Survey also found that the number of Americans who belonged to civic associations, environmental groups, women's groups, or peace groups increased from 6 percent in 1980, to 18 percent in 1990, to 33 percent in 1999—producing a higher rate of membership than in Britain, France, or Germany (see figure 3.1).

European political norms have traditionally placed less emphasis on group activities, and the structure of European political systems does not encourage direct citizen contact with government officials. But there is strong evidence

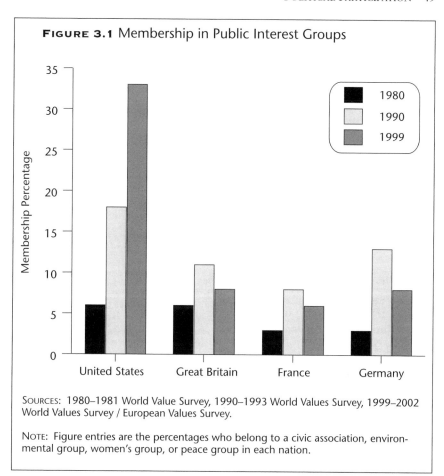

FIGURE 3.1 Membership in Public Interest Groups

Legend: 1980, 1990, 1999

SOURCES: 1980–1981 World Value Survey, 1990–1993 World Values Survey, 1999–2002 World Values Survey / European Values Survey.

NOTE: Figure entries are the percentages who belong to a civic association, environmental group, women's group, or peace group in each nation.

that communal participation has grown in these democracies as well. Other analyses demonstrate a growth of British participation in social groups, contacting and other forms of nonelectoral participation over the past several decades (Curtice and Seyd 2003; Hall 2002), and the World Values Survey similarly finds a general upward trend from 1980 to 1999 (see figure 3.1). Communal activity also has increased in Germany (Wessels 1997; Offe 2002). Voluntary civic associations were an innovation for German politics in the 1970s, but now these groups have expanded to become a regular aspect of politics. Again, the World Values Survey tracks this increase: in 1980, 3 percent claimed to belong to a civic association or political group; this figure bumped up to 12 percent in 1990, and was still 7 percent in 1999. By most accounts, communal activity is more limited in France. Tocqueville, for example, contrasted American social cooperation with the individualism of the French political culture. Even in France, however, the World Values Survey tracks an increase in civic group membership over time.

Putnam has identified important changes in the American political process, but I am not convinced that his findings mean that political involvement of all sorts is declining, or that the patterns he describes for the United States apply to other democracies. Especially within the three European nations we examine, participation in social and civic groups seems to be increasing, introducing more direct citizen involvement in the political process. (Furthermore, many of the factors that Putnam uses to explain the American trends have also occurred in Europe, but apparently without the same effects; see Putnam 2002.) Even if Americans are less likely to participate in institutionalized forms of social or political action, there is some evidence that engagement in informal groups, social movements, and local initiatives are filling part of this void (Putnam 2000, ch. 10). In summary, communal political involvement seems to be an increasingly common aspect of political action in contemporary democracies.

WHO PARTICIPATES?

The question of who participates in politics is as important as the question of how many people participate. First, the characteristics of participants help us to interpret the meaning of political activism. For example, dissatisfaction may stimulate individuals to participate in order to redress their grievances, or it may lead to alienation and a withdrawal from politics. Whether the satisfied or dissatisfied participate more casts a much different light on how we interpret participation. Second, if participation influences policy results, then the pattern of action suggests which citizens are making their voices heard by policymakers and which interests are not being represented. Finally, comparing the correlates of action across nations and modes gives us insights into the political process in each nation and how it shapes citizen choices on how to participate.

Verba, Schlozman, and Brady (1995) summarized previous theories of participation in terms of what they term the "civic voluntarism model." This model includes three types of influences on political participation: *personal characteristics, group effects,* and *political attitudes.* Under the first heading, political scientists stress social status (e.g., education and income) as the personal characteristic that is most strongly related to political action. Higher-status individuals, especially the better educated, are more likely to have the time, the money, the access to political information, the knowledge, and the ability to become politically involved. It is not social status, per se, that stimulates participation, but social status as it relates to skills and orientations that directly influence participation (Nie, Junn, and Stehlik-Barry 1996; Verba, Schlozman, and Brady 1995). So widespread is this notion that social status is sometimes described as the "standard model" of political participation (Verba and Nie 1972, chap. 8). Therefore, social status is the first variable to add to our list of the potential causes of participation.

Another personal characteristic is the individual's position in the life cycle. For many young people, politics is a remote world. As individuals age, however, they take on social responsibilities that increase their motivation to follow politics: they become taxpayers and homeowners, their children enter public schools, and they may begin to draw benefits from government programs. Most studies thus find that political involvement increases with age.

Gender is another factor that may affect political activism. Men are often more politically active than women in democracies (Norris 2002). Differences in political resources, such as educational level, income, and employment patterns, explain a large part of this gap (Schlozman, Burns, and Verba 1994). In addition, early life learning often portrays politics as inappropriate to the female role, which undoubtedly lessens the motivation of women to participate and the willingness of the male world to accept female participation. In an age of changing gender roles, we can determine whether gender is still an important predictor of participation.

A second set of potential predictors reflect group-based forces. Some group influences may be psychological, such as attachment to one's preferred political party. Because campaigns and elections are largely partisan contests, party attachments can stimulate individuals into action. A sense of party identification motivates people to vote or participate in campaigns as a display of party support; they are concerned that their party wins. Conversely, people with weak or nonexistent party bonds are less concerned with election results and are less likely to participate.

Participation in social and voluntary groups provides another potential stimulant to action. Experience in the participatory decision making of a social club or volunteer organization develops skills and orientations that carry over to the world of politics (Putnam 2000; Verba, Schlozman, and Brady 1995). Social groups also provide a useful touchstone for judging whether participation is a worthwhile activity in stimulating action (Uhlaner 1989). In addition, certain social groups actively mobilize the involvement of their members. Therefore, participation in nonpolitical groups may stimulate political involvement.

Political values are a third possible influence on participation. For example, researchers continue to debate the causal role of political dissatisfaction. On the one hand, policy satisfaction may increase support for the political process and thereby for political participation; in these terms, high turnout rates show the public's basic support of the government. On the other hand, dissatisfaction may stimulate efforts to change policy; from this perspective, high turnout rates show widespread public dissatisfaction with the government. Although scholars disagree on the causal direction of policy dissatisfaction, they agree that it is an important potential influence on participation levels.

In a somewhat different vein, participation may be related to policy preferences or ideology (Verba, Nie, and Kim 1978; Verba, Schlozman, and Brady 1995). Do Democrats participate as much as Republicans, or do they participate in different ways? Do members of the British Conservative Party participate as much as Labourites? If participation has an influence on policymakers and the government, then the question whether activists are drawn equally across political camps has important implications for the representativeness of the democratic process. Political participation that is heavily concentrated among ideological extremists may distort the policy process. Therefore, it is important to consider the political orientations (and policy preferences) of participants.

Beliefs about the citizen's role and the nature of political action also may affect participation rates (Pattie, Seyd, and Whiteley 2004; Parry, Moyser, and Day 1992, ch. 8).[6] A sense of political efficacy—the feeling that one's political action can affect the political process—may stimulate individuals to participate. Conversely, a feeling of political cynicism may lead to political apathy and withdrawal: if one cannot affect the political process, why bother to try?

Among the three kinds of potential predictors, the surveys available for analysis include the following factors:

- Educational level
- Age
- Gender
- Political party attachments
- Union membership
- Satisfaction with the democratic process
- Left/Right position
- Political efficacy

This set of predictors is also typically used in other national studies of participation. One of the lessons of the civic voluntarism model is that the effects of these variables overlap. Social status, for example, should have an independent influence through its impact on voters' cognitive skills, as well as through the values and norms that education stimulates. To determine the separate influence of each variable, we combined them in a summary multiple regression analysis predicting political participation. The analysis measures the causal importance of each factor on political activism, independent of the effects of the other variables. We conducted the analysis separately for voting, campaign activity, and communal activity to compare the causal patterns across participation modes.

Voting

Who is more likely to vote? We compared participation rates in the 1996 U.S. presidential election and in the 1999 European Parliament elections (see figure 3.2).[7] The thickness of the arrows in the figure illustrates the magnitude of differences for each factor.

The thick arrows connecting age and voting show that turnout increases significantly with age in all four nations—this is a pattern of more electoral disillusionment among the young (Franklin 2004; Wattenberg 2003). The

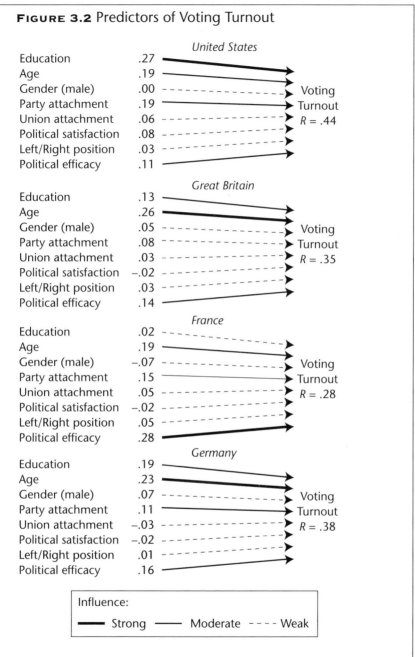

FIGURE 3.2 Predictors of Voting Turnout

United States

Education	.27	
Age	.19	
Gender (male)	.00	Voting
Party attachment	.19	Turnout
Union attachment	.06	R = .44
Political satisfaction	.08	
Left/Right position	.03	
Political efficacy	.11	

Great Britain

Education	.13	
Age	.26	
Gender (male)	.05	Voting
Party attachment	.08	Turnout
Union attachment	.03	R = .35
Political satisfaction	−.02	
Left/Right position	.03	
Political efficacy	.14	

France

Education	.02	
Age	.19	
Gender (male)	−.07	Voting
Party attachment	.15	Turnout
Union attachment	.05	R = .28
Political satisfaction	−.02	
Left/Right position	.05	
Political efficacy	.28	

Germany

Education	.19	
Age	.23	
Gender (male)	.07	Voting
Party attachment	.11	Turnout
Union attachment	−.03	R = .38
Political satisfaction	−.02	
Left/Right position	.01	
Political efficacy	.16	

Influence:
━━━ Strong ——— Moderate ‑‑‑‑ Weak

SOURCES: United States, Comparative Study of Electoral Systems, Module I; Great Britain, France, and Germany, 1999 European Election Study.

NOTE: Analyses are based on vote in the 1999 European Parliament elections and the 1996 U.S. presidential election.

figure expresses these causal effects as statistical coefficients, where the influence of age is estimated independent of the effects of the other predictors in the model. If the simple relationship is expressed in percentage terms, over 80 percent of Americans in their fifties claim to have voted, compared to 58 percent among those under age thirty. Voting turnout follows a sharp age gradient in all four nations.

Another personal characteristic that has a strong relationship to turnout is education. The better-educated are more likely to vote in all three European nations, although educational differences are much more pronounced among Americans. This illustrates the importance of political skills and resources as facilitators of political action.

Because elections are partisan contests, those who identify strongly with a party are more likely to show up at the polls (and presumably cast a ballot for their own party). Another organizational influence, union membership, shows a weak influence in stimulating turnout.

Feelings of political efficacy exert a modest impact in each nation. Those who feel that participation can influence politics are more likely participate. Other political values—satisfaction with democracy and Left/Right position—have a negligible impact on turnout.[8] In this most common of political activities, the ideological bias in participation is minimal.

Campaign Activity

Because the characteristics of campaign activity differ from the simple act of voting, we expect that the type of people who participate in campaign activity also differs. We combined several measures of campaign activism into a single index.[9] Then we used our standard set of predictors to explain campaign activism.

Figure 3.3 shows that individuals with strong partisan attachments are more likely to be active in campaigns. Because campaign work is an intensely partisan activity, partisan ties exert an even stronger force on this mode than on voting turnout. For example, 53 percent of strong partisans in the United States participated in at least one campaign activity in 1996, compared to only 14 percent of nonpartisans.

The greater initiative required by campaign activity also means that the political skills and resources represented by education have more influence on participation rates. Campaign activists in all four nations are disproportionately drawn from the better educated. There is also a tendency for older citizens in Great Britain and the United States to be more involved in campaigns, even while holding constant the other variables in the model.

Is there a gender gap? For both voting and campaign activity, gender differences in participation are small and inconsistent. Males vote at a higher rate in Britain and Germany in the EP elections, while females are more frequent voters in France—but the differences are modest and tend to vary across elections. The effects of gender on campaign activity are equally limited across nations. Furthermore, other research suggests that gender differences in participation

FIGURE 3.3 Predictors of Campaign Activity

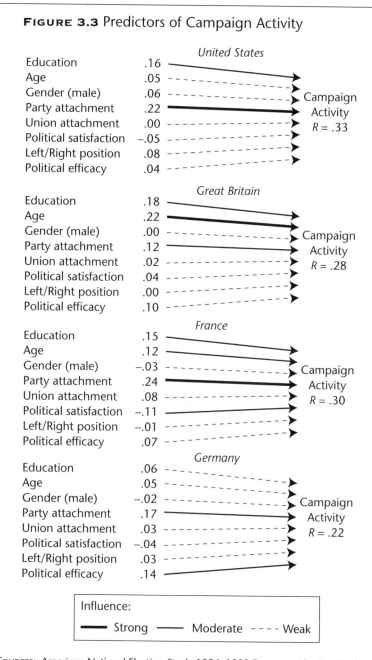

United States

Education	.16
Age	.05
Gender (male)	.06
Party attachment	.22
Union attachment	.00
Political satisfaction	−.05
Left/Right position	.08
Political efficacy	.04

Campaign Activity
R = .33

Great Britain

Education	.18
Age	.22
Gender (male)	.00
Party attachment	.12
Union attachment	.02
Political satisfaction	.04
Left/Right position	.00
Political efficacy	.10

Campaign Activity
R = .28

France

Education	.15
Age	.12
Gender (male)	−.03
Party attachment	.24
Union attachment	.08
Political satisfaction	−.11
Left/Right position	−.01
Political efficacy	.07

Campaign Activity
R = .30

Germany

Education	.06
Age	.05
Gender (male)	−.02
Party attachment	.17
Union attachment	.03
Political satisfaction	−.04
Left/Right position	.03
Political efficacy	.14

Campaign Activity
R = .22

Influence:

━━━ Strong ——— Moderate - - - - Weak

SOURCES: American National Election Study 1996; 1999 European Election Study.

NOTE: Great Britain, France, and Germany analyses are based on three-item index of campaign participation in the European Parliament elections (see table 3.5); the U.S. analyses are based on an index of the five items in table 3.3.

may be decreasing (Inglehart 1990, ch. 10). The gender image of politics may be lessening as more women enter the political process and gender roles in society narrow.

Again, the only political attitude that is consistently related to campaign activism is political efficacy. Neither ideology or political dissatisfaction systematically stimulates campaign activity.

Communal Activity

Participation in citizen-action groups requires a great deal of initiative and sophistication from the participant. As a result, figure 3.4 shows that the better educated are much more likely to participate in communal activities in all three European nations.[10] The other personal factors—age and gender—generally exert little influence. It is significant that in this least partisan of modes, youth participate at almost the same rate as older citizens (see also Dalton 1996, ch. 3).

Working with a community group is distinct from voting and campaign activity because communal participation is generally not a partisan activity. In fact, in many instances participants are drawn to communal groups because they lack strict party allegiances. Consequently, the figure shows that party ties have less impact on communal participation than on voting or campaign activities. We also find that union membership is less influential than for the other two participation modes because citizen-action groups lie outside the normal domain of union-based politics.

Political attitudes exert only a limited influence on communal activity. Feelings of efficacy tend to encourage participation, but these effects are modest. And again, Left/Right differences in this form of political action are insignificant. Communal activity transcends ideological position.

The correlates of activity for the three participation modes are fairly similar across nations, but two national deviations deserve attention. For all three modes, educational differences in participation are greater in the United States than in most other nations. American differences in voting by education ($\beta = .27$), for instance, are far greater than in Great Britain ($\beta = .13$), France ($\beta = .02$), or Germany ($\beta = .19$). Moreover, educational differences in turnout are increasing in the United States (Wattenberg 2002). We expect some differences in participation rates between social strata, but too large a gap implies that certain groups are excluded from the democratic process.

Most European democracies have avoided the problem of large social-status differences in voting turnout. Strong labor unions and working-class parties mobilize the working class and the less educated so that participation rates are similar across social strata. Indeed, union membership is more strongly related to participation among European electorates, and the extent of union membership is much greater among the European working class. The weakness of these same organizations in the United States, when coupled with the restrictive registration requirements of the American electoral sys-

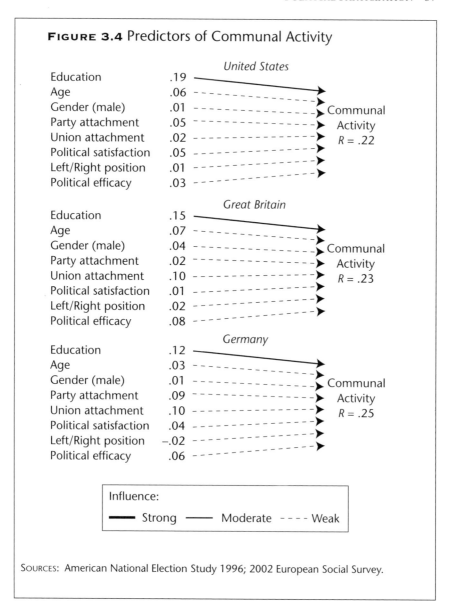

FIGURE 3.4 Predictors of Communal Activity

United States

Education	.19	
Age	.06	
Gender (male)	.01	Communal
Party attachment	.05	Activity
Union attachment	.02	R = .22
Political satisfaction	.05	
Left/Right position	.01	
Political efficacy	.03	

Great Britain

Education	.15	
Age	.07	
Gender (male)	.04	Communal
Party attachment	.02	Activity
Union attachment	.10	R = .23
Political satisfaction	.01	
Left/Right position	.02	
Political efficacy	.08	

Germany

Education	.12	
Age	.03	
Gender (male)	.01	Communal
Party attachment	.09	Activity
Union attachment	.10	R = .25
Political satisfaction	.04	
Left/Right position	−.02	
Political efficacy	.06	

Influence:
▬▬ Strong ── Moderate - - - - Weak

SOURCES: American National Election Study 1996; 2002 European Social Survey.

tem, has created a serious participation gap between social groups. Frances Fox Piven and Richard Cloward (2000) even went so far as to argue that this class bias was an intentional consequence of the U.S. system of voter registration. Regardless of the intent, the U.S. electoral system limits participation by the poor and the less educated. This large participation gap in the United States shows the need for some method of equalizing the involvement of all social groups in American politics.

A second national difference involves the age variable. The age gap in participation is most pronounced for both voting turnout and campaign activity, where the young are distinctly less likely to participate. This pronounced gap is a cause of concern, because it suggests the young are disengaging from electoral politics. However, age differences in communal participation are very small, and for participation in some civil society groups the young are even more active. In addition, new evidence from the 2002 British Citizenship Study suggests that the young in that nation are participating more in contacting, group activities, political consumerism, and protest—while campaign involvement remains low among youth (Pattie, Seyd and Whiteley 2004, ch. 6). Taken together, this evidence suggests that young voters may not be participating less but are participating in different ways than their elders, especially outside of the electoral process.

CHANGING PUBLICS AND POLITICAL PARTICIPATION

There are a variety of ways in which people can become involved in the democratic process, and we have demonstrated these differences in this chapter. Voting turnout is high in most Western democracies, averaging more than 70 percent in most nations. In addition, sizable proportions of the populace are involved in more demanding political activities, such as campaigns, communal participation, or directly contacting government officials. New forms of political consumerism are further expanding the boundaries of political action.

Each of our four nations displays a different mix of these various methods of citizen influence. Americans come closest to the pattern of multimodal participants: turnout in U.S. elections is relatively low, but Americans are active in campaigns and community activities at relatively high levels. Germans also are a relatively participatory public: turnout rates in German elections are much higher than in the United States, and Germans are also involved in campaign and communal activities. The British patterns of participation focus on voting, with modest involvement beyond the ballot box. In their more extensive analysis of British participation patterns, Geraint Parry, George Moyser, and Neil Day (1992, ch. 10) noted with some dismay that a quarter of the British public are almost completely inactive. However, Charles Pattie, Patrick Seyd, and Paul Whiteley's (2004) more recent study is more optimistic about the range of political activity in Britain. Based on the scarce available evidence, the French appear to have limited involvement in group activities, focusing their conventional participation on voting.

Our findings show that contemporary electorates are involved in politics in various ways. Yet a paradox remains. Political information, interest, and sophistication have clearly increased over the past generation (see chapter 2), and these rising levels of education and increased media consumption should increase political participation (Teixeira 1992; Wattenberg 2002). In overall terms, however, conventional participation levels are not increasing significantly; participation is actually declining for some modes of action.

Voting turnout rates have decreased in most advanced industrial democracies, and campaign activity has similarly eroded. Richard Brody (1978) refers to this as "the puzzle of political participation." Why are some aspects of political participation decreasing, if the public's political skills and resources are increasing?

This is a paradox with many possible explanations. Steven Rosenstone and John Hansen (1993) suggested that the decline in turnout in the U.S. is due to the decreasing ability of political organizations to mobilize individuals into action. The political parties are less active in bringing individuals to the polls and getting the public involved in campaigns. Growing social isolation and the decline of community is another explanation (Putnam 2000; Teixeira 1992, ch. 2). Although these arguments carry some weight, they are partially circular in their logic: People are less active in partisan politics because fewer people (and organizations) are mobilizing them to be involved. Moreover, if electoral activity is generally decreasing across nations, this observation leads us to ask why are political organizations generally less engaging?

I think we need to look beyond the electoral arena and reconsider how political sophistication and participation patterns are interrelated. Increasing political sophistication does not necessarily imply a growth in the level of all forms of political activism; rising sophistication levels may be more important in changing the *nature* of participation. Voting, for example, is an area where elites and political organizations traditionally can mobilize even disinterested citizens to turn out at the polls. High turnout levels often reflect the organizational skills of political groups rather than the public's concern about the election. Moreover, citizen input through this participation mode is limited by the institutionalized structure of elections, which narrows (and blurs) the choice of policy options and limits the frequency of public input. A French environmental group bluntly stated its disdain for elections with a slogan borrowed from the May Revolts of 1968: *Élections—piège à cons* (Elections—trap for idiots). When citizens can cast only a handful of votes over a four- or five-year period, as in Europe, this mode is not a channel for active policy engagement. An increasingly sophisticated and cognitively mobilized electorate is not likely to depend on voting and campaign activity as the primary means of expanding its involvement in politics.

The growing political skills and resources of contemporary electorates have had a more noticeable impact on increasing participation in areas where activity is citizen-initiated, less constrained, directly linked to government, and more policy-oriented (Dalton 1984; Inglehart 1990, ch. 10). The self-mobilized individual favors referendums over elections, and communal activity over campaign work. Similarly, participation in citizen lobbies, single-issue groups, and citizen-action movements is increasing in nearly all advanced industrial democracies (Meyer and Tarrow 1998). Verba, Schlozman, and Brady (1995, ch. 3) similarly find that issue-based contacting of political elites has significantly increased among Americans.

In summary, the trends in political activity represent changes in the style of political action, not just changes in the level of participation. The new style of citizen politics seeks to place more control over political activity in the hands of the citizenry. These changes in participation make greater demands on the participants, and, at the same time, increase public pressure on political elites. Citizen participation is becoming more closely linked to citizen influence.

SUGGESTED READINGS

Blais, André. *To Vote or Not to Vote? The Merits and Limits of Rational Choice Theory.* Pittsburgh: University of Pittsburgh Press, 2000.

Conway, M. Margaret. *Political Participation in the United States.* 3rd ed. Washington, D.C. : CQ Press, 2000.

Franklin, Mark. *Voter Turnout and the Dynamics of Electoral Competition in Established Democracies since 1945.* New York: Cambridge University Press, 2004.

Koch, Achim, Martina Wasmer, and Peter Schmidt, eds. *Politische Partizipation in der Bundesrepublik Deutschland: Empirische Befunde und theoretische Erklärungen.* Oplade: Leske + Budrich, 2001.

Parry, Geraint, George Moyser, and Neil Day. *Political Participation and Democracy in Britain.* Cambridge: Cambridge University Press, 1992.

Pattie, Charles, Patrick Seyd, and Paul Whiteley. *Citizenship in Britain: Values, Participation and Democracy.* New York: Cambridge University Press, 2004.

Putnam, Robert. *Bowling Alone: The Collapse and Renewal of American Community.* New York: Simon and Schuster, 2000.

———. *Democracies in Flux: The Evolution of Social Capital in Contemporary Society.* Oxford: Oxford University Press, 2002.

Van Deth, Jan, et al., eds. *Social Capital and European Democracy.* New York: Routledge, 1999.

Verba, Sidney, Kay Schlozman, and Henry Brady. *Voice and Equality: Civic Voluntarism in American Politics.* Cambridge, Mass.: Harvard University Press, 1995.

Wattenberg, Martin. *Where Have All the Voters Gone?* Cambridge, Mass.: Harvard University Press, 2002.

NOTES

1. Parry, Moyser, and Day (1992) add items on contentious politics that form another mode of British participation; the 2000 Citizenship survey (Pattie, Seyd, and Whiteley 2004) found three dimensions of individual actions (consumerism, contributing, and elections), contacting, and protest. Political consumerism—buying or boycotting a product for a political reason—appears to be a common activity in most contemporary democracies, and something missing from earlier participation studies. The 2002 European Social Survey found that more than a quarter of British and German respondents reported boycotting a product for political reasons in the previous 12 months, and more than a third had bought a product for political reasons.

2. Verba and Nie (1972) originally found only 4 percent of the American public was active primarily through contacting officials on personal matters. These individuals tended to be sophisticated, but also unconcerned with broad political

issues. We do not include this fourth participation mode in our analysis because empirical evidence is limited.

However, it appears that participation in this mode is increasing over time. Parry, Moyser, and Day (1992, chap. 3) found that contacting is common in Great Britain, and this is reiterated by Pattie, Seyd, and Whiteley (2004, chap. 3). Verba, Scholzman, and Brady (1995, chap. 3) also showed that issue-based contacting among Americans almost doubled between 1967 and 1987, involving almost a quarter of the public. The 2002 European Social Survey reports that significant numbers have contacted a politician or government official in the previous 12 months: 13 percent in Germany and 18 percent in Britain.

3. The British voting opportunities included local council and county elections, the 2001 House of Commons election, and the 2004 European Parliament election. The American voter's opportunities included both primary and general elections: three votes in the primary for federal offices and two for state offices (these five offices were filled in the general election), three votes for the junior college school district, two for the local school district board, three for city government, one for the water district, and nineteen initiatives and referendums. For additional cross-national evidence, see Dalton and Gray (2003).

4. Comparisons between eastern and western Germany suggest that Easterners lag a bit behind on measures of party and campaign involvement but display comparable levels of political interest and discussion (Dalton 2005; van Deth 2001).

5. Information on the 2000 Social Capital Survey is available at http://www.cfsv.org/communitysurvey/index.html.

6. To measure political efficacy, in the European Parliament survey and the CSES we used a question on whether voting matters; another item on whether politics is too complex to understand yielded essentially comparable results.

7. The analyses in figures 3.2, 3.3, and 3.4 are based on multiple regression analyses; figure entries are standardized regression coefficients. The coefficients measure the impact of each variable, while statistically controlling for the effects of the other variables in the model. We interpret coefficients of .10 or less as a weak relationship, .10–.20 as a modest relationship, and .20 or larger as a strong relationship.

The European Parliament elections attract less interest than national parliamentary elections, which may affect our findings. Turnout as reported by our respondents is 31 percent for Britain, 70 percent for France, and 59 percent for Germany. These turnout rates are comparable to U.S. elections. We decided to use this election because it was held simultaneously in all three European nations, and we have comparable public opinion data from the European Election Survey.

8. Political satisfaction was measured by a question on the respondent's satisfaction with the way democracy functions in the nation.

9. Campaign activity in the European samples was drawn from the 1999 European Parliament elections (see table 3.5). Activism was measured by summing: talked to friends about the campaign, attended a meeting, and looked up a web site. Campaign activity in the 1996 American National Election Survey was measured by counting the activities listed in table 3.3.

10. The group participation item is taken from a measure of participation in community groups in the European Social Survey; the 1996 ANES asked if the respondent worked with others or joined an organization in your community to do something about some community problem in the last 12 months.

CHAPTER 4

Protest Politics

OCCASIONALLY, CITIZEN participation bursts beyond the bounds of conventional politics to include demonstrations, protests, and other forms of unconventional activity. The demonstrations that accompanied the civil rights movement in the United States during the 1960s, the antiglobalization protests of the past decade, and the people-power protests that brought democracy to Eastern Europe illustrate how the public can force political systems to respond and change.

Protest is not new to Western democracies. The United States has repeatedly experienced political conflict throughout its history. The colonial period saw frequent revolts against taxation, property restrictions, and other government policies. When rural elements allied themselves with the urban poor and middle class, an American revolution against British control became inevitable. After independence, political conflict continued with the growth of agrarian/populist movements and workers' movements in the 1800s. Abolitionists, suffragettes, and other political groups used large-scale, nonviolent protests to promote their causes throughout the past century. The early half of the twentieth century was a period of often intense and violent industrial conflict.

A revolutionary tradition is even more deeply ingrained in the French political culture. Many French leftists trace the foundations of French democracy to the revolutions of 1789, 1830, and 1848, as well as the Paris Commune of 1871. Beyond these dramatic political events, French society displayed a high level of protest and collective violence for most of the past century (Tilly et al. 1975, ch. 2). A call to the barricades stirs the hearts of many French citizens, contributing to historically high levels of protest activity. In the words of one expert, protest in France is a national way of life.

Protest and collective action occurred on a more limited scale in Germany and Great Britain, although political conflict was still relatively common. Conflicts over industrial policy during the Wilhelmine Empire and the Weimar Republic often manifested themselves in mass protests. The Weimar Republic suffered from violent clashes between rival political groups. Even Britain, with its tradition of gradual political change, has a history of violence and political conflict that is often overlooked by political scientists (Marsh 1977, ch. 2).

Historically, protest and collective action have often appeared to be the last desperate acts of the public, arising from feelings of frustration and deprivation. Concentrated among the socially disadvantaged, repressed minorities, or groups alienated from the established political order, protest has long been an outlet for those who lack access through conventional channels. The

Internet Resource

Visit the Initiative and Referendum Institute web site for information on the use of referendums in the U.S. and other democracies:

http://www.iandrinstitute.org

expression of outrage or resistance remains a political resource for minorities and repressed groups, and demonstrations by racial minorities (foreign workers in Europe), the economically disadvantaged, and similar groups will continue. Perhaps the most graphic illustration of this form of protest was the democratic revolution that spread through Eastern Europe, the Philippines, South Africa, and other democratizing nations in the late 1980s. When citizens are blocked from exercising political influence through legitimate participation channels, protest politics exists as an option.

Within advanced industrial societies, however, the nature of protest has changed in at least three ways. First, since the student movements of the 1960s, the use of the tactic has broadened from the disadvantaged to include a wider spectrum of political groups. Gray Panthers protest for senior citizen rights, consumers actively monitor industry, environmentalists call attention to ecological problems, and citizen groups of all types are proliferating.

Second, with the changing social base of protest has come a shift in the focus of political action. Protests and demonstrations historically indicated revolutionary ferment and thus often challenged the basic legitimacy of political institutions. Food riots, tax revolts, and socialist worker uprisings are examples of such antigovernmental activity. The new forms of protest in advanced industrial societies, however, are seldom directed at overthrowing the established political order—for the affluent and well-educated participants are some of the primary beneficiaries of this order. Reformism has therefore replaced revolutionary fervor.

Third, before modern times, collective political action was often a spontaneous event, such as a disorderly crowd attacking a tax collector or sparking a riot. Modern protest, in contrast, is typically a planned and organized activity in which political groups consciously orchestrate their activities to occur when the timing will most benefit their cause. The protests outside the 2004 Republican National Convention in New York illustrate this new style. *The Economist* (September 4, 2004) reported that many of the protest leaders were veterans of major political protests ranging from the opposition to the Vietnam War to the antiglobalization movement's "Battle in Seattle." In New York, months of meetings, negotiations, and court decisions were required to shape the terms for protest permits. Protestors then marched along designated routes and received discount coupons for food and shopping, while protest leaders coordinated their activities by text messaging and cell-phone communications. And the mix of protestors ranged from antiwar activists, to anticapitalism, anti-imperialism, anti–gender discrimination, and anti–Fox News groups, to a long list of advocates for other causes. Said one of the protestors: "No matter who wins [the election], I will protest the inauguration." Protest has become simply another political resource for mobilizing public opinion and influencing policymakers.

The spread of protest politics not only expands the repertoire of political participation; it also represents a style of action that differs markedly from conventional politics (see table 3.1, p. 37). Protest can focus on specific issues or policy goals—from protecting whales to protesting the policies of a local government—and can convey a high level of political information with real political force. Voting and campaign work can seldom focus on a single issue because parties represent a package of policies. Instead of participating within an elite-defined framework, citizen activists themselves initiate the action, controlling the timing and location of their protest activities. Sustained and effective protest is a demanding participation mode that requires initiative and cooperation with others. Thus the advocates of protest argue that the public can strengthen its political influence by adopting a strategy of direct action.

MEASURING PROTEST

Although protest and other forms of collective action are a regular feature of democratic politics, these activities were absent from early surveys of political participation. This omission reflected the low level of protest in the 1950s and early 1960s, as well as the unusual nature of these activities. The growing wave of protest in subsequent years stimulated research to fill this void in our knowledge.

The first task was to measure protest participation. Edward Muller (1972) and Alan Marsh (1974) developed a model of this participation mode, ordering the various forms of protest politics along a continuum from least to most extreme. This continuum is marked by several thresholds (see figure 4.1). The first threshold represents a transition between conventional and unconventional politics. Signing petitions and participating in lawful demonstrations are unorthodox political activities but are still within the bounds of accepted democratic norms.

Ian McAllister (1992, 63–69) emphasized the importance of the second threshold because it marks the changeover to techniques involving direct action that are only semilegal, such as boycotts. Activities at this level or beyond exceed the boundaries of conventional, institutionalized political action. A third level of activity involves illegal but nonviolent acts, such as unofficial strikes or peacefully occupying a building. A final, fourth threshold introduces violent activities such as personal injury or physical damage. At this fourth level, political action clearly exceeds what is accepted or tolerable in a

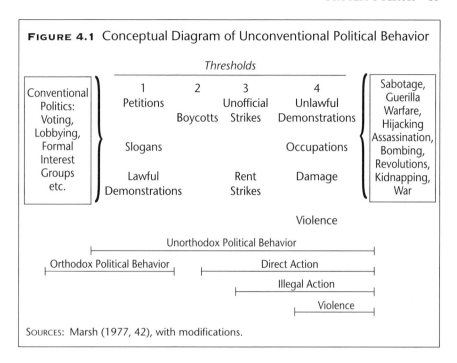

FIGURE 4.1 Conceptual Diagram of Unconventional Political Behavior

Thresholds

Conventional Politics: Voting, Lobbying, Formal Interest Groups etc.	1 Petitions	2	3 Unofficial Strikes	4 Unlawful Demonstrations	Sabotage, Guerilla Warfare, Hijacking Assassination, Bombing, Revolutions, Kidnapping, War
		Boycotts			
	Slogans			Occupations	
	Lawful Demonstrations		Rent Strikes	Damage	

Violence

Unorthodox Political Behavior

Orthodox Political Behavior   Direct Action

Illegal Action

Violence

SOURCES: Marsh (1977, 42), with modifications.

democracy. Research shows that protest action is cumulative: individuals active at any threshold also generally participate in milder forms of protest.

To provide an overview of protest activity, table 4.1 describes cross-national levels of action.[1] The column on the left ranks nations according to the percentage who have signed a petition—the most modest and most common form of protest. Indeed, by democratic standards, this activity is a conventional part of politics. The column on the right ranks nations by public involvement in any of four more challenging types of protest: attending a lawful demonstration, joining in boycotts, taking part in unofficial strikes, or occupying buildings.

Signing a petition is a very mild form of protest that now involves a large share of the public in most Western democracies. The petition has a long and venerable heritage in British and American politics, and political groups of every orientation use it. One can hardly enter a Kmart or a Marks & Spencer without being asked to sign a petition. Thus most Americans (81 percent) and Britons (79 percent) have signed a petition, and this form of action is commonplace in most other nations as well.

A more telling test of the public's willingness to transcend conventional political bounds is participation in the four challenging acts represented in the righthand column of the table. The French engage in relatively high levels of protest activity, exceeded by only a few other Western democracies. More than two-fifths of the French have participated in at least one of the four

TABLE 4.1 Cross-National Levels of Protest Activity (in percentages)

Signed a petition		Participated in a challenging act	
New Zealand	91	Greece	55
Sweden	87	Sweden	48
UNITED STATES	81	Denmark	46
GREAT BRITAIN	79	FRANCE	43
Australia	78	Netherlands	40
Canada	73	Belgium	39
FRANCE	68	Italy	37
Belgium	68	UNITED STATES	36
Norway	65	Norway	34
Switzerland	64	GERMANY	30
Japan	63	Australia	30
Ireland	60	Canada	30
Netherlands	59	Spain	29
Denmark	57	New Zealand	28
Austria	57	GREAT BRITAIN	25
Italy	53	Ireland	25
GERMANY	51	Finland	22
Finland	50	Switzerland	22
Greece	50	Austria	21
Spain	28	Portugal	17
Portugal	22	Japan	14

SOURCE: 1999–2002 European Values Survey / World Values Survey.

NOTE: Entries in the second column are the percentages who have engaged in at least one of the following acts: a lawful demonstration, a boycott, an unofficial strike, or occupying a building.

protest activities, and there is a widespread willingness to engage in these activities among nonparticipants. This finding verifies our earlier description of the French as disdaining conventional politics and relishing protest. In a much earlier work, William Kornhauser (1959) argued that the very weakness of social groups and conventional participation channels in France encourages support for protest. Michel Crozier (1964) described a French aversion to interpersonal interaction that also restricts political participation. Indeed, the French do not rank so highly in the signing of petitions, a political activity that requires face-to-face contact. To this personal aloofness is added a cultural tradition that enshrines France's revolutionary history. In just the single year following the 1999 French survey, truckers opposed to fuel increases blockaded gas stations, citizens demonstrated in support of a sheep farmer who had ransacked a McDonalds restaurant, bus and subway workers disrupted transportation systems in a dispute over shorter workweeks, scientists staged mass resignations in opposition to cuts in government funding, farmers protested the potential introduction of genetically modified crops, non-Christian religious groups demanded greater tolerance of minorities, and prostitutes demonstrated before government offices against unfair competition from immigrants. French protest knows few social bounds.

Most other nations display a modest level of protest, involving 20–30 percent of the public in at least one of these activities (Norris 2002, ch. 10). Mediterranean and Scandinavian nations are at the top of this ranking, while the Japanese evince a marked aversion to such political activities. It is notable that Britain and the United States rank lower in challenging activities than for signing petitions. We return to this point shortly.

Many western Germans (25 percent) have participated in one of these activities, since in their society protest is an accepted form of action by groups ranging from neighborhood associations to the environmental movement, but participation has been more variable in the East. A 1990 survey conducted just after Germany unified found that protest activity was exceptionally high in eastern Germany. In fact, the "peaceful revolution" of 1989 was not so peaceful; massive public demonstrations were required to topple the old regime. Protest activity in the East declined after the democratic transition, but it then grew again in the late 1990s as easterners increasingly expressed their dissatisfaction with the policies of a government whose capital is now located in the East. In 1999 more eastern Germans (45 percent) than westerners were active in protest politics (Watts 2001).

On the whole, most people in Western democracies participate in some form of protest action, if only in the mildest form, by signing a petition. Participation in higher forms of protest politics—such as participating in a lawful demonstration or joining a boycott—actually rivals levels of campaign activity (see chapter 3).

In his critique of American civic engagement, Robert Putnam (2000) suggests that protest participation is declining in the United States along with other forms of action. Certainly protest seems less newsworthy than it was a decade or two ago. But because protest politics and demonstrations now have broader usage, the overall level of protest has risen in most advanced industrial democracies. Table 4.2 tracks the development of protest activity over time for our four core nations.[2] Because it begins in 1974, this series undoubtedly misses the initial growth of such activities that occurred during the 1960s. It is clear, however, that protest generally increased in most advanced industrial democracies over the last quarter of the twentieth century (Inglehart 1997, ch 8; Norris 2002, ch. 10).

This growth of protest activity probably reflects a general increase in small demonstrations over highways, schools, neighborhood issues, and other specific concerns, rather than a few large-scale movements. In addition, the creation of citizen lobbies, environmental groups, consumer advocacy groups, and other NGOs provides an institutional basis for organizing future protests. These new opposition groups may be crucial in permanently changing the style of citizen politics. Protest is becoming a more common political activity in advanced industrial democracies and the era of protest politics is not passing.

TABLE 4.2 Protest Participation (in percentages)

	United States				Great Britain				West Germany				France		
	1975	1981	1990	1999	1974	1981	1990	1999	1974	1981	1990	1999	1981	1990	1999
Sign a petition	58	61	70	81	22	63	75	81	30	46	55	47	44	51	68
Participate in lawful demonstrations	11	12	15	21	6	10	13	13	9	14	25	22	26	31	39
Join in boycott	14	14	17	25	5	7	14	17	4	7	9	10	11	11	13
Participate in unofficial strike	2	3	4	6	5	7	8	9	1	2	2	2	10	9	12
Occupy building	2	2	2	4	1	2	2	2	*	1	1	1	7	7	9
Damage property	1	1	—	—	1	2	—	—	*	1	—	—	1	—	—
Engage in personal violence	1	2	—	—	*	1	—	—	*	1	—	—	1	—	—

SOURCES: 1974–1975 Political Action Study; 1981–1983, 1990–1993, 1999–2002 World Values Surveys; 1999–2002 European Values Survey.

NOTE: Table entries are the percentages who say they have done the activity. An asterisk denotes less than 1 percent; a dash indicates that the question was not asked in this study.

These time trends may also explain why the United States ranks relatively low in recent cross-national comparisons (see table 4.1) despite its reputation for a high level of protest activity. The American public exhibited high levels of protest in the first systematic studies of unconventional political action done in the 1970s (Barnes, Kaase, et al. 1979), and participation has gradually increased since that time, but its use has spread even more rapidly in Great Britain, France, Germany, and other Western democracies. For instance, Americans' frequency of participation in a boycott grew from 14 percent in 1975 to 25 percent in 1999; meanwhile, the British began at only 5 percent but increased to nearly U.S. levels by the end of the series. American participation has not declined, but participation in other nations has grown at a faster rate and thus is overtaking American activity levels.

Although we have generally spoken about protest in positive terms, the dark side of protest politics arises when citizens pass the fourth threshold to engage in violent behavior. The abortion clinic bombers and the terrorist activities of the Irish Republican Army or Spanish separatists go far beyond the tolerable bounds of politics, into actions that are fundamentally different from the protest behavior of most citizens. Table 4.2 also describes the level of violent political action in our four nations, showing that although protest politics is widely accepted, the number who participate in violent activities remains minimal. In 1981, for example, 44 percent of the French public had signed a petition and 26 percent had participated in a lawful demonstration, but only 1 percent had damaged property or engaged in personal violence. Democratic citizens want to protest the actions of their government, not destroy it.

WHO PROTESTS?

Why do citizens protest? If you have ever attended a protest, why did you go? Every protester has an individual explanation for his or her action. A commitment to an issue or ideology stimulates some people to act. General opposition to the government and political system leads other protestors to search for opportunities to display their feelings. Still others are caught up in the excitement and sense of comradeship that protests produce, or they simply accompany a friend to be where the action is. Social scientists have tried to systematize these individual motivations to explain the general sources of protest activity.

The *deprivation approach* maintains that protest is primarily based on feelings of frustration and political alienation. Political analysts have historically seen personal dissatisfaction and the striving for better conditions as the root cause of political violence. For Aristotle, the principal causes of revolution were the aspirations for economic or political equality on the part of the common people who lack it or the aspirations of oligarchs for greater inequality than they have. Much later, Tocqueville linked the violence of the 1789 French Revolution to unfulfilled aspirations expanding more rapidly than objective conditions, thereby increasing dissatisfaction and the pressure for change. Karl Marx similarly saw personal dissatisfaction arising from the competition between the haves and have-nots as the driving force of history and the ultimate source of political revolt.

Modern social scientists have echoed and quantified these themes. The theory has a psychological base: frustration leads to aggression. Therefore, dissatisfaction with society and politics can lead to political violence. The seminal study in the area is the work of Ted Robert Gurr, who stated that "the primary causal sequence in political violence is first the development of discontent, second the politicization of discontent, and finally its actualization in violent political action against political objects and actors" (1970, 12–13). Gurr based his conclusions on analyses of cross-national levels of political violence. Public opinion data also show that policy dissatisfaction increases the likelihood of participation in protest activities (Norris 2002).

This model implies that political dissatisfaction should predict protest activity. Indirectly, the theory suggests that protest should be more common among lower-status individuals, minorities, and other groups who have reasons to feel deprived or dissatisfied.

The *resource approach* is a second general explanation of protest. This model does not view protest and collective action as an outburst by a frustrated public. Instead, protest is as another political resource (like voting, campaign activity, or communal activity) that individuals may use in pursuing their goals. Protest is seen as a normal part of the political process, as competing groups vie for political influence.

The resource model provides alternative suggestions about who resorts to protest behavior, drawing upon the civic voluntarism model of Sidney Verba, Kay Schlozman, and Henry Brady (1995; also see chapter 3 above). The resource model implies that protest activity should be higher among the better educated and politically sophisticated—those who have the political skills and resources to engage in these demanding forms of activity. One also might view involvement in social groups as providing resources and experiences that encourage activities across other participation modes.[3]

And consistent with the civic voluntarism model, several personal characteristics may stimulate protest. Research routinely shows that the young are more likely to protest. Gender may also influence participation in protests (Schlozman, Burns, and Verba 1994). The confrontational style of protest politics appears to involve a disproportionate number of men, although there is evidence that this pattern is changing with a narrowing of gender roles.

Finally, political attitudes may also stimulate protest. Protest is often seen as a tool for liberals and progressives who want to challenge the political establishment and who feel the need to go beyond conventional politics to make their views heard. Recently, however, protest has broadened across the political spectrum, and it may no longer be the primary domain of the Left. For each pro-choice protest, there is now a pro-life demonstration; groups that protest liberal causes are matched by counter-protest among conservatives. Thus we should consider whether there is a political bias in the use of protest.

We used six predictors of conventional political participation from chapter 3 to tap these contrasting models of protest behavior: education, age, gender, union attachments, political satisfaction, and Left/Right position. Figure 4.2 presents these analyses based on the World Values Survey/European Values Survey.[4]

Distrust in parliament has only a modest impact on the willingness to engage in protest. Distrustful citizens are only slightly more willing to protest than those who trust the government. Furthermore, the pattern of other predictors tends to undercut the dissatisfaction model. For example, the willingness to protest is more common among males and the better educated than among women and the less educated.[5]

In short, protest in advanced industrial democracies is not simply an outlet for the alienated and deprived; often, just the opposite appears. The general pattern of protest activity is better described by the resource model. Protesters are individuals who have the ability to organize and participate in political activities of all forms, including protest. The clearest evidence of this is the strong tendency for the better educated to engaged in protest in all four nations.[6]

In one important area, however, the correlates of protest differ from conventional activity. Voting and campaign participation routinely increase with age, as family and social responsibilities heighten the relevance of politics. In contrast, protest is the domain of the young. In the United States, for example, only 11 percent of those under age twenty-five are not willing to engage in at least one challenging action, compared to 24 percent among those over age sixty-five. Age has been among the strongest predictors of the willingness to engage in protest.

Political scientists differ in their interpretations of this age relationship. On the one hand, the pattern may reflect life-cycle differences in protest. Youth is a period of enthusiasm and rebellion, which may encourage participation in protests and other such activities. Young people also may be more accessible to protest because of their free time and concentration in university settings. This explanation would predict that an individual's protest activity should decline with age.

On the other hand, age differences in protest may represent a generational pattern of changing participation styles. That is, today's young people protest, not because of their youth, but because their generation has adopted a new style of political participation: the increasing educational levels, political sophistication, and participation norms among younger generations are producing support for direct-action techniques. If this is true, age differences in protest represent a historical change in participation patterns. Thus youthful protesters should gradually mature into middle-aged activists and not fade with the passage of time.[7] Indeed, the impact of age has weakened over

FIGURE 4.2 Predictors of Protest Potential

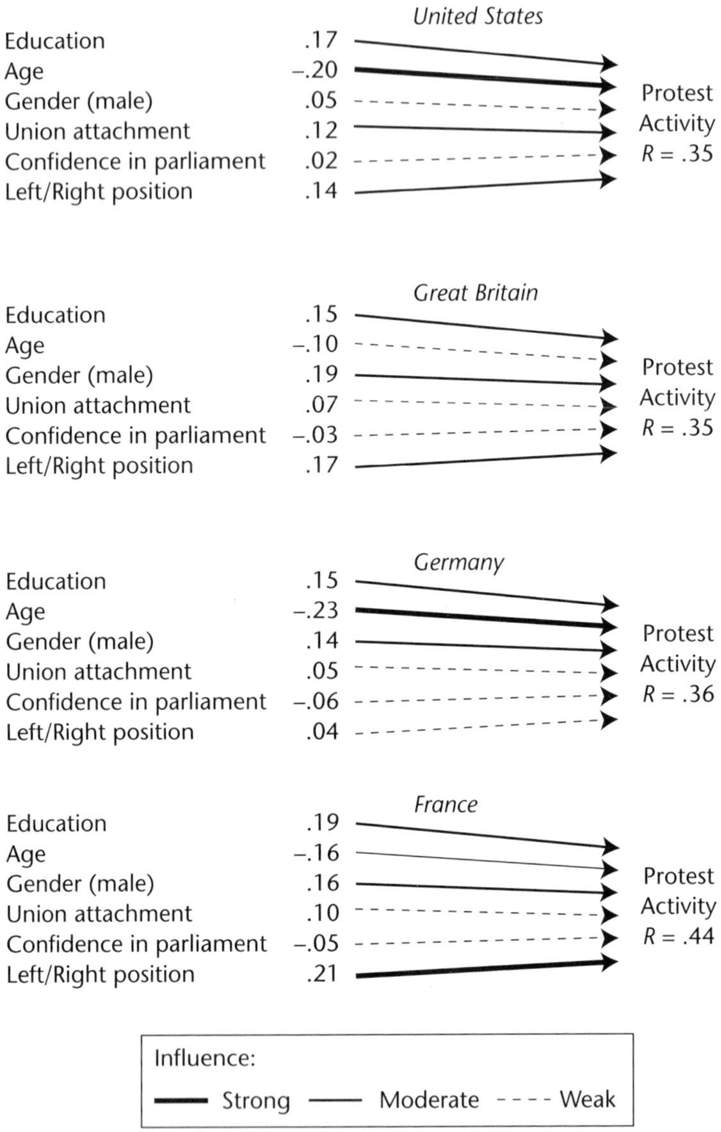

United States

Education	.17
Age	−.20
Gender (male)	.05
Union attachment	.12
Confidence in parliament	.02
Left/Right position	.14

Protest Activity
R = .35

Great Britain

Education	.15
Age	−.10
Gender (male)	.19
Union attachment	.07
Confidence in parliament	−.03
Left/Right position	.17

Protest Activity
R = .35

Germany

Education	.15
Age	−.23
Gender (male)	.14
Union attachment	.05
Confidence in parliament	−.06
Left/Right position	.04

Protest Activity
R = .36

France

Education	.19
Age	−.16
Gender (male)	.16
Union attachment	.10
Confidence in parliament	−.05
Left/Right position	.21

Protest Activity
R = .44

Influence:

━━━ Strong ⎯⎯ Moderate - - - - Weak

SOURCES: 1999–2002 European Values Survey / World Values Survey.

NOTE: The figure presents measures of the independent impact of each variable while controlling for the other variables (standardized regression coefficient). The model predicts a count of the number of challenging protest acts that the respondent has done or is willing to do (see table 4.1).

time as acceptance of protest has spread throughout society. Even seniors are now willing to take to the barricades.

Another important correlate of protest is Left/Right position. Although protest has spread throughout the political process and is used by groups on the Left and Right, the willingness to engage in these activities remains more common among leftists in each nation. These effects are stronger than the ideological biases in conventional forms of political action, and they are consistent even though three nations—the United States, Great Britain, and Germany—were headed by leftist governments at the time the data were collected, and France by a conservative government. Protest politics is still disproportionately the domain of the Left.

PARTICIPATION AND CONTEMPORARY DEMOCRACIES

Robert Putnam (2000, 2002) has argued that citizen involvement in society and politics is waning, and that this trend has serious and dangerous consequences for democracy. The evidence presented in this chapter and the previous chapter questions this conclusion, however. Citizen interest and participation in politics is not generally decreasing in advanced industrial societies—instead, *the forms of political action are changing.* The old forms of political participation—voting, party work, and campaign activity—are in decline. Conversely, participation in citizen-initiated and policy-oriented forms of political activity has increased. Chapter 3 discussed the growth of citizen-action groups, communal participation, and direct democracy methods. This chapter documents the expansion of protest.

Protest can take many forms. The most dramatic examples are the attention-getting events orchestrated by citizen groups to draw attention to an issue or organization. Greenpeace, for instance, has become famous for using its rubber boats to disrupt whaling and protect the harp seals from hunters, as well as other spectacular actions, and its galvanizing tactics have been adopted and expanded by other environmental organizations. But the larger significance of protest is seen in how it has broadened to involve a variety of other citizen groups, such as consumers dissatisfied with a company's product, taxpayers unhappy with the actions of local government, or students disgruntled by university policies. The general acceptance of protest has transformed the style of citizen politics.

Increases in these activities are especially significant because they place greater control over the locus and focus of participation in the hands of the citizenry. Political input is not limited to the issues and institutionalized channels determined by elites. A single individual, or a group of citizens, can organize around a specific issue and select the timing and method of influencing policymakers. These direct-action techniques also are high-information and high-pressure activities. Therefore, they serve some of the participation demands of an increasingly educated and politically sophisticated public, far more so than do voting and campaign activities (Cain, Dalton, and Scarrow 2003, ch. 12).

A major goal of democratic societies is to expand citizen participation in the political process and thereby increase popular control of government. Therefore, increases in communal participation, protest, and other citizen-initiated activities are generally welcomed. This changing pattern of political action is an important element of the new style of citizen politics in advanced industrial democracies.

In addition, however, these changing participation patterns create some new problems for modern democracies. The growing complexity and technical nature of contemporary issues requires that citizens have substantial political sophistication to cope with the world of politics. Participation in citizen-initiated activities—such as protest, communal activity, and direct contacting—is more demanding of the individual than voting or campaign activity. Electoral participation by the less sophisticated is often mobilized by political groups (such as unions or religious/ethic associations), but communal activity and protest politics require greater personal initiative. Consequently, involvement in politics is becoming ever more dependent on the skills and resources represented by social status.

This situation may increase the participation gap between lower-status groups and higher-status individuals. Differences in voting turnout by education, for example, are modest. Differences in communal participation and protest by educational level are substantial; the better educated are the benefactors of these new participation opportunities. Ironically, overall increases in political involvement may mask a growing social-status bias in citizen participation and influence, which runs counter to democratic ideals (see, e.g., Hall 2002).

The solution to this inequality problem is to raise the participation levels of lower-status groups, not to limit the activity of the better educated. Political leaders must facilitate participation by a broader spectrum of the public and lower the remaining barriers to participation. The dictum of "maximum feasible citizen participation" needs to be followed more closely.[8]

Charles Pattie, Patrick Seyd, and Paul Whiteley (2004) have also noted that the new forms of political action such as contacting and even citizen interest groups tend to be more individualistic, replacing the collective actions of election and party work. They are worried that atomistic participation will decrease attention to the collective needs of society and upset the necessary balancing of individual interests. Individuals (and groups) will participate to maximize their own specific interests while downplaying their collective responsibilities. Indeed, this is a problem we discuss in chapter 12 in the context of decreasing trust in government. But the solution is to construct new methods of aggregating political interests to balance the expansion of interest articulation that has already occurred.

Direct-action methods pose another challenge to contemporary democracies. By their very nature, direct-action techniques disrupt the status quo. These activities occasionally challenge the established institutions and procedures of contemporary democracies. This disruptive potential has led some critics to ask whether rapidly expanding citizen participation, especially in protest activities, is placing too many demands on already overburdened political systems (Huntington 1981; Zakaria 2003). Policy cannot be made in the streets, they argue. Efficient and effective policymaking requires a deliberative process, where government officials have some latitude in their decisions. A politicized public with intense policy-focused minorities lobbying for their special interests would strain the political consensus that is a requisite of democratic politics. Indeed, as citizen demands for influence are increasing, a survey of Washington political elites suggests that those who make and implement policy doubt the abilities of the American public.[9]

In short, some analysts argue that it is possible to have too much of a good thing—political participation. Some even cite the empirical evidence accompanying elitist theory of democracy as a basis for this position (see chapters 2 and 12). Citizen activism must be balanced against the needs for government efficiency and rational policy planning, they contend, and the expansion of participation in recent years may have upset this balance, leading to problems of governability in Western democracies. These arguments were commonplace in the 1980s, and even after the democratization wave of the 1990s there are still too many who would limit the rights of others.

Those who caution about an excess of participation display a disregard for the democratic goals they profess to defend; they seem to have more in common with the former regimes of Eastern Europe than with real democratic principles. The associate editor of *The Economist* noted the irony of worrying about the excesses of democracy as we simultaneously celebrated the fall of communism:

> The democracies must therefore apply to themselves the argument they used to direct against the communists. As people get richer and better educated, a democrat would admonishingly tell a communist, they will no longer be willing to let a handful of men in the Politburo take all the decisions that govern a country's life. The same must now be said, with adjustment for scale, about the workings of democracy. As the old differences of wealth, education and social condition blur, it will be increasingly hard to go on persuading people that most of them are fit only to put a tick on a ballot paper every few years, and that the handful of men and women they thereby send to parliament must be left to take all the other decisions. (Beedham 1993, 6)

Contemporary calls for direct citizen action are not antidemocratic behavior. Typically, they are attempts by ordinary citizens to pressure the political system to become more democratic. Protesters are often pressing entrenched elites to open the political process and to be responsive to new issue interests. Furthermore, very few citizens subscribe to the extreme forms of violent political action that might actually threaten a democratic system.

I favor a Jeffersonian view of the democratic process. The logic of democratic politics is that expanding political involvement also can expand citizens' understanding of the political process. Citizens learn about the responsibilities of governing and the choices facing society by becoming involved—and that makes them better citizens. Geraint Parry, George Moyser, and Neil Day (1992, ch. 13), for instance, provide empirical evidence that participation increases the public's knowledge about politics. A study of environmental groups similarly stressed the educational role of citizen-action groups (Pierce et al. 1992). In the long run, involving the public can make better citizens and better politics.

Ironically, there is some evidence from Britain that active citizens also become more critical of politicians and the political process (Parry, Moyser, and Day 1992, ch. 13). Thus the educational role of participation can lead to further challenges to the political status quo. But one hopes that a responsive political system could build positive experiences with the democratic process, thus making progress by addressing the demands of a critical public.

Contemporary democracies clearly face important challenges, and their future depends on the nature of the response. That response should not be to push back the clock, to re-create the halcyon politics of a bygone age. Democracies must adapt in order to survive, ideally by maximizing the advantages of increasing citizen participation while minimizing the disadvantages. The experience of the past several years suggest that this is the course we are following. Institutions are changing to accommodate increased citizen participation (Cain, Dalton, and Scarrow 2003), and politicians and bureaucrats are becoming more comfortable with an expanded form of democracy. Democracy is most threatened when we fail to take the democratic creed literally and deal creatively with the challenges posed by the new style of citizen politics.

SUGGESTED READINGS

Barnes, Samuel, Max Kaase, et al. *Political Action.* Beverly Hills, Calif.: Sage, 1979.
Cain, Bruce, Russell Dalton, and Susan Scarrow, eds. *Democracy Transformed? Expanding Political Access in Advanced Industrial Democracies.* Oxford: Oxford University Press, 2003.
Jennings, M. Kent, and Jan van Deth, eds. *Continuities in Political Action.* Berlin: de-Gruyter, 1989.
Norris, Pippa. *Democratic Phoenix: Reinventing Political Activism.* Cambridge: Cambridge University Press, 2002.

NOTES

1. Protest activity in table 4.1 appears very common because the question asked whether the respondent had ever engaged in the activity. By comparison, the 2002 European Social Survey asked whether the respondent had participated in the activity in the past twelve months. This yields a markedly lower level of protest, but also lower participation in conventional forms of action (such as

working for a party or donating money). The British and German results are presented for comparison:

	Great Britain	Germany
Signed a petition	40%	31%
Participated in a lawful demonstration	4	11
Participated in an illegal protest	1	1
Worked for a political party	3	4
Donated money to a political organization	8	9

2. When Putnam recently asked a differently phrased protest question that replicated an earlier study by Verba, Schlozman, and Brady (1995), he found that the percentage of Americans who had participated in a protest or demonstration during the past year had remained constant at 6 percent in 1987 and 7 percent in 2001. For information on the 2000 Social Capital Survey, see http://www.cfsv.org/communitysurvey/index.html.

3. Research also demonstrates that mobilization by friendship networks encourages individuals to participate in protests, but this is not a factor we can examine with our survey.

4. The protest measure is a simple additive scale of the respondent's willingness to participate in the four challenging activities of table 4.1. The model differs slightly from those in chapter 3 because the World Values Survey lacked a measure of party attachments and had a different measure of political satisfaction (confidence in parliament). The analyses in figure 4.2 are based on multiple regression; figure entries are standardized regression coefficients.

5. We conducted comparable analyses with the European Social Survey, which allowed us to match the predictors of chapter 3 but without data for the United States. Our measure of protest counts signing a petition, attending a legal demonstration, or attending an illegal demonstration. The results are generally consistent with those from the World Values Survey:

Predictor	Great Britain	Germany
Education	.16	.16
Age	−.06	−.01
Gender (male)	.06	.02
Party attachment	.12	.14
Union attachment	.07	.08
Political satisfaction	−.09	.01
Left/Right position	.03	.16
R	.26	.33

6. Union activity is also related to protest. However, the different union measure in the World Values Survey produces very few union activists (about 10 percent), which may affect the influence of this factor.

7. For evidence on the endurance of this new style of protest politics, see Jennings's (1987) national study of youth and Putnam's (2000) generational comparisons of protest. Putnam's findings suggest that the generational shift toward greater protest activity has reversed among the youngest age groups. The World Values

Survey finds lower participation in protests among the younger age groups when compared to the middle-aged, but the young also display a broad willingness to engage in protest politics.

8. This term is identified with the Great Society programs initiated by the Johnson administration to increase the participation of minorities and low-income groups. These institutionalized participation channels have been adopted by a range of citizen groups and governments in the United States and other democracies.

9. The Pew Research Center (1998b) surveyed members of Congress, top presidential appointees, and members of the Senior Executive Service to find out how leaders view the public. Among members of Congress, just 31 percent think Americans know enough about issues to make wise decisions about public policy. Even fewer presidential appointees (13 percent) and senior civil servants (14 percent) feel this way.

PART TWO

POLITICAL ORIENTATIONS

CHAPTER 5

Values in Change

Human values define the essence of our lives. Our values tell us what is important, to us and society. They provide the reference standard for making our decisions. We structure our lives around our beliefs about what is important to us: whether it is the choice of a career, a marriage partner, or a movie on Saturday night.

Politics often involves human values. Values identify what people feel are—or should be—the goals of society and the political system. Shared values help define the norms of a political and social system, while the clash between alternative values creates a basis for political competition over which values should shape public policy. For instance, should welfare programs be constructed in terms of economic efficiency or in terms of empathy for the families in need? Should attitudes toward stem-cell research be linked to moral views about abortion or to concern for those suffering from disease? In a real sense, politics regularly involves conflicts over values.

The new style of citizen politics includes a fundamental shift in some of the basic political values of many people. A comparison of contemporary societies to those of a generation ago would uncover strong evidence of changing social norms: hierarchical relationships and deference to authority are giving way to decentralization, self-expression, and a desire to participate in the decisions affecting one's life. Previous chapters have described how participatory norms are stimulating greater political involvement, but the consequences of value change are much broader. The new values affect attitudes toward work, lifestyles, and the individual's role in society.

The definition of societal goals and the meaning of "success" are also changing. Until recently, many Americans measured success almost solely in economic terms: a large house, two cars in the garage, and other signs of affluence. The late Malcolm Forbes said that life was a contest, and the winner was the person who accumulated the most possessions before he or she died (he is dead now). In Europe, the threshold for economic success might have been lower, but material concerns were equally important.

Once affluence became widespread, however, many people realized that bigger is not necessarily better. The consensus in favor of economic growth is now tempered by a concern for improving the quality of life. A new desire to protect the environment has spread throughout society. Instead of just income, careers are measured by the feeling of accomplishment and the freedom they offer. Social relations and acceptance of diversity are additional examples of values in change. Progress on racial, sexual, and religious equalities are transforming American and European societies.

Internet Resource

Visit the World Values Survey web site for information on this global survey of values:

http://www.worldvaluessurvey.org

Evidence of value change is all around us, if we look. We think in the present, however, and so the magnitude of these changes is not always appreciated. One can get a sense of these changes by comparing contemporary American lifestyles to the images of American life depicted on vintage television reruns from the 1950s and 1960s. Series such as *Ozzie and Harriet, Father Knows Best,* and *Leave It to Beaver* reflected the values of a bygone era. How well would the Nelsons or the Cleavers adjust to a world transformed by women's liberation, the new sexual morality, racial desegregation, rap music, and alternative lifestyles? Imagine the Cleavers and the Bundys as next-door neighbors—or Wally Cleaver hanging out with the guys from *The O.C.*

This chapter examines the evidence that values are systematically changing in advanced industrial societies. Then we consider some of the implications of this process of value change for democratic politics.

THE NATURE OF VALUE CHANGE

We study citizen values because they provide the standards that guide the attitudes and behaviors of the public. Values signify a preference for certain personal and social goals, as well as the methods to obtain these goals. One individual may place a high priority on freedom, equality, and social harmony—and favor policies that strengthen these values. Others may stress independence, social recognition, and ambition in guiding their actions.

Many personal and political decisions involve making choices between valued goals that lie on opposite sides of a given situation. One situation may create a choice between independence and obedience or between polite evasiveness and blunt sincerity. A national policy may present conflicts between the goals of world peace and national security or between economic growth and protecting nature.

People develop a general framework for making these decisions by arranging values in terms of their importance to the individual. Citizen behavior may appear inconsistent and illogical (see chapter 2) unless the researcher considers the values of each person and how they apply these values in specific situations. To one citizen, the issue of busing schoolchildren for racial balance taps values of social equality and civil rights; to another, it concerns freedom and providing for one's family. Both perspectives are reasonable, and attitudes toward busing are determined by how people weigh these conflicting values.

Value systems should include the salient goals that guide human behavior. Milton Rokeach (1973) developed an inventory of eighteen instrumental values dealing with the methods of achieving desired goals and eighteen terminal values defining preferred end-state goals. A complete list of important human goals, which should be much longer, would be necessary to explain individual behavior fully.

Social scientists have focused their attention on questions of value change as the evidence of the public's changing priorities became apparent in several areas. In reaction to the individualization of society, researchers described the shift from group solidarity and other-directed values to self-actualizing and inner-directed goals (Riesman 1950; Sennet 1978). Alex Inkeles and David Smith (1974) traced a more general process of value change, linking developed and modern societies, and this model has been updated by recent research on modernizing societies (Inglehart 1997; Inglehart and Welzel 2005).

Ronald Inglehart has developed a systematic approach to describe the value changes that are occurring in advanced industrial societies (Inglehart 1977, 1990; Abramson and Inglehart 1995). Inglehart bases his theory of value change on two premises. First, he suggests a *scarcity hypothesis*: individuals "place the greatest value on those things that are in relatively short supply" (1981, 881). That is, when some valued object is difficult to obtain, its worth is magnified. If the supply increases to match the demand, then the object is taken for granted and attention shifts to things that are still scarce. For example, water is a precious commodity during a drought, but when normal rains return, the concern over water evaporates. Similarly, the modern concern for clean water arose when pollution became widespread and the availability of clean water became uncertain. This general argument can be applied to other items valued by society.

The second part of Inglehart's theory is a *socialization hypothesis*: "to a large extent, one's value priorities reflect the conditions that prevailed during one's preadult years" (1981, 881). These formative conditions include both the situation in one's own family and broader political and socioeconomic conditions. Value change may continue after this formative period as people move through the life cycle or are exposed to new experiences. Nevertheless, Inglehart assumes that later learning must overcome the inertia of preexisting orientations.

The combination of both hypotheses—scarcity and socialization—produces a general model of value change. Individuals initially form their basic value priorities early in life and then emphasize those desired goals that are in short supply. Once these values priorities develop, they tend to endure in the face of later changes in personal and social conditions.

Chapter 1 described how advanced industrial societies are now characterized by unprecedented affluence, greatly increased educational levels, expanding information opportunities, extensive social welfare systems, and other related attributes that changed dramatically during the later twentieth century. We have linked these trends to the growing sophistication, cognitive mobilization, and participation of modern publics. In addition, Inglehart maintains that these social forces are changing the public's basic value priorities by altering socioeconomic conditions. Thus, as the relative scarcity of valued objects changes, this trend produces parallel changes in what the public values most.

To generalize the scarcity hypothesis into a broader theoretical model, Inglehart draws on the work of Abraham Maslow (1954), who produced a hierarchical ordering of human goals.[1] Maslow suggested that people are first driven to fulfill basic subsistence needs—water, food, and shelter. When these needs have been met, they continue searching until enough material goods are acquired to attain a comfortable margin of economic security. Having accomplished this goal, people may turn to higher-order needs, such as the need for belonging, self-esteem, participation, self-actualization, and the fulfillment of aesthetic and intellectual potential. Thus, social conditions generally predict the broad values emphasized by the public.

The CBS television show *Survivor* presents the Maslovian value hierarchy in practice. Once the group of relatively affluent Americans reach the island, their priorities shift toward subsistence needs: finding water, ensuring that there is enough rice for the day, and maybe even hunting rats for additional protein. The aesthetic, quality-of-life concerns they probably focused on at home are overtaken by the need to survive. This is Maslow as Robinson Caruso.

Inglehart applies the logic of Maslow's value hierarchy to political issues (see figure 5.1). Many political issues, such as economic security, law and order, and national defense, tap underlying sustenance and safety needs. Inglehart describes these goals as *material* values. In a time of depression or civil unrest, for example, security and sustenance needs necessarily receive maximum attention. If a society can make significant progress in addressing these goals, attention can then shift toward higher-order values, reflected in issues such as individual freedom, self-expression, and participation. Inglehart labels these goals *postmaterial* values.

Inglehart contends that this material/postmaterial continuum is a general framework for understanding the primary value changes now occurring in advanced industrial democracies. In his more recent writings, Inglehart describes this development as the shift from survival values to self-expressive values (Inglehart 1997; Inglehart and Welzel 2005). The broad nature of these value changes leads others to describe the process as a transition from "Old Politics" values of economic growth, security, and traditional lifestyles to "New Politics" values of individual freedom, social equality, and the quality of life. One sign of the significance of this concept is the large number of other studies that have examined the postmaterial theory (see the extensive literature cited in Van Deth and Scarbrough 1995).

The major challenges to Inglehart's theory of value change have come in two areas. First, several studies have questioned whether socioeconomic

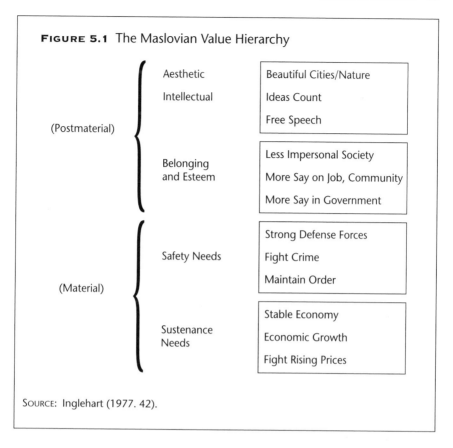

FIGURE 5.1 The Maslovian Value Hierarchy

(Postmaterial)

Aesthetic	Beautiful Cities/Nature
Intellectual	Ideas Count
	Free Speech

Belonging and Esteem	Less Impersonal Society
	More Say on Job, Community
	More Say in Government

(Material)

Safety Needs	Strong Defense Forces
	Fight Crime
	Maintain Order

Sustenance Needs	Stable Economy
	Economic Growth
	Fight Rising Prices

SOURCE: Inglehart (1977. 42).

conditions are linked to citizen values as Inglehart predicts. For example, Harold Clarke and Nitish Dutt (1991) demonstrated that Inglehart's simple value index is closely related to the ebb and flow of economic conditions, instead of consistently reflecting the conditions of earlier formative environments. Raymond Duch and Michael Taylor (1993, 1994) similarly raised questions about whether formative conditions are the key determinants of values (also see Inglehart's response, in Abramson and Inglehart 1995). In large part, I see these as narrow methodological questions about the measurement of values, such as whether educational attainment primarily represents formative conditions or present social position. But these questions do sensitize us to the fact that values are dependent on formative conditions *and* present circumstances.

A second critique asks whether advanced industrial societies are changing only along the single material/postmaterial dimension. Scott Flanagan (1982, 1987; Flanagan and Lee 2003) has argued that values are shifting along at least two dimensions: one that involves a shift from material to noneconomic values, and a second that involves a shift from authoritarian to libertarian values (also see Nevitte 1996). V. Braithwaite, T. Makkai, and Y. Pittelkow (1996) have similarly suggested that these societies are shifting from security-based values toward harmony-based values. Undoubtedly Inglehart's framework oversimplifies the process of value change, since societies are changing in multiple ways that tap different parts of people's value systems. This is clearly an area where further research is warranted. But Inglehart's framework generally overlaps with the value dimensions that these other researchers have suggested. For instance, Flanagan's two dimensions can be seen as subelements of Inglehart's broader framework. Regardless of how we conceptualize this process, however, there is general agreement that the value priorities of modern publics are changing.

THE DISTRIBUTION OF VALUES

When we measure citizen values, we must realize that most people attach positive worth to both material and postmaterial goals. The average person favors both economic growth and a clean environment, social stability and individual freedom. Politics, however, often involves a conflict between separately valued goals. Therefore, rather than study one set of values in isolation from another, we must identify which goals take priority in the public's mind when values come in conflict.

Surveys use a variety of methods to measure values. Indeed, because values are deeply held and relatively pure feelings, it is complicated to tap them with a simple public opinion survey question. In addition, researchers debate whether we should measure values in terms of personal life conditions or phrased as political goals that are linked to political behaviors. This measurement debate is ongoing (Van Deth and Scarbrough 1995; Bean and Papadakis 1994).

Following Inglehart's model of the Maslovian value hierarchy, the 1990–1991 World Values Survey assessed value priorities by asking respondents to rank the importance of twelve possible political goals. Table 5.1 presents the top priorities of American, British, French and German citizens across these items.

Most citizens on both sides of the Atlantic cited material goals as their first priority. Americans most often emphasized economic growth, a stable economy, and crime prevention. Europeans stress the same material needs. The responses from East Germans in 1990 are especially revealing: after suffering through a decade of mounting economic and social problems, East Germans stressed the need to improve economic conditions. Consistent with Maslow's theory, economic needs and security take precedence over postmaterial goals such as participation, free speech, and the environment—even though these were also severe problems in the East. As Bertolt Brecht once wrote: *"Erst kommt das Fressen, dann die Morale"* (first comes the food, then morals). In the Western democracies, however, many people also gave high rankings to postmaterial goals such as participating in job-related and political decision

TABLE 5.1 The Distribution of Value Priorities (in percentages)

	United States	Great Britain	France	West Germany	East Germany
High level of economic growth (M)	76	67	72	65	86
A stable economy (M)	71	62	47	66	86
More say in work/community (PM)	55	69	68	59	59
Fight against crime (M)	65	64	55	49	45
Protect free speech (PM)	48	45	63	61	51
Maintain order in nation (M)	57	46	44	55	60
More say in government (PM)	55	51	38	50	58
More humane society (PM)	33	43	57	55	47
Fight rising prices (M)	44	52	50	28	27
Make cities/country beautiful (PM)	23	36	38	42	49
Ideas count more than money (PM)	27	27	35	25	18
A strong defense (M)	38	19	12	12	2

SOURCE: 1990–1991 World Values Survey.

NOTE: Table entries are the percentage of respondents listing the item as first or second choice among items presented in sets of four. Missing data were included in the calculation of percentages. M = material value; PM = postmaterial value.

making, and protecting free speech. A majority of West Germans and French greatly valued progress toward a more humane society.

Using the choices made among these twelve items, we created a single index that scores individuals by the relative weight they attach to postmaterial goals.[2] Materialists place high priority on the six economic and security goals, while postmaterialists stress participation and the other postmaterial goals. Table 5.2 displays the percentages of postmaterialists on this twelve-item index over time.

In the early 1970s, postmaterialists were a relatively small minority in every nation. Using this index, only 13 percent of Germans and 18 percent of the British scored high on the postmaterial scale. The proportion of materialists was even more pronounced with Inglehart's four-item index (1977, 1990). The greater number of materialists is not surprising since the conditions fostering postmaterial value change were still developing. In historical perspective, the development of advanced industrialism is a relatively recent phenomenon.

By the 1990s, the proportion of postmaterialists had increased in each nation for which long-term data are available. The percentage of postmaterialists in western Germany, for example, had grown to 43 percent by 1995. More time points are available for the four-item postmaterial index. These trend data show a general shift toward postmaterial values for a large set of advanced industrial societies (Abramson and Inglehart 1995; Inglehart and Welzel 2005, ch. 4).

Evidence from other sources underscores the value shift among these publics. For instance, between 1949 and 1975, Germans reversed the priority

TABLE 5.2 The Shift in Postmaterial Values over Time (in percentages)

Country	1973	1990	1999
Belgium	38	38	—
Canada	—	29	30
Denmark	19	32	—
FRANCE	33	27	—
GERMANY (West)	13	36	43
GREAT BRITAIN	18	19	—
Ireland	15	23	—
Italy	16	33	—
Japan	—	31	28
Netherlands	35	39	—
Spain	—	37	29
Sweden	—	31	29
UNITED STATES	—	21	23
Norway	—	17	20
8-nation average	23	31	—

SOURCES: 1973 European Communities Study; for first U.S. time point: 1974 Political Action Study; 1990–1991 World Values Survey; 1999–2002 World Values Survey; for last German time point: 1995–1998 World Values Survey.

NOTE: Figure entries are the percentages placing a higher priority on postmaterial goals, using the 12-item values index in table 5.1, p. 87. See footnote 2 on scale construction.

they attached to two freedoms: freedom from want and freedom of speech (Dalton 1993, 118). In the insecure climate of the immediate postwar period, 35 percent of West Germans emphasized freedom from want, and 26 percent gave priority to free speech. After the Economic Miracle had transformed German lifestyles, only 23 percent stressed freedom from want, and 54 percent emphasized free speech. Similar trends are apparent in the values German parents say they would emphasize in raising their children (Nevitte 1996). Trend surveys conducted by the Japanese government also display a shift in values over the postwar period from what Inglehart would label material goals to postmaterial concerns (Inglehart 1990).

Even if there is uncertainty about the exact proportion of postmaterialists because of the debate on how to measure these values, the trend toward postmaterial goals is clear. Larger proportions of the public—often a third— now give priority to postmaterial goals in most advanced industrial democracies. Because many other individuals favor both kinds of values, the number of people exclusively preferring material goals is a minority in most nations. Thus value priorities in these societies are now characterized by a mix of material and postmaterial objectives.

For nearly three decades critics have claimed that postmaterialism is a "sunshine" issue that will fade with the next economic downturn or period of political uncertainty. In the 1970s, the OPEC increases in oil prices stimulated global recessions that some claimed would end the liberalism of the

1960s. The 1980s were heralded as the "me" decade. The 1990s were years of economic strains in Germany, Japan and many other nations. Despite these potential countertrends, public opinion surveys document the slow and relatively steady growth of postmaterial values over time. An evolutionary change in values is transforming the nature of citizen politics.

MODELING THE PROCESS OF VALUE CHANGE

How do we know expressed support for postmaterial goals really reflects an ongoing process of societal value change? At first, the evidence was tentative. With time, however, the evidence in support of postmaterial value change has grown. The trends cited here provide one sort of evidence.

The most telling evidence supporting the postmaterial thesis comes, however, from analyses that test the two hypotheses underlying Inglehart's theory. The scarcity hypothesis predicts that the socioeconomic conditions of a nation are related to the priorities of its citizens. The socialization hypothesis predicts that values become crystallized early in life. Thus the overall values of a society reflect the conditions decades or more earlier, when values were being formed.

We can test these ideas by comparing national levels of postmaterial values to the socioeconomic conditions of each nation. If scarcity breeds a concern for material values, then these concerns should be more common in nations with lower living standards. Conversely, the affluence of advanced industrial societies should increase support for postmaterial goals. Moreover, according to the socialization hypothesis, these effects should occur with a time lag. Thus, the best predictor of values should be national conditions a generation ago, when values were forming.

Figure 5.2 displays a clear relationship between national affluence (GNP per capita in 1965) and the distribution of material/postmaterial values in 1990–1991 for thirty-three nations.[3] In general, postmaterialists are most common in nations (including the four core nations in this book) that had relatively high living standards during the formative years of the average adult surveyed in 1990. In contrast, low levels of postmaterialism are found in less affluent nations, such as Nigeria, India, China, and other less developed nations (including several nations in Eastern Europe). Moreover, this is not simply a correlation between measures from the same year, as Abramson and Inglehart presented (1995, 128). We are comparing economic conditions a generation ago with value priorities in the 1990s.

The figure also describes a curvilinear relationship between economic conditions and value change.[4] The greatest value shift occurs during the transition from a subsistence economy to an industrial society, such as that found in postwar Western Europe. Once this level of affluence is achieved, further increases in living standards produce progressively smaller changes in values. This implies that the process of value change will continue at a slower rate in the future, but a gradual shift in values should continue.

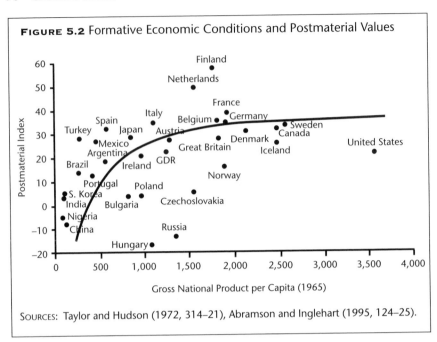

FIGURE 5.2 Formative Economic Conditions and Postmaterial Values

SOURCES: Taylor and Hudson (1972, 314–21), Abramson and Inglehart (1995, 124–25).

Another test of the postmaterial theory involves generational differences in values. Older generations, reared in the years before World War II, grew up in a period of widespread uncertainty. These individuals suffered through the Great Depression of the 1930s and endured two world wars and the social and economic traumas that accompanied these events. Because of these conditions, older generations in most Western democracies should have been socialized into a greater concern with material goals: economic growth, economic security, domestic order, and social and military security.

Conversely, younger generations in Europe and North America were raised in a period of unprecedented affluence and security. Present-day living standards are often several times higher than those experienced before World War II. The expansion of the welfare state now protects most people from even major economic problems. Postwar generations also have a broader worldview, reflecting their higher educational levels, greater exposure to political information, and more diverse cultural experiences. Furthermore, the end of the Cold War capped one of the longest periods of international peace in modern European history. Under these conditions, the material concerns that preoccupied prewar generations should diminish in urgency. Growing up in a period when material and security needs seem relatively assured, younger generations should shift their attention toward postmaterial goals.

Furthermore, Inglehart's socialization hypothesis predicts that values formed early in life should persist through the life span. That is, if values are enduring, different age groups should retain the mark of their formative generational experiences even if family or societal conditions change. Older Europeans should still stress security concerns even if their present lifestyles reflect a high level of affluence. Generations socialized in the conditions of the postwar Economic Miracle should retain their greater concern for post-material values even as they age and assume greater family and economic responsibilities.

Thus a crucial test of the value-change thesis involves tracking the value priorities of generations over time. Figure 5.3 describes the value priorities of several European generations from 1974 until 1997, using Inglehart's four-item value index.[5] The oldest generational cohort—those born between 1885 and 1909 (who were 65–88 years of age in 1974)—is located near the bottom of the figure. In 1974 the proportion of materialists in this cohort outweighs postmaterialists by nearly 50 percent. In contrast, the youngest cohort in 1974—those born between 1940 and 1954—is almost evenly balanced between material and postmaterial values.

Not only is the relative ranking of generations important evidence in support of Inglehart's theory, but so is the persistence of this pattern. The level of values fluctuates over time in response to random sampling variation and the sensitivity of the four-item values index to inflation levels (which I consider a

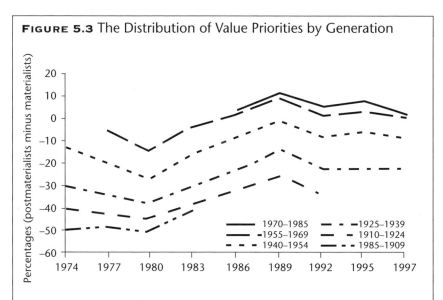

FIGURE 5.3 The Distribution of Value Priorities by Generation

Sources: Cumulative file for the Eurobarometers, 1974–1997.

Note: The data are based on a combined weighted sample of European Community Surveys carried out in six nations (Belgium, France, Great Britain, Italy, the Netherlands, and West Germany). The total sample size is 383,681. The values plotted in the figure are the percentages of postmaterialists minus the percentages of materialists, aggregated for six generational groups. Surveys across three-year time spans were combined to provide more reliable results.

methodological imperfection in the four-item measure).[6] Most important, the generational gaps in value orientations remain fairly constant over time—as seen in the parallel movement of each generation—although all cohorts are moving through the life cycle. The youngest age group from 1974, for example, has reached middle age by the end of the survey series (42–57 years of age); yet their average level of material/postmaterial values does not change significantly between 1974 and 1997. Life-cycle experiences normally modify, but do not replace, the early learning of value priorities.

The size of the generational differences in values across nations provide supplemental support for the value-change thesis. West Germany, for example, experienced tremendous socioeconomic change during the past few generations. Consequently, the value differences between the youngest and oldest German cohorts are larger than for many other nations. Conversely, in nations that experienced less socioeconomic change over the several decades, age groups should display smaller differences in their values. Abramson and Inglehart (1995, 134) demonstrated that there is a strong relationship between rates of economic growth and the size of the age gap in value priorities. Large social changes produce large changes in values.

Education is another indirect measure of an individual's economic circumstances during adolescence, when value priorities were being formed, because access to higher education often reflects the family's social status during an individual's youth.[7] In addition, education also may affect value priorities because of the content of learning. Contemporary Western educational systems generally stress the values of participation, self-expression, intellectual understanding, and other postmaterial goals. Moreover, the liberal orientation of the modern university milieu may encourage a broadening of social perspectives. And finally, the effects of education overlap with those of generation; the young are better educated than the old.

Figure 5.4 presents the differences across educational groups in the percentages expressing postmaterial values in 1999. In each nation, there is a positive relationship between educational level and support for postmaterial goals. In France, for instance, only 8 percent of the lesser-educated are postmaterialists, compared to 31 percent of those with higher education. One could argue that the American educational system is the most egalitarian of those portrayed in the figure, and thus the link between educational level and early life conditions is weaker than in the other two nations—consequently the relationship between education and values is also weaker.

The concentration of postmaterial values among the young and better-educated gives added significance to these orientations. If Inglehart's theory is correct, the percentage of postmaterialists should gradually increase over time, as older materialist cohorts are replaced by younger, more postmaterialist generations.[8] Similarly, if expanding educational opportunities continue to increase the public's educational level, support for postmaterial values should continue to grow. Furthermore, because postmaterialists are more active in politics, their political influence is greater than their numbers imply.

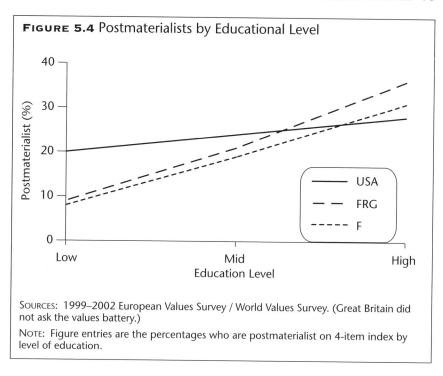

FIGURE 5.4 Postmaterialists by Educational Level

SOURCES: 1999–2002 European Values Survey / World Values Survey. (Great Britain did not ask the values battery.)

NOTE: Figure entries are the percentages who are postmaterialist on 4-item index by level of education.

Indeed, among the group of future elites—university-educated youth—post-material values predominate.[9] As these individuals succeed into positions of economic, social, and political leadership, the impact of changing values should strengthen. Value change appears to be an ongoing process.

THE CONSEQUENCES OF VALUE CHANGE

Postmaterialists now constitute only a minority of the population in most advanced industrial democracies, but the impact of these values is already apparent, extending beyond politics to all aspects of society. Indeed, one of the most impressive aspects of Inglehart's book *Culture Shift in Advanced Industrial Society* is the range of political phenomena he links to postmaterialism.

At the workplace, for example, these new value orientations fuel demands for a more flexible and individually oriented work environment. Rigid, hierarchical, assembly-line systems of production are being challenged by worker participation (codetermination), quality circles, and flexible working hours. The 1999 European Values Survey, for instance, finds that materialists emphasize good pay and job security as important characteristics of a job, while postmaterialists emphasize goals such as having the opportunity to use initiative, holding a job that is useful to society, and working with pleasant people. Many business analysts bemoan the decline of the work ethic, but it is more accurate to say that the work ethic is becoming motivated by a new set of goals.

Social relations are changing in reaction to these new value orientations. Neil Nevitte (1996) convincingly demonstrates that deference to authority of all kinds is waning: bosses, army officers, university professors, and political leaders all decry the decline in deference to their authority. But the postmaterial credo is that an individual earns authority, rather than having it bestowed by a position. Similarly, many citizens are placing less reliance on social norms—class, religion, or community—as guides for behavior. Parents today are stressing greater independence as they educate their children, and this is especially the case among postmaterialists. The public's behavior in all aspects of social and political life is becoming more self-directed. This increasing independence is reflected in the declining brand-name loyalty among consumers and in the decline of political party loyalty among voters. In short, contemporary lifestyles reflect a demand for greater freedom and individuality, which appears in fashions, consumer tastes, social behavior, and interpersonal relations.

This broader process of value change includes religious values and sexual mores (Inglehart 1997; Nevitte 1996). Materialists are significantly more likely to hold restrictive attitudes on sex-related issues, such as extramarital sex, abortion, and homosexuality. In short, materialists are not concerned only with economic matters; these values tap a broader set of traditional social norms.

In the realm of politics, postmaterial values are often linked to the new social movements of advanced industrial societies. Postmaterialists champion a new set of political issues—environmental quality, nuclear energy, women's rights, and consumerism—that the political establishment has often overlooked. Debates in Washington about acid rain, the safety of nuclear plants, and gender equality have close parallels in the capitals of Europe. Proponents of these issues have similar characteristics: they are young, better educated, and postmaterialist (Dalton 1994a, ch. 3; Inglehart 1990).

Value change also affects political participation. Postmaterial values stimulate direct participation in the decisions affecting one's life—whether at school, in the workplace, or in the political process. Postmaterialists are more interested in politics than are materialists and more likely to translate this interest into political action. In the 1999–2002 World Values Survey/European Values Survey (WVS/EVS), for example, postmaterialists are more likely than materialists to say they discuss politics and are interested in political matters.

The participatory orientation of postmaterialists adds to the puzzle of participation noted in chapter 2: if postmaterialism stimulates political involvement, why are voting and some other forms of action declining? Our answer to this puzzle reinforces the contention that the style of political action is changing in advanced industrial societies. The participatory orientation of postmaterialists has not affected all participation modes equally. Postmaterial values do not necessarily stimulate voting or campaign activity; in some nations, voting turnout is actually lower among postmaterialists.[10] This is partially because the established parties have responded ambiguously to postmaterial issues. In addition, postmaterialists are skeptical of formal hierarchical procedures and organizations, such as elections and most political parties.

Instead, postmaterial values stimulate participation in citizen initiatives, protests, and other forms of direct action. The 1999 WVS/EVS, for instance, found postmaterialists are much more likely than materialists to participate in protest (see figure 5.5). These nonpartisan participation opportunities provide postmaterialists with a more direct influence on politics, which matches their value orientations. Most postmaterialists also possess the political skills to carry out these more demanding forms of political action. As chapters 3 and 4 noted, along with increasing levels of citizen involvement has come a change in the form of political participation.

VALUE CHANGE AND VALUE STABILITY

This chapter has described the changing values of Western publics, but a more accurate description would stress the increasing diversity of the public's value priorities. More people still give primary attention to material goals, and the socioeconomic issues deriving from these values will continue to

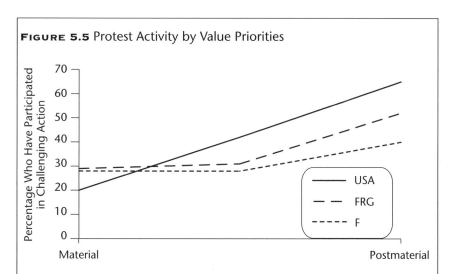

FIGURE 5.5 Protest Activity by Value Priorities

SOURCES: 1999–2002 European Values Survey / World Values Survey. (Great Britain did not ask the values battery.)

NOTE: Figure entries are the percentages who have engaged in at least one of the challenging activities in table 4.1 (lawful demonstration, boycott, strike, or occupying a building).

dominate political debate for decades to come. The persistence of material values should not be overlooked.

At the same time, postmaterial values are becoming more common. A sizable proportion of the public is willing to sacrifice further economic growth for a clean environment. Many people value the opportunity to participate in the decisions affecting their lives more than they value procedures that ensure stability and order at the possible cost of citizen input. Public values are changing.

The current mix of values sometimes makes it difficult for political analysts and politicians to know what the public wants. For nearly every example of the persistence of traditional material value patterns, there is now a counterexample reflecting postmaterial values. For every citizen lobbying a local town council to stimulate the economy, there is another who worries that growth will mean a loss of green space or a diminution in the quality of life. The diversity of values marks a major change in the nature of citizen politics: political debates again involve definition of goals and not just means to reach consensual goals.

The mix of values also makes it difficult for journalists to discern the public's priorities. During the 1960s, for instance, media reports made it seem that every young person was joining the counterculture. In the 1980s, images of the Yuppie in pursuit of an MBA and a BMW were equally pervasive. Now, Generation X is defined, in part, by the lack of either identity. The strength of empirical research is that we can track the values of the public in a more scientific manner. And what we find is a slow evolution toward postmaterial goals.

This process of value change has several consequences for contemporary politics. The issues of political debate are shifting. Concerns about environmental protection, individual freedom, social equality, participation, and the quality of life have been *added* to the traditional political agenda of economic and security issues. Some of the most telling evidence comes from a study of legislation in the U.S. Congress by Jeffrey Berry, who found that a majority of the congressional agenda was concerned with material issues in 1963, but that this emphasis had shifted to a predominately postmaterial agenda by 1991 (Berry 1999, ch. 4–5). Similarly, Inglehart has tracked a marked increase in the attention that political parties devote to environmental and other "New Politics" issues over time (Inglehart 1997). At present and for the foreseeable future, politics in most advanced industrial societies will address a mix of material and postmaterial issues.

As we noted earlier, value change also contributes to the reshaping of political participation. Postmaterialists are unlikely to embrace the structured electoral politics of representative democracy. Instead, they are advocates for direct participation and new forms of direct democracy, which also contributes to the development of an active civil society with a diverse range of public interest groups. Such groups have proliferated both in the United States and in Europe (Meyer and Tarrow 1998). The public's participatory demands have led to reforms within established political parties to increase the role of members, such as the convention reforms of the U.S. Democratic Party and the increased role for constituency associations in the British Labour Party.

Inevitably, changes in value priorities carry over to the institutions of the political process. Nevitte (1996) restated the political science premise that the values of society are eventually reflected in the values and institutions of the political system. Today, political parties are no longer the sole or even the primary agents of political representation in modern democracies. Public interest groups are now widely involved in the policymaking process, from the national government down to local governments and administrative boards. They are assuming some of the roles that political parties once performed. Postmaterialists also advocate a greater use of initiative and referendum, the opening up of administrative processes, and the expansion of the legal rights of citizen groups (Cain, Dalton, and Scarrow 2003). These institutional reforms increase the political influence of these groups, as well as producing even more fundamental changes in the process itself that affect all participants. In summary, postmaterialists favor expanding the democratic process and more directly involving citizens in the political process.

One other question involves the impact of these new values on the political parties and citizen voting behavior. Most of the established political parties are primarily oriented to traditional social divisions, and at least initially they resisted attempts to incorporate postmaterial issues into a partisan framework. Since the first edition of this book, several of the established political parties have become more sensitive to postmaterial issues. A generation ago, few politicians claimed to speak for the environment. Today, politicians of all colors claim to be green at election time. But it is still unclear whether the political parties will deliver on these promises once elected, or choose to focus instead on their traditional materialist constituencies (see chapters 7 and 8).

Only a few skeptics still doubt that value priorities are changing among Western publics; the evidence of change is obvious. It is more difficult to anticipate the many consequences of these new values. By monitoring these trends, however, we may get a preview of the nature of citizen politics in advanced industrial democracies.

SUGGESTED READINGS

Abramson, Paul, and Ronald Inglehart. *Value Change in Global Perspective.* Ann Arbor: University of Michigan Press, 1995.

Clark, Terry Nichols, and Vincent Hoffmann-Martinot, eds. *The New Political Culture.* Boulder, Colo.: Westview, 1998.

Inglehart, Ronald. *Culture Shift in Advanced Industrial Society.* Princeton, N.J.: Princeton University Press, 1990.

Inglehart, Ronald, and Christian Welzel. *Modernization, Cultural Change and Democracy: The Human Development Sequence.* New York: Cambridge University Press, 2005.

Nevitte, Neil. *The Decline of Deference.* Petersborough, Canada: Broadview, 1996.
Van Deth, Jan, and Elinor Scarbrough, eds. *The Impact of Values.* New York: Oxford University Press, 1995.

NOTES

1. Inglehart's early work was closely linked to the Maslovian value hierarchy, but this influence is less prominent in his recent research. As Inglehart has broadened his interests and empirical evidence beyond advanced industrial societies, he has become more sensitive to how cultural forces and local conditions can shape what values are considered scarce, and thus are valued by the public.

2. We counted the emphasis placed on the six material goals and the six postmaterial goals in table 5.1; entries are the percentages in each nation who place a higher priority on postmaterial goals. This one table uses a different method than Inglehart's standard 12-item index so that we can begin the trend with the 1970s surveys that used a different question format. Inglehart's 12-item index is a count of postmaterial items, excluding the beautiful cities item.

   Several of the analyses in this chapter use a four-item subset of the twelve items to construct a single index of material/postmaterial values (Inglehart 1990, chap. 2; 1977). The disadvantage of this index is that it is based on only four items, and this yields a narrow basis for tapping a broad dimension of human values. In some surveys, however, this is the only index available.

3. We use 1965 GNP/capita because this is roughly when values were being formed for many of the adults surveyed in 1990. In addition, we used Abramson and Inglehart's (1995, 124–125) summary index of values in order to be directly comparable to their analysis of the relationship between current GNP/capita and values.

4. There is a strong relationship ($r = .44$) between GNP/capita in 1965 and values in 1990, and this correlation is even stronger if modeled as a curvilinear relationship ($r = .49$). See Abramson and Inglehart (1995).

5. Figure 5.3 is based on the combined results of samples from six nations: Great Britain, West Germany, France, Italy, Belgium, and the Netherlands. The results were combined to produce age-group samples large enough to estimate values precisely. For additional discussion of generational effects, see Abramson and Inglehart (1995) and Inglehart and Welzel (2005).

6. One weakness of the Inglehart measure is that it attempts to measure basic values by means of items dealing with specific political issues. Thus it is not surprising that the four-item index is sensitive to inflation rates because one of the items taps concern about rising prices (Clarke and Dutt 1991; Clarke et al. 1999). A broader measure of values, such as Inglehart's twelve-item index or the social priorities question of Flanagan (1982), would be less susceptible to these measurement problems.

7. Duch and Taylor (1993) used multivariate analysis to argue that formative conditions do not influence current value priorities. Abramson and Inglehart (1995) challenged this interpretation, arguing that Duch and Taylor had distorted the results by their selection of timepoints and had misinterpreted the meaning of educational effects (also see Duch and Taylor 1994). I believe that the evidence of generational change is predominant, and that educational effects are another measure of formative life conditions, especially in Europe.

8. Even during this relatively brief time span, generational turnover has contributed to a postmaterial trend (Abramson and Inglehart 1995). For instance, in 1970, the pre–World War I generation constituted about 16 percent of the West German public; by 1980, this group constituted about 5 percent, and by 1990, they had essentially left the electorate. In the place of these older citizens, young Germans, socialized in the affluent post–World War II era, had entered the electorate.

9. Inglehart (1981) finds that European political elites (candidates for the European Parliament) are nearly three times more postmaterialist than the total public. Postmaterialists are also more common among younger elites.

10. Markus Crepaz (1990) shows that the presence of a green or New Left party increases voting rates, presumably by encouraging postmaterialists to turn out at the polls.

CHAPTER 6

Issues and Ideological Orientations

Issues are the everyday currency of politics. Issue opinions identify the public's preferences for government action and their expectations for the political process. Political parties are largely defined by their issue positions, and elections provide a means for the public to select between the competing issue programs they offer. As citizens become more sophisticated and involved in politics, issue beliefs have an increasing influence on voting choice and the policy process. Moreover, researchers find a significant relationship between the public's issue preferences and policy outcomes in democratic systems. Issues are what politics is about.

Issue opinions also represent the translation of broad value orientations into specific political concerns. Issues are partially determined by the values examined in the last chapter, as well as by other factors: cues from political elites, the flow of political events, and the contexts of specific situations. For example, a person may favor the principle of equal rights for all citizens; but attitudes toward voting rights, job discrimination, school busing, open housing, and other civil rights legislation represent different mixes of values and practical concerns. Consequently, issue opinions are more changeable and varied than broad value orientations.

Another important characteristic of issues is that people focus their attention on a few areas—they are members of one or more "issue publics" (see chapter 2). Some people are especially concerned with education policy; others are more interested in foreign affairs, civil rights, environmental protection, immigration, or another issue. In general, only a minority of the public is interested and informed on any specific issue, although most people are members of at least one issue public. Members of an issue public are relatively well informed about their issue and generally follow the actions of politicians and the political parties on that issue. The salient issue for an individual has a strong impact on his or her political behavior.

Issue opinions are a dynamic aspect of politics, and the theme of changing popular values can be carried over to the study of issues. In some areas, contemporary publics are obviously more liberal than their predecessors. The issues of women's rights, environmental protection, social equality, and individual lifestyles were unknown or highly divisive a generation ago, but a growing consensus now exists on many of these issues. In other areas, people remain divided on the goals of government. Support for tax revolts, neoconservative revival, "family values," and supply-side economics suggest that conservative values have not lost their appeal for many people. This chapter

Internet Resource

The International Social Survey Program (ISSP) web site has additional information on these surveys:

www.issp.org

describes the present issue opinions of Western publics and highlights, where possible, the trends in these opinions.

DOMESTIC POLICY OPINIONS

At one time, domestic policy was synonymous with economic matters, and economic issues still rank at the top of the public's political agenda for most elections. More recently, however, the number of salient domestic issues has proliferated. Many people are now concerned with such noneconomic issues as social equality, environmental protection, and immigration. This section provides an overview of the wide range of domestic policy concerns.

Socioeconomic Issues and the State

For most of the twentieth century, the political conflicts that emerged from industrialization and the Great Depression dominated politics in democratic party systems. This debate revolved around the question of the government's role in society and the economy, especially the provision of basic social needs.

A prime example of this policy area is the set of government-backed social insurance programs that most governments administer (such as Social Security in the United States, or government health care programs in Europe). European social programs protect individuals from economic calamities caused by illness, unemployment, disability, or other hardships. In some nations, the government's involvement in the economy also includes public ownership of major industries and active efforts to manage the economy.

Labor unions favor the extension of government social policy as a way to improve the life chances of the average person. Business leaders and members of the middle class frequently oppose these policies as an unnecessary government intrusion into private affairs. At stake is not only the question of government involvement in society but also the desirability of certain social goals and the distribution of political influence between labor and business. To a large extent, the terms *liberal* and *conservative* have been synonymous with one's position on these questions. Attitudes toward these issues provide the major source of political competition in most elections. Class-based opinions on socioeconomic issues are the primary policy concerns of many voters.

Despite expanding government policy efforts in these areas, or perhaps because of them, new questions about the scope of governmental activity arose in the 1980s. Conservative politicians on both sides of the Atlantic championed a populist revolt against big government. Margaret Thatcher, Ronald Reagan, and Helmut Kohl attempted to turn back the growth of government, privatizing government-owned businesses or government-run programs and reducing government social programs. Political observers interpreted their electoral successes as evidence of a new conservative trend in public attitudes toward government.

There is abundant evidence that support for the principle of big government has lessened in recent years. For instance, between 1964 and 1980, the number of Americans who believed that the federal government was too powerful rose from 30 to 49 percent (although it declined to 39 percent in 2000). The American public also became more critical of taxation levels and the use of their tax money. The Gallup surveys show that in the 1950s, less than half of the American public felt they were paying an unfair amount of taxes; since the late 1970s, however, more than three-quarters believe their share of taxes is too high. Similarly, the American National Election Study finds an increase in the proportion believing that government "wastes a lot" of tax dollars, from two-fifths in 1958 to two-thirds in the 1980s (although this percentage has recently declined following the tax cuts of the George W. Bush administration). These opinions fueled popular opposition to tax policy among Americans, and widespread feelings that tax levels are too high. Moreover, the Republican Party has successfully appealed to these antitax sentiments as a basis of its electoral support.

Some signs of a growing cynicism about big government also appear among Europeans. Longitudinal British public opinion trends uncover increasing criticism of big government beginning in the late 1970s (Heath and McMahon 1992). British desires for the denationalization of some industries grew during the early Thatcher years, parallelling the government's privatization of several government-owned enterprises and a general attempt to reduce the scope of British government.[1] The German government attempted to reduce the size of government in similar ways, and by the end of the 1980s, the French government had also begun a retrenchment in its programs. This policy debate about the proper scope of government has continued to the present day on both sides of the Atlantic.

Despite this new conservative policy activity, recent public opinion surveys show that many people still believe that government is responsible for promoting individual well-being and guaranteeing the quality of life for its citizens (Borre and Scarbrough 1995). Table 6.1 displays the percentages of citizens who think the government is "definitely responsible" for dealing with specific social problems. The British and the French have very high expectations of government: more than half believe the government is definitely responsible for providing health care, ensuring a decent standard of living for the elderly, and maintaining strict environmental laws. There is also strong

TABLE 6.1 Government Responsibility for Dealing with Policy Areas (in percentages)

	United States	Great Britain	France	Germany
Provide health care for sick	39	82	53	55
Provide decent living standard for the elderly	38	73	51	52
Strict environmental laws	46	63	67	62
Give aid to needy college students	35	38	59	31
Keep prices under control	25	44	42	28
Provide job for everyone who wants one	14	29	40	36
Reduce income differences between rich and poor	17	36	49	31
Provide housing for those who need it	20	37	44	25
Provide a decent living standard for the unemployed	13	29	34	22
Provide industry with help	17	41	36	20
Average	26	47	48	36

SOURCE: 1996 International Social Survey Program.
NOTE: Table entries are the percentages who say that each area should definitely be government's responsibility. Missing data were excluded from the calculation of percentages.

support for government action on price controls, public housing, and even aid to college students. Many Germans also believe that government is responsible in these policy areas—and the percentages are even higher among the residents of the former East Germany.[2] Data from other European nations show that support for government action to resolve social needs is a core element of the European political culture (Taylor-Gooby 1998).

In comparison to most Europeans, Americans are more reserved in their acceptance of government action. Even in areas where government is a primary actor, such as care of the elderly and unemployment, only a minority of Americans views these problems as definite government responsibilities (see table 6.1). The United States is a major exception among Western democracies in its limited support for activist government. The state never attempted to own a significant portion of industry, and most Americans oppose nationalization on even a limited scale. Popular support for basic social programs remains low by European standards. These conservative socioeconomic attitudes are often explained by the individualist nature of American society and the absence of a socialist working-class party.

Another measure of citizens' expectations of their government involves preferences for government spending. One of the great contradictions in public opinion is that even as people are critical of taxes and the overall size of government, support for increased spending on specific policy programs remains widespread. Table 6.2 displays the percentages of Americans who favor more government spending in a policy area minus those who want to spend less. These data describe a long-term consensus in favor of increased government spending on education, crime prevention, health care, preventing drug addiction, and environmental protection. Only welfare, the space program, and foreign aid are consistently identified as candidates for budget cuts. Moreover, although specific spending priorities change over time, the average preference for increased government spending listed across the bottom of the table has varied surprisingly little across seven administrations.

Americans' priorities for spending on specific programs do, however, respond to changes in the federal budget and the political context in a manner consistent with Benjamin Page and Robert Shapiro's (1992) description of a rational public. For instance, the perceived military weakness of the Carter administration stimulated calls for greater defense spending; 56 percent of Americans thought the government was spending too little on defense in the spring of 1980, while 11 percent said too much was being spent, and these attitudes supported the large defense expenditures of the early Reagan administration. Then, as examples of Pentagon waste became commonplace—accounts of $500 hammers and $7,000 coffeepots—popular support for defense spending was replaced by endorsement of the status quo or even a cut in defense budgets. Similarly, limitations on social spending enacted by the Reagan administration exceeded the wishes of many Americans. Between 1980 and 1991, support increased for *more* spending in the areas of health care, environmental protection, education, urban problems, and minority aid. Even while the George W. Bush administration was attempting to cut government spending, the American public wanted more spending on these programs in 2002.

Cross-national opinion polls indicate that budgetary support for specific policy programs such as health care, environmental protection, education, housing, and social services is widespread among Europeans as well (see table 6.3). The British favor increased spending in most areas, especially on policies identified with the welfare state. Germans display modest support for increased spending, but this attitude must be seen in the context of already large public expenditures and the economic uncertainties accompanying German unification. The other European nations in this survey generally support increased government spending (Kaase and Newton 1998). Americans also favor increased government spending on various government programs, despite their general reservations about the scope of government.

This contrast between the general skepticism about government and the endorsement of increased spending on specific areas reflects a common con-

TABLE 6.2 Budget Priorities of the American Public over Time (in percentage difference scores)

Priority	1973	1976	1980	1984	1988	1991	1996	2000	2002
Halting rising crime rate	60	57	63	62	64	59	61	55	50
Protecting the nation's health	56	55	47	51	63	66	60	69	71
Dealing with drug addiction	59	51	52	57	64	50	48	53	49
Protecting the environment	53	45	32	54	60	63	50	55	53
Improving the educational system	40	41	42	59	60	62	65	67	69
Solving problems of big cities	36	23	19	31	36	35	45	40	30
Improving the condition of blacks	11	2	0	19	19	20	13	21	15
The military and defense	−27	−3	45	−21	−22	−13	−15	−2	9
Welfare	−31	−46	−43	−16	−19	−15	−43	−19	−20
Space exploration program	−51	−51	−21	−27	−16	−26	−32	−29	−26
Foreign aid	−66	−72	−64	−65	−63	−68	−69	−52	−59
Average	13	9	16	19	22	21	16	23	22

SOURCE: NORC General Social Survey, various dates.

NOTE: Table entries are the percentages saying "too little" being spent on the problem minus the percentages saying "too much."

TABLE 6.3 Cross-National Comparison of Citizen Budget Priorities (in percentage difference scores)

Priority	United States	Great Britain	France	Germany
Education	72	84	56	48
Health	61	91	36	52
Police and law enforcement	51	72	26	56
Old-age pensions	41	79	23	51
Environment	36	39	37	53
Unemployment benefits	5	16	−12	21
Culture and arts	−31	−59	−21	−19
Military and defense	−12	−14	−59	−61
Average	28	39	11	25

SOURCE: 1996 International Social Survey Program.

NOTE: Table entries are the percentages saying "too little" being spent on the problem minus the percentages saying "too much." Missing data were excluded from the calculation of percentages.

tradiction in public opinion. The motto for government is clear: tax less, and spend more. Seymour Martin Lipset and Everett Ladd (1980) describe this paradox as the combination of "ideological conservatism" and "programmatic liberalism." Americans and Europeans continue to demonstrate an ambiguous mix of support for and opposition to government action.

The most accurate description of popular attitudes toward government might be that citizens are now critical of "big" government, but they also are accustomed to, and depend on, the policies of the modern state. When people confront the choice between cutting taxes and maintaining government services, many surveys find that a plurality prefer the services option even in the midst of the so-called tax revolt. The mix of opinions limits initiatives for dramatic increases in public spending, yet the massive tax reduction introduced by the Bush administration has stimulated public worries that this policy will reduce benefits in many desired government programs.

Race and Equality

The world is getting smaller, and Western democracies are becoming more racially and ethnically diverse. The politicization of this issue began in the United States in the mid-1960s; after generations of dormancy, the issues of civil rights and racial equality inflamed American politics. For most of the next two decades the civil rights issue preoccupied the attention of many Americans and became a major source of political conflict. Racial issues continue to be a central issue in American politics, for the success of the civil rights movement among African Americans has encouraged similar activity among Hispanics, Asian Americans, and other minorities.

Europe has also begun to confront issues of racial tolerance and civil rights as immigration has increased the diversity of these societies. Decolonialization by Great Britain and France created a steady inflow of black and brown immigrants from former colonies (Hollifield 1993). Labor-force shortages led the West Germans to invite "guestworkers" from less developed Mediterranean countries to work in German factories. Nonwhites now account for 5–10 percent of the population in these three nations, and as much as a quarter of the workforce in some cities. Moreover, the new wave of immigrants during the past decade has introduced greater cultural differences, and greater political tensions, as these newcomers often differ from the indigenous populations in race, religion, and social status.

Western democracies have struggled to address these issues, and there are too many examples of public backlashes against minorities. For example, tensions between French and North Africans have occasionally erupted into violence in southern France, and the National Front Party espouses antiforeigner policies. German unification produced a surge of violence against foreigners, the emergence of the xenophobic Republikaner Party, and eventually a tightening of German immigration and asylum laws. Perhaps the most dramatic example was the emergence of the List Pim Fortuyn in the Netherlands, headed by an otherwise liberal gay activist who was extremely critical of the presence of Muslim fundamentalists in Dutch society.

Although racial and ethnic conflicts are part of contemporary politics, the trends in racial attitudes over the past generation document a massive change in the beliefs of Americans. In the 1940s, a majority of white Americans openly endorsed racial segregation of education, housing, transportation, and employment (see figure 6.1). The values of freedom, equality, and justice that constitute the American creed did not apply to blacks. A phenomenal growth in support for racial integration occurred over the next four decades, however, as integration of housing, education and employment won widespread endorsement. General approval of the appointment of Colin Powell as Secretary of State and of Condoleezza Rice's accession to various positions of power within the George W. Bush administration illustrates how much has changed.

In a provocative book on public opinion, Paul Sniderman and Thomas Piazza (1993) examine racial attitudes in contemporary America. They show that as racial integration became accepted, the politics of race broadened to include a new set of proactive issues—affirmative action, government social programs, and equity principles—on which the American public remains divided. Some actions aimed at redressing racial inequality—affirmative action policies (such as school busing and preferential treatment) and racial quotas—are opposed by most Americans (Schuman

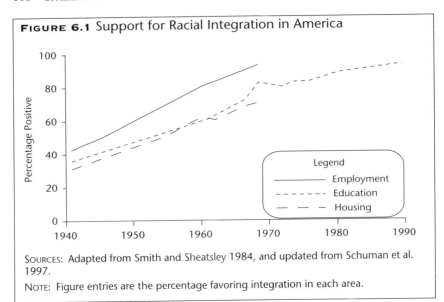

FIGURE 6.1 Support for Racial Integration in America

SOURCES: Adapted from Smith and Sheatsley 1984, and updated from Schuman et al. 1997.

NOTE: Figure entries are the percentage favoring integration in each area.

et al. 1997). Current controversies over affirmative action programs illustrate this discontent. Many political analysts claim that these divided opinions are signs of a new racism in America. Based on an innovative set of survey experiments, Sniderman and Piazza conclude that although a minority of Americans still harbor racial prejudice, the contemporary clash over racial policies is more attributable to broader ideological conflicts over the scope of government, beliefs about equality, and other political values.

European attitudes toward racial and ethnic minorities seem to reflect a similar mix of two factors (Sniderman et al. 2000, 2003). One factor is simple prejudice toward individuals of a different race or religion—though such sentiments appear among only a minority of Europeans. The other factor is a clash of interests or goals that is analogous to class, regional, or other social interests. For instance, middle-class individuals can disagree with policies to benefit the working class, without being prejudiced against the working class. While prejudice is difficult to address or correct, differences in interests are more open to reconciliation and compromise. Thus, the mix of factors is important in judging the potential resolution of these issues.

Perhaps the best way to compare opinions cross-nationally is to focus on attitudes toward immigrants (McCrone and Surridge 1998; Sniderman et al. 2003; Alba, Schmidt, and Wasmer 2003). Table 6.4 indicates that citizens in all four nations are concerned about issues of immigrant and minority relations. Surveys routinely find that most people say that immigration is a major problem in their nation and that the levels of immigration should be reduced. The first item in the table indicates that the majority of Europeans favor limits on immigration and that Americans are only slightly more open despite their immigrant heritage. Europeans also favor an assimilation policy, whereby immigrants assume the values of their new country rather than maintaining their culture and customs. Indeed, these are the differences in values that lead to contemporary culture clashes in Europe (and the United States).

At the same time, tolerance toward immigrants is apparent in other survey items in the lower half of the table. Majorities in each of these European nations feel a moral duty to help immigrants, and nearly equal proportions say they feel a sense of sympathy for immigrants. However, worries about the impact of immigrants on jobs, crime, and society are commonplace. For instance, most people still favor giving a priority to native workers over immigrants if jobs are scarce (though Europeans are more liberal on this view than respondents in other regions in the World Values Survey). It is this juxtaposition of abstract support for the principles of equality and tolerance, with the fears over concrete problems in the clash between different cultures that makes racial and ethnic conflicts so difficult for Americans and Europeans.

Although the climate of opinion now accepts more racial and ethnic diversity, one must be cautious not to overlook the real racial problems that persist in many nations. Support for the principle of equality coexists with the remnants of segregation in the United States; racial conflict can still flare up

TABLE 6.4 Cross-National Comparison of Attitudes toward Immigrants (in percentages)

	United States	Great Britain	France	Germany
Attitudes toward immigration				
Anyone can come	12	4	6	5
Come if there are jobs	45	34	34	33
Strict limits	39	49	50	56
Prohibit immigration	4	13	10	7
Multicultural vs. assimilation of immigrants				
Can maintain customs	—	45	27	24
Should assimilate	—	55	73	76
Attitudes toward immigrants				
Moral duty to help immigrants	—	59	62	60
Feel sympathy for immigrants	—	63	53	67
If jobs are short, priority to native population	49	58	54	59
Immigrants bad for nation	43	50	50	60

SOURCES: 1999–2002 European Values Survey / World Values Survey; final item, Pew (2003).

NOTE: Table entries are the percentages agreeing with each statement. Missing data were excluded from the calculation of percentages.

in Brixton, Marseilles, or Berlin. Problems of housing segregation, unequal education, and job discrimination are real. Public opinion alone is not sufficient to resolve these problems, and, undoubtedly, some survey respondents overstate their tolerance level. Still, the shift of social norms toward support of racial equality makes these problems more solvable than when discrimination was openly practiced.

Gender Issues

Another social dimension concerns equality between men and women. A short generation ago, traditional gender roles were deeply entrenched on both sides of the Atlantic. American women faced limited career opportunities, and German housewives were expected to devote their efforts to *Kinder, Kirche, und Küche* (children, church, and kitchen). The status of women in Great Britain, France, and other advanced industrial societies was equally constrained.

These traditional attitudes underwent a profound transformation in the latter half of the twentieth century. The women's movement grew most rapidly in the United States, and a parallel increase in women's groups occurred in Europe (Lovenduski and Norris 1996). These groups, along with individual women, raised society's consciousness about the different treatment of men and women and changed societal values. As political action led to legislation equalizing the rights of both sexes, the public at large became more sensitive to gender issues, and social norms have gradually changed.

Most Americans now express belief in equal opportunities for men and women. For example, one question asks whether one approves of a married woman working if she has a husband to support her, by implication condoning the norm that married women belong at home (see figure 6.2). In 1938 when this question was first asked, only 22 percent of Americans approved

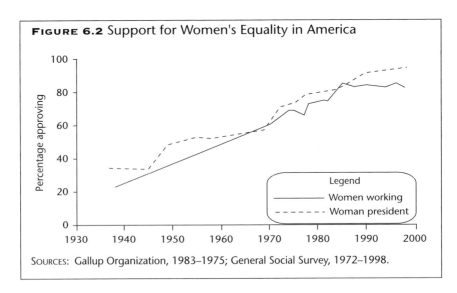

FIGURE 6.2 Support for Women's Equality in America

Percentage approving (y-axis: 0, 20, 40, 60, 80, 100)

x-axis: 1930, 1940, 1950, 1960, 1970, 1980, 1990, 2000

Legend
——— Women working
– – – – Woman president

SOURCES: Gallup Organization, 1983–1975; General Social Survey, 1972–1998.

of a woman working in these circumstances; this figure had increased to 80 percent or more by the end of the 1990s. Similarly, Gallup data show that in 1936, only 31 percent of Americans said they would vote for a woman as president; by the 1990s this figure had risen above 80 percent.

Table 6.5 provides further evidence on how Americans and Europeans think about gender-related issues (also see Inglehart and Norris 2003; Scott, Braun, and Alwin 1998). The items focused on the role of women are a good example of these changing attitudes. Most people believe that a working woman can establish close ties with her children and that a job can establish a woman's independence. Most now disagree with the proposition that men have first right to employment when jobs are scarce. Furthermore, differences between men and women on these issues are relatively small in most instances, and, in some cases, men express more liberal opinions.

These findings initially suggest that gender norms are changing, and in one sense it is amazing that gender roles developed over centuries have shifted so rapidly. At the same time, this transformation has been incomplete. Evidence

TABLE 6.5 Attitudes toward Gender Equality (in percentages)

	United States	Great Britain	France	Germany
Situation of women has improved	70	68	60	68
Women's role				
Working/non-working mothers can establish same relationship with children	79*	73	77*	67*
Having a job is best way for woman to be independent	—	66	84*	81*
Men have more right to a job (Disagree)	82	64	68	57*
A women needs children to be fulfilled (Disagree)	85	79	33	46
3-item Average	82	72	59	57
Action				
Member of women's group	14	2	>1	4
Volunteer work for a women's group	8	1	>1	2
Political role				
Country would be better governed if more women politicians (Disagree)	57	51	59	51

Sources: 1999–2002 European Values Survey / World Values Survey; first and last items, European Community, "European Men and Women Study 1995."

Note: Table entries are the percentages who agree (or disagree) with each statement. Asterisks denote women's role items on which there are substantial differences between genders (Tau-b greater than .10).

from European surveys indicates that most men still feel that women are primarily responsible for housework and a man has more right to a job (Scott, Braun, and Alwin 1998). Other survey data indicate that many working women feel their situation is worse that men's in regard to wages, promotion prospects, job opportunities, and job security. Traditional images of the social role of women still exist in the minds of many people. Ultimately, the legacy of the women's movement may be the creation of a choice for women—both work and family are now accepted options—instead of limitation to a single role.

The lower part of table 6.5 focuses on politics. Americans are more likely to be members of women's group and to participate in voluntary activities for these groups. This reflects the stronger participatory norms of Americans discussed in previous chapters, as well as the earlier origins of the women's movement in the United States. We also find support for the political equality of women. Majorities in each nation reject the notion that politics is better left to men, and most express equal confidence in male and female politicians. Although women remain underrepresented within the top stratum of political officials, old stereotypes of politics as an exclusively male domain have eroded. Even if these expressed opinions are not fully matched by the reality of actions, the changes in political norms are having real effects on the status of women and encouraging further policy change.

Environmental Protection

Environmental protection represents one of the new issue concerns of advanced industrial democracies. Environmentalism was initially stimulated by a few very visible ecological crises, after which these concerns persisted and expanded. Separate issues were linked together into environmental programs, citizen groups mobilized in support of environmental issues, and new green parties formed in several nations (Rootes 1999; Dalton 1994a). Gradually these societies developed an awareness of how human activity and economic development could threaten the natural environment, lessen the quality of life, and threaten the sustainability of our progress.

The broadest sign of public concern is interest in the host of environmental issues that have reached public consciousness (Dalton and Rohrschneider 1998). Issues of global warming, the ozone hole, and biodiversity have become global concerns (except at 1600 Pennsylvania Avenue). Interest in environmental issues translates into support for environmental protection; contemporary publics broadly support government actions to protect the environment (table 6.6). Just as table 6.1 demonstrated disproportionate support for increased government spending on environmental protection, a Gallup survey conducted before the 1992 environmental summit at Rio de Janeiro found that more than 90 percent of the public in these nations favored stronger environmental protection laws for business and industry. Nearly equal numbers favored laws requiring that all citizens conserve resources and reduce pollution (see Dunlap, Gallup, and Gallup 1993).

TABLE 6.6 Environmental Attitudes (in percentages)

	United States	Great Britain	France	Germany
Policy support				
Government should reduce pollution	57	77	84	68
Trade-off questions				
Would give up part of income to prevent pollution	69	49	46	33
Would pay more taxes to prevent pollution	61	50	37	29
Action				
Member of environmental group	20	2	2	3
Volunteer work for an environmental group	9	8	1	2

SOURCES: 1999–2002 European Values Survey / World Values Survey.

NOTE: Table entries are the percentages who agree with each statement. Missing data were excluded from the calculation of percentages.

Many political analysts discount these environmental opinions because such popular views can be expressed in a survey without concern for the actual costs of a policy. However, when people are asked to balance their environmental beliefs against the potential economic costs of environmental protection, there is still considerable support. The data in the middle panel of table 6.6 indicate that roughly half of the public (except in Germany) would give up part of their income or pay higher taxes to prevent pollution. A clear majority of Americans favor protection of the environment even if it risks holding back economic growth; and most Europeans agree (Dalton and Rohrschneider 1998).

Another sign of public support for environmental reform is participation in the environmental movement. The lower panel in the table demonstrates that membership in environmental groups is relatively high in the United States, and the movement involves a small but vocal minority in most European nations. Other less demanding examples of consumer behavior demonstrate even broader levels of environmental activism among European publics.[3]

This environmental advocacy indicates that people are now interested in new political issues that tap the noneconomic concerns typical of postmaterial values. In earlier periods, economic needs superseded concerns about the environment; today, many people say they are willing to sacrifice financially to improve the environment. These concerns reflect more than just a growing awareness of the hidden health and economic costs of pollution. In a broad cross-national study of attitudes toward the environment, Ronald Inglehart

(1995) notes that the citizens of prosperous countries with relatively cleaner environments are most willing to make sacrifices for the environment. Material success allows the citizens in these nations to shift attention to the quality of their lives. Similarly, support for environmental protection is more common among the young, the better-educated, and postmaterialists. Environmentalism thus reflects the processes of value change that are part of the new style of citizen politics.

Social and Moral Issues

Another set of domestic policy issues involves the turbulent debate over social and moral norms associated with interpersonal relations and life choices. In the late 1960s and early 1970s, young people began to question traditional values by making symbolic statements, such as the use of drugs or the choice of hairstyles, clothing, and music. This youth movement tested the extent of individual freedom on matters such as abortion, divorce, homosexuality, and pornography. These issues entered the political debate in a variety of ways.

These social lifestyle issues differ from most other policy concerns because of their moral content. Unlike economic issues involving negotiable monetary benefits, social issues such as abortion or homosexuality address situations in which basic moral principles of right and wrong are at stake. Several consequences follow from this moral dimension. People find it is difficult to compromise on social issues because moral views are intensely felt. The issue publics for social policy questions often are larger than might otherwise be expected. In addition, religious values are an important determinant of opinions on social issues. The active interest groups on social issues are religious organizations and Christian Democratic parties, not labor unions and business groups.

Table 6.7 presents public opinion data on several social and moral issues. Until recently, traditional value orientations led many people to be highly critical of divorce; scandal, dishonor, and religious isolation often accompanied the divorce decree. As the table indicates, however, these attitudes have changed dramatically; nearly everyone now believes that divorce is sometimes justified. As attitudes toward divorce have become more tolerant, nearly all Western democracies have changed their laws to remove the stigma of divorce and provisions discriminating against women.

Attitudes toward sexual relations evoke differing responses, depending on the context. What stands out in the table is the more conservative orientation of Americans compared to the European respondents. Only a minority in each nation now criticizes homosexuality as always unjustified, and longitudinal data from the World Values Survey suggest that these opinions are becoming more tolerant over time. The majority in each nation even see circumstances in which euthanasia is now justifiable.

Abortion also has been a divisive social issue in several nations. Proponents and opponents of abortion are intense in their beliefs and oriented toward political action. Furthermore, this issue has periodically been the

TABLE 6.7 Attitudes on Social and Moral Issues (in percentages)

	United States	Great Britain	France	Germany
Divorce is sometimes justified	81	87	89	93
Euthanasia is sometimes justified	76	79	88	72
Extramarital sex is sometimes justified	—	45	62	59
Homosexuality is sometimes justified	68	74	77	81
Abortion attitudes				
Abortion is not wrong:				
If child may have birth defect	47	63	81	49
If parents are poor	31	34	53	22
Religious attitudes				
Believe in God	96	72	62	67
Believe in life after death	81	58	45	39
Believe in heaven	88	56	31	31
Believe in hell	75	35	20	20
Religious attitudes average	85	55	40	39

SOURCES: 1999–2002 European Values Survey / World Values Survey; abortion items, 1998 International Social Survey Program.

NOTE: Table entries are the percentages who agree with each statement. Missing data were excluded from the calculation of percentages.

subject of major legislative or judicial action in all four nations. Most people today believe that abortion is sometimes justified, as when the health of the baby is at risk. (Other surveys show broad support for abortion when the health of the mother is endangered). Fewer people approve of abortion when it is based on economic factors. Despite the dramatic ebbs and flows in public events on this issue, there does not appear to be a strong trend in these attitudes over time (Page and Shapiro 1992; Ashford and Timms 1992).

These findings lead to two broad conclusions. First, Americans are generally more conservative than Europeans on social and moral issues. This pattern is likely the result of national differences in religious feelings, as seen in the bottom panel in the table. Despite the affluence, high mobility rates, and social diversity of its citizens, the United States is among the most religious of Western societies. American church attendance and religious feelings are among the highest in the world. A full 96 percent of Americans considered say they believe in God, compared to 60–70 percent among Europeans. Even more striking are the patterns on other religious beliefs: three-quarters of Americans believe in the existence of hell, compared to only a third of Britons and a fifth of Germans and French. The antireligious policies of the GDR created an even more secular society in eastern Germany.[4]

Second, public opinion has generally become more tolerant on social issues as the processes of modernization and secularization have transformed
Western societies. Long-term opinion series for the United States and Germany indicate a gradual liberalization of attitudes toward sexual relations
and homosexuality over the past generation.

Underlying these longitudinal changes has been the diminishment of religious values in these societies. Church attendance has decreased and religious
attachments have weakened. For example, the 1980 World Values Survey
found that nearly half of the public in each European nation said that God
played an important part in their lives; more than 80 percent of Americans
expressed this same opinion. Over the next two decades these measures of religiosity dropped off markedly in each nation. If the time series had begun in
the 1950s or 1960s, the value shift would be markedly greater.[5]

This change in values has mixed effects on politics. The decline in religiosity may prompt greater tolerance of different lifestyle choices, especially
those involving abortion rights and alternative lifestyles. At the same time,
weakening religious attachments are probably linked to declining respect for
and acceptance of authority, as well an erosion in moral and ethical standards. A more secular public sees humankind in a different light.

FOREIGN POLICY OPINIONS

Foreign policy has undergone dramatic political changes in recent years, and
it tends to be an area of shifting issue opinions. After decades of silent conflict during the Cold War, the collapse of the Soviet Union dramatically reshaped the international order. The democratic revolution that spread
throughout Eastern Europe also altered the international distribution of
power and values in a fundamental way. Then, just as a new stability was
emerging, the world was shocked by the horrific terrorist attacks on the
World Trade Center and the Pentagon in September 2001. The war to liber-
ate Afghanistan was followed by the American overthrow of the Iraqi regime
of Saddam Hussein. The world is changing rapidly, and governments and
people are unsure about what lies ahead and what policies governments
should follow. This section describes contemporary foreign policy opinions
in several areas.

Conflict and Cooperation

Although the Cold War is over, the world can still be a brutish place. Regional
and local conflicts—such as those in Bosnia or Sudan—threaten individual
and international security. Yet the end of the Cold War has transformed peace
and conflict issues in the current world. Potential conflict between the U.S.
and Russia no longer is the central theme of international relations; public attention has shifted toward other sources of international conflict.

In a cross-national survey conducted in 2002, less than half of the European public felt that nuclear weapons were the greatest danger in the world

today (see table 6.8). This is a dramatic change from a time when nuclear Armageddon hung over Europe as a constant threat.

Contemporary European publics instead see ethnic and religious hatred as the greatest threat in the contemporary world; people worry about the threat of attack from terrorists—named as a concern by a majority in each nation. This survey was done in the year following the 9/11 attacks, which were then followed by bombings around the world and by the war in Afghanistan. Concerns about terrorism are now near the top of the foreign policy agenda in most Western democracies.

We cite surveys from 2002 because the Iraq war subsequently polarized transatlantic opinions, although the beginnings of this U.S./Europe gap can also be seen in table 6.8. In 2002 most Europeans supported the U.S. war against terror, because it was focused on dismantling Al Qaeda and liberating Afghanistan from the Taliban. But even then, many Europeans felt that America was acting on its own, without consulting its allies. These sentiments became more negative with the buildup to the Iraq war, and Europeans began to advocate a foreign policy more independent of the United States. The ultimate resolution of the Iraq war may reshape how Europeans and Americans think of each other and deeply affect the potential for international cooperation.

Another new element of foreign policy opinion is the positive sentiment toward international organizations. Table 6.8 demonstrates, for example, that most people express confidence in the United Nations—even in the United States, where conservative politicians have long denounced the UN. The majorities in the table may seem modest, but as a reference point, the citizens of all four nations place more confidence in the United Nations than in their own national parliaments! In contrast to the past criticism the UN has received from some prominent American politicians, this support may be an indicator of a new spirit of international cooperation—although the potential for such a development is being tested by the Iraq conflict. Support for the North Atlantic Treaty Organization (NATO) is also high in the three member-states. These data and other survey evidence over the past decade suggest that support for internationalism is now common among Western democracies, reflecting part of a new world order.

Another example of international cooperation is the process of globalization, which involves both economics and other international exchanges. There has been an active, organized opposition to globalization in recent years, especially among liberals in the Western democracies, but this attitude is not shared by the citizens of these four nations. Very large majorities say that global trade has had a positive impact on their nation. Similarly, people are generally favorable to international organizations that are the vehicles for globalization and to multinational corporations (which often receive less favorable treatment in the press). The antiglobalization protestors, in contrast, garner much less support. Certainly globalization represents new economic, social, and cultural challenges to Western democracies, but most people appear to believe that the positives outweigh the negatives.

TABLE 6.8 Attitudes on Foreign Policy Issues (in percentages)

	United States	Great Britain	France	Germany
Major international threats				
Nuclear weapons the greatest danger	59	40	29	41
Ethnic/religious hatred the greatest danger	52	69	59	61
Terrorism				
Worried about terrorist attack	67	56	60	63
Support U.S. war on terror (2002)	—	69	75	70
U.S. acts on its own in war on terror	41	73	80	85
Europeans should be more independent of U.S. (2002)	—	47	60	51
International cooperation				
Confidence in UN	57	60	54	52
Confidence in NATO	53	59	—	51
Confidence in European Union	—	26	49	37
Globalization				
Global trade has positive impact	78	87	88	91
International organizations have positive influence on nation	60	67	66	66
Multinational corporations have positive influence on nation	55	61	50	57
Antiglobal protestors have positive influence on nation	30	39	44	34

SOURCES: 1999–2002 European Values Survey / World Values Survey; Pew (2002, 2003).
NOTE: Table entries are the percentages agreeing with each item.

We are in a period in which international relations are in flux, and new threats to world order have emerged since the ending of the Cold War. Although it is too early to discern the exact shape that foreign policy opinions will take in this new context, it appears that Western publics are broadening their perspectives and thinking about foreign policy in more cooperative and international terms. As one illustration, a 1995 survey found that a substantial proportion of the publics in Great Britain, Germany, and France felt that nuclear weapons were no longer necessary, and a differently worded question in the United States found nearly half of Americans shared these views.[6] Instead, new challenges to peace and international stability have emerged onto the agenda.

LEFT/RIGHT ORIENTATIONS

People are changing their opinions on many issues. Attitudes on equality issues display a dramatic shift over the past generation; overt discrimination against racial minorities, women, and other minority groups is no longer condoned by most people. Tolerance of nonconformity is also more common, whether the objects of tolerance are political or social minorities (McClosky and Brill 1983; Thomassen 1995). Liberal attitudes toward new issues such as environmental quality and alternative lifestyles are also commonplace. Moreover, there is a broad consensus in support of the basic social programs provided by the modern state, although voters do not endorse a further growth in these programs and would welcome a reduction in their taxes.

Still, it is difficult to use specific issue opinions to make sweeping generalizations about the changing political orientations of the public. Citizens are now interested in a wider range of issues than just socioeconomic concerns, and so a general assessment of overall political tendencies must weigh several different issues. The rate of social change across various issues is uneven: support for environmental protection has grown rapidly over time, while attitudes toward abortion have been more stable. Finally, the content of ongoing political controversies also changes over time. For instance, the racial issues that were intensely fought over in the 1960s—school desegregation, open housing, and public accommodations—now register overwhelmingly liberal responses; but new racial issues—quotas and affirmative action programs—divide the American public. This change represents progress in the development of racial tolerance, but racial policy remains politically contentious. One of the major points we have (re)learned from recent political trends is that new issues of conflict inevitably replace old consensual issues.

One way to generalize about the overall political orientations of Western publics is to examine broad ideological orientations that extend beyond specific issues. Political scientists frequently measure such broad orientations in terms of Left/Right attitudes (Fuchs and Klingemann 1989). Political issues are often discussed or summarized in terms of Left/Right or liberal/conservative philosophies. Republicans attack what they call the "loony Left," while Democrats rail against the "reactionary Right." These labels provide reference points that help voters interpret and evaluate political activities, but the ability to think of oneself in Left/Right terms does not imply that citizens possess a sophisticated conceptual framework or theoretical dogma. For many individuals, Left/Right attitudes summarize their positions on the political issues of greatest concern (also see chapter 11 on issue voting).

Figure 6.3 presents the distribution of Left/Right orientations across several nations in the early 1980s (lower figure) and at the end of the 1990s (upper figure). The survey asked respondents to place themselves on an 11-point scale, extending from Left to Right. The figure plots the average Left/Right self-placement of these electorates.

The United States is one of the more conservative nations in overall Left/Right terms; few advanced industrial democracies are farther to the right (for additional nations, see Inglehart 1997). This placement on the political scale reaffirms the impression derived from many of the specific issue areas examined in this chapter. Germany and most other advanced industrial

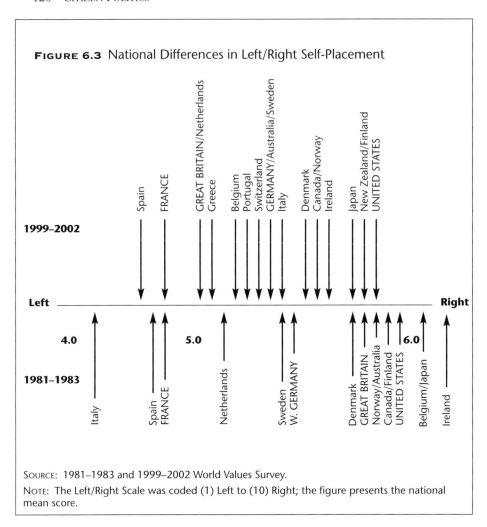

FIGURE 6.3 National Differences in Left/Right Self-Placement

SOURCE: 1981–1983 and 1999–2002 World Values Survey.
NOTE: The Left/Right Scale was coded (1) Left to (10) Right; the figure presents the national mean score.

democracies are clustered around the midpoint of the scale. At the liberal pole are Mediterranean nations—France and Spain—that have significant leftist traditions.

There is some evidence that Left/Right attitudes are more often moving in a liberal direction over time, although the cross-national pattern is varied. For example, between 1981 and 1999, there was a significant leftward shift by Australia, Belgium, Britain, Canada, Ireland, Japan, Norway, and the United States. Only Italy moved decisively in a conservative direction. Generational comparisons provide even stronger indication of political change; the young are consistently more liberal than their elders (Ashford and Timms 1992, appendix). This generation gap suggests that democratic publics are gradually becoming more liberal in their overall political orientations.[7] But even these data tell only a partial story.

As we suggested above, the content of Left and Right orientations reflects the issues of salience to the public, and this is another source of political change. The meaning of the terms themselves varies across age and political groups (Inglehart 1984; Fuchs and Klingemann 1989). For older citizens, these terms are linked to attitudes on socioeconomic issues: *Left* indicates support for social programs, working-class interests, and the influence of labor unions; *Right* is identified with limited government, support for middle-class interests, and the influence of the business sector. Among the young, the New Politics issues of environmental protection, social equality, and lifestyle freedoms are added to socioeconomic interests. For the young, the term *Left* can mean opposition to nuclear energy, support for sexual equality, internationalism, or endorsement of social programs.

Therefore, it is difficult to speak in simple terms about whether contemporary publics are becoming more liberal or conservative in an overall sense. Indeed, the best longitudinal evidence from the United States suggests that these broad orientations shift in both directions, depending on the issues of controversy and the political currents of the time. James Stimson (1999) shows that the 1960s were a period of liberal ascendance, while the 1980s were a decade of conservative swing. But underlying these overall trends, it appears that the Left/Right placement of young citizens differs from their elders, and the meaning of *Left* and *Right* in political discourse is also changing.

PUBLIC OPINION AND POLITICAL CHANGE

A significant feature of contemporary issue opinions is that more people are interested in more issues. Opinions on socioeconomic issues were once the predominant concern of voters and political elites; one could realistically describe political competition in terms of a single overarching policy area, such as the New Deal in the United States or capitalist/socialist conflicts in Europe. In recent years, however, the number of the public's distinct issue interests has diversified. Socioeconomic matters still attract widespread attention, but in addition, issues of social equality, environmental protection, social morals, and foreign policy capture the interest of large numbers of citizens.

The expansion of the boundaries of politics to include these new issues has several implications for the nature of contemporary politics. Governments have increased the scope of their activity: now they must worry not only about economic policy but also whether the environment is clean and whether personal life choices are tolerated. This expansion of the government's role has rekindled ongoing debates about the appropriate scope of government, although the policy content of the current debate is much different from prior debates about the economic role of the state.

The proliferation of issue publics also changes the structure of political representation and decision making. Issue publics focus their efforts to maximize representation on their issues, but the proliferation of such focused interests probably increases the complexity of the governing process. A majority of (differing) voters want government to spend more on (differing) specific programs; a majority also want government to tax them less. Policymakers thus see conflicting signals emanating from the public, without a method (or perhaps motivation) to resolve these conflicts systematically. Government responses to the demands of one issue public may conflict with the demands of another. Policy proliferation can lead to issue-by-issue decisions rather than broad programmatic planning. One of the challenges facing contemporary governments is how to adapt the democratic process to this different pattern of interest representation.

What can we say about the overall political orientations of contemporary publics? Journalists and social commentators frequently refer to a liberal or conservative mood sweeping a nation. The early 1960s and early 1970s supposedly were a time of radical change and liberal ascendance. Similarly, discussions of a new conservative mood in Western democracies became commonplace in the 1980s, exemplified by the electoral strength of Reagan, Thatcher, Kohl, and Chirac. Bill Clinton's victory in 1992 was called a signal of a new era, but just two years later the Republican midterm victories supposedly marked another new era, which in turn quickly came to an end with Clinton's reelection in 1996. The pundits were then surprised again when George W. Bush took the White House in 2000, with Republicans controlling both houses of Congress (while Blair and Schröder's victories moved Britain and Germany to the left).

Tested against actual public opinion data, such generalizations are often difficult to substantiate. The counterculture movement of the 1970s was not as widespread as the media suggested, and the conservative revival of the 1980s was equally overdrawn. The visible public actions of political groups can distort our perception of the broader currents of public opinion.[8] Furthermore, there are many issues of potential interest to the public, not all of them moving in a consistent direction over time.

Still, some general trends emerge from our findings. One apparent trend has been the shift toward what might be termed *libertarian attitudes*. Contemporary publics are becoming more tolerant of individual diversity and more concerned with the protection of individual freedoms. This applies to the rights of minorities and women, as well as to a general acceptance of individual freedom in social relations. These trends are manifested in attitudes toward social equality, moral issues, and the quality of life. Paralleling these changes have been a decline in respect for authority and concern about social order.

The counterevidence is *socioeconomic attitudes*. Concerns about the excessive cost and bureaucracy of government are now commonplace (even if people favor greater government spending on a wide variety of programs). The end of socialism and the retrenchment of the welfare state in the West have made it impossible for the Left to attain its traditional goals of state control of the economy and state guarantees of basic social needs. There has been a conservative shift on these aspects of the socioeconomic issue.

In a period of increasing issue proliferation, such conflicting trends are not surprising. There can be a gradual liberalization of political values on social issues, with a conservative tilt on socioeconomic matters. But even this generalization would be difficult to sustain because the meaning of such ideological labels has changed as part of the process of issue proliferation. No longer does liberalism stand for the creation of social programs, the nationalization of industry, and peaceful coexistence with the communist world—it may just as well mean protection of a clean environment or women's rights legislation. No longer does conservatism represent the prohibition of government social programs or the defeat of the Soviet empire—it may instead mean advocacy of term limits or supporting family policies.

The content of contemporary political debate is therefore difficult to compare to the political conflicts of the New Deal era of the 1930s or even those of the Great Society of the 1960s. Perhaps this shift in the content of the political debate is what most directly indicates how advanced industrial societies are modernizing and progressing politically in the new millennium.

SUGGESTED READINGS

Alba, Richard, Peter Schmidt, and Martina Wasmer, eds. *Germans or Foreigners? Attitudes toward Ethnic Minorities in Post-reunification Germany.* New York: Palgrave Macmillan, 2003.

Borre, Ole, and Elinor Scarbrough, eds. *The Scope of Government.* New York: Oxford University Press, 1995.

Inglehart, Ronald, and Pippa Norris. *A Rising Tide: Gender Equality and Cultural Change around the World.* New York: Cambridge University Press, 2003.

Jowell, Roger, et al., eds. *British—and European—Social Attitudes: The 15th Report.* Brookfield, Vt.: Ashgate, 1998.

Niedermayer, Oskar, and Richard Sinnott, eds. *Public Opinion and International Governance.* New York: Oxford University Press, 1995.

Norris, Pippa, and Ronald Inglehart. *Sacred and Secular: Religion and Politics Worldwide.* New York: Cambridge University Press, 2004.

Schuman, Howard, et al. *Racial Attitudes in America: Trends and Interpretations.* Rev. ed. Cambridge, Mass.: Harvard University Press, 1997.

Sniderman, Paul, et al. *The Outsider: Prejudice and Politics in Italy.* Princeton, N.J.: Princeton University Press, 2000.

Stimson, James. *Public Opinion in America: Moods, Cycles, and Swings.* 2nd ed. Boulder, Colo.: Westview, 1999.

NOTES

1. As the Conservative government sold off public enterprises, the public responded to the changing political context—support for further privatizations decreased over this same time span (Heath and McMahon 1992, 118–119).
2. For more on East-West contrasts, see Bauer-Kaase (1994).

3. A majority of Americans say they have avoided products that might harm the environment (Dunlap et al. 1993). The percentage of green consumers is also high in Europe, where waste problems and recycling efforts are more common. The 2000 International Social Survey found that 93 percent of Germans said they sort their trash for recycling, as do 51 percent of the British and 57 percent of Americans. The same survey showed significant numbers who claim to have signed an environmental petition: 22 percent in the U.S., 30 percent in Britain, and 31 percent in Germany; nearly equal numbers say they have contributed to an environmental group: 23 percent in the U.S., 24 percent in Britain, and 20 percent in Germany.

4. Religious attitudes illustrate the occasional inconsistency of public opinion. Citizens in all five surveys are more likely to believe in heaven than in hell (is this wishful thinking?). Eastern Germans are also more likely to believe in miracles than in the existence of God.

5. Most advanced industrial societies have experienced a long-term trend toward secularization. Church enrollment, for instance, has dropped off in most nations, as have other forms of involvement in the churches (Norris and Inglehart 2004, ch. 4).

6. These data are from the *Index to International Public Opinion 1995–1996*, 563 and 641.

7. These generational differences might be due to life-cycle effects, implying that younger people will become more conservative as they age. We could determine this if we had access to data over a longer time period, but the length of the available series is too brief for this purpose. Even if longer-term data were available, however, this would not address questions about the changing content of the terms *Left* and *Right* as discussed later.

8. Elections provide a poor indicator of ideological trends except in a very long-term perspective. Elections measure the positions of parties and candidates relative to the electorate, but not the overall distribution of opinion on any specific issue. A party that moves too far left can lose votes, as can one that moves too far right. Furthermore, the combination of issues in an election makes it difficult to make simple estimations of the voters' intentions on specific policies.

PART THREE

THE ELECTORAL CONNECTION

CHAPTER 7

Elections and Political Parties

C itizens use various ways to influence politics, but the electoral connection through political parties is the primary basis of public influence in representative democracies. Elections are one of the few methods that enable a society to reach a collective decision based on individual preferences. The choice between (or among) parties aggregates the preferences of individual voters, thereby converting public opinion into specific political decisions. Other forms of citizen participation may exert substantial influence on government, but they lack this representative quality.

Elections also are important because of what they decide. Electoral outcomes determine who manages the affairs of government and makes public policy.[1] The selection of leaders—along with the ability to "throw the rascals out" at the next election—is the public's penultimate power (one step short of protest/violence). Political elites may not always deliver what they promise, but the selection of a government provides some popular control over these elites.

Elections attract disproportionate attention from social scientists for several other reasons. Elections involve a majority of the public, so they enable us to see how most people make political decisions. Voting also provides an opportunity to study how political attitudes are linked to actual behavior—the casting of a ballot. Individuals translate their beliefs and opinions into a specific voting decision, so voting choices are likely to be relatively well thought out, intelligible, and predictable. The electoral connection thus offers a good setting for studying political thoughts and behavior beyond a simple response to a public opinion survey. If there is one political act that provides a window into the mind of most citizens, it is voting.

To study elections, one must start by understanding the political parties that provide the foundation of the electoral process. Parties are the primary institutions of representative democracy, especially in Europe (Luther and Mueller-Rommel 2002; Webb, Farrell, and Holliday 2002). Parties define the choices available to voters. Candidates in most European nations are selected by the parties and elected as party representatives, not as individuals. Open primaries and independent legislators are virtually unknown outside the United States. A large proportion of Europeans (including the Germans) vote directly for party lists rather than for individual candidates.

Political parties also direct the content of election campaigns. Party programs help define the issues that are discussed during a campaign (Klingemann, Hofferbert, and Budge 1994; Budge, Robertson, and Hearl 1987). In many European nations, it is the parties, not individual candidates, that

127

Internet Resource

Virtually all democratic political parties have web sites that can be found at:

http://www.electionworld.org

---

control campaign advertising. Political parties and party leaders thus exercise a primary role in articulating the public's concerns.

Once in government, parties control the policymaking process. Leadership of the executive branch and the organization of the legislative branch are decided on the basis of party majorities. The parties' control is often absolute, as in the parliamentary systems of Europe, where representatives from the same party vote as a bloc. American parties are less united and less decisive, but even here parties actively structure the legislative process. Because of the centrality of political parties to the democratic process, political scientists describe many European political systems as examples of "responsible party government."

Political parties thus provide the focus for our study of the electoral connection, and ultimately of the workings of democratic representation. A well-known political scientist, E.E. Schattschneider (1942), concluded that "modern democracy is unthinkable save in terms of political parties." Similarly, James Bryce (1921, 119) stated that "parties are inevitable. No one has shown how representative government could be worked without them." These are refrains echoed by many contemporary political scientists.

Beginning a new section on electoral choice, this chapter summarizes the history and social bases of contemporary party systems. This discussion presents a framework for understanding the party options available to the voters, as well as the characteristics of the major parties as political organizations and agents of representative democracy.

AN OVERVIEW OF FOUR PARTY SYSTEMS

To introduce the party systems in our four core nations, we begin by describing the characteristics of the major parties in each nation. Parties vary in size, structure, and governmental experience, as well as in political orientation.[2]

As table 7.1 shows, the American party system is atypical in many ways. The single-member-district electoral system encourages the development of a two-party system of Democrats and Republicans because seats are awarded only to the largest vote-getter in each district. A party system based on only two parties is unusual, since most democracies have multiparty elections, and thus multiparty coalitions are necessary to form a government majority. In the United States, in contrast, power shifts back and forth between the two

TABLE 7.1 Party Characteristics

Party	Year founded	Legislative election vote %	Seats	Party structure	Years in government (1970–2004)
United States (2004)					
Democrats	1832	47.4	201	Decentralized	23
Republicans	1856	49.9	233	Decentralized	11
Great Britain (2001)					
Labour	1900	40.7	413	Centralized	16
Liberal Democrats	1987	18.3	52	Decentralized	0
Conservatives	1830	31.7	166	Mixed	18
Regional parties		6.2	24	Mixed	0
France (2002)					
Communist Party (PC)	1920	4.8	21	Centralized	5
Socialists (PS)	1905	24.1	140	Centralized	13
Greens	1978	4.5	3	Decentralized	5
Union for Popular Movement (UPM)	1947	33.7	357	Mixed	21
UDF (Union for French Democracy)	1978	4.8	29	Mixed	21
National Front (FN)	1972	11.3	0	Personalistic	0
Germany (2002)					
Party of Democratic Socialism (PDS)	1990	4.8	2	Centralized	0
Social Democrats (SPD)	1863	38.5	251	Centralized	18
Greens	1980	8.6	55	Decentralized	6
Free Democrats (FDP)	1948	7.4	47	Decentralized	26
Christian Democrats (CDU/CSU)	1950	38.5	248	Mixed	16
Republikaner	1983	0.6	0	Mixed	0

SOURCE: Compiled by the author; election statistics from http://www.electionworld.org.

major parties. The Republicans' dramatic breakthrough in the 1994 congressional elections ended forty years of Democratic rule. For the past decade, the national electorate has been fairly evenly divided between the parties, although the Republicans hold control of both houses of Congress. The fluctuation in congressional vote totals over time is relatively small, averaging less than a 3 percent vote change between elections.

The results of presidential elections are more varied, however. For instance, Lyndon Johnson won a huge Democratic landslide in 1964, and Ronald Reagan won an equally impressive Republican majority in 1984. In contrast, the presidential elections of 2000 and 2004 demonstrated the rough parity of party support in more recent times. Presidential elections are heavily influenced by the candidates' own attributes, and voting results often fluctuate sharply as the candidates change. Therefore, our cross-national analyses of electoral patterns in subsequent chapters analyze American congressional elections rather than the presidential contests because they are more similar to Western European parliamentary contests.

Another distinctive aspect of the American political system is the decentralized nature of party organizations. Because of the federal system of American government, instead of one Democratic Party (or Republican Party) there are really fifty—one in each state. National party meetings are something like medieval gatherings of feudal states, rather than the conclaves of a unitary organization. The presidential nominating conventions are not controlled and directed by the national party committees but are taken over every four years by the personnel of the winning candidates. Even in Congress, American legislators are more likely to cross party lines than are parliamentarians in disciplined party systems. This means that there is considerably more diversity and fluidity within the American party system. The institutional weakness of the parties is also apparent in their small memberships (see chapter 3).

Great Britain presents a different partisan pattern—often described as a two-and-a-half-party system. The Labour Party is the major force on the left, and the Conservative Party is the representative of the right. Each of these major parties routinely receives around 40 percent of the national vote. The smaller Liberal Democratic Party, located near the center of the political spectrum, garners 10–15 percent.[3]

The diversity of the British party system has increased during the past two decades. Revived regional movements strengthened the nationalist parties in Scotland (Scottish Nationalist Party) and Wales (Plaid Cymru) in the 1970s, and the development of regional parliaments in the 1990s further strengthened these regional parties. At the end of the 1980s the historic Liberal Party was reformed as the Liberal Democrats, combining traditional conservatism on economic issues with more liberal policies on social issues. And other minor parties have periodically won significant vote shares, especially in the European Parliament elections, which are proportional representation elections. Despite these changes in the party system, the competition between Labour and the Conservatives still structures British electoral competition for the House of Commons.

The British political parties also are more highly organized and centralized than the major American political parties. Because Britain, like most other democracies, lacks the system of primaries that select candidates in the United States, the national party organizations play an important role in selecting candidates and determining the strategies and activities of election campaigns there. Once elected, members of Parliament (MPs) generally follow party lines in policy debates and in their voting behavior. Thus, party unity has great rewards.

Another feature of parliamentary systems is the constant emphasis on the party rather than on individual politicians. For instance, British voters do not directly cast a vote for the chief executive (the prime minister), as Americans vote for president. Under the procedures of its parliamentary system, the party group that controls Parliament elects the prime minister, who heads the executive branch. Even when it comes to electing a local district representative, British voters choose a party, often without knowing much about the candidate who represents the party in the district. The British political system is based on a model of strong party government.

The German party system is even more diverse. The electoral system is based on proportional representation: a party's share of the votes determines its share of the seats in parliament.[4] As a result, Germany has a multiparty system, with two major parties and several smaller parties. The Christian Democrats (CDU/CSU) are the major conservative party, and the Social Democrats (SPD) are the major leftist party. The CDU/CSU controlled the government for the first two decades of the Federal Republic (1949–1969), and again from 1982–1998. The SPD, which is the historical successor to the pre–WWII Social Democratic Party, controlled the national government from 1969 until 1982, and has held power again since the 1998 election in a coalition with the Green Party.

Several smaller parties also compete in German elections. The Greens emerged on the partisan stage in the 1980s as representatives of a postmaterial agenda (Poguntke 1993). Now in a coalition with the SPD, the Greens use their position within the government to advocate a variety of New Politics causes. The small Free Democratic Party (FDP), which captures between 5 and 10 percent of the vote, was a junior coalition partner in earlier governments.

German unification in 1990 further changed the political landscape, adding millions of new voters from the East. The Party of Democratic Socialism (PDS) emerged as a successor to the communist and socialist values of the German Democratic Republic; it attracts the bulk of its support from the East. In 2002 the PDS fell below the 5 percent hurdle required to win proportional representation in parliament, and thus its representation in the Bundestag is limited to the two district seats it did win. The Republikaner, a right-wing party that advocates nationalist and anti-foreigner sentiments, has not won seats in the national parliament, though its presence has affected the climate of political debate in contemporary Germany.

The German political system emphasizes the role of political parties to a greater degree than does the U.S. system. For example, parties control the candidate selection process. In Bundestag elections, the voter casts two votes. The first vote (*Erststimme*) is for a district candidate who is nominated by a small group of official party members or by a committee appointed by the membership (not through a primary election). The second vote (*Zweitstimme*) is directly for a party, which leads to the selection of half the Bundestag deputies from lists created by the parties. In addition, election campaigns are generously financed by the government, which allocates funding and access to public radio and television to the parties and not to the individual candidates. Government funding for the parties also continues between elections, to help them perform their educational functions as prescribed in the Basic Law. Within the Bundestag, parties caucus in advance of major legislation to decide the party position, and most legislative votes follow strict party lines. With the notable exception of the Greens, the German political parties are highly organized and centralized institutions. Therefore, it is not surprising to hear Germany described as a system of "party government."

France has an even more highly fragmented multiparty system. Instead of one party on the left, there are several: the Communist Party (PC), the Socialist Party (PS), and various smaller extreme leftist parties. Instead of one major party on the right, there are several: the Gaullist tradition is now represented by the Union for a Popular Movement (UPM; formerly the Rally for the Republic, or RPR), while the Union for French Democracy (UDF) represents a more center-right position. During the 1980s, the National Front (FN) emerged as an extreme right-wing party that attracts voters opposed to social changes occurring in France. A new environmental party also formed in the early 1980s, then reformed in mid-decade, and reformed again in the early 1990s. Now running under the label of the Green Party, it attracts some support for young, postmaterialist voters. Added to this mix are miscellaneous small centrist or extremist parties. In the 2002 election, for example, more than nine party groups won representation in the parliament, and many more ran for office.

The electoral history of the Fifth Republic is one of party change and electoral volatility. The Gaullist Party, now UPM, was originally the major party on the right and participated in conservative governments for the first two decades of the Fifth Republic. Eventually it was joined by the UDF, another major conservative party. The tide shifted toward the left in the 1980s, especially toward the Socialists, with their broad program of Old Politics and New Politics reforms. The Socialist Party won a majority in the 1981 legislative elections. The conservatives controlled Parliament from 1986 to 1988, and then a leftist majority reestablished itself. The conservatives swept the parliamentary elections of 1993, and then a Socialist/Green/PC majority formed after the 1997 elections. A conservative majority won legislative control in 2002. Analysts expected the 2002 presidential election to be a showdown between the Left and the Right, but the final contest was between the UPM and the National Front, which had finished 1-2 in the first *tour*. In short, the French party system is exceptionally fluid.

It is difficult to describe the French system in terms of a theoretical model of responsible party government. On the one hand, the French party system offers voters greater ideological choice than is available to American, British, or German voters. Political parties also play a major role in running political campaigns and directing the activities of the parliament. On the other hand, the fragmentation of the party system typically requires coalition politics, wherein parties are forced to negotiate and compromise on their programs. This process weakens the chain of party responsibility that is found intact in the British or German governments. Moreover, it is often the party leader, rather than the national party organization, who defines a party's goals and strategies. French parties are often highly personalistic—even a highly centralized party such as the PC. The French party system thus might be characterized as a party system in constant transition.

THE HISTORY OF PARTY SYSTEMS

Discussions of political parties normally focus on the present: the policy positions and political leaders that define current party images. We often think of each election in terms of the issues of the day. But across elections, parties normally take consistent positions that reflect their historical roots based either in an ideology or a connection with enduring social interests. Many voters repeatedly support the same party across elections for the same reasons. The Democratic tendencies of American Catholics, for example, result from their class position when they first emigrated to America, and the history of how Catholics were integrated into society and politics. The Republican leanings of Cuban-Americans can be traced to their unique historical experiences, which linked them to the Republican Party.

Seymour Martin Lipset and Stein Rokkan (1967) described the development of modern party systems in terms of the historical conditions of national and socioeconomic development. Table 7.2 summarizes their analyses and outlines the voting implications of this framework. Lipset and Rokkan maintained that two successive revolutions in the modernization of Western societies—the *National Revolution* and the *Industrial Revolution*—created divisions among certain social groups that still structure partisan competition today. Although their discussion dealt primarily with Western Europe, the approach is relevant to other Western democracies, including the United States.

The National Revolution comprised the process of nation building that transformed the map of Europe in the eighteenth and nineteenth centuries. The National Revolution spawned two sets of competing social groups (social cleavages) that are represented in the middle column of table 7.2. The *center/periphery* cleavage, which pitted the dominant national culture against ethnic, linguistic, or religious minorities in the peripheral regions, involved conflicts over values and cultural identities. For example, were Alsatians to become Germans or French; was Scotland a separate nation or a region within Britain? The diverse state histories within the United States generated similar tensions between regional cultures, even leading to a civil war. This cleavage is visible today in persistent regional differences in political orientation: between the English, Welsh, and Scots; between Bretons and the Parisian center; between the "Free State of Bavaria" and the Federal Republic of Germany; between the "old" Federal Republic and the new

German states in the East; and between the distinct regional cultures in the United States.

The second social cleavage associated with the National Revolution is the *church/state* conflict, which casts the centralizing, standardizing, and mobilizing forces of the national government against the traditional influence of the Catholic Church. In the face of a growing secular government, the church often sought to protect its established privileges by resisting the new national government. Furthermore, Protestants often allied themselves with nationalist forces in the struggle for national autonomy. Contemporary divisions between religious denominations and between secular and religious groups are a continuation of these earlier social divisions.

The Industrial Revolution in the nineteenth century also generated two new social cleavages, as seen in table 7.2. The *land/industry* cleavage pitted rural and agrarian interests against the economic concerns of a rising class of industrial entrepreneurs. For instance, the Ruhr industrialists challenged the power of the Prussian Junkers; the landed gentry of Britain and the United States were challenged by the barons of industry. We see this cleavage in contemporary conflicts between rural and urban interests.

As industrialization progressed, a second cleavage developed between *owners and workers* within the industrial sector. This cleavage reflected class conflict between the working class and the middle class (composed of business owners and the self-employed). The struggle for the legitimization and representation of the working-class movement often generated intense political conflict in the late nineteenth and early twentieth centuries. Today this cleavage is seen in the political competition between labor unions and business associations, and more generally between members of the working class and the middle class.

These historical events may seem far removed from contemporary party systems, but Lipset and Rokkan (1967) claimed that a linkage exists. These four cleavages define the major bases of social conflict existing within our four core nations. As social groups related to these cleavages developed—

TABLE 7.2 Social Cleavages and Voter Alignments

Historic era	Cleavage	Voting groups
National Revolution	Center/periphery Church/state	Region Religious denomination Religious/secular
Industrial Revolution	Land/industry Owners/workers	Urban/rural Middle/working class
Postindustrial Revolution	Cultural values	Material/postmaterial

SOURCE: Compiled by the author.

such as labor unions or farmer associations—they won access to the political process before the extension of the voting franchise. When mass voting rights were granted to most Europeans around the turn of the century, this structure of group competition was already in place. In most instances new voters were mobilized to support the party groups that already were politically active. New voters thus entered the electorate with preexisting partisan tendencies. The Conservative Party in Britain, for example, became the representative of the middle-class establishment, while the Labour Party catered to the interests of the working class. The working class in France and Germany supported the Communist and Socialist parties. The American party system developed more gradually, because the voting franchise was granted earlier and because social groups were less polarized. Still, the modern party system reflects political cleavages that are connected to the Civil War and the Great Depression. The Democratic Party, for instance, still draws upon the New Deal coalition that formed its basis in the 1930s.

The formation of mass political parties thus tended to institutionalize the existing group alignments, creating the framework for modern party systems. Once voters formed party loyalties and interest groups established party ties, these relationships became self-perpetuating. At each election, parties turned to the same social groups for their core support, and most voters in these groups habitually supported the same party. In one of the most often cited conclusions of comparative politics, Lipset and Rokkan stated that "the party systems of the 1960s reflect, with but few significant exceptions, the cleavage structures of the 1920s" (1967, 50).

Early electoral research substantiated Lipset and Rokkan's claims. Regional voting patterns from early in the twentieth century were mirrored in recent election returns. Survey research found that social cleavages, especially class and religious differences, exerted a potent effect on voting. For example, Richard Rose's (1969) comparative study of voting patterns in the 1960s found that voting choices were often frozen around the cleavages that Lipset and Rokkan described.

Just as this theme of partisan stability was becoming the conventional wisdom, dramatic changes began to affect these party systems. The established parties were presented with new demands and challenges, and evidence of partisan change mounted (Dalton, Flanagan, and Beck 1984).[5] New parties emerged to compete in elections, and some of the established parties fragmented. Voting results became more changeable from election to election, and voter choices appeared less frozen and predictable.

At the root of this development was a weakening relationship between traditional social cleavages and partisan choice. In their comparative study of Western democracies, Mark Franklin, Tom Mackie, and Henry Valen (1992) found broad evidence that traditional social divisions were losing their ability to predict voting choices (also see chapter 8). Because of this erosion in traditional social group–based politics, voting choices became more fluid. Partisan volatility increased at the aggregate and individual levels. Popular attachments to political parties weakened and discussions of party dealignment became commonplace (see chapter 9). In summary, the major research question changed from explaining the persistence of historical patterns in contemporary party systems to explaining their instability.

Several unique national circumstances contributed to the disruption of these patterns: the Vietnam War and Watergate in the United States, regional and economic tensions in Britain, or the green movement in Germany. The party systems of Europe and North America also experienced their normal share of political crises and economic problems that often rocked the incumbent parties.

In addition, a Postindustrial Revolution introduced a new set of postmaterial issues onto the political stage in these nations (see table 7.2). The established parties faced the new issues of environmental protection, social equality, nuclear energy, sexual equality, and alternative lifestyles. People began to demand more opportunities for participation in the decisions affecting their lives and to press for a further democratization of society and politics. Once these trends began, they provoked a conservative counterattack that opposed the liberalization of social norms and other postmaterial issues. Sometimes this backlash has led to a reassertion of traditional value conflicts based on religion or other historic social cleavages. These new postmaterial conflicts are now an important aspect of contemporary politics.

The initial inability or unwillingness of the major parties to respond fully to the new demands was a major factor in the destabilization of modern party systems. As a result, several new parties formed specifically to represent the new political perspectives. The first wave included environmental parties, such as the Green parties in Germany and France or Left-libertarian parties (Richardson and Rootes 1995). This development was followed by a counterwave of New Right parties, such as the National Front in France and the Republikaner in Germany (Ignazi 2003). It is unclear whether these new parties reflect temporary adjustments to new issues or a more long-lasting realignment of political conflict. American history is filled with third-party movements that were eventually incorporated into the established parties. Is the present partisan instability in advanced industrial democracies just another case of this recurring pattern?

Party systems are in a state of flux, and it is difficult to determine how fundamental and long-lasting these changes will be. It is clear, however, that the new political conflicts arising in advanced industrial societies have contributed to this unstable situation. While we wait for history to determine the significance of these trends, we can look more closely at the political alignments that now exist in America, Britain, Germany, and France.

THE STRUCTURE OF POLITICAL ALIGNMENTS

Most parties and party systems are still oriented primarily toward the traditional political alignments described by Lipset and Rokkan—which we shall refer to collectively as the *Old Politics* cleavage because it is based on the political conflict between Old Left and Old Right coalitions. Lipset and Rokkan considered the social class cleavage to be the primary factor in structuring the Old Politics cleavage because class issues were the most salient during the period when the franchise was being extended. The Old Left identifies itself with the working class and labor unions, as well as with secular groups and urban interests. The Old Right is synonymous with business interests and the middle class; in some nations this conservative coalition also includes religious and rural voters. When political issues tap the concerns of the Old Politics cleavage—for example, wage settlements, employment programs, social security programs, or abortion legislation—class and religious characteristics are strongly related to voting preferences.

The political conflicts of advanced industrial societies also include a new dimension of postmaterial cleavage (see chapter 5). This *New Politics* dimension involves conflict over new issues such as environmental quality, alternative lifestyles, minority rights, participation, social equality, and other postmaterial issues. This dimension represents the cleavage between proponents of these issues, the New Left, and citizens who feel threatened by these issues, the New Right.

The Old Politics cleavage is likely to remain the primary basis of partisan conflict in most advanced industrial democracies for the immediate future. The New Politics dimension is significantly affecting these party systems, however, because it can cut across the established Old Politics cleavage. Despite their differences, labor unions and business interests often join forces to fight the opponents of nuclear energy. Farmers and students sometimes become allies to oppose industrial development projects that may threaten the environment. Fundamentalist blue-collar and white-collar workers unite to oppose challenges to their moral code. The emergence of New Left and New Right interests may restructure social-group alignments and party coalitions in new and contrasting ways. In sum, the simple dichotomy between Old Left and Old Right is no longer adequate to describe present patterns of political competition. The contemporary political space is now better described by at least two dimensions (or more).

We can illustrate the separation of the Old Politics and New Politics cleavages with examples drawn from the American experience. For much of the past century, the Old Politics cleavages defined the primary basis of party competition in the U.S. party system. The New Deal coalition created in the 1930s in response to the Great Depression determined the social bases of party support: the Democratic Party and its working-class supporters against the Republicans and big business. Religious differences were muted because of the formal separation of church and state in the United States.

In the 1960s, the New Politics introduced a new set of issues into the American political process. Student protesters, the women's movement, and the alternative lifestyles movement challenged the symbols of the political establishment. Herbert Weisberg and Jerold Rusk (1970) described how this cultural conflict introduced a new dimension of cleavage, as represented by dissident Democratic candidates in the late 1960s and early 1970s. These researchers found, however, that Democrats and Republicans were not clearly divided on New Politics issues, which divided parties internally rather than separating them politically (also see Inglehart 1984).[6]

The policies of the Reagan and first Bush administrations stimulated a convergence of Old Politics and New Politics alignments over the 1980s and early 1990s. The Reagan administration's taxing and spending priorities sharply favored business and the more affluent sectors of society, which reinforced ties between business interests and the Republican Party. Furthermore, the Reagan administration pursued a conservative social agenda and developed political links to religious groups such as the Moral Majority and other fundamentalist organizations, thus injecting religion into partisan politics to an extent atypical of modern American politics.

The Reagan and first Bush administrations also clarified party positions on the New Politics agenda. Environmental protection had some roots in the Republican Party; Richard Nixon, for example, had established the Environmental Protection Agency during his first term and had introduced a variety of environmental legislation. Reagan, however, openly speculated that "killer trees" were a major cause of air pollution, and the policy initiatives of his administration demonstrated its hostility toward the environmental movement. Although George H.W. Bush claimed to be "the environmental president" while campaigning in 1988, the assault on environmental protection legislation continued under his administration. Similarly, the Reagan and Bush administrations were openly antagonistic toward feminist organizations. The abortion issue became a litmus test of Republican values in the appointment of federal judges and the selection of candidates.

As the Republicans grew more critical of the New Politics agenda, the Democrats became advocates of these same causes. The Democrats served as the partisan supporters of the environmental movement in congressional legislation, and they were the first to nominate a woman and feminist for national political office—Geraldine Ferraro, who ran for vice president in 1984. Bill Clinton's "New Democrats" coalition attempted to unite the old constituency of labor unions and the new constituency of environmentalists and feminists in the 1990s. Similarly, the Republican Party attempted to bring together its traditional middle-class and business supporters with its new voters among cultural conservatives. George W. Bush has moved even farther in this direction to strengthen the conservative identity of the Republican Party.

We can illustrate the current social and partisan alignments with data from the 2004 American National Election Study. The survey asked respondents about their feelings toward a set of sociopolitical groups and the political parties.[7] We used a statistical analysis method to represent the interrelationship of group perceptions in graphic terms.[8] This technique maps the political space as perceived by Americans: when there is a strong similarity in how two groups are evaluated, they are located near each other in the space; when groups are evaluated in dissimilar terms, they are positioned a distance apart. Thus one can think of the resulting figure as the political map that voters use to orient themselves to social groups and political parties.

The American sociopolitical space in 2004 is depicted in figure 7.1. The traditional Left/Right cleavage of the Old Politics is quite evident as the horizontal dimension in the figure. John Kerry is located at the left, along with the Democratic candidate for the House of Representatives in the survey respondent's district (Dem Hse), and both politicians are seen as close to the labor unions. In contrast, George W. Bush is located at the very opposite end of the continuum, and the nearest groups are business, the Christian Coalition, and the Republican candidate for the House.

The figure also portrays the position of other political groups in this political space. New Left groups, including feminists and environmentalists, are seen as close to Kerry and the Democrats in 2004—a closer proximity because of Kerry's more leftist politics than occurred for either Bill Clinton or Al Gore. The positioning of these New Left groups near the Democrats, and the Christian Coalition near the Republicans, may be an indication that cultural issues are being integrated into American party politics, at least with the candidate choices in 2004.

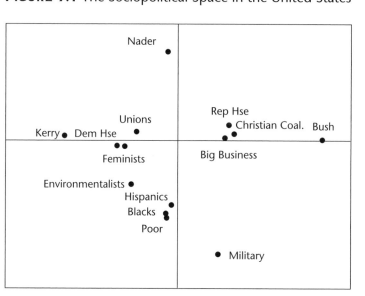

FIGURE 7.1 The Sociopolitical Space in the United States

SOURCE: 2004 American National Election Study.
NOTE: The figure presents a multidimensional scaling of thermometer scores.

Another part of the political space is occupied by minority groups—blacks, Hispanics, and the poor—who are perceived as closer to the Democratic Party, but distinct from either Old Left or New Left groups. Finally, the opposite ends of a second political continuum are represented by Ralph Nader, the former Green Party candidate who ran as an antiestablishment independent in 2004, and the military, which Americans see as the group most opposite to Nader. This contrast between Nader and the military also suggests that an establishment/antiestablishment dimension still exists within the American political space.[9]

Comparable current data on the sociopolitical space in Britain, Germany, and France are not available, but another study uses a different method to illustrate party positions on Old Politics and New Politics issues in all four party systems. Michael Laver and W. Ben Hunt (1992) asked experts to position the parties in their respective nations on a set of policy dimensions. Figure 7.2 presents party positions on two issues: taxes versus social spending as a measure of the socioeconomic issues of the Old Politics, and the environment versus economic growth as a measure of New Politics priorities.

The top panel of the figure locates parties on the spending/taxes issue. Here we find a traditional Left/Right party alignment in each nation. The Democratic Party in the United States is located at the left end of this continuum, following the pattern found earlier in mapping the sociopolitical space. At the opposite end of the Old Politics dimension is the Republican Party. From Ronald Reagan to the 1994 "Contract with America" to the George W. Bush campaigns, the Republicans have developed a strong commitment to cutting public services and cutting taxes that is now ingrained in the Republican policy image.

In Great Britain, the Labour Party is the historic representative of the working class and the advocate for socialist policy. The party's working-class orientation is institutionalized through formal ties to the labor unions. Normally, membership in a union automatically includes a dues-paying membership in the Labour Party; union leaders also control this large bloc of votes at Labour Party conventions. Past Labour governments nationalized several major industrial sectors, expanded social welfare programs, and vigorously defended the interests of their working-class supporters. The Labour Party is located to the left of both the American Democrats and the German SPD on this dimension.[10] The British Liberal Democrats are a small centrist party that occupies a midpoint on this dimension. Traditionally a representative of liberal, middle-class values, this party has formed and reformed itself in recent years, but it still holds a centrist position on issues of the government's socioeconomic role.

Since Margaret Thatcher's first election in 1979, the Conservative Party has aggressively attempted to roll back the scale of national government. Conservative governments privatized many government-owned industries, reduced government social and educational programs, sold off public housing, and generally tried to lessen the scope of the government's involvement in society. These policies reinforced the Conservatives' traditional image as a party that favors business interests and draws disproportionate support from middle-class voters. Even now, more than a decade after Thatcher left the party leadership, these images remain part of the Conservative Party's public image, placing it to the right on this economic dimension.

The major representative of the Old Left in Germany is the Social Democratic Party (SPD), which emerged from the socialist working-class movement and still consistently represents working-class interests. Although German labor unions no longer have institutional ties to the SPD, the relationship nevertheless remains close.[11] Because of these liberal traditions, the SPD is seen as favoring increased social spending—though this policy preference may have moderated a bit since the early 1990s. The SPD government of Gerhard Schröder has tried to temper its leftist image, but the party remains a strong advocate of government social spending. The German Greens are described as a Left-libertarian party because they combine a distinctly liberal position on many traditional issues of social spending and the welfare state with an advocacy of New Left causes. Thus political experts position the Greens to the left of the SPD on the social-spending dimension in figure 7.2.[12]

The Christian Democratic Union/Christian Social Union (CDU/CSU) is the major political force on the right in Germany. The CDU was formed after the war as a conservative-oriented catchall party (*Volkpartei*); in the state of Bavaria the CSU runs as the party of the conservative bloc. In national politics, the CDU and CSU act as a single party. As their names imply, both conservative parties represent religious voters on the church/state cleavage. The Union parties also advocate conservative economic policies and a free-market economy. The CDU/CSU and the smaller Free Democratic Party (FDP) occupy similar conservative positions on the services/taxes dimension. Indeed, during the sixteen years (1982–1998) when the two parties shared control of the government, they pursued conservative economic programs that limited the size of government and stimulated economic development. The exceptional costs of German unification forced these parties to turn temporarily away from these welfare policies, but their commitment to smaller government remains strong. The National Democratic Party (NPD) is a very small, extreme-right party known for its nationalistic and reactionary policies; it has not won representation in the Bundestag. Experts locate the NPD at the conservative end of the social services dimension.

France has two major parties that represent traditional Old Left positions: the Communist Party (PC) and the Socialists (PS). The PC strongly believes that the government is responsible for social needs and is the most extreme leftist party in all four nations. The PC depends very heavily on working-class votes and has formal ties with the communist labor union, the CGT. Furthermore, while other communist parties have lost their Marxist ideology since the collapse of the Soviet Union, the French Communist Party remains committed to its principles. The French Socialists, by comparison,

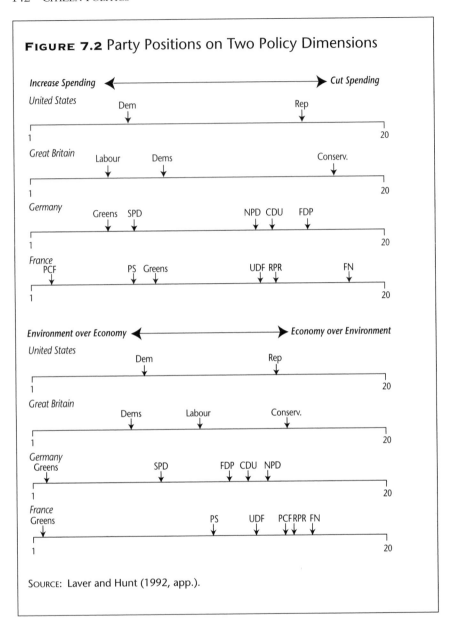

FIGURE 7.2 Party Positions on Two Policy Dimensions

SOURCE: Laver and Hunt (1992, app.).

have moderated their ideological image to appeal to liberal middle-class voters. Still, political experts see the PS as strongly committed to extensive governmental social programs.

France has two major conservative parties. Until recently, the Rally for the Republic (RPR) was the successor to the Gaullist forces that created the Fifth

Republic, and the current Gaullist successor party, the Union for a Popular Movement (UPM), follows in this same tradition. (The president of France, Jacques Chirac, transformed the RPR into the UPM in 2002.) The party is a representative of conservative business interests and the middle class; it favors reduction of government social programs and taxes. The Union for French Democracy (UDF) is a moderate conservative party that attracts liberal elements of the middle class. At the far right of the political spectrum is the National Front (FN), an example of a New Right party, focusing its attention on cultural and social issues, such as opposition to foreigners, a nationalistic foreign policy, and traditional social values. Its identity is formed more as a backlash to the liberal themes of the New Politics than by traditional economic issues; but on issues of social spending it is perceived as sharply conservative.

If Old Politics issues, such as government social spending, were the only factors structuring electoral competition, then Lipset and Rokkan would still be correct in describing contemporary party systems in terms of the cleavages of the 1920s. The class-based Left/Right party alignment that historically structured partisan politics remains clearly visible in political experts' positioning of the contemporary parties on the services/taxes dimension.

The content of the political agenda, however, now includes more than the economic and security concerns of the Old Politics. As the New Politics has introduced postmaterial interests into the political debate, this issue expansion has led to a different alignment of parties. The partisan alignments along the New Politics cleavage are displayed in the bottom panel of figure 7.2, which positions parties on the environment/economy policy dimension.

In the United States, we find the same Left/Right ordering of the parties. The Democrats are seen as the advocates for environmental protection, while the Republicans are perceived as more concerned with protecting the economy even at a cost to the environment. This party cleavage was aptly illustrated in the 2000 presidential election, in which the Democrats nominated Al Gore, a political figure closely identified with environmental protection and author of a best-selling book on the subject, as their candidate. Meanwhile, the Republicans' candidate, George W. Bush, expressed concern for environmental quality, but he also promised to roll back what he considered excessively strict environmental regulations and to balance environmental protection against the nation's economic and energy needs. In the United States, the alignment of the two parties is now similar on both Old Politics and New Politics dimensions.

In most other party systems, the environmental issue creates a new pattern of partisan alignment. In Britain, for example, the Liberal Democrats have distinguished themselves as the party most sympathetic to the environmental issue. In Germany, the Green Party is seen as a strong advocate for environmental causes and is located at the far end of this continuum. Over time, the SPD has become more sympathetic to the environmental movement, but experts still position it near the center of this policy scale. The Social Democrats are closer to the conservative CDU/CSU and FDP on this dimension than they are to the

Greens. The extremist NPD is on the far right of this continuum, which illustrates where this party and the New Right Republikaner would be located on the New Politics dimension. As the Greens are advocates for modernization and liberal issues, the NPD (and more recently the Republikaner) are the most vocal critics of social and cultural change. Overall, the major cleavage on the environmental dimension separates the Greens from *all* the other German parties.

The ability of New Politics to transform party alignments is most clearly illustrated in the French party system. The French Greens are strong supporters of the environment, occupying an extreme New Left position. The traditional leftist parties are neutral or critical of environmental protection. The Socialists are at the center of this scale; the Communists, who are extremely leftist on Old Politics issues, are positioned between the conservative UDF and RPR on the environmental dimension. Indeed, the Communists and the National Front hold similar positions on the environmental dimension in France. Overall, as we saw in the German party system, the New Politics cleavage separates the Greens from all the other French parties.

While figure 7.2 locates the political parties at the end of the 1980s, a more recent study by Gary Marks and Marco Steenbergen (2004) asked a new panel of experts to locate the European parties along similar Old Politics and New Politics issue dimensions as of 2000. Their findings are quite similar to the results presented here. The traditional economic cleavage is still quite apparent in the three European party systems, echoing the Left/Right positions described earlier. The introduction of the Party of Democratic Socialism (PDS) in Germany has increased polarization along this dimension, as has the growth of the National Front in France, but the relative positions of the major parties remain fairly consistent. Similarly, the environmental/libertarian issue dimension continues to divide political parties in different ways. In France, for instance, the Greens are on the proenvironment end of this dimension, while the Communist PC is located near the two major conservative parties (UDF and RPR). In Germany, the economically very conservative FDP shifts dramatically toward the liberal end of the continuum on environmental/libertarian issues, while the communist-successor PDS moves toward the conservative end.

By combining the evidence in this section, we can begin to map the sociopolitical space that voters use to orient themselves to partisan politics. In each nation there is a clear representation of political positions along the traditional socioeconomic issues that formed the initial structure of party competition in these democracies. In addition, the emergence of new issues is prompting the formation of new parties or the realignment of the established parties to represent these issues. Much of the current research on electoral politics attempts to assess the relative position of the political parties on both dimensions, as well as the relative weight of both dimensions in structuring political choice for the electorate. The mix of these old and new dimensions is one of the forces that fuels the current processes of electoral change in these nations.

CONTEMPORARY PARTY SYSTEMS

This chapter has described broad similarities in the ideological structure of contemporary party systems. Most political parties are still oriented to the Old Politics cleavages of class and religion. Even if these cleavages have become less salient, the political ties between social groups and political parties perpetuate these images. Parties are, after all, still turning to the same interest groups and associations for the core of their support. Contemporary publics see rightist parties as linked to business interests (and sometimes the Catholic Church), while leftist parties are seen as allied with the labor unions.

While major party differences exist on the Old Politics dimension, there are indications that the New Politics cleavage is taking on increasing importance. Earlier chapters (5 and 6) found that people are developing postmaterial values that lead to new policy interests. These new issues initially were represented outside the established parties through public interest groups, but they are now gaining representation within partisan politics, which places new demands on the established parties.

Some indications of partisan change along the New Politics dimension are already evident. New parties, such as the German and French Greens, have emerged to represent New Politics concerns. These small parties draw their support from the young, the better educated, and postmaterialists—key groups defining the New Politics cleavage. And in response, New Right parties have emerged in many Western party systems, typically advocating conservative values, social order, and often a criticism of immigration and minority politics.

A more basic change would occur if the larger established parties were to adopt clearer positions on New Politics issues, and there is some evidence of such a change in the policies and electoral strategies of the major leftist parties in several nations. Some established parties are attempting to combine Old Left and New Left issue appeals into a single program, though this is a difficult coalition to maintain because of their contrasting interests. Similarly, some conservative parties have attempted to appeal to both Old Right and New Right groups, and have experienced the same tensions in pulling this coalition together.

Many established parties have been hesitant to formalize close ties to New Left or New Right groups, however, especially in Western Europe, where the Old Politics ties remain strong. Parties are naturally cautious about taking clear stands on a new dimension of conflict before the costs and benefits are clear. The major European leftist parties, for example, are internally split on many Old Politics/New Politics conflicts: while most industrial labor unions favor economic development projects that will strengthen the economy and produce jobs, leftist environmentalists often oppose these same projects because of their ecological consequences. Many conservative parties also face divisions between conservative business elites, new cultural conservatives, and liberal middle-class voters.

Added to these uncertainties are the new questions of partisan identity in the post–Cold War era. The end of communism requires a rethinking of the foreign policy stances of many parties. Many conservative parties that used anticommunism as part of their political image must now replaced it with other political themes. Similarly, the collapse of East European socialism has weakened the ability of social democratic parties to advocate expanding the role of government. In short, parties of the Left and the Right are rethinking some of the themes that have long furnished their electoral identities.

Because of the uncertainties facing the parties and the difficulties in integrating a new political cleavage into the existing party systems, future partisan change is likely to follow an uncertain course. Continuing changes in citizen values and issue interests mean that the potential for further partisan change is real.

SUGGESTED READINGS

Abramson, Paul, John Aldrich, and David Rohde. *Change and Continuity in the 2000 and 2002 Elections.* Washington, D.C.: CQ Press, 2003.

Clarke, Harold, et al. *Political Choice in Britain.* Oxford: Oxford University Press, 2004.

Evans, Geoffrey, and Pippa Norris, eds. *Critical Elections: British Parties and Voters in Long-Term Perspective.* Thousand Oaks, Calif.: Sage, 1999.

Hampton, Mary, and Christian Soe, eds. *Between Bonn and Berlin: German Politics Adrift?* Lanham, Md.: Rowman & Littlefield, 1999.

LeDuc, Lawrence, Richard Niemi, and Pippa Norris, eds. *Comparing Democracies: New Challenges in the Study of Elections and Voting.* 2nd ed. Thousand Oaks, Calif.: Sage, 2002.

Lewis-Beck, Michael S., ed. *The French Voter.* New York: Palgrave, 2004.

Luther, Richard, and Ferdinand Mueller Rommel, eds. *Party Change in Europe.* Oxford: Oxford University Press, 2002.

Norris, Pippa, ed. *Britain Votes 2001.* Oxford: Oxford University Press, 2001.

Norris, Pippa. *Electoral Engineering: Voting Rules and Political Behavior.* New York: Cambridge University Press, 2004.

Rohrschneider, Robert, and Russell Dalton, ed. "Judgment Day and Beyond: The 2002 Bundestagswahl." Special issue, *German Politics and Society,* summer 2003.

Webb, Paul, David Farrell, and Ian Holliday, eds. *Political Parties in Advanced Industrial Democracies.* Oxford: Oxford University Press, 2002.

NOTES

1. There are several good analytic studies of recent American elections (Abramson, Aldrich, and Rohde 2003; Pomper 2001), British elections (Clarke et al. 2004; Norris 2001), German elections (Rohrschneider and Dalton 2003; Hampton and Soe 1999; Klein et al. 2000), and French elections (Lewis-Beck 1999; Boy and Mayer 1993).

2. Vote share is based on the most recent national election: United States (2004), Britain (2001), Germany (2002), and France (2002). The computation of years in

government is complicated by the separation of powers in the United States and France; we decided to count the number of years a party was part of the legislative majority between 1970 and 2004 as the most comparable cross-national statistic.

3. Because of the single-member-district electoral system, the Liberal Democrats are routinely disadvantaged in winning seats in Parliament. In 2001, for example, the party won 18 percent of the popular vote nationwide but received only 8 percent of the seats in the House of Commons.

4. The German electoral law requires that a party win 5 percent of the national vote on the second ballot, or three district seats, in order to share in the proportional distribution of Bundestag seats. In 2002 the PDS won only two district seats and less than 5 percent nationally, so it did not receive additional parliamentary seats based on its national share of the vote.

5. Bartolini and Mair (1990) forcefully argue that earlier historical periods were also marked by high levels of partisan volatility. But their methodology underestimates the degree of the current levels of partisan change (Dalton and Wattenberg 2000, chap. 3).

6. For instance, the 1984 Democratic primaries featured a confrontation between Old Left and New Left Democrats. Walter Mondale, who was identified with the traditional New Deal policies of the Democratic Party, won early endorsements from labor unions and the party establishment. Gary Hart, in contrast, explicitly claimed that he was the New Politics candidate, the representative of new ideas and a new generation. Hart's core voters were the Yuppies—young, urban, upwardly mobile professionals—one of the groups linked to the New Politics cleavage.

7. These are the so-called feeling thermometer questions that measure positive and negative feelings toward each object. Respondents are given a thermometer-like scale to measure their "warmth" or "coldness" toward each group.

8. The feeling thermometers were analyzed using a multidimensional scaling program, and the solution was then rotated so the Kerry-Bush dimension was aligned horizontally in the scale. For earlier analyses of similar sociopolitical spaces, see Barnes, Kaase, et al. (1979); Inglehart (1984); and previous editions of this text.

9. Ideally, what is needed is a tracking of sociopolitical alignments over time to see if there has been a systematic change in the Democrats' and Republicans' electoral alliances.

10. Other evidence suggests that the Labour Party moved dramatically to the center in the 1997 campaign in an attempt to attract moderate voters and win a parliamentary majority (Budge 1999). Even with this movement to the center, however, the party still retained its distinct orientation on class issues.

11. The German portion of the Cross National Election Project also contained a question on the partisan leanings of social groups. About three-quarters of the German public saw labor unions as leaning toward the SPD, and an equal number saw business associations and the Catholic Church as leaning toward the CDU/CSU; nearly 80 percent saw environmental groups as favoring the Greens. See Dalton (1993a, 266); and Wessels (1993).

12. The Party of Democratic Socialism (PDS) is a successor of the communist party of the German Democratic Republic. The PDS would be positioned on the far left of this scale.

CHAPTER 8

The Social Bases of Party Support

There is a well-worn saying that people act politically as they are socially, and this has been the case for electoral politics. The preceding chapter discussed how party systems were formed to provide political representation for class, religious, and other social groups. Contemporary political parties maintain ties to their clientele groups and project images in group terms: Labour is a working-class party, the Republicans are the party of business, the Christian Democrats represent religious voters, and so forth. Although the campaign issues and personalities change from election to election, parties generally retain their institutional and ideological connections to specific social groups. Most parties depend on the votes of their clientele groups to provide a stable base of electoral support.

From its beginnings, electoral research has stressed social-group attachments as an important influence on voting behavior. One of the first empirical studies of American voting focused on the social bases of partisanship (Lazarsfeld, Berelson, and Gaudet 1948). This study found that an "index of political predispositions" based on social class, religion, and rural/urban residence was strongly related to voting choice. Social stratification is even greater in Europe, producing even sharper group differences in voting patterns. A common cliché notes that social class is the basis of British politics, and all else is just embellishment and detail. Both class and religion are strong correlates of voting in Germany and France.

This chapter begins our analysis of voting behavior by studying the group basis of voting that evolves from the social alignments described in chapter 7. We highlight both stability and change in group-based voting. On the one hand, the partisan loyalties generated by social characteristics produce stable party coalitions, since the parties routinely attract the same kinds of core voters; this constancy in the bases of party support reinforces the partisan images presented in chapter 7. On the other hand, there is strong evidence that modernization processes in advanced industrial societies are eroding the group bases of party preferences (Franklin, Mackie, and Valen 1992). In addition, the increasing sophistication of contemporary electorates may lessen voter reliance on social cues, as individuals make their own political decisions. We examine these theories by tracking group voting patterns over time and across nations.

THE SOCIAL GROUP MODEL OF VOTING

Social characteristics such as class and religion influence a voter's choice of party in several possible ways. First, a person's social position often indicates

---

Internet Resource

Visit the web sites of the American National Election Study and the British Election Study:

US: www.umich.edu/~nes/
GB: www.essex.ac.uk/bes/

---

his or her values and political beliefs. A French steelworker is more likely than a shopkeeper, for example, to favor an expansion of social services or government regulation of business. Opposition to liberal abortion laws is more likely among devout Catholics than among the nonreligious. Thus social characteristics are an indirect measure of attitudinal differences between groups of voters and their perceptions of which party best represents their policy positions.

Second, social characteristics also indicate some of the political cues to which an individual is exposed. A British mineworker, for example, hears about politics from his coworkers or other working-class neighbors and friends, and he also receives political persuasion from the union representative at work and from union publications at home. Thus his working-class milieu provides repeated cues on which policies will benefit people like him, and which party best represents his interests; a strong Labour Party bias in these cues is inevitable. Similarly, a Bavarian Catholic hears about political issues at weekly church services, from Catholic social groups, and from predominately conservative Catholic friends; this information generally encourages a favorable opinion of the Christian Social Union and its program.

Third, social groups can be an important reference point in orienting voters to political issues and providing information about politics. Even if an individual is not a member of a labor union or a regular churchgoer, the knowledge that unions favor one party and the Catholic Church another can help voters locate themselves in relation to the parties. The cues provided by social networks and group-party associations help to guide many citizens' political orientations and voting behavior.

Voter reliance on social-group cues is an example of the satisficing decision making described in chapter 2. Social cues can narrow voters' choices to parties that are consistent with their social position. Voters thus enter an election favoring the party (or parties) that historically supports the class or religious groups to which they belong, while excluding parties with unsupportive records. Political parties nurture such ties, communicating their group loyalties to the voters by calling themselves "Labour" or "Christian Democrats."

Voters thus may decide between competing parties based on the cues that social groups provide—the endorsements of labor unions, business associations, religious groups, and the like—as well as the group appeals of the parties themselves. The parties' stable alliances with specific social groups mean that many voters develop standing partisan predispositions that endure across elections, simplifying the decision process still more. When British industrial workers cast their votes for Labour because the party represents people like themselves, this is a reasonable electoral decision.

Reliance on social characteristics thus is a shortcut in making voting decisions. A citizen who is knowledgeable about all the issues and all the candidates is well prepared to make an informed voting choice and to justify this decision in issue-oriented and ideological terms. Social characteristics provide a simpler, although less certain, method of choosing which party represents the voter's interests. Still, when strong social-group identities are matched by clear party positions on these social cleavages, as they are in most European nations, then social characteristics can provide a very meaningful guide for voting behavior.

SOCIAL CLASS AND THE VOTE

Class politics taps the essence of what we have described as the Old Politics— an economic conflict between the haves and the have-nots. The class cleavage represents the economic and material problems of industrial societies: improving standards of living, providing economic security, and ensuring a just distribution of economic rewards. Issues such as unemployment, inflation, social services, tax policies, and government management of the economy reinforce class divisions.

Social scientists have probably devoted more attention to the relationship between social class and voting than to any other social characteristic. Theoretically, the class cleavage involves some of the most basic questions of power and politics that evolve from Marxian and capitalist views of societal development. Empirically, one's position in the class structure is often a strong predictor of voting choice. Seymour Martin Lipset's early cross-national study of electoral politics described the class cleavage as one of the most pervasive bases of party support:

> Even though many parties renounce the principle of class conflict or loyalty, an analysis of their appeals and their support suggests that they do represent the interests of different classes. On a world scale, the principal generalization which can be made is that parties are primarily based on either the lower classes or the middle and upper classes. (1981a, 230)

Most early empirical studies of voting choices generally supported these conclusions.

Research on the class cleavage normally defines social class in terms of occupation. Following Karl Marx's writings, occupations are typically classified on the basis of their relationship to the means of production. The bourgeoisie are the owners of capital and the self-employed; the proletariat are the workers who produce capital through their labor. This schema is then generalized to define two large social groupings: the middle class and the working class. These class differences provided the basis for the creation of socialist and communist parties that represent the interests of the working class; conservative parties, in turn, defend the interests of the middle class.

While this Marxian dichotomy once defined the class cleavage, the changing nature of advanced industrial societies has reshaped the class structure. The traditional bourgeoisie and proletariat have been joined by a "new" middle class—what others have called a "salatariat"—that consists primarily of salaried white-collar employees and civil servants (Heath, Jowell, and Curtice 1991). Daniel Bell (1973) defined a "post-industrial" society as one in which most of the labor force holds new-middle-class positions; by the 1980s nearly all Western democracies had passed that threshold.

The new middle class is an important addition to the class structure because it lacks a clear position in the traditional class conflicts between the working class and the old middle class. The separation of management from capital ownership, the expansion of the service sector, and the growth of government (or nonprofit) employment creates a social stratum that does not conform to Marxian class analysis. The new middle class does not own capital as the old middle class did, and it differs in lifestyle from the blue-collar workers of the traditional proletariat. Members of the new middle class seem less interested in the economic conflicts of the Old Politics and more attuned to the New Politics issues we examined in chapter 5 and 6. Consequently, the political identity of the new middle class differs from both the bourgeoisie and the proletariat.

Table 8.1 presents the voting preferences of these social classes in the most recent election for which data are available.[1] Historical class alignments persist in each nation. The working class in each nation gives disproportionate support to leftist parties, ranging from 56 percent voting for the Democrats in the United States to 66 percent voting Labour in Britain. At the other extreme, the old middle class is the bastion of support for conservative parties. This traditional proletariat/bourgeoisie cleavage remains strong in each nation—although less than half of the electorate in each nation now belongs to either of these two classes.

The new middle class now constitutes the majority of voters and, more important, holds ambiguous partisan preferences. It is normally located between the working class and the old middle class in its Left/Right voting preferences. In addition, the new middle class gives disproportionate support to parties that represent a New Politics ideology, such as the German Greens and the French Greens. The new middle class is a key element in the changing political alignments of advanced industrial democracies.[2]

Although social class can still influence voting choice, class cues carry much less weight than they did in the mid-twentieth century (Nieuwbeerta and de Graaf 1999). This long-term pattern can be seen in figure 8.1, which presents the Alford index of class voting in our four core nations. To maximize

TABLE 8.1 Social Class and Party Support (in percentages)

	Working class	New middle class	Old middle class
United States (2004)			
Democrats	56	55	48
Republicans	44	45	52
Total	100	100	100
Great Britain (2001)			
Labour	66	40	36
Liberal Democrats	14	25	17
Conservatives	20	35	47
Total	100	100	100
France (2002)			
PC/Far Left	12	7	3
Socialists	43	39	28
Greens	15	14	16
UDF	2	10	11
RPR	22	27	38
National Front	6	3	3
Total	100	100	99
Germany (2002)			
PDS	3	3	4
Greens	2	7	4
SPD	49	50	38
FDP	10	6	8
CDU/CSU	36	34	44
Total	100	100	98

SOURCES: United States, 2004 American National Election Study (CSES); Great Britain, 2001 British Election Study; Germany, German Election Study 2002 (CSES); France, 2002 International Social Survey (ISSP).

NOTE: U.S. data are based on congressional vote; German data are for East and West electorates combined. Social class is based on occupation of the respondent.

comparability, this index measures the Left/Right voting patterns of the working class versus those of the combined middle class (old and new). It calculates class voting as the simple difference between the percentage of the working class voting for the Left and the percentage of the middle class voting for the Left.[3]

The general trend in figure 8.1 is obvious; class differences are declining. The size of the class voting index has decreased by almost half in Britain during the past fifty years, and by a greater proportion in Germany.[4] Class voting patterns follow a varied decline in American congressional elections; in

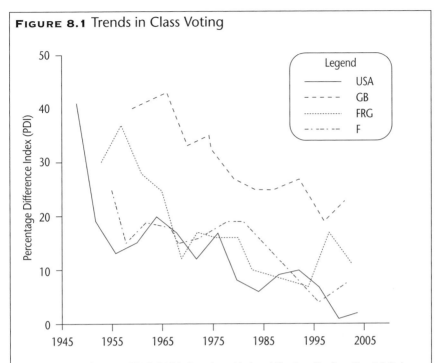

FIGURE 8.1 Trends in Class Voting

SOURCES: United States, 1948–2004, American National Election Studies; Great Britain, 1955, Heath et al. (1985); 1959, Civic Culture study; 1964–2001, British Election Studies; Germany, 1953–2002, German Elections Studies (Western Germany only, 1990–2002); France, 1955, MacRae (1967, 257); 1958, Converse and Dupeux survey; 1962, IFOP survey; 1967, Converse and Pierce survey; 1968, Inglehart survey; 1973–1988, Eurobarometer; 1996 and 2002, ISSP.

NOTE: Figure entries are the Alford Class Voting index, i.e., the percentage of the working class preferring a leftist party minus the percentage of the middle class voting for the Left. U.S. data are based on congressional elections, except for 1948, which is based on president vote.

the 2000 and 2004 elections, the gap was virtually nonexistent. Paul Abramson, John Aldrich, and David Rohde (2003, ch. 5) show that the erosion of class voting is even more pronounced in U.S. presidential elections. In France, social class had a modest impact on voting during the French Fourth Republic, but the turbulent events accompanying the formation of the Fifth Republic—including the creation of a broad-based Gaullist Party—abruptly lowered class voting in 1958. During the early elections of the Fifth Republic, class voting stabilized at a level significantly below pre-1958 levels (Lewis-Beck and Skalaban 1992). Then class voting has declined again in more recent French elections (also Cautrès 2004).

To place the current levels of class voting in our four nations in cross-national perspective, figure 8.2 compares the strength of class differences in

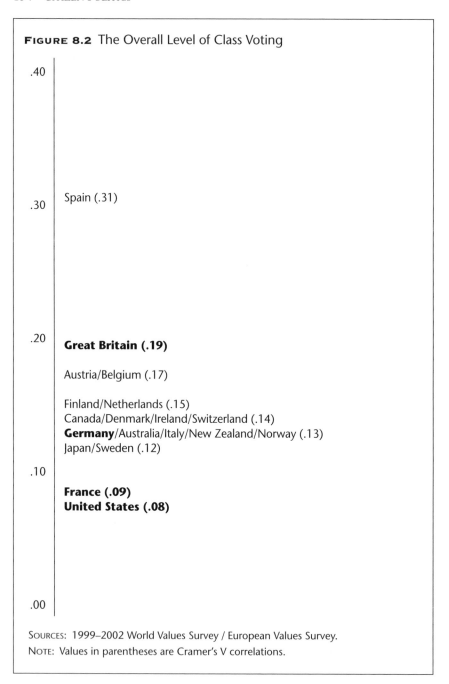

FIGURE 8.2 The Overall Level of Class Voting

.40

.30   Spain (.31)

.20   **Great Britain (.19)**

Austria/Belgium (.17)

Finland/Netherlands (.15)
Canada/Denmark/Ireland/Switzerland (.14)
Germany/Australia/Italy/New Zealand/Norway (.13)
Japan/Sweden (.12)

.10

France (.09)
United States (.08)

.00

SOURCES: 1999–2002 World Values Survey / European Values Survey.
NOTE: Values in parentheses are Cramer's V correlations.

partisan preferences for nineteen advanced industrial democracies. We compare the party support of six class groups to allow for greater variation in the composition of the class structure.[5] The Cramer's V correlation measures the size of class voting differences among these class groups. Across four editions of *Citizen Politics,* we have tracked the downward trend in class voting; today, class is only modestly related to vote choice. The greatest degree of class polarization exists in Spain, which is still a consolidating democracy. The formerly high levels of class voting in Scandinavia and Britain have gradually eroded over time, until the class cleavage is now weak even in these nations.

In terms of our four core nations, British class differences rank in the upper tier, reflecting the relative importance of class interests in British politics—and the influence of class cues on voting. Germany displays moderate levels of class voting, slightly less than the cross-national average, and French class differences are distinctly smaller than in the past. The United States also has weak class differences in party preferences. As other scholars have previously observed, the American party system blurs the influence of social class on voting choice, as both parties draw substantial parts of their support from across class lines (Clark, Lipset, and Rempel 1993).

Despite this evidence that class voting differences are narrowing, some researchers argue that the new class alignments of advanced industrial societies are perpetuating class voting, albeit in new forms (Evans 1999, 2000; Hout, Brooks, and Manza 1993). John Goldthorpe (1987), for example, proposed a new categorization of social class incorporating notions of job autonomy and authority relationships into traditional class criteria such as income level and manual labor. Others create an expanded list of class categories that reflect new social contexts, such as the middle-class salatariat or affluent blue-collar workers (Hout et al. 1995; Heath, Jowell, and Curtice 1991; Wright 1997). Researchers also explore criteria other than employment as potential new bases of socioeconomic cleavage: some suggest that education may form the basis of a political cleavage separating the information-rich, technologically sophisticated voter from the information-poor, unskilled voter. Others maintain that conflicts between the public and private sectors are supplanting traditional class conflicts. Other innovative research defines social position by lifestyle characteristic, distinguishing between industrial employees and Yuppies, for example (Pew Center 1999; Delli Carpini and Sigelman 1986).

This reconceptualization of social class implies that social cues now function in more complex and differentiated ways than in the past. Still, the empirical reality remains: even these complex new class frameworks have only a modest value in explaining how citizens vote. Richard Rose and Ian McAllister (1986, 50–51), for instance, compared several of these alternative models for British voting behavior in the 1983 election and found that each explains only a very modest share of the vote. Harold Clarke and his colleagues (2004, ch. 3) used three different statistics to estimate class voting in Britain from the 1960s to the present, finding that all three trace a very similar downward trend. Paul Nieuwbeerta (1995; Nieuwbeerta and de Graaf 1999) showed that alternative statistical measures of class voting do not change these long-term trends across a large set of Western democracies. Similarly, the analyses of figure 8.2 are based on a more extensive measure of social class that includes a separate new middle-class category, yet the average level of class differences in these nations is quite modest (Cramer's V = .14). The most persuasive evidence comes from the longitudinal comparative analyses of Mark Franklin, Tom Mackie, and Henry Valen (1992, ch. 19), who combined occupation, union membership, income, education, and other class traits and found a general decline in the ability of these social characteristics to explain electoral choice in most Western democracies.

David Butler and Donald Stokes (1969, 85–87) developed a conceptual framework of group-based voting that may help to identify the source of the decline in class voting. They describe group-based voting as a two-step process: voters are first linked to a social group, and then the group is linked to a political party. The combined strength of these two links determines the overall level of group-based voting. Using this framework, we can look to see if there have been changes either in the relationship between voters and class groupings or in the relationship between class groupings and the political parties. The first explanation, for example, highlights how the changing class structure of contemporary societies may be weakening the link between individuals and class groupings. Members of the traditional social strata—industrial workers, farmers, and the self-employed—often remain integrated into class networks and remain distinct in their voting preferences. But there are simply fewer of these voters today. The growth of the new middle class reduces the percentage of the electorate for whom traditional class ties are directly relevant.[6]

The blurring of the relationship between voters and class groupings also can arise from a general narrowing in the life conditions of social classes. On the one hand, the spread of affluence leads to the *embourgeoisement* of some sectors of the working class—some workers have incomes and living standards that overlap with those of the middle class. On the other hand, the expanding ranks of low-paid and low-status white-collar employees and the growth of white-collar unions are producing a *proletarianization* of part of the middle class. Few individuals now possess exclusively middle-class or working-class social characteristics, and the degree of class overlap is increasing over time. In sum, a convergence of life conditions contributes to the convergence of class voting patterns.

Increasing social and occupational mobility also may weaken the link between individuals and traditional social classes. Each of the nations in this study saw a decline in the number of farmers and an increase in middle-class employment during the second half of the past century; dramatic changes in the size of economic sectors often occurred within a few decades. High levels of social mobility mean that an individual's ultimate social position is often different from that of his or her parents. Many farmers' children moved a conservative political upbringing into unionized, working-class environments in the cities, just as many working-class children went from urban, socialist backgrounds into traditionally conservative, white-collar occupations. Some socially mobile adults will change their class identity and voting behavior to conform to their new social contexts; others will not. This mix of social forces blurs traditional class and partisan alignments.

A second broad explanation for declining class voting involves changes in the relationship between class groups and the political parties. Over the past generation, many political parties have tried to broaden their electoral appeal, partially to attract new middle-class voters, and this outreach process has led to more moderate party positions on traditional class-based issues. Socialist parties in Europe shed their Marxist programs and adopted more moderate domestic and foreign policy goals. Conservative parties also tempered their views and accepted the basic social programs proposed by the Left. Socialist parties vied for the votes of the new middle class, and conservative parties sought votes from the working class. Historical analyses of party programs document a general convergence of party positions on socioeconomic issues during the past half century (Budge, Robertson, and Hearl 1987; Caul and Gray 2000). With smaller class-related differences in the parties' platforms, it seemed only natural that class cues would become less important in guiding voting behavior.

Initially at least, this second theory appeared to be another plausible explanation for the decline in class voting differences. However, various studies show that party positions on the class cleavage remain clearly differentiated. For example, a survey of political experts documented a clear awareness of the continuing party differences on the socioeconomic issues that underlie the class cleavage (Laver and Hunt 1992; also see chapter 7). Furthermore, the American public still clearly perceives the partisan leanings of unions and business associations (chapter 7), and comparable data are available for Germany (Wessels 1994). In short, it does not appear that ambiguity about the class positions of the parties is the prime reason for decreased class voting; instead, these cues are simply less relevant to today's voters.

The decline in class voting patterns is therefore important for several reasons. First, it signals a change in the nature of political conflict, away from the class-based issues that once dominated elections. Second, these trends signal a change in how voters reach their decisions. It seems that the bonds linking voters to politically relevant class groups are weakening, even while the political cues provided by traditional class groups (and parties) persist. Union members, for example, realize that labor leaders want them to vote for parties of the Left, but they are now more likely to make their own decisions. Third, this social trend implies that the long-term decline in class voting should continue, while other factors are having a growing influence on voting decisions.

RELIGION AND THE VOTE

Religion is potentially another major basis of social division in contemporary party systems. The relationship between religion and parties arises from a centuries-old interplay of these two forces. As the Reformation created divisions between Catholics and Protestants that carried over into politics, control of the nation-building process often became intermixed with religious differences (see chapter 7). In England, for example, the Anglican Church supported national independence and became identified with the dominant national culture. In Germany, the tensions between Lutherans and Catholics were a continuing source of conflict and even open warfare. Gradually the political systems of Europe accommodated themselves to the changes wrought by the Reformation, and a new status quo developed. Then the French Revolution renewed religious conflicts in the nineteenth century. Religious forces—both Catholic and Protestant—defended church interests against the liberal, secular movement spawned by the events in France. Conflicts over church/state control, the legislation of mandatory state education, and disestablishment of state religions occurred across Europe.

As was true with the class cleavage, disagreements over religion structured elite conflict and acted to define the political alliances existing in the late nineteenth century. The political parties that formed during this period often allied themselves with specific religious interests: Catholic or Protestant, religious or secular. Thus the party alignments that developed at the start of the twentieth century institutionalized the religious cleavage, and many features of these party systems have endured to the present (Lipset and Rokkan 1967).

Early empirical research on voting behavior underscored the continuing importance of the religious cleavage. Richard Rose and Derek Urwin's examination of the social bases of party support in sixteen Western democracies concluded that "religious divisions, not class, are the main social bases of parties in the Western world today" (1969, 12). Numerous other cross-national and longitudinal studies have documented the persisting importance of the religious cleavage, and in recent years there have been signs that cultural conflicts and religious fundamentalism are renewing the importance of religion in the political world (Norris and Inglehart 2004; Leege et al. 2002).

Measuring the impact of religious cues on voting behavior is more complex than the study of class voting. The class composition of most industrial democracies is similar, but their religious composition is varied. Britain is largely Protestant, and nearly two-thirds of the population are nominally Anglicans. In contrast, nearly all French citizens are baptized Catholics, and the Protestant minority is very small. Germany has a mixed denominational system, with Lutheran Protestants slightly outnumbering Catholics. The United States lacks a dominant national religion; instead, there are significant numbers of Catholics, Reformation-era Protestants, Pietist Protestants, other Protestant and Christian groups, Jews, and the nonreligious.

In addition to the diverse religious composition of nations, the partisan tendencies of religious denominations can vary cross-nationally. Catholics normally support parties on the right, and Protestants normally support parties on the left. But historical events have sometimes led to different religious alignments. Thus, the voting cues provided by religious affiliation may differ across nation in contrast to the consistent working-class/middle-class pattern for social class.

We begin by examining the relationship between religious denomination and party support in the four core nations. As table 8.2 shows, religious differences in voting are often substantial, but each nation displays a unique pattern. The historical conflict between the Catholic Church and the Liberal/Socialist parties still appears in Germany. Most Catholics support the CDU/CSU, which defends traditional values and the church's prerogatives. A majority (51 percent) of Catholics voted CDU/CSU in 2002, and this increases to 79 percent among Catholics who attend church weekly. In contrast, Protestants and the nonreligious give greater support to the leftist parties: SPD, Greens, and PDS.

Although more than 80 percent of the French population are baptized Catholics, sizable differences in voting behavior still separate French Catholics and non-Catholics. In 2002 only 17 percent of those without a religion favored conservative parties, compared to 56 percent among Catholics. However, because the French public is overwhelmingly Catholic, the political impact of this imbalance on election outcomes is limited.

In Britain the religious cleavage follows another pattern. The Church of England historically allied itself with the political establishment; thus Anglicans are relatively more likely to vote for the Conservative Party. Catholics lean toward the Labour Party because of their minority status and their interest in the issue of Irish independence. Presbyterians give disproportionate support to Labour and the Liberal Democrats.

Religious and moral conflicts are a recurring theme in American history (Wald 2003; Layman 2001; Kohut et al. 2000); yet the formal separation of church and state limits the impact of religion on partisan politics. Table 8.2 shows that the Reformation-era Protestant denominations (Anglicans, Calvinists, Lutherans, etc.) predominately supported the Republicans in 2004, while Baptists and other Protestant groups leaned toward the Democrats. These differences are modest, however, and may reflect factors other than religion per se. Similarly, the slight Democratic leanings of American Catholics reflect the historical legacy of ethnic and class influences rather than explicitly religious values. Jewish Americans also historically give disproportionate support to the Democrats, and they continued to do so in 2004.

Placing these religious voting patterns into a cross-national context, the left side of figure 8.3 displays the levels of denominational-based voting in

TABLE 8.2 Religious Denomination and Party Support (in percentages)

United States (2004)	No religion	Jewish	Catholic	Reformation Protestant	Baptist	Other Protestant
Democrats	65	73	52	41	56	51
Republicans	35	27	48	59	44	49
Total	100	100	100	100	100	100

Great Britain (2001)	No religion	Catholic	Presbyterian	Anglican
Labour	51	62	48	43
Liberal Democrats	25	14	19	19
Conservatives	24	24	33	38
Total	100	100	100	100

France (2002)	Catholic	No religion
PC/Far left	3	16
Socialists	32	49
Greens	9	19
UDF	13	3
RPR	38	11
National Front	5	3
Total	100	101

Germany (2002)	No religion	Protestant	Catholic
PDS	9	2	0
Greens	10	5	5
SPD	49	57	37
FDP	7	6	7
CDU/CSU	25	30	51
Total	100	100	100

SOURCES: United States, 2004 American National Election Study (CSES); Great Britain, 2001 British Election Study; Germany, German Election Study 2002 (CSES); France, 2002 International Social Survey (ISSP).

NOTE: U.S. data are based on congressional vote; German data are for East and West electorates combined.

several nations. The starkest religious differences are often found in religiously divided societies, such as Germany and Canada and the Netherlands. In a set of Scandinavian nations—Denmark, Finland, and Sweden—the correlation largely results from differences between religious voters (of all denominations) and those without any religious affiliation. The impact of reli-

FIGURE 8.3 The Overall Level of Religious Voting

Religious Denomination	*Church Attendance*
	Austria (.46)
	Netherlands (.44)
.40	
	Belgium (.33)
	Finland/Norway/Swiss (.31)
.30	Denmark (.29)
	Spain (.28)
Denmark (.27)	Ireland (.27)
	Italy (.26)
Canada/Finland (.24)	
Great Britain (.23)	
	France (.22)
Netherlands (.21)	New Zealand (.21)
.20	**Germany/Great Britain**/Canada (.19)
Germany/USA/Spain/Sweden (.17)	
France/Belgium/Ireland/Norway/Swiss (.16)	
Austria (.15)	
Japan (.14)	
	USA/Japan (.14)
New Zealand (.12)	
Australia (.11)	
	Australia (.11)
.10	
Italy (.08)	

SOURCES: 1999–2002 World Values Survey / European Values Survey.
NOTE: Values in parentheses are Cramer's V correlations.

gious denomination on party preferences is slightly greater (average Cramer's V = .17) than the impact of social class. The persisting strength of religious differences is surprising, because in many nations religious matters are not explicitly discussed in elections. However, religion taps value orientations that provide a basis of cultural issues such as the role of women, abortion, or other moral concerns.

Another aspect of the religious cleavage is the influence of religiosity, such as church attendance or religious feelings separate from denominational affiliation. In predominately Catholic nations, such as France, this dimension represents a voter's integration into the Catholic culture. In mixed denominational systems, the secularization process has often stimulated an alliance between Protestants and Catholics in a joint defense of religious interests, so denominational differences are replaced by a secular/religious cleavage. In Germany, for example, the Christian Democratic Union unites active Catholics and Protestants against secular interests in society. Even in the United States, similar patterns have developed. George W. Bush has actively campaigned for the votes of religious conservatives of all denominations. The Bush campaign hoped to tap a common concern for the preservation of traditional values and opposition to abortion, even among social and ethnic groups that were traditionally affiliated with the Democratic Party.

Table 8.3 presents the relationship between religious involvement, measured by the frequency of church attendance, and party preference. The voting gap between religious and nonreligious citizens is considerable in both France and Germany. For instance, only 15 percent of French citizens who attended church weekly preferred the Socialists or the Communists in 2002, compared to 58 percent among those who never went to church. Because of the Church of England's relationship to the government, religious conflicts have not been a major factor in British electoral politics since early in the twentieth century.

There has been considerable debate about the role of religion in American elections, especially in recent elections. Many analysts argue that George W. Bush's emphasis on his evangelical beliefs and deliberate appeal for religious voters produced his margin of victory in the 2004 popular vote. Table 8.3 indicates, however, that those who actively attend religious services were only slightly more likely to vote for a Republican congressional candidate in 2004 (Cramer's V = .08). Even in the presidential election, the impact of church attendance was limited (Cramer's V =.09). Because of the multiplicity of denominations and the complexity of religious attachments in America, it is an oversimplification to claim that religious feelings exert a strong partisan influence in the United States (Kohut et al. 2000; Layman 2001).

The cross-national pattern of secular/religious voting displayed on the right-hand side of figure 8.3 shows that the secular/religious divide (average correlation = .26) is a stronger explanation of the vote than either class or religious denomination. Despite the paucity of explicitly religious issues in most campaigns, religious attachments are often a strong predictor of party

TABLE 8.3 Church Attendance and Party Support (in percentages)

	Never	Occasionally	Weekly
United States (2004)			
Democrats	57	58	46
Republicans	43	42	54
Total	100	100	100
Great Britain (1997)			
Labour	56	49	46
Liberal Democrats	18	18	21
Conservatives	26	33	34
Total	100	100	101
France (2002)			
PC/Far left	11	5	1
Socialists	47	32	14
Greens	16	12	8
UDF	5	11	21
RPR	17	36	53
National Front	5	4	4
Total	101	100	101
Germany (2002)			
PDS	6	2	0
Greens	7	7	2
SPD	53	50	29
FDP	7	8	3
CDU/CSU	27	33	65
Total	100	100	99

SOURCES: United States, 2004 American National Election Study (CSES); Great Britain, 1997 British Election Study; Germany, German Election Study 2002 (CSES); France, 2002 International Social Survey (ISSP).

NOTE: U.S. data are based on congressional vote; German data are for East and West electorates combined.

choice. In Scandinavia, for instance, religion reflects continuing controversies over lifestyle issues, such as temperance and moral values. In other nations, the religious/secular cleavage is related to issues such as abortion or other moral questions (see chapter 6). Religion constitutes a hidden agenda of politics, tapping differences in values and moral beliefs that might not be expressed in a campaign but nevertheless influence voter choices. Indeed, a variety of evidence indicates that moral or religious images continue to divide the parties in many Western democracies.[7]

Our analyses also underscore the diversity of religious voting patterns across the four core nations at the end of the twentieth century. Both religious denomination and church attendance are significantly related to partisan preferences in Germany. The religious cleavage in France is based on the voting differences between practicing Catholics and the nonreligious. In both the United States and Britain there are only modest partisan differences by church attendance. The limited degree of religious voting in the United States illustrates the continued separation of church and state, despite the attempts by some to politicize religion.

Despite this evidence of strong relationship between religious values and partisan preferences in contemporary democracies, we might expect the religious cleavage to follow the same pattern of decline as the class cleavage. Social modernization may disrupt religious alignments in the same manner that social-class lines have blurred. Changing lifestyles, and religious beliefs, have decreased involvement in church activities and diminished the church as a focus of social (and political) activities. Most Western nations display a steady decline in religious involvement over the past fifty years (Franklin, Mackie, and Valen 1992, ch. 1). In the Catholic nations of Europe, for instance, frequent church attendance has decreased by nearly half since the 1950s. Predominately Protestant countries, such as the United States and the nations of northern Europe, began with lower levels of church involvement but follow the same downward trend. By definition, this secularization trend means that fewer voters are integrated into religious networks and exposed to the religious cues that can guide the vote.

The expectation of a decline in religious voting can be tested by observing the pattern of religious voting over time. Similar to the class voting index, figure 8.4 plots a religious voting index based on the difference in party preferences between religious denominations. For instance, the differences in Conservative Party support between Anglicans, nonconformist Protestants, and Catholics in Britain have slowly narrowed since 1959. Similarly, the gap in leftist voting between German Catholics and Protestants averages in the 25-point range for the first half of this series. However, this gap narrowed during the 1980s, and the merger with a secular eastern electorate (two-thirds of whom express no denominational affiliation) has further dampened religious voting differences since unification.

Partisan differences between American Catholics and Protestants vary across elections; the religious cleavage intensified with John Kennedy's candidacy in 1960, while other elections display weak religious voting. In addition, despite the stress on religious voting blocks in recent American elections, there is actually a slight convergence in Protestant/Catholic voting in congressional elections (see Abramson, Aldrich, and Rohde 2003, ch. 5, for evidence on presidential elections).

The long-term trends in voting differences between religious and nonreligious citizens are relatively stable over time (data not shown). Religious involvement in France has a strong and persisting impact on voting preferences, averaging a more than 40 percent difference in leftist party support. The religious cleavage in Germany was relatively strong and sta-

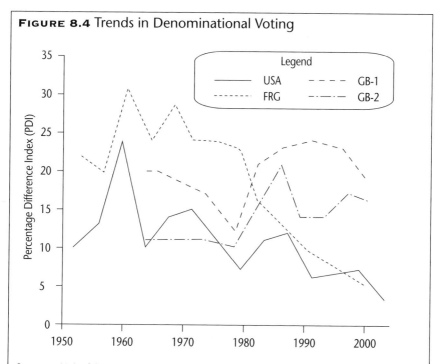

FIGURE 8.4 Trends in Denominational Voting

SOURCES: United States, 1948–2004, American National Election Studies; Great Britain, 1964–2001, British Election Studies; Germany, 1953–2002, German Election Studies (western Germany only, 1990–2002).

NOTE: Comparisons for the United States and Germany are between Protestants and Catholics. GB-1 is a comparison of the Labour Party vote of Angelicans and Catholics; GB-2 is a comparison of the Conservative Party vote of Angelicans and nonconformists.

ble until the 1980s; it has weakened in the past two decades, especially since unification. British party differences on the religious voting index are initially quite small and display little change over time. The recent attempts of the Republican Party to court religious voters has heightened attention to religion in recent U.S. elections—but the magnitude of this gap remains limited.[8]

In summary, the trends for religious voting do not show the sharp drop-off found for class voting. Denominational differences have narrowed slightly in several nations, though denomination remains a stronger predictor of vote choice than social class. The secular/religious divide is an even stronger correlate of voting preferences. This continued pattern of religious voting is all the more surprising because advanced industrial societies have become more secular during the past few decades. In addition, many of the societal changes that weakened the class cleavage presumably should have the same effect on religious voting.

Despite these appearances, the importance of religion as a basis of voting behavior is declining, but the pattern of decline is less obvious than for class voting. Comparisons of the voting patterns of religious denominations appear to be moderating slightly, but these relationships include only those voters with religious attachments. Individuals who attend church regularly remain well-integrated into a religious network and maintain distinct voting patterns; however, there are fewer of these individuals today. By definition, the growing number of secular voters do not turn to religious cues to make their electoral choices. Thus, as the number of individuals relying on religious cues decreases, the partisan significance of religious characteristics and their overall ability to explain voting are slowly weakening.

OTHER SOCIAL GROUP DIFFERENCES

The decline of social group–based voting is most apparent for class and religion, but a similar erosion of influence has occurred for other social characteristics.

Regional differences occasionally flare up as a basis of political division. Great Britain, the United States, and now the unified Germany have seen regional interests polarize over the past generation. In other societies, such as Spain, Canada, and Italy, sharp regional differences from the past have persisted to the present (e.g., Rose 1982; Clarke, Kornberg, and Wearing 2000). In most nations, however, region exerts only a minor influence on voting. Similarly, urban/rural residence displays only modest differences in voting patterns. Furthermore, the impact of such social traits on voting preferences has generally weakened as social modernization decreases the gap between urban and rural lifestyles or regional differences.

The media and some political analysts have devoted considerable attention to the gender gap in voting. The available empirical evidence, however, suggests that gender is seldom a major explanation of voting patterns, normally averaging less than a 10 percent gap in party preferences between men and women. Moreover, the gender gap traditionally has run in the opposite direction from that of the current gender gap in the United States—that is, women historically have favored parties of the right. As feminists have changed the political orientations of some younger women, male/female voting differences have narrowed as more women support parties of the left (Studlar, McAllister, and Hayes 1998; Jelen, Thomas, and Wilcox 1994). But even in recent U.S. elections, the gender gap has been quite modest compared to other influences on vote choice. Significant voting differences begin to emerge, however, if one combines gender and life-status measures, such as employment status (Norris 1999a).

One possible exception to the pattern of declining social cleavages is race and ethnicity. There are sharp racial differences in partisan support within the American electorate, and these differences have widened over time (Tate 1993; Abramson, Aldrich, and Rohde 2003). For instance, 92 percent of

African Americans cast their congressional votes for Democrats in 2004, compared to 71 percent of Hispanics and 44 percent of white Americans. The minority immigrant populations in Europe may produce similar differences in these party systems. Ethnicity has the potential to be a highly polarized cleavage because it often involves sharp social differences and strong feelings of group identity. Yet most societies remain relatively homogeneous in terms of ethnicity, and this limits the impact of race or ethnicity as an overall predictor of vote choice. For example, the Cramer's V correlations for race and vote is significant in the United States (.25) but quite modest in a nation such as Britain (.10 in 2001), which has only a small minority population (Saggar and Heath 1999).

This evidence leads to one of the most widely repeated findings of modern electoral research: sociological factors have declining influence on voting behavior. Mark Franklin, Tom Mackie, and Henry Valen (1992) compiled the most comprehensive evidence supporting this conclusion by tracking the ability of a set of social characteristics (including social class, education, income, religiosity, region, and gender) to explain partisan preferences. Across fourteen democracies, they found a marked and consistent erosion in the voting impact of social structure. The rate and timing of this decline varies across nations, but the end product is the same. In party systems such as the United States and Canada, where social-group–based voting was initially weak, the decline has occurred slowly. In other electoral systems—such as Germany, the Netherlands, and several Scandinavian nations—where sharp social divisions once structured the vote, the decline has been steady and dramatic. Franklin, Mackie, and Valen (1992, 385) conclude with the new "conventional wisdom" of comparative electoral research:

> One thing that has by now become quite apparent is that almost all of the countries we have studied show a decline during our period in the ability of social cleavages to structure individual voting choice.

NEW POLITICS AND THE VOTE

As traditional social group influences decrease in importance, the New Politics (or postmaterial) cleavage may provide the basis for a new partisan alignment. The erosion of Old Politics cleavages is at least partially the result of the increasing salience of New Politics issues (Knutsen 1995b). Environmental protection, women's rights, and other social issues are not easily related to traditional class or religious alignments. Furthermore, New Politics issues attract the attention of the same social groups that are weakly integrated into the Old Politics cleavages: the young, the new middle class, the better educated, and the nonreligious.

The development of a new basis of partisan cleavage can be a long and difficult process. Groups must organize to represent New Politics interests and mobilize voter support, but the group bases of these issues are still ill-defined.

The environmental and women's movements, for example, have multiple groups representing them, they seldom speak with a single voice, and the voters' bonds to specific groups are weaker than to class and religious groups. The political parties also must develop clear policy images on these issues. Many established parties are hesitant to identify themselves with these issues because the stakes are still unclear and the parties are often internally divided on the issues (Rohrschneider 1993b; Dalton 1994a, ch. 9).

Despite these limiting factors, the potential impact of New Politics values on voting has increased in recent years. Small green or New Left parties now compete in many European democracies (Richardson and Rootes 1995). In response, the established parties are gradually becoming more receptive to the political demands of New Politics groups. The inclusion of green parties in the government coalitions in France (1997) and Germany (1998), and Al Gore's candidacy in the 2000 U.S. elections signal how the established parties are accepting green issues.

People also seem willing to base their voting choices on New Politics concerns. Harvey Palmer (1995), for example, found that postmaterial values were gradually becoming a better predictor of British party preferences than either income or occupation. Postmaterialism has also exercised a significant impact on German voting preferences, at least until unification created a new set of policy concerns (Fuchs and Rohrschneider 1998). Oddbjorn Knutsen's research (1995a; Knutsen and Scarbrough 1995) similarly points to a growing relationship between postmaterial values and party choice in most European nations. In addition, many Europeans express a willingness to vote for an environmental party—the potential electorate for a green party rivals that of socialist and Christian Democratic parties (Inglehart 1990, 266)!

Chapter 7 suggested that the initial structure of this new cleavage may focus on the conflict between New Politics and Old Politics adherents. Therefore, we used the material/postmaterial values index (chapter 5) to see if these orientations influence voting. Materialists emphasize security, stability, economic well-being, and other Old Politics objectives, while postmaterialists place greater stress on such New Politics goals, such as participation, social equality, and environmental protection.

Table 8.4 displays the relationship between these value priorities and party preferences. In every nation, postmaterialists favor the Left, while materialists lean toward the Right. The influence of changing values is especially clear for the New Left environmental parties in France and Germany. For example, 30 percent of French postmaterialists supported the Greens, compared to only 10 percent of materialists.

The overall size of these voting differences is considerable, often exceeding the Alford index scores for class or religious voting. The four-item postmaterialism index tends to understate the impact of these values (compared to the 12-item index). Still, there is a 22 percent gap in Left/Right support in Germany and France. Significant percentage difference scores also appear in

TABLE 8.4 Value Priorities and Party Support (in percentages)

	Materialists	Mixed	Postmaterialists
United States			
Democrats	57	62	62
Republicans	43	38	38
Total	100	100	100
Great Britain			
Labour	43	48	58
Liberal Democrats	19	20	29
Conservatives	38	32	12
Total	101	101	99
France			
PC	4	4	6
Socialists	43	34	37
Other Left	2	2	8
Greens	10	23	30
UDF	11	8	5
RPR/UPM	23	24	11
National Front	7	5	2
Total	100	100	99
Germany			
PDS	3	5	7
Greens	2	6	12
SPD	36	33	44
FDP	1	4	3
CDU/CSU	59	51	35
Total	101	99	101

SOURCES: 1999–2002 World Values Survey/European Values Survey; 1997 British Election Study.

NOTE: Value priorities are measured with the four-item index (see chapter 5).

Britain (15 percent), while value differences are less pronounced in the United States (5 percent).

The extent of postmaterial values–based voting in advanced industrial democracies is described in figure 8.5. As other studies have noted, postmaterialism has an exceptionally strong influence in Denmark and the Netherlands, where established political parties have responded to these new issue concerns. Postmaterial values–based voting is also significant in Germany and France, exceeding the influence of class-voting differences (compare to figure 8.1). Repeating a pattern we have seen for other cleavages, New Politics values only weakly affect American electoral behavior.

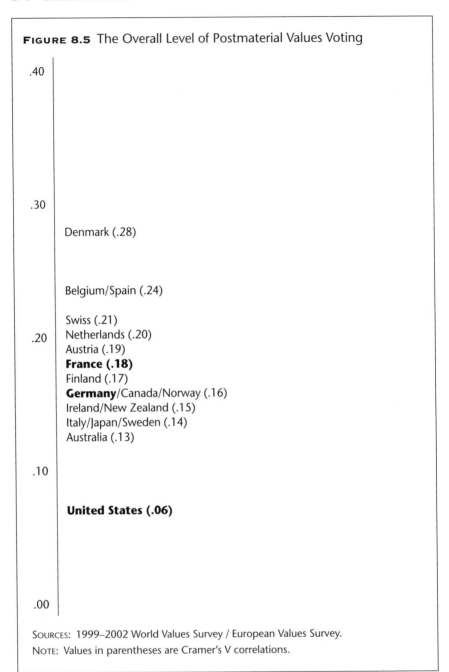

FIGURE 8.5 The Overall Level of Postmaterial Values Voting

.40

.30

Denmark (.28)

Belgium/Spain (.24)

Swiss (.21)
.20   Netherlands (.20)
Austria (.19)
France (.18)
Finland (.17)
Germany/Canada/Norway (.16)
Ireland/New Zealand (.15)
Italy/Japan/Sweden (.14)
Australia (.13)

.10

United States (.06)

.00

SOURCES: 1999–2002 World Values Survey / European Values Survey.
NOTE: Values in parentheses are Cramer's V correlations.

Previous electoral research found that the extent of values polarization is partially a function of the diversity of choice in a party system; with more parties, it is more likely that one will choose to represent these New Politics concerns. In addition, affluence stimulates postmaterial concerns. This is most clearly evident in the East/West German comparisons: postmaterial values have a significant influence on the voting choices of many westerners (Cramer's V = .21), but eastern Germans are less likely to possess postmaterial values and are preoccupied with the economic problems that accompanied German union. Thus postmaterial values play a smaller role in the voting behavior of easterners (Cramer's V = .14) even though they are voting on the same party choices. Figure 8.5 also shows that across the advanced industrial democracies, the average weight of postmaterial value priorities (Cramer's V = .17) now exceeds the weight of social class in determining party choice (figure 8.1).

In contrast to the impact of social characteristics that are weakening over time, we expect the impact of postmaterial values to increase as these new issues enter the political agenda and parties respond by offering policy choices on environmentalism, quality-of-life issues, and other postmaterial concerns. The postmaterial values index is not routinely included in national election study surveys, but we can track the impact across European nations using the Eurobarometer timeseries. Figure 8.6 presents the Cramer's V correlations between postmaterial values and party preference for Great Britain, France, and West Germany, with the data cumulated for five year periods to emphasize the broad trends. In contrast to class voting, which is decreasing over time, the impact of postmaterial values is increasing, albeit with some variability in the trends. For example, the voting difference between materialists and postmaterialists in West Germany produced a .13 correlation in the early 1970s; this increased to a .19 correlation by the end of the 1990s (with a spike in the early 1980s when the Greens first ran for parliament). Thus the sources of partisan cleavage are changing in advanced industrial democracies—the long-standing Old Politics cleavages are being joined by a new values cleavage.

It would be a mistake to assume that the growing salience of New Politics issues in voting means an inexorable increase in support for leftist parties. The Old Politics cleavages will remain as major forces structuring party competition for some time. Furthermore, the partisan consequences of the New Politics depend on how parties respond to these issues. For instance, while American environmentalists normally feel closer to the Democratic Party, an early Republican president (Teddy Roosevelt) nurtured the modern environmental movement and another Republican president (Richard Nixon) created the Environmental Protection Agency. Similarly, Margaret Thatcher linked her Conservative government to the issue of global warming, while the Labour Party has been less visible on many environmental issues. Environmentalism is not a Left or Right issue in the traditional Old Politics meaning of these terms; the partisan effects of these issues depends on how the parties

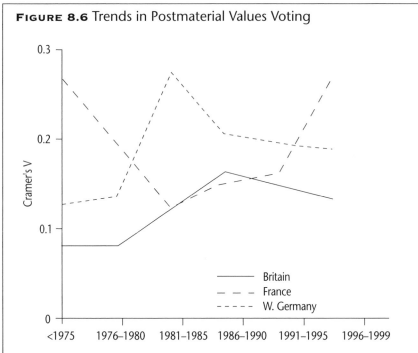

FIGURE 8.6 Trends in Postmaterial Values Voting

SOURCES: Eurobarometer cumulative file, 1970–1999.

NOTE: Figure entries are the Cramer's V correlations between the four-item postmaterial values index and party preference, cumulated for five-year intervals. Nonpartisans were not included in the calculation of correlations.

respond (see Dalton 1994a, ch. 9). The real lesson is that public interests and party alignments are changing, and the party systems in advanced industrial democracies are affected by these trends.

THE TRANSFORMATION OF SOCIAL CLEAVAGES

Harold Clarke and his colleagues (2004) began their study of voting choice in the 2001 British election with a vignette that captures the spirit of our findings in this chapter:

> Jim Hill voted Labour in the 1955 general election. Jim worked as a welder
> . . . and made castings for the motor industry. He belonged to the Transport and
> General Workers' Union. He rented a house . . . from the local council. . . . Jim
> did not think much about politics—although he paid his union dues and occa-
> sionally talked politics with his mates in the local pub. Like most people he
> knew, Jim had always thought of himself as "Labour."

Jim's granddaughter, Melanie, still lives today in the Midlands town where her grandfather spent his life, although the foundry where he worked closed in the early 1980s. She lives in her own terraced house, which she is buying with her partner, in an area where 40 percent of the population is Asian. After graduating from university in the early 1990s, she became a teacher. She left in 1996, disillusioned with work in the public sector, to become a customer services manager at a nearby airport. . . . In the 1997 general election, Melanie voted Labour. In 2001, she thought about not voting at all, but finally opted for the Liberal Democrats.

The transformation of social conditions between Jim and Melanie Hill—and consequently the political choices of the Hill family across three generations—encapsulates the social transformations that have affected all advanced industrial democracies to some degree.

This chapter has described a general decline in the relationship between social characteristics and voting choice. Throughout much of the twentieth century, the dominant social cleavage in most democracies separated working-class and middle-class parties. But the socioeconomic transformation of these societies has weakened class alignments. Similarly, the number of churchgoers available for mobilization by confessional parties is decreasing, leading to a declining influence of religion on voting behavior. These class and religious trends are often accompanied by declines in the influence of regional, residential, and other social cleavages.

Since there is a natural logic (and political rationale) to thinking about party systems as the representation of social-group differences, one response to the erosion of Old Politics group divisions has been to search for potential new social bases of alignment. Political scientists term this a *partisan realignment,* defined as a significant shift in the group bases of party coalitions, usually resulting in a shift in the relative size of the parties' vote shares.

There have been many prior examples of realignment in Western party systems, in which one system of group cleavages is supplanted by another (Dalton, Flanagan, and Beck 1984, ch. 1). For example, the 1930s New Deal realignment in the United States is traced to the entry of large numbers of blue-collar workers, Catholics, and blacks into the Democratic Party coalition. Realignments have been a regular feature of American electoral politics for well over a century, and probably since the emergence of the first mass-party coalitions around 1800. Similar historical realignments have occurred in European party systems, such as the Labour Party's rise in the early 1900s and the Gaullist realignment at the beginning of the French Fifth Republic.

Some analysts suggest that New Politics issues—environmental protection, nuclear energy, sexual equality, consumer advocacy, and human rights—may provide the basis of a new partisan alignment. These issues are attractive to voters who are weakly integrated into Old Politics alignments. Eventually, these interests may coalesce into political movements that will realign electorates and party systems. The growing partisan polarization along the New Politics value cleavage apparently supports this realignment thesis. Value priorities have become a more important influence on voting choice, and new parties now represent these perspectives.

I am not convinced, however, that it is accurate to think of contemporary partisan politics in the same terms as past partisan realignments. The process of partisan realignment is normally based on clearly defined and highly cohesive social groups that can develop institutional ties to the parties and provide clear voting cues to their members. A firm group base provides a framework for parties to develop institutional ties to social groups, and for groups to socialize and mobilize their members.

There are few social groupings comparable to labor unions or churches that might establish the basis of a New Politics realignment. For instance, generational differences in support for New Politics parties might indicate an emerging New Politics cleavage, but age groups provide a very transitory basis for mobilizing voters. Other potential group bases of voting cues, such as education or alternative class categorizations, so far remain speculative, without firm evidence of realigning effects.

Postmaterial values are related to partisan preferences, but these values are unlikely to provide a basis for a new group-party alignment. Values define clusters of like-minded people, but one cannot identify a postmaterialist in the same way that class, religion, or region provides a basis of personal identity and group mobilization. Indeed, postmaterial values are antithetical to such traditionally structured organizations as unions and churches. Instead, a vast array of single-issue groups and causes represent New Politics concerns—from the women's movement to peace organizations to environmental groups. These groups generally are loosely organized with ill-defined memberships that wax and wane.

The lack of a group basis for the New Politics cleavage highlights another aspect of the new style of citizen politics. The kinds of cleavages that divide modern electorates and the kinds of groups they define are changing. Electoral politics is moving from cleavages defined by fixed social groups to value and issue cleavages that identify communities of like-minded individuals. The growing heterogeneity, secularization, and *embourgeoisement* of society is weakening social-group ties generally. Increasing levels of urbanization, social mobility, and geographic mobility work against the continued existence of exclusive, cohesive social groups. The revolutions in education and cognitive mobilization work against the dominance of disciplined, hierarchic, clientelist associations.

In summary, two kinds of changes are affecting contemporary electoral politics. First, there is shift from the Old Politics cleavages toward the New Politics, which implies that the content of political debate will change, and many of the traditional class-based issues must share the political stage with debates over the quality of life and cultural issues. Such a change in the group bases of party support is consistent with the changing orientations of contemporary publics discussed in chapters 5 and 6.

A second change involves the weakening of most political bonds. Social groups may still represent some of the changing political interests of contemporary electorates, but we are witnessing a transformation from social-group cleavages to issue-group cleavages. Because issue-group cleavages are more difficult to institutionalize or "freeze" via social-group ties to mass organizations, they may not be as stable. In addition, because many of the new issue concerns involve only a narrow sector of the public, the linkage between these issues and party support may remain unclear. Some parties may adopt vague issue stands to avoid offending specific interests; other parties may cater to special interest groups and lose their broader programmatic image.

As a result of this second change, the bases of political mobilization are becoming more individualized in advanced industrial societies. Interest mobilization along any political dimension—Old Politics or New Politics—will be characterized by more complex, overlapping, and crosscutting associational networks; more fluid institutional loyalties; and looser, more egalitarian organizational structures. Thus the question is not whether labor union leaders support leftist parties (they do) or whether labor union members perceive these cues (they do)—but whether the union rank and file will follow their leaders anymore. The fact is that fewer individuals are following such external cues, and this change affects the breadth, effectiveness, and stability of any future partisan alignment.

The new style of citizen politics therefore should include a more fluid and volatile pattern of party alignments. Political coalitions and voting patterns will lack the permanence of past class and religious cleavages. Without clear social cues, voting decisions will become a more demanding task for voters—more dependent on the individual beliefs and values of each citizen.

SUGGESTED READINGS

Anderson, Christopher J., and Carsten Zelle, eds. *Stability and Change in German Elections: How Electorates Merge, Converge, or Collide.* Westport, Conn.: Praeger, 1998.

Clark, Terry Nichols, and Seymour Martin Lipset, eds. *The Breakdown of Class Politics: A Debate on Post-industrial Stratification.* Baltimore: Johns Hopkins University Press, 2001.

Clarke, Harold, et al. *Political Choice in Britain.* Oxford: Oxford University Press, 2004.

Dalton, Russell, Scott Flanagan, and Paul Beck, eds. *Electoral Change in Advanced Industrial Democracies.* Princeton, N.J.: Princeton University Press, 1984.

Evans, Geoffrey, ed. *The End of Class Politics? Class Voting in Comparative Context.* New York: Oxford University Press, 1999.

Franklin, Mark, Tom Mackie, and Henry Valen, eds. *Electoral Change.* New York: Cambridge University Press, 1992.

Judis, John, and Ruy Teixeira. *The Emerging Democratic Majority.* New York: Scribner, 2002.

Norris, Pippa. *Electoral Change in Britain since 1945.* Cambridge, Mass.: Blackwell, 1997.

NOTES

1. Most American voting studies analyze presidential elections. Because of the importance of candidate image, presidential elections reflect a different set of electoral forces than are normally found in European parliamentary elections. To assure comparability of American and European results, the U.S. data in this chapter are based on voting in congressional elections.

2. In earlier editions, we noted that class voting patterns were reversed in East Germany, as these voters responded differently to the party choices because of their history in dealing with the Communists. However, by 2002 the Left/Right alignment of working-class/middle-class voters had realigned to follow the general pattern shown in table 8.1 (Dalton and Bürklin 1996; Dalton 2003).

3. In the United States, this is the percentage voting Democratic in congressional elections; in Britain, the percentage voting Labour; in Germany, the percentage voting SPD of the two-party vote (SPD and CDU/CSU) before 1980, and leftist percentage (SPD, Greens, and PDS) in later elections; in France, the percentage voting for leftist parties (PC, Socialist, and other Left).

4. We measured social class by the occupation of the head of household coded into the following categories: (1) managers/owners, (2) professional, (3) nonmanual, (4) manual worker, (5) farming, and (6) other occupations/no occupation.

5. Generational patterns in class voting also reinforce the argument for the long-term erosion in this cleavage (Franklin, Mackie, and Valen 1992, ch. 19). Research generally finds strong relationships between class and vote among older generations, while among younger generations, these relationships are weak and decreasing.

6. In support of this interpretation, new middle-class voters have been a major source of electoral volatility in the United States (Hout et al. 1995; Abramson, Aldrich, and Rohde 2003) and Germany (Dalton 2003). The following table shows that the French new middle class has also shifted its vote preferences for the Left over time:

1962	1967	1968	1973	1978	1981	1988	1996	2002
42%	40%	42%	54%	51%	57%	56%	60%	46%

7. Laver and Hunt (1992) and Marks and Steenbergen (2004) show that political elites in most Western democracies still perceive significant party differences on dimensions such as pro- and anticlerical and the permissiveness of social policy. There is evidence that Germans can clearly differentiate the parties in their religious leanings, and these perceptions have grown more distinct over time (Dalton 1993b, 60; Wessels 1994). Finally, chapter 7 found that the American public perceives conservative religious groups as closer to the Republican Party.

8. The gap in party support between those who never attend church and those who attend on a weekly basis was 18 percent in 2000 and only 11 percent in 2004. This is within the range of the level of religious polarization in elections of the 1950s and 1960s, but is still half the level of religious differences in nations such as Germany and France.

CHAPTER 9

Partisanship and Electoral Behavior

Social cleavages may provide the foundation of modern party systems, as seen in the two previous chapters, but this represents only the beginnings of electoral decision making. Each election presents voters with choices over policy proposals and candidates for office. While social characteristics and group cues may be a basis for making decisions, citizens also hold a variety of political beliefs and values that affect their electoral calculus. Often, these considerations go beyond group ties or the perceptions derived from group cues.

Consequently, contemporary electoral research emphasizes the attitudes and values of voters as key factors in understanding electoral choice. Most voters do not regard elections as conflicts over historical cleavage alignments, but as opportunities to deal with more contemporary problems (which may reflect long-term conflicts). Citizens make judgments about which party best represents their interests, and these perceptions guide voting behavior. Attitudes toward the issues and candidates of an election are thus a necessary element in any realistic model of voting. Attitudes are also changeable, and their incorporation into a voting model helps explain variation in party results across elections.

A Sociopsychological Model of Voting

Faced with the limitations of a purely sociological approach to voting, early electoral researchers developed voting models to include psychological factors, such as attitudes and values, as influences on voting decisions and other political behavior. A team of researchers at the University of Michigan first formalized a model integrating both sociological and psychological influences on voting (Campbell et al. 1960, 1966). This sociopsychological model describes the voting process in terms of a *funnel of causality* (figure 9.1). At the wide mouth of the funnel (on the left side of the figure) are the socioeconomic conditions that generate the broad political divisions of society: the economic structure, social divisions such as race or religion, and historical alignments such as the North/South division in the United States. These factors influence the structure of the party system (see chapter 7), as represented by the arrows in the figure, but are distant from the actual voting decisions of individual citizens.

As we move through the causal funnel, the arrows signify that socioeconomic conditions influence group loyalties and basic value orientations. For instance, economic conditions may bond an individual to a social class, or

Internet Resource

The Institute for Democracy and Electoral Assistance (IDEA) has data on election turnout around the globe:

http://www.idea.int/vt/index.cfm

regional identities may form in reaction to social and political inequalities. Thus social conditions are translated into attitudes that can directly influence the individual's political behavior.

The causal funnel narrows further as group loyalties and value priorities are linked to more explicitly political attitudes. Angus Campbell and his colleagues explained individual voting decisions primarily in terms of three attitudes: party attachment, issue opinions, and candidate images. These attitudes are closest to the voting decision and therefore have a direct and very strong impact on the vote. In addition, the events of the campaign—media influence, campaign activity, economic and political conditions—influence the voter's issue opinions and candidate images.

Although the funnel of causality appears simple by contemporary standards of social science, it represented a major conceptual breakthrough for voting research. This model provides a useful device for organizing the factors that potentially influence voting behavior. To understand voting decisions, one has to recognize the causal relationship between the many factors

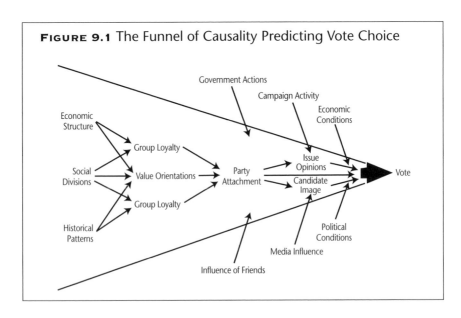

FIGURE 9.1 The Funnel of Causality Predicting Vote Choice

involved. The wide end of the funnel represents broad social conditions that structure political conflict but are temporally and psychologically far removed from the actual voting decision. As we move through the funnel, attention shifts to factors that are explicitly political, involve individual beliefs, and are more proximate to voting choice. Social characteristics are therefore seen as an important aspect of the voting process, but their primary influence is in forming broad political orientations and group loyalties; most of the direct impact of social characteristics on voting is mediated by attitudinal dispositions. Attitudes, in turn, depend on the group loyalties and value orientations of the individual, as well as external stimuli such as friends, media, government actions, and the activities of the campaign. There is a place in the funnel of causality for each element of the voting process, and we can understand each element in relation to the others.

In addition to the descriptive value of the model, the sociopsychological approach is very successful in predicting voting choices. Attitudes toward the parties, issues, and candidates of an election are psychologically very close to the actual voting decision and therefore are strongly related to voting choices. In fact, the model can predict voting decisions more accurately than individuals can predict their own behavior (Campbell et al. 1960, 74)!

The sociopsychological model has defined a paradigm of voting behavior that structures how we think about elections and how researchers analyze the voting process. Researchers have tested and applied the basic elements of the model in a variety of nations. This chapter examines partisan attachments as a central concept in the sociopsychological model of voting. Then, chapter 10 examines how specific issue opinions provide another element in this model.

PARTISAN ATTITUDES

The sociopsychological model was developed to focus on the specific issue opinions and candidate evaluations that determine voting behavior. Yet it soon became clear that partisan loyalties strongly influenced many of the specific political beliefs and behaviors of the citizenry. As one elderly Tallahassee voter once commented to me while waiting to vote, "I vote for the candidate and not the party. It just seems like the Democrats always choose the best candidate." Many voters begin each electoral season with already-formed partisan predispositions. These partisan loyalties are a central element in an individual's belief system, serving as a source of political cues for other attitudes and behaviors.

The Michigan researchers described these partisan attachments as a sense of *party identification,* similar to identifications with a social class, religious denomination, or other social group. Party identification is a long-term, affective, psychological identification with one's preferred political party (Campbell et al. 1960, chap. 6; Warren Miller 1991).[1] These party attachments are distinct from voting preferences, which explains why some Americans vote for the presidential candidate of one party while expressing loyalty to another party. Indeed, it is the conceptual independence of voting and party identification that initially gives the latter its theoretical significance.[2]

The discovery of party identification is one of the most significant findings of public opinion research. Partisanship often provides the starting point for individual belief systems, as discussed in chapter 2. Partisanship is also the ultimate heuristic, because it provides a reference structure for evaluating many new political stimuli—what position does "my" party take on this issue—and making political choices. As seen in chapter 3, partisanship is also a stimulus for engagement in campaigns and elections. The functional importance of partisanship was emphasized by the developers of the concept:

> The present analysis of party identification is based on the assumption that the . . . parties serve as standard-setting groups for a significant proportion of the people in this country. In other words, it is assumed that many people associate themselves psychologically with one or the other of the parties, and that this identification has predictable relationships with their perceptions, evaluations, and actions. (Campbell, Gurin, and Miller 1954, 90)

More recently, Herbert Weisberg and Steve Greene (2003, 115) have concluded that "party identification is the linchpin of our modern understanding of electoral democracy, and it is likely to retain that crucial theoretical position."

After the description of party identification in the United States, the concept was exported to other democratic nations. In several cases, researchers had problems finding an equivalent measure of partisanship in multiparty systems or in nations where the term *partisanship* holds different connotations for the voters (Budge, Crewe, and Farlie 1976). The concept of a partisan "independent" is not as common in other electoral systems as it is in the United States. Thus researchers could not simply translate the American party identification question into French or German; they had to find a functional equivalent for partisan attachments.[3] Still, most public opinion specialists agree that voters hold some party allegiances that endure over time and strongly influence other opinions and political behavior. Equivalent measures of party identification are now included in the election studies of virtually all contemporary democracies.

The Learning of Partisanship

The importance of party identification for understanding political behavior results in part from the early origins of these attachments. Socialization studies find that children develop basic partisan orientations at a very early age, often during the primary school years (Hess and Torney 1967, 90). Children learn party loyalties before they can understand what the party labels stand for—a process similar to the development of many other group ties. These early party attachments then provide a reference structure for future political learning (which often reinforces early partisan biases).

The early-life formation of party identities means that parents play a central role in the socialization of these values. The transmission of partisanship within the family can be seen by comparing the party identifications of parents and their children. A cross-national socialization study interviewed parents and their children to compare their opinions directly (table 9.1). This research found relatively high levels of partisan agreement within American, British, and German families.[4] In the United States, for example, 70 percent of the 16–20-year-old children of Democratic parents are themselves Democrats, and 54 percent of Republican parents have Republican children. Less than a sixth of the children actually favor the party in opposition to their parents. These levels of partisan agreement are similar to those found in a larger and more representative study of American adolescents (Jennings and Niemi 1973). The British and German surveys also show that the party attachments of parents are frequently re-created in the values of their offspring. Parents apparently have a strong formative influence on the partisan values of their children, even before most children become active in the political process.

There are many reasons why parents are so successful in transmitting their partisanship to their children. Partisan loyalties are formed when parents are the dominant influence in a child's life and exposure to partisan cues from the parent is common. Parties are very visible and important institutions in the political process, and virtually all political discussion includes some partisan content: we identify candidates and judge them by their party affiliation, and we evaluate policies by their party sponsor. It does not take long for a child to identify the parents' partisan leanings from their reactions to television news and statements in family discussions. Furthermore, most parents have strong party attachments that endure across elections; children are thus exposed to relatively consistent and continuous cues on which party their parents prefer. For example, one of my university colleagues was openly proud that he had conditioned his preschool child to groan each time a specific former president appeared on television. Either through explicit reinforcement or subconscious internalization of parental values, many children learn of their parents' partisan preferences and take them as their own.

Once individuals establish party ties, later partisan experiences often follow these early predispositions. Democrats tend to vote for Democratic candidates; Republicans vote for Republicans. Thus electoral experience normally reinforces these partisan tendencies because most citizens cast ballots for their preferred party.[5] The accumulated experience of voting for the same party and the political agreement that leads to such partisan regularity both tend to strengthen partisan ties. Consequently, researchers generally find that partisan loyalties strengthen with age—or, more precisely, with continued electoral support of the same party (Converse 1969, 1976).[6]

Figure 9.2 displays this increasing percentage of those with a party identification by age.[7] Regardless of which party one supports, party bonds are stronger among older age groups. Most people in the United States, Britain, and France develop a strong sense of party identity by middle age, which continues to strengthen through the rest of the life cycle. For example, only 43 percent of the youngest French age group say they are partisans, compared to 75

TABLE 9.1 The Transmission of Parental Partisanship (in percentages)

	United States		
	Parental Party Preferences		
	Democrat	Republican	Independent
Child's party preference			
Democrat	70	25	40
Republican	10	54	20
Independent	20	21	40
Total	100	100	100

	Great Britain			
	Parental Party Preference			
	Labour	Liberal	Conservative	None
Child's party preference				
Labour	51	17	6	29
Liberal	8	39	11	6
Conservative	1	11	50	6
None	40	33	33	59
Total	100	100	100	100

	West Germany			
	Parental Party Preference			
	SPD	FDP	CDU/CSU	None
Child's party preference				
SPD	53	8	14	19
FDP	4	59	1	3
CDU/CSU	9	—	32	12
None	34	33	53	66
Total	100	100	100	100

SOURCE: Political Action Survey.

percent among the old age group. The same general age pattern is evident for British and American electors. Measures of the strength of partisanship depict a similar pattern of party bonds intensifying with age (or more precisely, with accumulated experience of supporting the same party in successive elections).

In the previous edition of this study, the Federal Republic of Germany was an exception to this general pattern. Residents of communist East Germany obviously had not had the same opportunity over the decades prior to unifi-

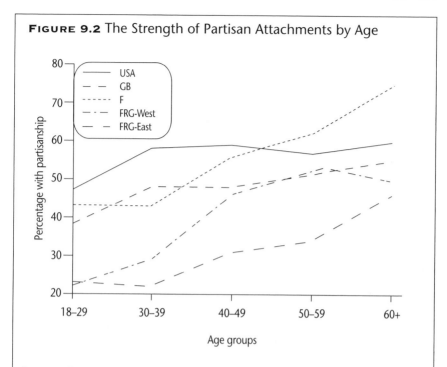

FIGURE 9.2 The Strength of Partisan Attachments by Age

SOURCES: Comparative Study of Electoral Systems, modules I and II; United States, 1996 American National Election Study; Great Britain, 1997 British Election Study; Germany, 2002 German Election Study; France, 2002 French Election Study.

NOTE: The CSES uses a comparably worded question on partisanship, so direct comparisons of the level of partisan attachments cross-nationally are appropriate.

cation to develop attachments to the democratic parties of the West. Their direct experience with the current party system dated only to 1990. Thus the overall level of partisan attachments was significantly weaker in the East. In addition, there was relatively little difference in the strength of partisan ties between young easterners and those over age fifty.

As we predicted, as eastern Germans are accumulating more experience with democratic electoral politics, the life-cycle pattern of partisan learning is becoming more apparent. This learning process has probably been accelerated by the deliberate attempt by the PDS to appeal to easterners, which has apparently served to integrate these new citizens into the electoral system of the Federal Republic. The East/West gap in partisanship consequently has narrowed from the levels of the early 1990s, and the pattern of greater partisanship among the old now applies to both halves of Germany.

Thus, partisan attachments are normally learned early in life, become deeply embedded in a child's belief system, and then are reinforced by later partisan experiences. Partisanship may change in reaction to later life experiences, but these attachments are not easily altered once they have formed. For example, party identification is one of the most stable political attitudes, far exceeding the stability of opinions on long-standing national issues such as race relations, economic programs, and foreign policy (Converse and Markus 1979). Additional evidence of long-term partisan stability comes from a panel study of high school seniors and their parents. M. Kent Jennings and Greg Markus (1984) found that 78 percent of American adults and 58 percent of adolescents kept their partisan ties constant across one of the most turbulent political periods in recent American history (1965–1973).

Evidence from other nations mirrors this pattern. British party attachments are significantly more stable than other political beliefs (Schickler and Green 1997). On the average, between 80 and 90 percent of the British public retain constant party ties from one election to the next. Hilde Himmelweit and her colleagues (1981) interviewed a sample of British middle-class males over a twelve-year period. They found that most voters supported the same party in 1959 and 1974 (a fifteen-year time span); conversions between Labour and Conservative partisanship were exceedingly rare. Longitudinal studies in Germany also have found that partisanship is a very stable political attitude (Baker, Dalton, and Hildebrandt 1981). The limited evidence for France shows that below the surface of substantial turbulence in the actions of party leaders, there is considerable continuity in the partisan orientations of the French public (Converse and Pierce 1986, ch. 3).

Important evidence on the relative constancy of partisan attachments comes from comparing the stability of partisanship and voting preferences (see table 9.2). For instance, re-interviews with the same American voters in 1972 and 1976 found that 93 percent had stable party identifications, while only 75 percent had stable congressional voting preferences. Moreover, when there was some variability, more voters maintained a stable party identification while changing their vote (22 percent) than the other way around (4 percent). Party preferences were also more stable than voting preferences in Great Britain and Germany, but this difference was more modest than in the United States (LeDuc 1981; cf. Heath and Pierce 1992). In Europe there is a greater tendency for partisanship and vote to travel together; when one changes, so does the other (Holmberg 1994). Because of their limited amount of voting opportunities, Europeans are less likely to distinguish between long-term partisanship and current voting preferences. Still, partisanship generally is a political orientation that continues over time, even in the face of vote defections.[8]

In sum, electoral research stresses the importance of partisanship in shaping the political orientations of the public. Partisanship is a central element in an individual's belief system and a basis of political identity. These orientations are formed early in life and may condition later life learning. Thus it is easy to see why researchers give it a central role in a sociopsychological model of voting choice.

TABLE 9.2 The Relative Stability of Party Attachments and Vote (in percentages)

Party Identification	United States, 1972–76	
	Vote	
	Stable	Variable
Stable	71	22
Variable	4	3
N = 539		

Party Identification	Great Britain, 1970–74	
	Vote	
	Stable	Variable
Stable	75	10
Variable	5	10
N = 795		

Party Identification	West Germany, 1976	
	Vote	
	Stable	Variable
Stable	71	22
Variable	4	3
N = 707		

SOURCE: LeDuc (1981, 261); Berger (504)

Note: The tables present percentages of the total N based on those who were voters and identified with a political party at each time point. American and British results are based on changes between two elections; West German data are based on changes during a three-wave 1976 election panel.

THE IMPACT OF PARTISANSHIP

In sports, loyalty to a specific team helps one know who to root for and which players to admire, and it motivates individuals to participate in support of their team. People often develop such ties early in life, and they endure through the ups and downs of the franchise. Moreover, in my case, my attachment to the Dodgers strengthens with repeated trips to root on my team, even if they lose.

It is the same with feelings of partisan attachment: parties help to make politics "user-friendly." When the political parties take clear and consistent policy positions, the party label provides a key informational short-cut on how "people like me" should decide. Once voters decide which party generally represents their interests, this single piece of information can act as a perceptual screen—guiding how they view events, issues, and candidates. A policy advocated by one's party is more likely to meet with favor than one advocated by the other team.

Moreover, in comparison to social-group cues such as class and religion, party attachments are a more valuable heuristic. Party cues are relevant to a much broader range of political phenomena because parties are so central to democratic politics. Issues and events frequently are presented to the public in partisan terms, as the parties take positions on the political questions of the day or react to the statements of other political actors. People vote for parties or party candidates at elections. Governments are managed by partisan teams. Thus reliance on partisanship may be the ultimate example of the satisficing model of politics.

The Washington Post performed an interesting experiment that illustrates the power of partisanship as a political cue (Morris 1995). They included a question on a fictitious government act in one of the newspaper's opinion surveys. One form of the question included reference to either President Clinton's or the Republicans' position on the issue, and another form discussed the act without any partisan cues. They found that the number of people expressing an opinion on this act increased when a partisan cue was given. Moreover, there were dramatic partisan effects. Democrats were far more likely to oppose the fictitious act when told Clinton wanted repeal; Republicans disproportionately opposed the act when told the Republicans in Congress wanted repeal.

An example from the 2000 American National Election Study demonstrates the power of partisanship to shape even nonpartisan opinions. Before the 2000 U.S. elections, the survey asked the public to judge whether the national economy would improve or worsen over the next twelve months. With the Democrats in the White House, Democrats were more optimistic about the nation's economic future than Republicans by an 8 percent margin. After the election, with Bush the apparent winner (although the election outcome was still in doubt), Republicans became more positive about the economy by a small margin.

This reversal of the relationship between preelection and postelection surveys illustrates the power of partisanship to shape citizen perceptions of the political world. Partisanship has an even stronger influence on opinions that are more closely linked to the parties, such as evaluations of governmental performance and candidate images (Abramson, Aldrich and Rohde 2003, ch. 8; Miller and Shanks 1996). Partisans root for the players (candidates) on their team and save their catcalls for the opponents.

Party ties also mobilize individuals to become politically active (see chapter 3). Just like a sports loyalty, attachment to a political party encourages an individual to become active in the political process to support his or her side. Voting turnout and participation in campaign activities are generally higher among strong party identifiers (chapter 3). The 2000 American Election Study, for example, finds that turnout was 23 percent higher among strong partisans than among independents. In addition, strong partisans are more likely to try to influence others, to display campaign paraphernalia, to attend a rally, or to give money to a candidate during the campaign. Partisanship functions in a similar way in other established democracies. For instance, strong partisans voted at a higher rate in the 2002 German Bundestag elections, and they were several times more likely to participate in campaign events and twice as likely to try to persuade others how to vote. While 88 percent of strong German partisans believed it makes a difference who controls the government, only 49 percent of weak partisans and 44 percent of nonpartisans shared this conviction.

The cue-giving function of partisanship is clearly seen for voting behavior. Partisanship means that voters enter an election with a predisposition to support their preferred party. Philip Converse (1966) described partisanship as the basis for a "normal vote"—the vote expected when other factors in the election are evenly balanced. If other factors come into play, such as issue positions or candidate images, their influence can be measured by their ability to cause defections from standing partisan commitments. For the unsophisticated voter, a long-term partisan loyalty and repeated experience with one's preferred party provides a clear and low-cost cue for voting. Even for the sophisticated citizen, a candidate's party affiliation normally signifies a policy program that serves as the basis for reasonable electoral choice.

There generally is a close relationship between partisanship and voting in parliamentary elections (Holmberg 1994). In the 2001 British elections, only 14 percent of partisans defected to vote for another party. Even with multiple parties to choose from, defection rates were low in the 2002 German Bundestag elections. A full 81 percent of German partisans voted for a district candidate from the party they identified with, and 78 percent cast a party vote on the second ballot even though many strategic voters supported a smaller party to help their own party's coalition chances. The limited voting opportunities in most European nations tend to lessen the separation between partisanship and vote.

The American elector, in contrast, "has to cope simultaneously with a vast collection of partisan candidates seeking a variety of offices at federal, state, and local levels; it is small wonder that he becomes conscious of a generalized belief about his ties to a party" (Butler and Stokes 1969, 43). Thus the separation between attitudes and behavior is most noticeable in American elections, especially when voters are asked to make a series of choices for local, state, and federal offices (Beck et al. 1992). In highly visible and politicized presidential elections, candidate images and issue appeals have the potential to counteract partisan preferences, and thus party defections are common in these elections. The success of Republican presidential candidates from Reagan to George W. Bush occurs because they have attracted defectors from the Democratic majority. Even in the highly divisive two-party contest of 2000, for instance, 7 percent of American partisans cast presidential votes contrary to their party identification.

A similar situation exists in France. The two-candidate runoff in French presidential elections is decided by the size of the vote the candidates can attract from parties other than their own (Boy and Mayer 1993). In French parliamentary elections, however, voting choice more closely conforms to standing partisan preferences.

In summary, it is easy to see why partisanship is the ultimate heuristic, because it performs a variety of functions for the partisan:

- Creates a basis of political identity
- Provides cues for evaluating political events, candidates, and issues
- Mobilizes participation in campaigns and election turnout
- Provides cues on voting preferences
- Stabilizes voting patterns, for the individual and the party system

Thus partisan attachments became the cornerstone to our understanding of how citizens manage the complexities of politics and make reasonable decisions on the questions they face at election time.

PARTISAN DEALIGNMENT

Because partisanship is a central variable in the study of many different aspects of citizen political behavior, it came as some surprise when researchers first noted that party ties were eroding in many advanced industrial democracies. The initial signs of partisanship decline appeared in the rising fluctuations of party outcomes from election to election (Crewe and Denver 1985). The erosion of the social-group basis of party support contributed to this trend of increasing party volatility; the frozen group alignments that Seymour Martin Lipset and Stein Rokkan (1967) had described were beginning to thaw (chapter 8). In addition, election surveys in several nations found that partisan identifications were weakening (Dalton, Flanagan, and Beck 1984).

At first, it was difficult to be certain that party bonds were eroding when this trend was intermixed with the normal patterns of partisan change between elections. Partisan change is a regular element of the electoral process, and periods of heightened partisan volatility and fragmentation dot the electoral histories of most democracies. As we argued above, however, relatively few voters do change their partisan preferences between adjacent elections.

The weakening of party ties first became apparent in the United States (see figure 9.3). American partisanship was extremely stable from the 1950s to the early 1960s; the percentage of party identifiers remained within the 70–75 percent range, and less than a quarter of the public claimed to be "independents" without fixed partisan ties. But partisan loyalties began to weaken after the 1964 election, and by the 1980s, more than a third of the electorate were nonpartisans. H. Ross Perot's candidacy pushed the percentage of partisans down still further in the 1990s (Wattenberg 1998). The percentage of partisans reached a new low (59 percent) in the 2000 election sur-

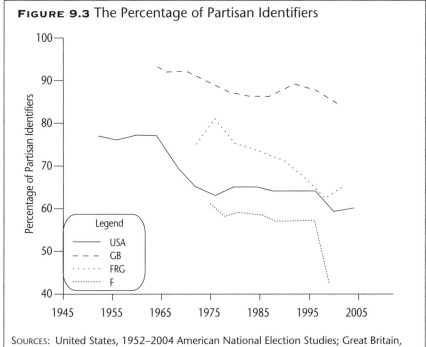

FIGURE 9.3 The Percentage of Partisan Identifiers

SOURCES: United States, 1952–2004 American National Election Studies; Great Britain, 1964–2001 British Election Studies; Germany, 1972–2002 German Elections Studies (western Germany only, 1990–2002); France, Eurobarometer Surveys (1975, 1978, 1981, 1986, 1988, 1993, 1996, and 1999).

vey, and this level continued into the 2004 election, despite the highly politicized and partisan nature of the campaign.

Several American politics experts questioned the existence and significance of these trends. For example, Bruce Keith and his colleagues (1992) doubted that the decrease in the percentage of party identifiers was a meaningful change. Donald Green, Bradley Palmquist, and Eric Schickler (2002, 31) examined a broad array of partisan behaviors in the ANES time series and concluded, "Partisanship is alive and well, and as far as we can tell, it is as influential for us as it was for our parents and grandparents." Other researchers claimed that the ability of partisan identities to predict presidential vote preferences had not significantly diminished over the five-decade series of the ANES (Miller and Shanks 1996; Bartels 2000). The significance of partisanship is so great that many doubted that party ties were really weakening.

The topic of partisanship is a good example of the value of cumulative research, and especially comparative analysis. As the body of evidence has grown, adding more elections and more nations, it is now clear that a general pattern of partisan decline is broadly affecting advanced industrial democracies (Dalton and Wattenberg 2000; Fiorina 2002; Webb 2002; Clarke and

Stewart 1998). Voters are not simply defecting from their preferred party in one or two elections, or just in the United States. Instead, there is an ongoing erosion in partisan loyalties across a wide set of nations—the same loyalties that electoral research emphasized as a core element in explaining citizen political behavior.

For instance, an almost identical pattern of declining party ties occurred in Great Britain (see figure 9.3). Because of the traditions of the British party system and the format of the British partisanship questionnaire, fewer Britons claim to be nonpartisans. In the 1964 British election study, 93 percent claimed a standing partisan preference; by the 1980s, the number of partisans had decreased by about 10 percent. Responses to questions about the strength of attachments among partisans display an even clearer pattern: more than 40 percent of the British public were strong partisans during the late 1960s, but less than 20 percent claim to be strong partisans in the most recent elections.

Germany initially deviated from the pattern of partisanship found in other advanced industrial democracies. There was a large increase in partisanship between 1961 and 1976, as West Germans developed initial commitments to the postwar party system (Baker, Dalton, and Hildebrandt 1981, ch. 8). But at some point in the late 1970s, the trend began moving in the opposite direction. Partisans were 81 percent of the public in 1976; by 2002 they accounted for 65 percent among westerners. Partisanship is even lower among easterners, because they lack prior partisan experience and are just beginning to develop party attachments. During the 2002 election, 45 percent of eastern Germans claimed to lack any party ties (Dalton and Bürklin 2003).

The series of comparable French survey data is much shorter and is drawn from the Eurobarometer surveys. Beginning in the 1970s, the percentage of partisans slowly decreased, and then there was a marked drop-off at the end of the 1990s (also see Haegel 1993).

This weakening of party ties in our four core nations typifies a pattern occurring in almost all advanced industrial democracies. An analysis of the nineteen advanced industrial democracies for which long-term survey data exist shows that the percentage of partisans has decreased in seventeen cases (Dalton 2000a; 2004a, ch. 2). Furthermore, if we focus on the strength of partisanship, it has decreased in all nineteen nations. In nations as diverse as Austria, Canada, Japan, New Zealand, and Sweden, the pattern is the same: the partisan attachments of the public weakened during the latter half of the twentieth century.

Other evidence points to growing public doubts about parties as political institutions. Several international surveys find that public confidence in political parties rates at the bottom of a list of diverse social and political institutions (Dalton and Weldon 2004). Similarly, data from Britain, Canada, Germany, Sweden, and other nations demonstrates that contemporary publics are significantly less trusting of political parties (Bromley and Curtice 2002; Carty 2002; Rieger 1994; Holmberg 1999). Indeed, the ebbing of public attachment to political parties is broadly evident in most contemporary democracies.

Advanced industrial democracies are experiencing a new period of *partisan dealignment,* which means that a significant proportion of the public is failing to develop party attachments or is becoming openly critical of political parties as institutions of government. Electoral analysts first thought that partisan dealignment was a temporary phenomenon, as parties and politicians struggled with problems that temporarily weakened their support among the public (like a sports team on a losing streak). Now, however, it appears to be a continuing feature of contemporary politics. After more than thirty years, for example, American partisanship remains below its highpoints in the 1950s and early 1960s. More important, if party identification is the most important attitude in electoral behavior research, then the breadth of these dealignment patterns should have major implications for these nations.

THE CONSEQUENCES OF DEALIGNMENT

Does it matter if fewer people now identify with a political party? It should, if our theories about the heuristic value of partisanship are correct. Because partisan ties are seen as so central to the workings of electoral politics and political behavior, the erosion of these ties should have obvious and predicable effects on citizen politics. Indeed, the evidence of partisan dealignment is visible in a range of different aspects of electoral behavior.

For instance, partisanship binds individual voters to a preferred party. Thus as these ties weaken, so should patterns of partisan-centered voting choice. For example, weakened party attachments lead fewer American and German voters to cast straight-party ballots, and the rates of split-ticket voting has risen in recent elections (figure 9.4). In the 1960s less than a sixth of Americans split their ballots between a presidential candidate of one party and a congressional candidate of another party; by the 1980s this proportion had risen to a quarter of the electorate. With Perot's third-party candidacy in 1992, 36 percent of Americans split their ballots. Even without Perot, split-ticket voting remained relatively high in the 2000 election, but then dropped off with the partisan 2004 contest. Split-ticket voting between House and Senate votes has also increased dramatically (Stanley and Niemi 2000). There is similar evidence of a rise in split-ticket voting in Germany between first and second ballots (Schoen 2000). Split-ticket voting appears to be a general consequence of the dealignment trend across other nations as well (Dalton and Wattenberg 2000, ch. 3).

Weakened partisanship is also increasing the fluidity of voting patterns. For instance, the number of political parties and the shift in vote shares between elections are generally increasing in advanced industrial democracies—including the four we are studying here (Dalton and Wattenberg 2000, ch. 3). Although most voters continue to support the same party over time, the number of floating voters is increasing in these party systems. Partisanship was

FIGURE 9.4 The Growth of Split-Ticket Voting

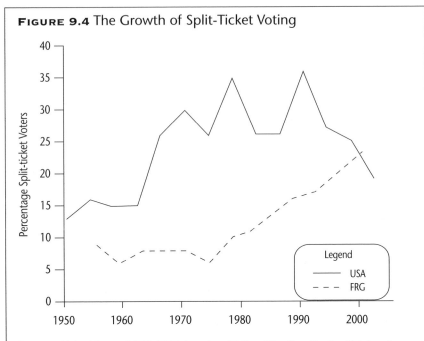

SOURCES: United States, 1952–2004 American National Election Studies (third-party presidential candidates counted as split voting); Germany, (Dalton and Bürklin 2003, 68), data for 1990–2002 are from western Germany.

once a stable guidepost for citizen political behavior, but now fewer individuals are following its guidance.

Since partisanship also mobilizes individuals to participate in politics, it is no surprise that dealignment has been accompanied by a decline in electoral participation (see chapter 3). Voter turnout has decreased in most advanced industrial democracies. Participation in campaign activities—going to meetings, working for candidates, and displaying party support—has also atrophied (Dalton and Wattenberg 2000, ch. 3). If politics is like sports, then the decreasing number of habitual fans means that there will be fewer to attend each game and participate in the sport.

Finally, when citizens do turn out to vote, the nature of the voting process is changed as a result of this decline in partisanship. As long-term party and social-group cues are decreasing in importance, the decision-making process shifts toward the issues and candidates of specific campaigns. As one indicator of this shift, trend data show a systematic tendency for voters to make their decisions later in the campaign (Dalton and Wattenberg 2000, ch. 3; Dalton and Bürklin 2003). Also, campaigns are now more likely to matter because fewer voters base their choices on standing partisan predispositions—voters are beginning to choose.

THE CAUSES OF DEALIGNMENT

There are several explanations for the dealignment trend. At least initially, researchers linked declining partisanship to political events and political crises. In the United States, the dramatic events of the 1970s initially turned many young people away from political parties. The antipartisan sentiments stirred by the Vietnam War, Watergate, and similar crises kept new voters from developing the early-life partisan attachments that could build over time. The student protests in Europe and an apparently increasing number of party scandals may have had a similar effect in these nations.

The cross-national breadth of dealignment trends, however, suggests that more than a series of coincidental political crises lies behind these trends. The sources of partisan dealignment more likely reflect broader patterns of social and political change that are common to advanced industrial democracies. The declining role of parties as political institutions seems to play a key part of this process. Many of the parties' traditional political functions have been taken over by other institutions. A myriad of special-interest groups and single-issue lobbies have developed in recent years, and political parties have little hope of representing all of them. Instead, these groups press their interests without relying on partisan channels. Party leaders are even losing some control over the selection of elected party representatives. The most advanced example is the United States, where the expansion of open primaries and nonpartisan elections is weakening the parties' hold on recruitment. The British Labour Party has experienced a similar shift in nominating power away from the party in Parliament to party conventions and local constituency groups. These and other developments lessen the importance of parties in the political process and therefore weaken the significance of parties as political reference points.

Changes in the mass media also contribute to dealignment trends. The mass media are assuming many of the information functions that political parties once controlled. Instead of learning about an election at a campaign rally or from party canvassers, prospective voters now turn to television and newspapers as the primary sources of campaign information (see chapter 2). Furthermore, the content of the mass media has changed to downplay the importance of political parties. The American media have shifted their campaign focus away from the political parties toward the candidates, and a weaker parallel trend is evident in several parliamentary democracies (Dalton and Wattenberg 2000, ch. 3).

Party performance in government and party policy positions can also contribute to dealignment (Zelle 1995; Thomassen 2005). On the one hand, contemporary parties are struggling with problems of maintaining social services in the face of mounting government deficits. Some of the economic and welfare issues traditionally associated with the class cleavage have not been fully resolved. On the other hand, the new issues of advanced industrial societies often appear unsuited for mass political parties. Many of these issues, such as nuclear energy, minority rights, or local environmental problems, are too narrow to affect mass partisan alignments on their own. The rise of single-issue interests does not translate well into partisan attachments, because the electoral impact of these issues is uncertain and because it is difficult to accommodate these issues within large political coalitions. In the United States, this lack of connection between issues and parties has led to a proliferation of citizen interest groups and direct-action politics; in Europe it has spawned similar groups, as well as a variety of small parties on the left and right. Analysts thus maintain that political parties have lessened their critical programmatic function of aggregating and articulating political interests. In a creative new study, Frode Berglund and colleagues (2005) show that the extent of distinct policy choices between the parties is related to the strength of partisanship across six European democracies; as the former has blurred, partisanship has weakened.

While these systematic factors are important, their ability to explain the dealignment trend has limitations. For instance, while it is true that some failures in party performance may have initially stimulated a dealignment trend, this trend did not reverse when a new party won control of the government or when policy failure was replaced by policy success. Furthermore, the research literature in each nation typically points to a unique set of policy failures, but the dealignment trend is a common feature across these diverse experiences. Thus one looks for general changes affecting advanced industrial societies. Even the emphasis on the changing role of the media overlooks the diverse role the media play across these nations, because of their different public/private ownership patterns and different journalist norms. Thus we believe that more fundamental changes in contemporary publics have contributed to partisan dealignment.

Cognitive Mobilization and Apartisans

Part of the dealignment literature begins by accepting the importance of partisanship as a heuristic that helps citizens orient themselves to politics (Shively 1979; Borre and Katz 1973). However, the process of cognitive mobilization means that voters' political sophistication is increasing, and therefore more people are able to deal with the complexities of politics without reliance on external cues or heuristics (chapter 2). In addition, the growing availability of political information through the media reduces the costs of making informed decisions.

The process of cognitive mobilization thus lessens the need for citizens to develop party identifications as a shortcut to help them handle difficult and often confusing political decisions. Indeed, the self-defined political interests of the cognitively mobilized may drive them away from habitual party cues that provide less room for individual choice.

The cognitive mobilization theory also implies that the recent increase in the number of independents will be concentrated among a distinct group of citizens: the better-educated, the better-informed, and those who are cognitively mobilized. In contrast, the early literature on partisanship held that nonpartisans were at the margins of the electoral process; they were uninvolved in elections and unsophisticated about politics (Campbell et al. 1960). If the growing numbers of independents are concentrated among the politically unsophisticated, which is possible in some explanations of dealignment (Milner 2002, ch. 2; Dimock 1998), it would contradict the cognitive mobilization theory—and potentially represent a negative development for the contemporary democracies.

However, research on the dealignment trends in advanced industrial societies tends to support the cognitive mobilization theory (Dalton 2000a). The greatest decline in partisanship occurs among the better-educated and the cognitively mobilized. In addition, in most nations dealignment is concentrated among younger generations, who are now less likely to be socialized into a partisan identity. At the same time, there is little evidence that policy dissatisfaction is driving dealignment, which suggests that it is the public's changing norms, rather than poor party performance, that is stimulating dealignment.

These empirical findings lead us to think of party mobilization and cognitive mobilization as two alternative ways that citizens can connect themselves to the political process (Dalton 1984). Some voters remain oriented to politics based on their partisan attachments—and this is a potent source of political cues. Cognitive mobilization produces another group of politically interested and well-educated voters who orient themselves to politics on their own. The combination of these traits defines a typology of four types of citizens (see figure 9.5). *Apoliticals* are neither attached to a political party nor cognitively mobilized; this group conforms to the independents originally described by Campbell and his colleagues (1960, 143–145). *Ritual partisans* are mobilized into politics primarily by their strong party attachments, and are not cognitively mobilized. *Cognitive partisans* are highly ranked on both mobilization dimensions: they have strong party attachments, and they are psychologically involved in politics even when party cues are lacking.

Apartisans are the "new independents." It is essential to distinguish them from traditional independents (apoliticals). Apartisans are cognitively mobilized, which implies high levels of political involvement and sophistication, though these citizens remain unattached to any political party. Apartisans are also concentrated among the young, the better-educated, and postmaterialists (Dalton 1984). Other research shows that the development of advanced industrial societies is increasing the proportion of apartisans within contemporary publics, as well as shifting the ratio of ritual and cognitive partisans. For instance, data from the American National Election Studies find that the number of apartisans has more than doubled over the past forty years—to a fifth of the electorate.[9] In addition, the number of cognitive partisans has grown slightly, while the proportion of ritual partisans has decreased by almost half. Ronald Inglehart found that the percentage of apartisans in Europe increased significantly over a single decade (1976–1987) (Inglehart 1990, 366). Furthermore, Inglehart found sharp differences in the percentage of apartisans across European generations, which

FIGURE 9.5 Patterns of Political Mobilization

		Strength of Partisanship	
		Independent	Party Identification
Cognitive Mobilization	High	Apartisan	Cognitive Partisan
	Low	Apartisan	Ritual Partisan

suggests that the number of apartisans will continue to grow. Longitudinal analyses of Swedish, German, and British partisanship yield similar findings (Holmberg 1994; Wolf 2002).

The recognition of apartisans has several implications for contemporary political behavior. Apartisans have the political resources to follow the complexities of politics, and they are free of affective party ties. Thus, these new independents are less consistent in their voting patterns because voting behavior is not dependent on long-standing party predispositions. This group may be expected to inject more issue voting into elections and to demand that candidates be more responsive to public opinion. Apartisans may also press for an expansion of citizen input beyond the narrow channel of elections and other party-related activities. The political skills of apartisans enable them to organize effective citizen-action groups, citizen lobbies, protest demonstrations, and other unconventional political activities. The nonpartisan, issue-oriented characteristics of these activities make them ideal participation modes for apartisans.

Finally, ongoing processes of socioeconomic change should gradually increase the number of apartisans. The actions of parties in specific elections may hasten or retard this process in the short term. Nevertheless, the evidence suggests a long-term trend toward partisan dealignment in advanced industrial societies.

POLITICS IN A DEALIGNED ERA

Most elections involve a choice among parties or their representatives, and so parties remain the central actors in the political process in most contemporary democracies. This chapter has argued that most citizens develop a psychological identification with a preferred political party, and these attachments are a potent guide for political behavior. And yet, the extent of these party ties is eroding in virtually all the advanced industrial democracies—producing a new characteristic of partisan dealignment. In addition, this decline in partisanship has been more pronounced among the better-educated and the politically engaged—as if the most sophisticated fans of the sport of politics are becoming disengaged with the partisan players they see on the field.

Furthermore, as with the weakening of the sociological model, the relative simultaneity of dealignment trends across various nations is striking. Long-term sources of partisan preference—social characteristics and partisanship—are weakening in most advanced industrial societies. In a single nation, such developments might be explained by the specific trials and tribulations of the parties. When a pattern appears across a wide variety of nations, however, it suggests that the causes are common to advanced industrial societies. Indeed, linking the process of cognitive mobilization to partisan dealignment seems to represent yet another feature of the new style of citizen politics. Cognitively mobilized citizens are better able to make their own political decisions—and more interested in doing so—without relying on heuristics or external cues. These new apartisans are producing the dealignment trend.

Weakening party bonds have real consequences for the operation of the political process. For instance, partisan dealignment is part of a general process of political change that is transforming the relationship between voters and parties. The personal connection between parties and voters is being replaced by professional organizations that rely on the media and direct mailing to connect to voters. Instead of depending on party members for staffing, election campaigns have become professionalized activities run by hired specialists. Instead of drawing on membership dues to fund party activities, many party systems are turning to public funding sources. As citizens' connections to the parties have weakened, the parties have sought alternative sources of support. Such changes in organizational style may exacerbate dealignment trends, by further distancing parties from the voters.

Weakened party-line voting also may contribute to the recent level of split-party control of both the federal and state governments in the United States (Brody et al. 1994). Between 1981 and 1986 different parties controlled the House and Senate for the first time since 1916, and this pattern recurred from 1994 to 2000, and again in 2001–2002. Most visible, of course, has been the division in partisan control of the presidency and the Congress. From 1952 to 2004, the same party controlled the presidency and the House for only twenty out of forty-eight years. Even the highly partisan

2004 election illustrates this diversity; while the Republicans made gains in the U.S. Congress, Democrats made gains in state legislative seats.

The Federal Republic of Germany also has a federal system, and the same pattern is found there. For the first twenty years of the FRG's history, the same party coalition controlled the Bundestag (the directly elected lower house of parliament) and the Bundesrat (which represents the majority of state governments). Between 1976 and 2004, however, federal and state control was divided for more than a third of this period. In Great Britain, one sees a growing regionalization of voting patterns, as local electoral results are less closely tied to national patterns.

Of course, one of the strongest signs of dealigned politics is the rise of new political parties that can draw on independents for their initial support. The number of political parties grew during the latter half of the twentieth century in most parliamentary democracies. Ross Perot's candidacy in the 1992 and 1996 U.S. presidential elections and Ralph Nader's 2000 and 2004 campaigns illustrate the potential to appeal to the growing number of nonpartisans. Perot, a candidate without prior political experience and without the support of a party apparatus, garnered 19 percent of the presidential vote in 1992.[10] The success of "flash parties"—such as Berlusconi's Forza Italia, Jorg Haider's Freedom Party in Austria, List Pym Fortuyn in the Netherlands—and the general rise of New Left and New Right parties in Europe are additional indicators of the volatility now present in contemporary party systems.

Finally, the eroding influence of long-term sources of partisanship would suggest that factors further along the funnel of causality can play a larger role in voter choice. Citizens are still voting, even if they are not relying on party cues or early-learned partisanship to the degree they once did. On the one hand, this new independence may encourage the public to judge candidates and parties on their policies and governmental performance—producing a deliberative public that more closely approximates the classic democratic ideal. On the other hand, the lack of long-standing partisan loyalties may also make electorates more vulnerable to manipulation and demagogic appeals (Holmberg 1994, 113–114). Dealignment has the potential to yield both positive and negative consequences for electoral politics, depending on how party systems and voters react in this new context. In the following chapters, we consider how the changing role of issues and candidate images is affecting the calculus of elections.

SUGGESTED READINGS

Dalton, Russell, and Martin Wattenberg, eds. *Parties without Partisans: Political Change in Advanced Industrial Democracies*. New York: Oxford University Press, 2000.

Green, Donald, Bradley Palmquist, and Eric Schickler. *Partisan Hearts and Minds: Political Parties and the Social Identities of Voters*. New Haven, Conn.: Yale University Press, 2002.

Jennings, M. Kent, and Thomas Mann, eds. *Elections at Home and Abroad*. Ann Arbor: University of Michigan Press, 1994.

Miller, Warren, and J. Merrill Shanks. *The New American Voter*. Cambridge, Mass.: Harvard University Press, 1996.

Rose, Richard, and Ian McAllister. *The Loyalties of Voters: A Lifetime Learning Model*. Newbury Park, Calif.: Sage, 1990.

Thomassen, Jacques, ed. *The European Voter*. Oxford: Oxford University Press, 2005.

Wattenberg, Martin. *The Decline of American Political Parties, 1952–1996*. Cambridge, Mass.: Harvard University Press, 1998.

NOTES

1. The standard party identification question is one of the most frequently asked items in U.S. public opinion surveys, measuring both the direction of partisanship and the strength of party attachments: "Generally speaking, do you think of yourself as a Republican, a Democrat, an Independent, or what? (For those expressing a party preference:) Would you call yourself a strong Republican/Democrat or a not very strong Republican/Democrat? (For Independents:) Do you think of yourself as closer to the Republican or Democratic Party?"

   The question yields a seven-point measure of partisanship ranging from strong Democratic identifiers to strong Republican identifiers.

2. One of the current debates in the American voting literature is the question of how closely aggregate levels of partisanship track current voting preferences. For the contrasting sides of this debate, see MacKuen, Erikson, and Stimson (1989); Abramson and Ostrom (1991, 1994).

3. For instance, the German version of the party identification question specifically cues the respondent that it is asking about long-term partisan leanings: "Many people in the Federal Republic lean toward a particular party for a long time, although they may occasionally vote for a different party. How about you?"

4. These data are drawn from the Political Action study, which supplemented its national sample of adults with additional parent-child interviews of families where a 16–20-year-old was still living in the parent's home. For additional analyses, see Jennings et al. (1979).

5. Morris Fiorina (1981) describes partisanship as a "running tally" of an individual's accumulated electoral experience. If early partisan leanings are reinforced by later voting experience, party ties strengthen over time. If voting experiences counteract partisanship, then these party loyalties may gradually erode. Also see Niemi and Jennings (1991).

6. Researchers have debated whether age differences in American partisanship represent generational or life-cycle effects (Converse 1976; Abramson 1979). We emphasize the life-cycle (partisan learning) model because the cross-national pattern of age differences seems more consistent with this explanation.

7. Part of these relationships are due to patterns of accumulated partisanship over the life cycle. In addition, the lower levels of partisanship among the young can partially be traced to decreasing initial attachments among younger generations.

8. While we stress the stability of partisanship, there is also evidence that this stability is eroding over the past several decades (Dalton and Wattenberg 2000, ch. 3).

9. We define cognitively mobilized citizens as having a combination of interests and skills—that is, being "very interested" in politics and/or having at least some college education. The following table presents the distribution of types using data from the American National Election Studies (also see Dalton 2004b):

	1964–1966	1980–1990	2000
Apartisans	10%	14%	20%
Cognitive partisans	27	29	33
Ritual partisans	47	36	27
Apoliticals	16	21	20

10. The 1992 American National Election Study found that Perot garnered 10 percent of the vote among Democratic identifiers, 17 percent among Republican identifiers, and 36 percent among pure independents. This pattern continued in the 1996 election, and in 2000 both Buchanan and Nader gained the greatest percentage of their votes from independents.

CHAPTER 10

Attitudes and Electoral Behavior

Electoral conflict may begin as the competition between rival social groups or party camps, but elections inevitably revolve around the issues and candidates of the campaign.[1] Think of your own voting decisions: you do not vote for a party because of your social class, your religion, or your party identity—you vote for a party for its policy positions. Issues and candidates give political meaning to the partisan attachments and social divisions we have discussed in earlier chapters. The electoral significance of partisanship (or class attachments) is expressed in the cluster of issue positions and candidate preferences that evolve from long-term partisan ties. Most Labour Party supporters, for example, support the party not out of blind loyalty, but because they share a belief in policies that the party normally advocates.

Issue beliefs and candidate images are also important because they represent the dynamic aspect of electoral politics. The distribution of partisanship may define the broad parameters of electoral competition, but specific campaigns are fought over the policies the contenders advocate, the images of the candidates, or the incumbent government's policy performance. The mix of these factors almost always varies across elections, and thus issue beliefs and candidate images explain the ebbs and flows of voting outcomes over time. This is why the funnel of causality locates issue beliefs and candidate images as proximate to voting choice (figure 9.1). Although partisanship may partially determine these attitudes, the content of a campaign also shapes these attitudes and thus the ultimate voting decision.

Finally, as the electoral impact of long-term partisan attachments and social cues is decreasing, many political scientists maintain that there is a corresponding increase in the influence of issue opinions on voting choice (e.g., Franklin, Mackie, and Valen 1992). Martin Wattenberg (1991) has written provocatively about the rise of candidate-centered choices by American voters, and the role of candidate images is now more widely debated in European party systems (Aarts, Blais, and Schmitt 2005; McAllister 1996).

This chapter examines the role of issues and candidate images in electoral choice. We consider both the conditions that determine the potential influence of these attitudes on the vote, as well as their actual impact in contemporary party systems. This evidence enables us to complete our model of voter choice and discuss the implications of our findings for the democratic process.

Internet Resource

Visit the Comparative Study of Electoral Systems web site to find a parallel survey of voters that was conducted in more than a dozen nations:

http://www.cses.org

PRINCIPLES OF ISSUE VOTING

The study of issue voting is closely intertwined with the scholarly debate on the political sophistication of the public. In theoretical terms, issue voting is presented as the defining feature of a sophisticated, rational electorate: the voter evaluates the government and the opposition and then thoughtfully casts a ballot for his or her preferred party. For the skeptics of mass democracy, this theoretical ideal seldom exists in reality. Instead, they see voters as lacking knowledge of the parties' positions, sometimes unsure of their own positions, and often voting on the basis of ill-formed or even incorrect beliefs (see chapter 2).

The early empirical voting studies criticized the electorate's ability to make informed choices. The authors of *The American Voter* maintained that meaningful issue voting is based on three requirements: citizens should be interested in the issue, they should hold an opinion on the issue, and they should know the party or candidate positions on the issue (Campbell et al. 1960, ch. 8). The *American Voter* researchers maintained that on most policy issues, most voters fail to meet these criteria; they classified a third of the public, or less, as possible issue voters on each of a long list of policy topics. When Paul Abramson, John Aldrich, and David Rohde (2003) updated these assessments of potential issue voters, they came to similar conclusions. Moreover, the Michigan researchers believed that these small percentages reflected the conceptual and motivational limits of the electorate—the lack of issue voting is presumably an intrinsic aspect of mass politics (Converse 1990). These political scientists therefore doubt the position that election results represent the policy choices of the public.

Even at the beginning of empirical voting research, however, there were critics of this negative image of issue voting. V. O. Key was one of the first to present survey evidence showing that citizens were "moved by concern about the central and relevant questions of public policy, of government performance, and of executive personality." In short, Key's unorthodox argument stated, "voters are not fools" (1966, 7–8). Key's position gradually has become less unorthodox as our understanding of citizen voting behavior has grown.

The fact that only a minority of the public may fulfill the criteria of rational issue voting for each specific issue does not mean that only a third of the total public are capable for any and all issues. Contemporary electorates are comprised of overlapping *issue publics*, groups of people interested in a specific issue (see chapter 2). These issue publics vary in size and composition. A large and heterogeneous group of citizens may be interested in basic political issues such as taxes, inflation rates, budget deficits, and the threat of war. On more specific issues—agricultural policy, nuclear energy, transportation policy, foreign aid—the issue publics normally are smaller and politically distinct. Most voters are politically attentive on at least one issue, and many voters may belong to several issue publics. Using open-ended questions about the likes and dislikes of the parties and candidates, Amy Gershkoff (2005) has classified Americans in terms of their self-interest in various issues. Her findings indicate that about a quarter of the public are not members of any issue public, and another quarter volunteer an interest in only one specific issue. But half of the electorate belong to two or more issue publics, and a seventh belong to four or more. Gershkoff concludes that voters are information specialists, focusing their attention on a few key issues, following the news on these issues and using them as a basis for electoral choice.

Moreover, when citizens define their own issue interests, they can fulfill the issue-voting criteria for their issues of interest. For example, David RePass (1971) found that only 5 percent of Americans were interested in medical programs for the elderly, but over 80 percent of this group could be classified as potential issue voters. One may assume that this issue public would be disproportionately comprised of older Americans; young college students do not follow the Medicate debate, but focus on other issues. This insight has been replicated and expanded in a series of articles by Jon Krosnick and his colleagues (Krosnick 1990; Amand and Krosnick 2003; also Gershkoff 2004). Thus adopting a more diversified view of the electorate—not all citizens must be interested in all issues—greatly strengthens the evidence of issue voting.

The conflicting claims about the nature of issue voting also may arise because researchers think of issue voting in different terms or use contrasting empirical examples to support their claims. Indeed, the literature is full of descriptions of how various types of issues function within the electoral process and why we should differentiate between these types of issues in terms of the demands they place on voters and their likely impact on electoral choices.[2] Issue voting may be more likely for some sorts of issues than for others; the implications of issue voting also may vary depending on the type of issue.

Figure 10.1 introduces a framework for thinking about issue voting. One important characteristic is the type of issue. *Position issues* define conflicts over policy goals (Stokes 1963). A typical position issue might involve debates over whether the U.S. Congress should support the Kyoto agreement on global warming, or whether Britain should privatize government-owned industries. Discussions of issue voting often focus on position issues that define the current political debate.

In contrast to position issues, *performance issues* involve judgments on how effectively the candidates or parties pursue widely accepted goals.[3] For instance, most voters favor a strong economy, but they may differ in how they

FIGURE 10.1 A Classification of Issues

Type of Issue

Time Frame	Position	Performance	Attribute
Retrospective	Policy Appraisal	Performance Evaluation	Attribute Voting
Prospective	Policy Mandate	Anticipatory Judgment	

evaluate a government's success in accomplishing this goal. Conflicting claims about performance judgments often lie at the heart of electoral campaigns. Finally, voters may judge the *attributes* of the parties or candidates: do they possess desired traits or characteristics? For example, a party must be considered trustworthy if its campaign promises are to be believed. As depicted in the figure's framework, these distinct issue characteristics reflect the different types of decisions being made and each type of issue voting has different implications for assessing voters' judgments and electoral outcomes.

We can also characterize issue voting by the time frame of the voters' judgments (Fiorina 1981; Miller and Borrelli 1992; Abramson, Aldrich, and Rohde 2003, ch. 7). *Retrospective* judgments occur when citizens rate political actors primarily on their past performance. For instance, evaluating Chancellor Gerhard Schröder in 2002 based on the performance of the economy—something he encouraged German voters to do when he was first elected in 1998—would be an example of retrospective voting. *Prospective* judgments are based on expectations of future performance. If a voter were to judge Schröder based on what his administration might do differently in the future, this would be an example of prospective voting.

Retrospective and prospective judgments hold different implications for the nature of voting choice. Retrospective judgments should have a firmer base in the facts, since they arise from past experience. Such political evaluations can be a relatively simple decision-making strategy: praise the incumbents if times have been good; criticize them if times have been bad. However, a pure reliance on retrospective judgments limits the scope of citizen evaluations. Elections enable voters to select a government for the future, and these decisions should include evaluations of a party's promises and its prospects for success. Therefore, voting decisions should include prospective judgments about a government's likely behavior in the future. Prospective judgments are based on a speculative and complex decision-making process.

Individuals have to make their own forecasts and link them to the expected performance of political actors—a task that imposes a considerable information burden on the voter. How citizens balance retrospective and prospective judgments thus reflects directly on the nature of voting choice.

The combination of both sets of characteristics provides a typology of the different types of issue calculations that voters may use in elections. Some issue voting involves a *policy appraisal* that assesses a party's (or candidate's) past position on a policy controversy. For instance, when some voters supported George W. Bush in 2004 because they favored his strong measures against terrorists, they were making a judgment about the past policies of the Bush administration. Alternatively, voters may consider what a party or candidate promises in policy terms as the basis of their voting decision. When Bush wanted voters in 2000 to support his plans to reduce taxes, he was asking for a *policy mandate* from the electorate.

Policy appraisals and policy mandates represent a sophisticated form of issue voting in which citizens are making choices between alternative policy goals for their government. This process places high requirements on the voters: they must inform themselves about the policy issue, settle on a preferred policy, and see meaningful choices between the contenders. This information may be acquired directly by the voter, or by using surrogate information sources (Popkin 1991; Lupia 1994).

In comparison, *performance evaluations* involve more general judgments about how a political actor (party, candidate, or government) has been doing its job in the past. If the political actor has been successful, voters support its return to office; if it has struggled, voters cast their ballots for an acceptable challenger to the incumbents. For example, in 1980 Ronald Reagan asked Americans to make a performance evaluation of Jimmy Carter's presidency when he asked: "Are you better off than you were four years ago?" In other instances, voters may make *anticipatory judgments* about the future performance of government. For instance, some analysts claim that the Labour Party lost in 1992 because some voters doubted the party's ability to function effectively as a governing party, although they favored many of Labour's policy proposals.

Finally, some aspects of issue voting may involve judgments about candidate or party attributes as a basis of choice. This type of voting is less often conditioned by a time frame. Voters judge candidates on their personal characteristics, which, although not immediately political in their content, are legitimate factors to consider in selecting a candidate (Kinder et al. 1980). Just as Carter's moral integrity helped him in 1976, Bill Clinton's "slick Willie" image hurt him at the polls in 1992—and both images were politically relevant although they did not involve explicit policy or performance calculations. Similar stylistic considerations can influence voter choices of a political party. For instance, Tony Blair's 1997 victory in Britain and Schroder's 1998 victory in Germany were at least partially attributed to each man's ability to project a more dynamic, forward-looking image than his electoral opponents.

Electoral researchers consign attribute voting to a low level of political sophistication because it does not involve explicit policy criteria. As we discuss later, however, many attributes involve traits that are directly relevant to the task of governing or to providing national leadership. Thus, we should consider attribute voting as a potentially meaningful basis of electoral choice.

The typology of figure 10.1 thus provides a useful framework for thinking about different aspects of issue voting. For example, Martin Wattenberg's (1991, ch. 6) analysis of support for Ronald Reagan provides an especially insightful example of how policy positions and performance evaluations reflect theoretically and empirically distinct aspects of issue voting. Some candidates win because of their policy promises; others win despite their program. There is evidence that a similar interplay of factors is at work in many elections.

We do not explicitly examine each type of issue voting in this chapter. But we do highlight how various types of issues can influence contemporary electoral outcomes, and the implications of each type for the nature of democratic politics.

POSITION ISSUES AND THE VOTE

Nearly a generation ago, some social scientists speculated about the imminent end of political conflict. They thought that advanced industrial societies would resolve the political controversies that had historically divided their populations (the controversies of the Old Politics), which would lead to the end of meaningful policy disagreements. We have witnessed just the opposite.

Contemporary electoral research documents increased levels of policy-based voting in modern party systems. Real changes in the nature of electorates (and politics itself) have facilitated issue voting. The process of cognitive mobilization increases the number of voters who have the conceptual ability and the political skills necessary to fulfill the issue-voting criteria. The growth of citizen-action groups, new issue-oriented parties, and the general renaissance of ideological debate at election time are obvious signs of the public's greater issue awareness. Political elites have become more conscious of the public's preferences and more sensitive to the results of public opinion polls.

Advanced industrialism obviously has not meant the end of policy differences within these societies. Contemporary issue voting still involves many long-standing policy debates. Economic cycles inevitably stimulate shifting concerns about the economic role of government and the nature of the modern welfare system. Indeed, the past few decades have seen a revival of economic controversy, spawned initially by economic recession and then by the "free market" programs of Reagan, Thatcher, Kohl, and other new conservatives. More recently, George W. Bush has renewed this debate in the United States with his conservative agenda. Similarly, political events can often revive latent conflicts, such as the current debate over affirmative action in the United States, or renewed regional tensions in many democratic societies.

Issue controversies also are born from the changing focus of political concern. This effect is most clearly illustrated in the area of foreign policy. The United States and other Western democracies are grappling with a new post–Cold War international system, with the new global threat of terrorism in the post–September 11 world, and with new international conflicts that challenge peace and stability throughout the world. Another set of recent political controversies includes New Politics concerns such as nuclear energy, women's rights, environmental protection, and related issues. These issues have entered the political agenda of most advanced industrial democracies over the past two decades, introducing new political controversies and a heightened degree of policy polarization. Until recently, politicians and voters did not even know that problems of global warming and ozone depletion existed. Furthermore, new issues play a special role in providing a political base for many new parties and reorienting the voting patterns of the young.

Faced with a diversity of issues across elections and electoral systems, it is difficult to provide a summary assessment of the impact of issues across time or nations. Indeed, the impact of specific issues should ebb and flow across time since they represent a dynamic part of elections. However, we can provide a general measure of the impact of policy preferences on voting behavior by examining the relationship between Left/Right attitudes and vote. Chapter 6 described Left/Right attitudes as a sort of "super issue," a statement of positions on the issues that are currently most important to each voter. Some voters' Left/Right attitudes may be derived from positions on traditional economic conflicts; others' Left/Right attitudes may reflect positions on New Politics controversies. In some cases, Left/Right attitudes may signify a mix of different types of issues. The specific issues of concern therefore may vary across individuals or across nations, but Left/Right attitudes can provide a single measure of each citizen's overall policy views.[4]

Most citizens can position themselves along a Left/Right scale, and their attitudes are linked to specific policy views, fulfilling the first two criteria of policy voting (Inglehart 1990, ch. 9). Figure 10.2 shows that citizens in each nation can also fulfill the third requirement: positioning the major political parties on this Left/Right scale. The figure presents the voters' average self-placements and the average scores they assign to the major political parties in their respective nations.

American voters are the most conservative, placing themselves to the right of the British, German, and French publics. Americans perceive modest political differences between the Democratic and Republican parties, although this polarization is greater than between Republican and Democratic voters themselves.[5] This discrepancy suggests that the growing divisions of American political parties at the elite level exceed the differences within the electorate. Morris Fiorina (2005) similarly argues that the supposed red/blue polarization in America is often overstated when compared to empirical reality.

FIGURE 10.2 Left/Right Placement of the Parties and Voter Self-Placement

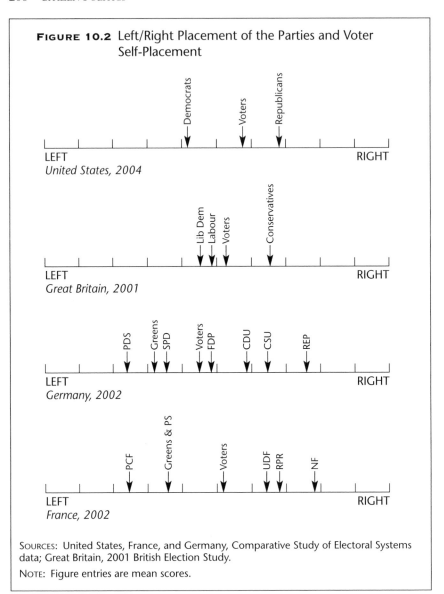

SOURCES: United States, France, and Germany, Comparative Study of Electoral Systems data; Great Britain, 2001 British Election Study.

NOTE: Figure entries are mean scores.

And while specific presidential candidates may be seen as relatively more or less ideological, the positions of the parties themselves change relatively little from election to election.

The perceived party differences are typically greater in European party systems. In France, for example, the political spectrum runs from the Communist Party at the leftist extreme to the National Front on the far right. By crude estimate, the French voter sees a range of party choices that extends more than twice as far across the political landscape than is represented by the differences between the major American political parties. Similarly, the German partisan landscape ranges from the PDS, the reformed communist party on the far left, to the extremist Republikaner on the far right. In Great Britain, the Labour and Conservative parties assume distinct positions on the Left/Right scale, although the Labour Party has moved distinctly toward the center under Blair's leadership.[6] Most political observers would agree that these party placements are fairly accurate portrayals of actual party positions (e.g., Laver and Hunt 1992, ch. 7). Therefore, in overall terms, citizens fulfill the third issue-voting criterion: knowing the party positions.

These Left/Right attitudes are strongly related to voting choice in each nation (table 10.1). The impact of Left/Right attitudes is greatest where a large number of parties offer clear policy options, as in France, where a full 96 percent of self-identified leftists favored a leftist party (Communists, Socialists, or Greens) in the 2002 legislative elections, compared to only 14 percent among self-identified rightists. Even in the United States, there is a 61-percentage-point gap in the Democrats' share of the vote as a function of Left/Right attitudes. These voting differences are much larger than the effects of social characteristics noted in chapter 8. The substantial influence of Left/Right attitudes is registered here because policy evaluations are located closer to the end of the funnel of causality.

The patterns of party support also confirm the relative positions of the parties along the Left/Right continuum. For instance, as the most extreme leftist party in France, the PC attracts the greatest share of its vote among the most extreme leftists, while the Socialists do best among more moderate leftists; this pattern is mirrored in support for the UDF and the RPR on the right. Another significant contrast is between the Greens in Germany and France. The German Greens' strong support from leftists reflects their position along the continuum, while the French Greens typically draw more support from the center.

We can add more detail to how issue positions affect vote by studying the relationship between specific policy attitudes and party preferences. Several surveys from the International Social Survey Program include different issue positions across several policy domains (see chapter 6 for additional discussion of these items). Table 10.2 describes the relationship between these issue positions and party choices in our four nations.[7] We should be cautious about over-interpreting these data, however, since the strength of each relationship reflects both the varying size of the relevant issue public and the clarity of party positions. The dynamic, short-term nature of issue beliefs means that either of these factors, and thus the impact of an issue, may greatly change between elections. These data therefore offer only a snapshot description of the relationship between issue opinions and party preferences, and not an explanation. Still, snapshots can provide a valuable picture of reality.

The traditional economic issues of the Old Politics—such as support for social services and government measures to lessen income inequality and

TABLE 10.1 Left/Right Attitudes and Party Support (in percentages)

Country	Left	—	Center	—	Right
United States (2004)					
Democrat	94	78	60	35	33
Republican	6	22	40	65	67
Total	100	100	100	100	100
Great Britain (2001)					
Labour	79	62	49	31	31
Liberal Democrats	18	30	29	12	5
Conservatives	3	8	22	57	64
Total	100	100	100	100	100
France (2002)					
PCF, extreme Left	24	8	15	5	4
Socialists	64	69	29	11	9
Greens	8	17	16	4	1
Center parties	2	1	3	1	1
UDF	0	1	6	12	10
RPR	1	2	23	55	52
NF, other Right	1	2	8	12	23
Total	100	100	100	100	100
Germany (2002)					
PDS	8	4	1	1	1
Greens	10	11	4	2	1
SPD	69	62	36	27	22
FDP	2	5	15	6	9
CDU/CSU	11	19	44	64	67
Total	100	101	100	100	100

SOURCES: United States, 2004 American National Election Study (CSES); Great Britain, 2001 British Election Study; France, 2002 French Election Study (CSES); Germany, 2002 German National Election Study (CSES).

manage the economy—display strong relationships with party preferences in all four nations. In each nation the strongest correlation involves an economic issue. This pattern occurs because economic topics have large issue publics and most political parties have clear policies on issues of the government's role in the economic and related economic policies (see figure 7.2, p. 142). In the United States, for example, the Republican Party has challenged social spending programs as part of the conservative legacy of the Reagan administration, and there have been similar challenges by conservatives in Great Britain and Germany. The conflict over economic issues, social programs, and the role of government remains a central theme in contemporary elections.

TABLE 10.2 The Correlation between Issue Opinions and Party Preferences

Issue	United States	Great Britain	France	Germany
Left/Right attitudes	0.39	0.34	0.40	0.27
Socioeconomic issues				
Social services over taxes	0.35	0.22	0.37	0.21
Government reduce inequality	0.19	0.17	—	0.13
Government control wages	0.16	0.17	0.20	0.14
Government control prices	0.15	0.14	0.17	0.14
Environmental issues				
Pay more for environment	0.19	0.19	—	0.15
Government responsible for environmental laws	0.14	0.12	0.16	0.12
Economic growth harms environment	0.07	0.13	—	0.07
GM foods are dangerous	—	0.13	—	0.10
Nuclear power is dangerous	0.11	0.12	—	0.13
Gender issues				
Husbands work/wife at home	0.08	0.12	0.14	0.14
If wife works, family suffers	0.08	0.09	0.12	0.14
If mother works, child suffers	0.08	0.10	0.14	0.16
Foreign policy				
Spend more on defense	0.14	0.15	0.26	0.15

SOURCES: 1996, 1998, 2000, and 2002 International Social Survey Program; Left/Right attitudes correlation, Comparative Study of Electoral Systems and 2001 British Election Study.
NOTE: Table entries are Cramer's V coefficients.

New Politics issues dealing with the environment have a modest impact on party choice. In Britain, for instance, the average correlation for socioeconomic issues is .18; for the environmental issues, the average is .14. Although many people are interested in issues such as environmental protection, the translation of these policy attitudes into party preferences remains secondary to economic concerns. Partially this is because material, economic issues still attract greater attention and because the established parties often offer less distinct policy choices on environmental and other New Politics issues. For instance, while the German and French Greens have a distinct profile on environmental issues, the positions of the remaining established parties are less clear-cut (figure 7.2).

Gender-related issues also often cut across established party lines. In the United States, for example, the party positions are clearly stated, but the parties are internally divided on issues such as abortion and the role of women; hence these issues are not strongly related to party preferences. In Europe, the impact of gender issues is somewhat stronger, especially in France and

Germany, where large Catholic voter blocs and/or Christian parties tend to polarize opinions on these issues. In sum, both environmental and gender issues tend to cut across traditional party lines. Still, these New Politics issues are significant more for their potential impact than for their present influence on electoral outcomes.

Foreign policy issues normally are weakly related to party preferences. France is the one nation where foreign policy issues often impact on partisanship; this effect reflects continuing conflicts over France's role in the international system, ranging from its relationship to NATO to the policies of European unification. Foreign policy can sometimes influence partisan choice (Amand and Krosnick 2003), but its impact is normally secondary to domestic issues. Foreign policy issues attract the primary attention of only a small share of the public, except at times of international crisis. Party differences on most foreign policy issues are also modest in comparison to party polarization on many other topics.

A much richer compendium of information on issue voting exists for each nation separately (Abramson, Aldrich, and Rohde 2003; Clarke et al. 2004; Boy and Mayer 1993; Anderson and Zelle 1998). This literature indicates that position issues often influence the voting preferences of contemporary electorates. Indeed, this is one instance in which we refrain from presenting relationships between issue opinions and party preference from the World Values Survey so that students can explore these relationships with the data described in Appendix B.

The impact of any one issue for the entire public is often modest, because not all issues are salient to all voters. However, a more refined analysis of specific issue publics would find that individual voting decisions are heavily influenced by each voter's specific issue interests (Krosnick 1990; Gershkoff 2005). Cognitively sophisticated voters are also more likely to rely on issues as a basis for their electoral choice, further magnifying the importance of issue voting. When these findings are combined with evidence of increasing issue voting overall, V. O. Key's positive assessments of the public's voting behavior no longer appear so unorthodox.

PERFORMANCE ISSUES AND THE VOTE

Another element of issue voting involves performance as a basis for electoral choice. Many voters say they turn to performance criteria, judging the success of incumbents or their prospects for the future, as part of their voting decision. Morris Fiorina (1981, 5) put it best: citizens "typically have one comparatively hard bit of data: they know what life has been like during the incumbent's administration. They do not need to know the precise economic or foreign policies of the incumbent administration in order to judge the results of those policies." In other words, performance-based voting offers people a reasonable shortcut for ensuring that unsuccessful policies are dropped and successful policies continued.

This literature argues that it is only important that voters dispense electoral rewards and punishments—regardless of whether the policies and the outcomes are connected. Benjamin Page (1978, 222), for example, wrote that "even if the Great Depression and lack of recovery were not at all Hoover's fault . . . it could make sense to punish him in order to sharpen the incentives to maintain prosperity in the future." Page acknowledged that although blame may be placed unfairly, yet "to err on the side of forgiveness would leave voters vulnerable to tricky explanations and rationalizations; but to err on the draconian side would only spur politicians on to greater energy and imagination in problem solving." Therefore, performance voting requires that voters have a target for their blame when the government falters in some respect. Typically, such blame is triggered by to poor economic performance, though voters can consider foreign policy performance or other policy areas as well.

The literature on performance-based economic voting has burgeoned in recent years. Considerable evidence documents the importance of macroeconomics on micropolitics, both in the United States (MacKuen, Erikson, and Stimson 1992) and in Europe (Lewis-Beck 1988; Lewis-Beck and Paldam 2000; Anderson 1995; Norpoth 1992).

Even a simple measure of performance evaluation—overall judgments about the performance of the national economy over the past twelve months—displays a significant correlation with party preferences. Figure 10.3 displays the relationship between perceptions that the economy is improving/worsening and support for the incumbent party. In each case there is a clear tendency for negative economic perceptions to hurt the incumbents, and for positive perceptions to benefit the party in power. In the 1997 British election, for example, John Major's Conservatives won 48 percent support among those who thought the economy was improving, versus only 5 percent among those who thought it was deteriorating.

One might ask, however, whether these relationships are really evidence of causality. As we noted in chapter 8, some people adjust their economic expectations to reflect their other images of the government (see pp. 186). Voters who like the incumbent are more likely to put a favorable spin on economic conditions; those who are critical of government for one aspect of policy may generalize this dissatisfaction to include their economic judgments. Such projections, which are a normal part of incumbent images, likely magnify the relationship between economic perceptions and party preferences, but the underlying relationship is still important. A rising economic tide benefits the incumbents, while a failing economy often spells defeat at the next elections.

Another factor involves the exact scope and nature of economic influences. One point of debate concerns whether voters base their political evaluations on their own personal economic situation (pocketbook voting) or on the performance of the broader national economy (sociotropic voting). Most of the evidence suggests that voters follow the sociotropic model,

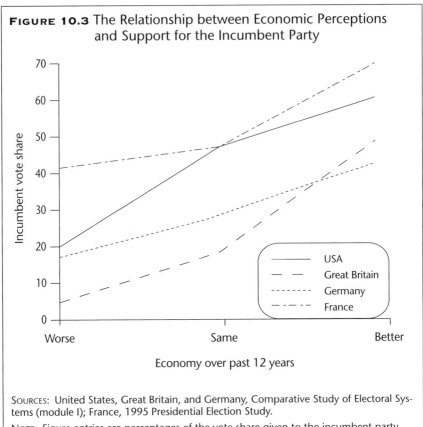

FIGURE 10.3 The Relationship between Economic Perceptions and Support for the Incumbent Party

SOURCES: United States, Great Britain, and Germany, Comparative Study of Electoral Systems (module I); France, 1995 Presidential Election Study.

NOTE: Figure entries are percentages of the vote share given to the incumbent party.

which implies that policy outcomes rather than narrow self-interest are the driving force behind performance voting (Kinder and Kiewiet 1981; Lewis-Beck 1988). Researchers also disagree on whether voters evaluate performance retrospectively or base their judgments on prospective expectations (see Fiorina 1981; MacKuen, Erikson, and Stimson 1992).

The state of the economy can be so important in some elections that it overrides other policy considerations. Many election analysts claim that incumbent parties are virtually unbeatable during strong economic upturns and extremely vulnerable during recessionary periods. For example, researchers argue that Americans and Britons elected conservative governments in 1979 and 1980 not for ideological reasons, but merely because they were the only instruments available for defeating incumbents who had failed to deliver the economic goods (Crewe and Searing 1988; Wattenberg 1991). Four years after coming to power, both Margaret Thatcher and Ronald Reagan won re-election on the basis of improved economic performance (and the success of the Falklands War in Thatcher's case)—in spite of continuing policy differences with most of their country's voters (Norpoth 1992). Other studies have documented the role of economic performance in other European states (Anderson 1995).

While narrow performance voting does not conform to democratic theory's emphasis on policy evaluation, researchers defend performance voting as entirely rational. Does it make sense, they ask, to pay attention to the policy positions of an ineffective administration that seemingly cannot make good on its promises and program? Retrospective voting theorists emphasize that the only really effective weapon of popular control in a democratic regime is the electorate's capacity to throw a party out of power.

CANDIDATE IMAGES AND THE VOTE

Democratic theorists describe issue voting in positive terms, but they view candidate-based voting decisions less positively. Some researchers view voting on the basis of personality characteristics as "irrational" (cf. Converse 1964; Page 1978). Candidates' images can be seen as commodities packaged by image makers who sway the public by emphasizing traits with special appeal to the voters. People's judgments about alternative candidates are, in this view, based on such superficial criteria as a candidate's style or looks (e.g., Sullivan and Masters 1988). Indeed, there is much experimental evidence indicating that it is possible to manipulate a candidate's personal appearance to affect voters' choices.

Recently, the voting literature has stressed a different approach to candidate assessments. This emerging view holds that candidate evaluations are not necessarily superficial, emotional, or purely short-term. Voters may focus on the personal qualities of a candidate to gain important information about characteristics relevant to assessing how the individual will perform in office (Kinder 1986; Miller, Wattenberg, and Malanchuk 1986; Rahn et al. 1990). This approach presumes that individuals organize their thoughts about other people into broad preexisting categories, or "prototypes," that are used in making judgments when limited factual information is available. Donald Kinder and his colleagues (1980), for example, explored the features that citizens use to define an ideal president. They showed that people can choose attributes they believe would make for an ideal president, but these prototypic conceptions are only related to ratings of the incumbent president.

Arthur Miller, Martin Wattenberg, and Oksana Malanchuk (1986, 536) presented data to support a rational voter interpretation of candidate evaluations: "candidate assessments actually concentrate on instrumental concerns about how a candidate would conduct governmental affairs." Analyzing candidate image data from the American National Election Studies, they found that the three most important dimensions of candidate image for Americans are integrity, reliability, and competence. Such criteria are hardly irrational, for if a candidate is too incompetent to carry out policy promises or too dishonest for those promises to be trusted, it makes perfect sense for a voter to pay attention to personality as well as policies. Interestingly, both David Glass (1985) and Miller, Wattenberg, and Malanchuk (1986) found that college-educated voters are the most likely to judge the candidates by their personal attributes.

The United States is certainly in the lead in developing a pattern of candidate-centered electoral politics (Wattenberg 1991). Presidents are the focal point of the quadrennial elections, and the large shifts in vote shares between presidential elections has often been traced to the effects of candidate images. Presidents (and chief executives in state and local governments) are elected independent of the legislature and largely run on personal platforms rather than as representatives of a fixed party position. Thus candidate image is one of their major electoral resources. To an extent, a similar personalization of politics occurs in France, where the president functions separately from the legislative majority and even from his own party within the legislature.

Electoral research on parliamentary systems initially suggested that popular images of party leaders had a minor impact on voting choice because these electorates did not directly vote for the chief executive. Recent research, however, finds significant effects. Clive Bean and Anthony Mughan (1989) showed that the perceived effectiveness of party leaders was moderately important in the British election of 1983 and possibly decisive in the Australian election of 1987. Analyses of German parliamentary elections similarly emphasized the growing role of candidate images (Ohr 2000). French politics has long valued the importance of a strong political leader, institutionalized in the directly elected presidency. Thus evidence from elections and from internal party politics points to the growing importance of candidate images even in parliamentary systems (Aarts, Blais, and Schmitt 2005; McAllister 1996; Ansell and Fish 1999). Anyone who has watched modern parliamentary campaigns, with candidates staging walkabouts for television and hosting discussion sessions with voters (in front of the cameras) must recognize that candidate images are a growing part of contemporary electoral campaigns in virtually all advanced industrial democracies.

THE END OF THE CAUSAL FUNNEL

When we reach the end of the causal funnel (figure 9.1), and people are ready to vote, it is difficult to come to a precise assessment of the influence of partisanship, issues, and candidate images on voting choices. Since candidate images are at the very end of the funnel of causality, they are very strongly related to voting preferences, at least in systems where voters cast a ballot for a specific candidate. But at the same time, candidate images are themselves the cumulation of prior influences. Long-term partisanship can have a potent effect in cueing voters on which politicians to like or dislike, just as voters' issue preferences can lead them toward a specific candidate. Thus, it is often difficult to determine the separate causal influences when there is such overlap. In the 2002 German election, for instance, among those who voted for the CDU/CSU, 63 percent thought Edmund Stoiber best represented their views; among SPD voters, 70 percent thought Gerhard Schröder best represented their views.

Furthermore, in parliamentary systems, partisan and candidate preferences are often closely intertwined because parliamentary candidates normally are chosen merely for the party they represent; in some nations citizens vote directly for parties. British voters did not elect Blair and German voters did not elect Schröder—both were selected by the partisan majorities in the parliament. Only in a system of direct election of candidates who can exercise autonomy from their party—such as the U.S. and French presidents—are we likely to see much separation between party preferences and candidate preferences.

So in the nexus of overlapping candidate, party, and issue preferences, it is difficult to assess the independent influence of each. But an illustration of the mix of factors at play can be drawn from comparing the weight of several core variables discussed in this chapter across our set of nations. Figure 10.4 combines Left/Right attitudes, evaluations of how good a job the government has done, and candidate images to explain voting choices. (Of course, there are other factors that should be considered, such as party identification and social group cues, but the figure summarizes the key variables at the end of the causal funnel.) The left side of the figure presents the impact of these factors in predicting legislative vote choices. The right side of the figure presents the relationships for presidential vote in the United States and France.

Each of the three factors is significantly related to legislative voting preferences in each example, but perhaps the most interesting feature is the relative pattern across nations and election types. The effect of candidate image—in this case, feelings toward George W. Bush and John Kerry—were strong in the American survey, even though we were predicting congressional voting preferences in 2004.[8] Although British elections are held to select members of Parliament, images of Tony Blair and William Hague (the respective Labour and Conservative party leaders) were also strongly related to voter choice in the 2001 election—although part of this relationship reflects the fact that the candidates mediate the effects of issues preferences (Clarke et al. 2004, ch. 4). Similarly, images of Schröder and Stoiber were strongly related to citizen choices in the 2002 Bundestag elections. Although it is difficult to estimate exactly the impact of candidate images on voter choice, the available evidence generally suggests that candidate images are an important basis of electoral choice in contemporary elections (Aarts, Blais, and Schmitt 2005; Ohr 2000; Wattenberg 1991).

Moreover, candidate images are even more important in presidential elections, where people are directly voting for the candidate, rather than a party group. Thus, the identical candidate variable has a .52 impact on congressional voting preferences in the United States but a .78 relationship with presidential vote choice. Similarly, the images of party leaders are more strongly

FIGURE 10.4 The Influence of Issues and Candidate Images on Vote

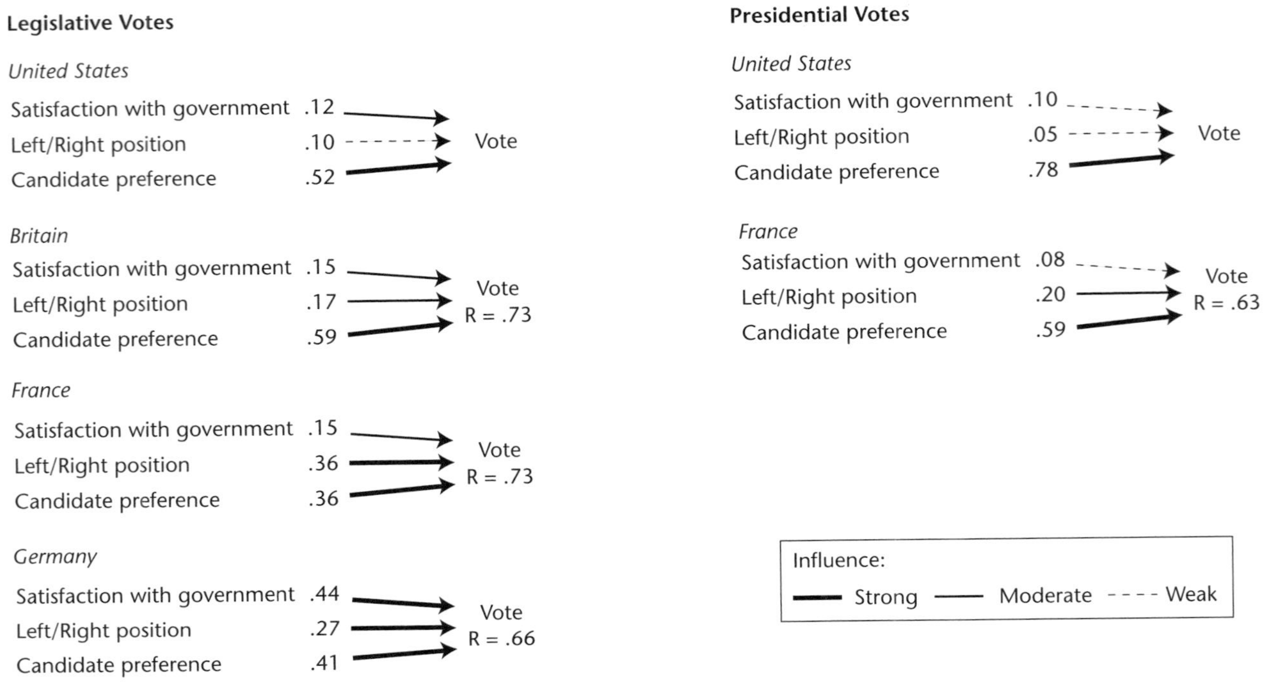

Legislative Votes

United States

Satisfaction with government .12
Left/Right position .10
Candidate preference .52
→ Vote

Britain

Satisfaction with government .15
Left/Right position .17
Candidate preference .59
→ Vote
R = .73

France

Satisfaction with government .15
Left/Right position .36
Candidate preference .36
→ Vote
R = .73

Germany

Satisfaction with government .44
Left/Right position .27
Candidate preference .41
→ Vote
R = .66

Presidential Votes

United States

Satisfaction with government .10
Left/Right position .05
Candidate preference .78
→ Vote

France

Satisfaction with government .08
Left/Right position .20
Candidate preference .59
→ Vote
R = .63

Influence:
—— Strong —— Moderate - - - Weak

SOURCES: United States, 2004 American National Election Study (CSES); Britain, 2001 British Election Study; France, 2002 French Election Study (CSES); Germany, 2002 German Election Study (CSES).

tied to vote choice in the French presidential elections than in National Assembly elections. In candidate-centered elections, candidate images are inevitably more important.

Issues—represented here by Left/Right attitudes and perceptions of the government's performance—generally carry more weight in European parliamentary elections, as is seen in the patterns for Great Britain and Germany. Since European parties offer clearer party choices than American parties do, and Europeans vote for a party more so than for a candidate, it is not surprising that the policy images of the parties are a stronger basis of voting in European elections. The specific mix of issue and candidate influences will be highly variable across elections because these are short-term elements of the vote, but these trans-Atlantic differences reflect institutional structures that are likely to endure over time.[9] Thus it is striking that in neither U.S. congressional nor presidential elections do liberal/conservative orientations have a strong relationship to vote independent of candidate image.

CITIZEN POLITICS AND VOTING BEHAVIOR

The past several chapters have described changes in the patterns of voting behavior in advanced industrial democracies. One major change is a general decline in the long-term determinants of voting choice. The influence of social class on voting preferences has decreased in virtually all Western democracies, as has the impact of religion, residence, and other social characteristics (see chapter 8). Similarly, dealignment has decreased the effect of party attachments on voting decisions; fewer voters now approach elections with standing party predispositions based either on social characteristics or early-learned partisan ties (chapter 9).

As the long-term determinants of party choice have decreased in influence, there has been a counterbalancing growth in the importance of short-term attitudes, such as issue opinions and candidate images (see Miller and Borrelli 1992; Franklin 1985; Rose and McAllister 1986). The most persuasive cross-national evidence comes from a study of voting behavior in seventeen Western democracies. In reviewing their findings, Mark Franklin, Tom Mackie, and Henry Valen (1992, 400) conclude: "if all the issues of importance to voters had been measured and given their due weight, then the rise of issue voting would have compensated more or less precisely for the decline in cleavage politics."

This trend toward greater issue voting and candidate voting in most advanced industrial democracies is a self-reinforcing process. Issue voting contributes to, and benefits from, the decline in partisanship-based voting. As party ties weaken, the potential increases for issue opinions to influence voting choice. In addition, as policy preferences become more important to the voter, this influence encourages some party defection and erodes the voter's party attachments still further.[10] Thus, the rise of issue voting and the decline of partisanship are interrelated trends.

This shifting balance of long-term and short-term voting influences represents another aspect of the new style of citizen politics. As modern electorates have become more sophisticated and politically interested, and as the availability of political information has expanded, many citizens can now reach their own voting decisions without relying on broad external cues such as social class or family partisanship. In short, more citizens now have the political resources to follow the complexities of politics; they have the potential to act as the independent issue voters described in classic democratic theory but seldom seen in practice.

Additional evidence in support of this interpretation comes from the work on cognitive sophistication by Paul Sniderman, Richard Brody, and Philip Tetlock (1991). These researchers find that better-educated and politically sophisticated voters place more weight on issues as a basis for their electoral decision making; less sophisticated voters rely more on partisanship and social cues. These findings conform to evidence from chapter 9 that locates sophisticated apartisans within the better-educated group, especially youth (also Dalton 2000a). Taking these two developments together, social change is shifting the basis of electoral choice by transforming the skills and resources of contemporary electorates.

We can illustrate the changing styles of citizen voting behavior by examining the changing impact of economics on the vote. Traditionally, economic conflicts were structured by social divisions: the working class versus the middle class, industrial versus agrarian interests. In this situation, one's social position was often a meaningful guide to voting decisions. As social divisions have narrowed and the group bases of political interests have blurred, however, social class has decreased as a source of voting cues. This does not mean that economic issues are unimportant-quite the opposite: contemporary evidence of economic voting is widespread, but now issue positions are individually based rather than group-derived. The political cues of a union leader or business association must compete with the voter's own opinions on economic policy and party programs. That a continuing concern for economic growth and security has not revived traditional class divisions provides compelling evidence that a new style of citizen politics now affects voting patterns.

This new style of individually based voting decisions may signify a boon or a curse for contemporary democracies. On the positive side, sophisticated voters should inject more issue voting into elections, increasing the policy implications of electoral results. In the long term, greater issue voting may make candidates and parties more responsive to public opinion. Thus, the democratic process may move closer to the democratic ideal.

On the negative side, many political scientists have expressed concerns that the growth of issue voting and single-issue groups may place excessive demands on contemporary democracies (see chapter 12). Without the issue-aggregating functions performed by party leaders and electoral coalitions, democratic governments may face conflicting issue demands from their voters. Governments may find it increasingly difficult to satisfy unrestrained popular demands.

Another concern involves the citizens who lack the political skills to meet the requirements of sophisticated issue voting. These people may become atomized voters if traditional political cues (party and social groups) decline in usefulness. Lacking firm political predispositions or a clear understanding of politics, these individuals may be easily mobilized by dynamic elites or fraudulent party programs. Many political analysts see the rise of New Right parties in Europe, especially those headed by charismatic party leaders, as a negative consequence of a dealigned electorate. Indeed, television facilitates unmediated one-on-one contacts between political elites and voters. Despite its potential for encouraging more sophisticated citizen involvement, this medium also offers the possibility of trivialized electoral politics in which video style outweighs substance in campaigning.

In summary, the trends discussed here do not lend themselves to a single prediction of the future of democratic party systems. But the future is within our control, depending on how political systems respond to these new challenges. The new style of citizen politics will be characterized by a greater diversity of voting patterns. A system of frozen social cleavages and stable party alignments is less likely in advanced industrial societies where voters are sophisticated, power is decentralized, and individual choice finds greater latitude. The diversity and individualism of the new style of citizen politics are major departures from the structured partisan politics of the past.

SUGGESTED READINGS

Aarts, Kees, André Blais, and Hermann Schmitt, eds. *Political Leaders and Democratic Elections.* Oxford: Oxford University Press, 2005.

Anderson, Christopher. *Blaming the Government: Citizens and the Economy in Five European Democracies.* Armonk, N.Y.: M.E. Sharpe, 1995.

Anderson, Christopher, and Carsten Zelle, eds. *Stability and Change in German Elections: How Electorates Merge, Converge, or Collide.* Westport, Conn.: Praeger, 1998.

Klingemann, Hans-Dieter, ed. *The Comparative Study of Electoral Systems.* Oxford: Oxford University Press, 2005.

LeDuc, Lawrence, Richard Niemi, and Pippa Norris, eds. *Comparing Democracies: New Challenges in the Study of Elections and Voting.* 2nd ed. Thousand Oaks, Calif.: Sage, 2002.

Miller, Warren, and J. Merrill Shanks. *The New American Voter.* Cambridge, Mass.: Harvard University Press, 1996.

Niemi, Richard, and Herbert Weisberg, eds. *Controversies in Voting.* 4th ed. Washington, D.C.: CQ Press, 2001.

Wattenberg, Martin. *The Rise of Candidate-centered Politics.* Cambridge, Mass.: Harvard University Press, 1991.

NOTES

1. I want to acknowledge my collaboration with Martin Wattenberg (Dalton and Wattenberg 1993, 2000), which helped to develop my thinking on many of these issues.

2. For example, Ted Carmines and James Stimson (1980) make a distinction between "hard" issues, which are complex and difficult to evaluate, and "easy" issues, which present clear and simple choices. Donald Kinder and Rod Kiewiet (1981) stress the distinction between narrow personal issues, such as voting on the basis of economic self-interest, and issues that reflect national policy choices, such as voting on the basis of what will benefit most Americans.

3. Bernard Berelson, Paul Lazarsfeld, and William McPhee (1954) described these as style issues; Donald Stokes (1963) used the term "valence issue." Later research made the further distinction between performance and attributes that we present here (Miller and Wattenberg 1985; Shanks and Miller 1990).

4. Anthony Downs conceived of Left/Right labels as a way to reduce information costs, rather than as fully-informed ideological orientations. As he explained, "With this short cut a voter can save himself the cost of being informed upon a wide range of issues" (1957, 98).

5. Americans who voted for the Democratic congressional candidate locate themselves at 4.9 on the Left/Right scale, much more toward the center than the average placement of the Democratic Party (4.1). Conversely, voters for the Republican presidential candidate were just as conservative (6.7) as the overall public's placement of the Republican Party (6.7).

6. The Labour Party pursued a conscious effort to moderate its leftist image in 1997 and even more so in 2001 (Clarke et al. 2004; Evans and Norris 1999, chs. 1 and 2). Moving closer to the voters was a key factor in propelling Labour to victory in 1997.

7. The relationship is described by a Cramer's V correlation statistic: a value of .00 means that issue opinions are unrelated to party preference. A Cramer's V of .20 is normally interpreted as a moderately strong relationship, and .30 is considered a strong relationship.

8. We measured affect toward Bush and Kerry in the United States, and toward Blair and Hague in Britain. For Schröder and Stoiber in Germany, we combined two questions on trust and competence. The French models used Chirac and Lionel Jospin as the major rival party leaders in the legislative elections, and Chirac and Jean-Marie LePen as the candidates in predicting the 2002 presidential runoff in which they were the two candidates. The government performance question asked about how good a job the government had done since the last election.

9. One productive new area of research examines how institutional context systematically affects the correlates of voting. For instance, candidate effects are predictably stronger in candidate-based systems than in party-based proportional representation. In addition, the ability of the electorate to identify party responsibility also affects the potential for issue voting. See, for example, Powell (2000); Anderson (2000); Miller and Niemi (2002); Whitten and Palmer (1999).

10. The conventional wisdom holds that partisanship is often a strong influence on issue opinions, while the reverse causal flow is minimal (figure 9.1). As issue voting has increased, however, researchers have found that issues can remold basic party attachments. Recent studies show that the causal influence of issues in changing partisanship can be quite large (Niemi and Jennings 1991; Fiorina 1981).

CHAPTER 11

Political Representation

Contemporary democracies owe their existence to a relatively modern invention: representative government. From the ancient Greeks up through the time of Jean-Jacques Rousseau, democracy was equated with the direct participation of the citizenry in the affairs of government. Political theorists believed that democracies must limit either the definition of citizenship or the size of the polity so that the entire public could assemble in a single body to make political decisions. The Greek city-state, the self-governing Swiss canton, and the New England town meeting exemplify this democratic ideal.

The invention of representative government freed democracies from these constraints. Instead of directly participating in political decision making, the public would select legislators to represent them in government deliberations. The functioning of the democratic process would depend on the relationship between the representative and the represented.

The case for representative government is largely one of necessity. Democracy requires citizen control over the political process, but in a large nation-state, the town-meeting model is no longer feasible.[1] Proponents of representative government also stress the limited political skills of the average citizen and the need for professional politicians. Citizen control over government is routinized through periodic, competitive elections to select these elites. Elections should ensure that elites remain responsive and accountable to the public. By accepting this electoral process, the public gives its consent to be governed by the elites selected.

Many early democratic theorists criticized the concept of representative government because they felt that it undermined the very tenets of democracy by transferring political power from the people to a small group of designated officials. Voters had political power only on the day their ballots were cast, and then had to wait in political servitude until the next election—four or five years hence—for the next opportunity to exercise that power. Under representative government, citizens may control, but elites rule. Rousseau warned "the instant a people allows itself to be represented it loses its freedom."

Recent proponents of direct democracy are equally critical of representative government. European green parties, for example, criticize the structure of representative government while calling for increased citizen influence through referendums, citizen-action groups, and other forms of "basic" democracy. Populist groups in the United States display a similar skepticism of electoral politics in favor of direct action. Benjamin Barber (1984, 145) articulated these concerns:

Internet Resource

Visit the Eurobarometer web site of the European Union for information on the latest citizen and elite surveys:

http://europa.eu.int/comm/dg10/epo/

> The representative government principle steals from individuals the ultimate responsibility for their values, beliefs, and actions. . . . Representation is incompatible with freedom because it delegates and thus alienates political will at the cost of genuine self-government and autonomy.

These critics worry that the democratic principle of popular control of the government has been replaced by a commitment to routinized electoral procedures—that democracy is defined by its means, not its ends. Thus, other opportunities for increasing public influence and control are not developed because elections provide the accepted standard of citizen influence. These critics are not intrinsically opposed to representative government, but they are critical of a political system that stops at representation and limits or excludes other (and perhaps more effective) methods of citizen influence.

The linkage between the public and the political decision makers is one of the essential questions for the study of democratic political systems. The commitment to popular rule is what sets democracies apart from other political systems. While we cannot resolve the debate on the merits of representative government, this chapter asks how well the representation process functions in Western democracies today.

COLLECTIVE CORRESPONDENCE

In the broadest sense of the term, the representativeness of elite attitudes is measured by their similarity to the overall attitudes of the public. Robert Weissberg (1978) referred to this comparison as *collective correspondence*: when the distribution of public preferences is matched by the distribution of elite views, the citizenry as a collective is well represented by elites as a collective.

The complexity of the representation process obviously goes beyond a definition based simply on citizen/elite agreement. Some political elites may stress their role in educating the public instead of merely reflecting current public preferences. In other instances, when voters hold contradictory opinions, the policymaking role of elites may lead them to adopt more consistent, but less representative, positions. Policy preferences also are not necessarily equivalent to policy outcomes. We could add other qualifiers to this list. Still, citizen-elite agreement is the normal standard for judging the representativeness of a democratic system. This is a meaningful test of representation because it determines whether political decision makers approach the policymaking process with the same policy preferences as the public. It is a basic goal of representative democracy.

Cross-national data comparing the beliefs of top-level political elites and the public are extremely rare. More common are studies that focus on public/elite comparisons in a single nation.[2] Thus, this chapter assembles a diverse mix of evidence comparing elite and public opinion within and across nations.

We begin with evidence from the United States. Table 11.1 compares the American public to members of the U.S. Congress in 1987 and 1998.[3] In 1987 the American public was more conservative than these elites on the issue of minority aid (-.83), for example, but more liberal than elites on the government providing needed services (+.57) (Herrera, Herrera, and Smith 1992). On overall liberal/conservative positions, the match between the public and elites was quite close, which is appropriate because this measure summarizes political positions on many policy matters. And as we note in other nations, members of Congress were slightly more liberal than the public overall in 1986–1987.

TABLE 11.1 The Distribution of Opinions for the American Public and Elites

	Citizens	Members of Congress	Difference
1986–1987			
Liberal/conservative position	4.26	4.05	–.21
Government provide services	3.57	4.14	.57*
Government guarantee living standard	4.47	4.01	–.46*
Government should aid minorities	4.17	3.34	–.83*
Spend more on defense	3.82	3.58	–.24
Cooperate more with Russia	4.35	3.58	–.77*
Intervene in Central America	3.31	2.98	.33
Attitudes toward abortion	2.13	1.69	–.44*
1998 (percentages)			
Maintain government programs	57	45	
Liberal/conservative position			
Conservative	37	47	
Moderate	40	31	
Liberal	19	7	

SOURCES: for top panel, 1987 House of Representatives Survey (Herrera, Herrera, and Smith 1992) and 1986 ANES; for bottom panel, 1998 Pew Center Survey of Members of Congress, Clinton Appointees, and Senior Civil Servants, done in association with *National Journal* (Pew Center 1998b).

NOTE: Entries in top panel are mean scores on a 7-point scale, with 1 = the liberal position; the abortion item is measured on a 4-point scale; differences marked by an asterisk are significant at .01 level. Entries in bottom panel are percentages agreeing with policy statement and self-identifying on a liberal/conservative scale.

In 1998 the Pew Center (1998b) surveyed members of Congress, but this study only included a few items that were comparable to questions in public opinion surveys. Only 45 percent of members of Congress said that federal government programs should be maintained to deal with important problems, but 57 percent of the American public supported this position—a finding similar to the gap reported in the earlier survey. On the standard liberal/conservative scale, Congress now had more self-identified conservatives than the public at large, and fewer liberals, but the percentage differences were modest on each response. These findings suggest that the balance of elite opinions had shifted away from the liberal tendencies of the 1986–1988 Democratic Congress, which is what might be expected, given the Republican majority in the 1996–1998 Congress.

While the public and elites differed somewhat in their policy views, there was not a large and systematic bias in the direction of these differences. In addition, previous comparisons of public opinion and opinions of members of Congress in 1978 and 1982 found that the two groups differed by only a few percentage points (Bishop and Frankovic 1981; Erikson and Tedin 2001, 267). Thus, the fit between the American public and congressional elites generally shows a high level of congruence.

Cross-national studies of mass and elite opinions in Europe are quite rare. Therefore, our comparative analyses must rely on an early study of European voters and candidates to the European Parliament (EP) (Dalton 1985). Where possible, we update these results with findings from more recent studies. Table 11.2 presents the distribution of citizen and elite opinions in Great Britain, Germany, and France. The broadest measure of political orientations is the Left/Right self-placement scale discussed in chapter 6. The first row in the table shows that EP elites in each nation are significantly more likely than the public to identify themselves as leftists. This liberal tendency among political elites is a common finding; a survey of voters and EP candidates in the 1994 election found a similar pattern (Thomassen and Schmitt 1997). Political elites often consider themselves to be more progressive than their constituencies.

Collective correspondence on specific issues varies across these three nations. The British elites were more liberal than the public on most issues. This elite bias was strongest for foreign aid and security issues, probably because these elites were candidates for the European Parliament. Abortion policy was the only area where the British public was much more liberal than the elites.

More recent data collected by the 1992 British Candidates Survey and the 1997 British Representation Study (Norris 1999d) show that the average British citizen and member of the British Parliament position themselves at virtually the same position on the Left/Right scale. On traditional economic issues—taxes versus services, privatization, and jobs versus prices—the MPs are slightly to the right of the British public. On the two noneconomic issues of European integration and the role of women, the MPs are to the left of the public.

TABLE 11.2 The Distribution of Opinions for the European Public and Elites (in percentages)

	Great Britain		West Germany		France	
	Public	Elites	Public	Elites	Public	Elites
Leftist self-placement	42	46	42	57	47	68
Old Politics						
Public ownership of industry	30	35	34	27	41	48
Government manages economy	44	38	45	32	56	44
Codetermination	52	54	69	60	73	52
Control multinationals	50	66	66	75	72	86
Reduce income inequality	65	64	76	88	93	93
Liberalize abortion	77	58	75	65	77	74
Foreign aid						
Aid EC regions	45	90	47	98	71	90
Aid Third World	35	85	40	93	52	82
Security						
Strengthen defense	18	25	30	22	34	32
Action against terrorists	5	29	12	30	8	15
New Politics						
Nuclear energy	21	23	34	19	34	15
Protest environment	94	92	88	97	94	92
Free expression	72	78	76	79	74	86
Average liberal issue response	46	57	53	60	60	62

SOURCE: 1979 Eurocandidate Survey, Eurobarometer 11; both studies have been weighted to produce representative national samples.

NOTE: Table entries are the percentages of respondents expressing a liberal opinion on each item.

Table 11.2 suggests that in 1979 the West German public was slightly more liberal than political elites on the Old Politics issue conflicts of economics and abortion. Conversely, elites were significantly more liberal on foreign aid, dealing with terrorists, and the free-speech issue. Recent German citizen/elite studies find similar patterns of agreement. When Bernhard Wessels (1993) compared the issue opinions of Bundestag deputies and the German public, he found close agreement on Old Politics issues such as economic growth and public order, and somewhat lower levels of agreement on New Politics goals (also see Herzog and Wessels 1990, ch. 3; Hoffmann-Lange 1992).

The closest overall match between citizen and EP elite opinions occurs in these French data. French citizens and elites generally favored liberal policies on Old Politics issues, and there were no consistent differences between political strata on these issues. The pattern on New Politics and security issues was equally mixed. Only on foreign aid issues were EP elites clearly more liberal than the French public (also see Converse and Pierce 1986, 597).

In summary, if we judge collective correspondence by substantive criteria—for example, a 10 percent difference or less in issue opinions—then citizen/elite agreement is fairly common.[4] Most economic, security, and New Politics issues fall within the 10 percent range for the British, German, and French comparisons to the European Parliament elites. Only foreign policy issues display sizable opinion differences between citizens and EP candidates. The samples of German and French elites appear most representative of their respective publics. Overall, an average of 53 percent of the German public gave liberal responses on the thirteen issue questions, compared to 60 percent of elites. The match of citizen and elite opinions is even closer in France (60 percent versus 62 percent). The voter/elite gap is harder to compare in the United States because 7-point scales were used, but there appears to be a mix of agreement and disagreement in mass/elite comparisons.

DYADIC CORRESPONDENCE

Collective correspondence between the issue opinions of the public and the political elites does not occur as a collective process. Some degree of popular control is necessary to ensure the responsiveness of elites. Citizen/elite agreement without popular control is representation by chance, not democracy. One method of popular control makes political elites electorally dependent on a specific constituency. Weissberg (1978) defined the pairing of constituency opinion and elites as *dyadic correspondence*—in simple terms, liberal constituencies presumably select liberal representatives and conservative constituencies select conservative representatives.

In studying the connection between citizens and elites, researchers initially treated the individual legislator as the primary means of dyadic linkage. One explanation for this approach lies in the historical development of political theory on representation. Edmund Burke's classic "Speech to the Electors of Bristol" in 1774 defined a paradigm of representation that still influences modern political science. Traditionally, a *delegate* model defined the legislator's role in a deterministic fashion. Representative government required that delegates be sent to Parliament and that voters instruct the delegate on constituency preferences; the legislator was obliged to follow the constituency's mandate. Burke proposed a more independent *trustee* role for legislators, arguing that, once elected, legislators should be allowed to follow their own beliefs about what they thought was best for their constituency and the nation.

This theoretical emphasis on the individual legislator was reinforced by the development of modern empirical research on political representation, which, especially from the American perspective, treated the legislator as the basis of political linkage (Miller and Stokes 1963). In part, this focus reflected the weakness of American parties and the open structure of the American political process, in which many legislators can, and do, act as individual entrepreneurs. Research concentrated on whether individual legislators followed the delegate or trustee model in representing their constituencies (Kuklinski 1978).

Warren Miller and Donald Stokes (1963) conducted the seminal study of political representation in America to incorporate these theoretical models of representation. Having designed a complex study of the relationship between public opinion and elite actions, they interviewed a small sample of the public in each of 116 congressional districts across the nation after the 1958 congressional elections, as well as members of the House of Representatives from these same districts. Finally, they assembled the voting records of the members of Congress for the next legislative session.

Miller and Stokes (1963) used this information to build a model of the representation process (figure 11.1). Broadly speaking, these researchers envisioned two pathways by which a constituency could influence the voting behavior of its representative. One pathway defined the trustee model of representation: the constituency can select a legislator who shares its views (path *a*), so that in following his or her own convictions (path *b*) the legislator represents the constituency's will. In this case, the constituency's opinion and the legislator's actions are connected through the legislator's own policy attitudes. A second pathway traces the delegate model:. A legislator turns to citizens in his or her district for cues on their policy preferences (path *c*), and then follows these cues in making voting choices (path *d*). In this case, the legislator's perception of constituency attitudes provides the linkage between actual constituency opinion and the legislator's voting behavior.

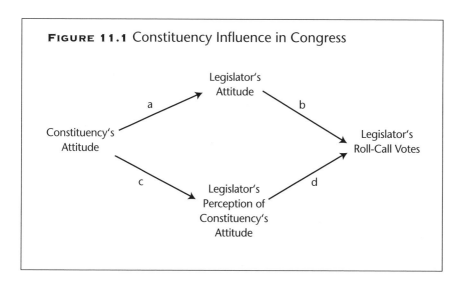

FIGURE 11.1 Constituency Influence in Congress

They applied the model to three policy areas: civil rights, social welfare, and foreign policy. Miller and Stokes found a strong relationship between constituency opinion and the legislator's voting record for civil rights and social welfare issues, and a weaker connection for foreign policy. In addition, the path of constituency influence varied between policy domains. Civil rights issues primarily functioned by a delegate model; the delegate path was at least twice as important as the trustee path. For social welfare issues, the trustee path through the legislator's own attitude was the most important means of constituency influence.

This study provided hard empirical evidence of the representation process at work. Moreover, the process seemed to work fairly well: most liberal constituencies were represented by liberal legislators, and most conservative constituencies chose conservative representatives. Although there have been many critics of the methodology of this study, its essential conclusions are still supported by most political scientists (for further discussion, see Erikson and Tedin 2001, ch. 10; Warren Miller et al. 1999).

Cheryl Lyn Herrera, Richard Herrera, and Eric Smith (1992) partially replicated the Miller and Stokes analyses with data from the 1986–1988 Congress. They compared the opinions of members of Congress from thirty-three districts to the opinions of their constituents who had been surveyed as part of the 1986 American National Election Study. Employing a variety of statistical measures, these researchers found that the fit between constituencies and their representatives is fairly high on most issues, especially issues that are likely to have large issue publics and polarized public opinion, such as abortion, minority aid, and government services. Moreover, they concluded that "dyadic representation is better today than was true 30 years ago" (p. 201), implying that the democratic process in the United States was working even better than during the Miller and Stokes study in the late 1950s.

Another example of dyadic congruence comes from a study by Stephen Ansolabehere, James Snyder, and Charles Stewart (2001a, 2001b), who examined path a in figure 11.1: the link between citizen attitudes and the attitudes of elected legislators. They measured the positions of congressional candidates from surveys conducted by the Vote Smart project in the mid-1990s, and then compared these data to measures of district opinions and the roll-call votes of the elected representatives in the following Congress. Figure 11.2 depicts the relationship between the liberal/conservative values of each congressional district and a summary measure of liberal/conservative values of the representative elected from the district.[5] There is a very strong congruence between district and representative opinions (r = .78), as one would expect if the democratic process is functioning. Moreover, when these researchers examined the next step in the representation process—path b in figure 11.1—there was an equally strong link between the representatives' attitudes and their overall voting pattern (r =.88 for Republicans and .85 for Democrats).[6] Elections thus provide a mechanism for voters to select candidates who broadly share their political values, and who then take these orientations to Washington.

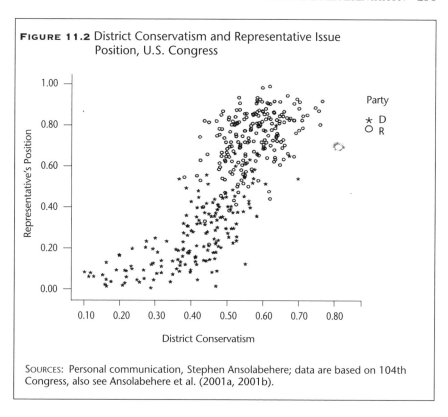

Figure 11.2 District Conservatism and Representative Issue Position, U.S. Congress

Sources: Personal communication, Stephen Ansolabehere; data are based on 104th Congress, also see Ansolabehere et al. (2001a, 2001b).

The Miller and Stokes model also was extended to representation studies in nearly a dozen other Western democracies (Holmberg 1989; Barnes 1977; Farah 1980; Converse and Pierce 1986; Higley et al. 1979). However, these studies typically found little evidence of policy agreement between constituencies and their legislators. For instance, Samuel Barnes found virtually no correspondence between the issue opinions of Italian deputies and public opinion in their respective districts (the average correlation across eight issues was .04). Barbara Farah documented a similar lack of correspondence between district opinions and the policy views of district-elected deputies in the German Bundestag (the average correlation across six issues was -.03). The French representation study also found a weak linkage between district and legislator opinions on specific policy issues (Converse and Pierce 1986, ch. 22).[7] It appeared that political representation did not occur in these European democracies—or that it worked through other means.

THE PARTY GOVERNMENT MODEL

Research on political representation in non-American political systems gradually deemphasized a theoretical model based on individual legislators and focused instead on the actions of political parties as collectives. This model of representation through parties—"responsible party government"—is built upon several principles:

- Elections should provide competition between two or more parties contending for political power.
- Parties must offer distinct policy options so voters have meaningful electoral choices.
- Voters should recognize these policy differences among the parties.
- At the least, voters should be sufficiently informed to award or punish the incumbent parties based on their performance.

National elections therefore serve as evaluations of the political parties and their activities, and representation occurs through parties rather than individual candidates.

This party government model also appeared more relevant to the study of parliamentary systems with strong political parties. In most European systems, candidates are selected by party elites rather than through open primaries, so they are first and foremost party representatives. The responsible party government model presumes that members of a party's parliamentary delegation will act in unison. Parties vote as a bloc in parliament, although there may be internal debate before the party position is decided. Parties exercise control over the government and the policymaking process through party control of the national legislature. In sum, the choice of parties provides the electorate with indirect control over the actions of individual legislators and the affairs of government.

While the representation process may be based on individual legislators in the United States, political representation in Europe largely follows the party government model. In comparison to the United States, the multiparty systems of most European democracies offer the voters greater diversity in party programs, which gives more meaning to party labels (see chapter 7). Most democracies are parliamentary systems, where unified legislative parties play a crucial role in determining control of the executive branch. The available evidence shows that party cohesion in European legislatures is considerably higher than in the American Congress (Bowler 2000; Thomassen 1994, 246). When a party votes as a united bloc, it makes little sense to discuss the voting patterns of individual legislators. Furthermore, public recognition of which party controls the government is more widespread in Western Europe than in the United States, probably as a result of the European parliamentary form of government. Giovanni Sartori (1968, 471) maintains that "citizens in Western democracies are represented *through* and *by* parties. This is inevitable" (italics in original).

The party government model thus directs the voters' attention to parties as political representatives, rather than to individual deputies (Warren Miller et al. 1999). Indeed, many Europeans (including Germans) vote directly for party lists. Dyadic correspondence is based more on a voter/party model than a district/legislator model. The voter half of the dyad is composed of all party supporters in a nation (even if there are geographic electoral districts); the elite half is composed of party officials as a collective. If the party government model holds, we should expect a close match between the policy views of voters and party elites taken as collectives.

We should stress one other point in considering dyadic correspondence. We occasionally speak in causal terms—voter opinions presumably influence party positions—but the causal flow works in both directions. Voters influence parties, as parties try to persuade voters. This is why researchers have adopted the causally neutral term *correspondence*. The essence of the democratic marketplace is that like-minded voters and parties search out each other and ally forces. Even if one cannot determine the direction of causal flow, the similarity of opinions between voters and party elites is a meaningful measure of the representativeness of parties.

Some of the best evidence of the correspondence between voters and their parties comes from the 1994 European Parliament Election Study. This study interviewed parliamentary candidates from political parties spread across Europe, as well as the voters for these same parties. Figure 11.3 compares the Left/Right

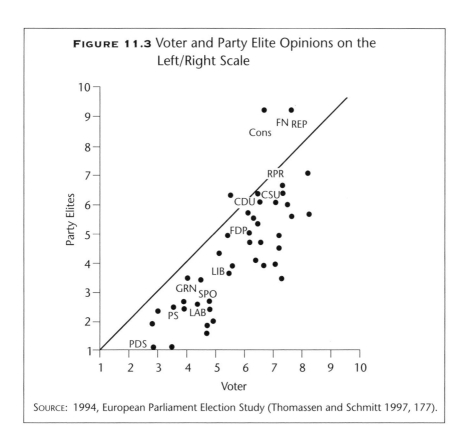

FIGURE 11.3 Voter and Party Elite Opinions on the Left/Right Scale

SOURCE: 1994, European Parliament Election Study (Thomassen and Schmitt 1997, 177).

self-placement of voters and elites in each party. The horizontal axis in the figure plots the average position of a party's supporters; the vertical axis plots the average opinion of the party's elites. These two coordinates define a party's location in the figure. The 45-degree line represents perfect intraparty agreement: when the opinions of party elites exactly match those of their supporters.

Two important patterns can be gleaned from this figure. First, there is a strong relationship between voter and elite opinions within parties ($r = .83$). Voters with leftist preferences and elites who share these views come together in the traditional leftist parties, such as the German SPD, the British Labour Party, and the French Socialists; and there is a similar congruence on the right. This pattern provides the evidence of party differences that underlie the party government model of representation. Second, there is a systematic tendency for party elites to say they are more leftist than their own voters (since most parties lie below the diagonal line).

Unfortunately, the 1994 EP Election Study contained very few issues, so in order to examine more detailed patterns of issue agreement, we turn to other data sources. In chapter 7 we used expert judgments to plot the party positions on an Old Politics / New Politics cleavage dimension. To measure voter opinions, we found comparable issue questions in the International Social Survey Program for both dimensions. Then we compared the opinions of party voters to the experts' judgment of political parties in a diverse set of nations available from the ISSP study.

Figure 11.4 displays party patterns on the Old Politics issue of cutting taxes versus support for the social services (see figure 7.2). We have voter and party positions for twenty-five party dyads, which demonstrate a strong correspondence on this dimension. The socialist and communist parties tend toward the lower-left quadrant; and their voters also hold liberal opinions on this issue. For example, the voters for the French Communist Party and the party itself are positioned at the bottom left corner of the figure; the UDF is located at the opposite corner of this continuum. The correlation between voters and parties is quite high ($r = . 65$). Because economic and religious issues are so important in structuring political conflict, research generally suggests that congruence on these issues remains high (Dalton 1985; Laver and Hunt 1992; Warren Miller et al. 1999).

Attitudes toward the environment exemplify a New Politics issue. We begin with a question on whether economic growth always harms the environment. Then we compare these voter opinions to the expert judgments of party positions on this dimension (see figure 7.2). Figure 11.5 shows a basic correspondence between party voters and party elites on this issue: a voter bloc concerned about development harming the environment is represented by party elites who generally share this concern. However, the relationship is substantially weaker here ($r = .217$) than on the Old Politics cleavage.

The pattern of party alignment on the environmental issue is also significant. There are modest differences in experts' positioning of the major established Left and Right parties on the environmental issue. We saw in chapter 7

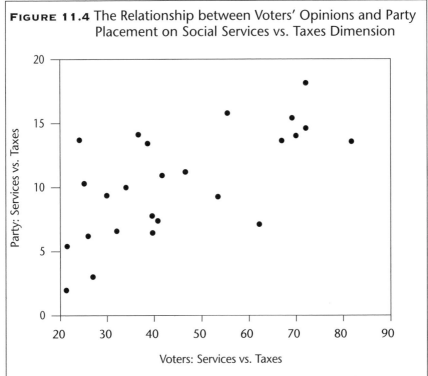

FIGURE 11.4 The Relationship between Voters' Opinions and Party Placement on Social Services vs. Taxes Dimension

SOURCES: The 25 dyads represent party voters from the International Social Survey (voter groups from Australia, Canada, Spain, France, Ireland, New Zealand, and the United States) and party positions from Laver and Hunt (1992).

that the major leftist parties—the German SPD, British Labour, and the French PS—all hold centrist positions on this issue, not much different from the positions of their conservative party rivals. In fact, the voters of the Italian Communist Party and the Italian Christian Democrats hold almost identical opinions, largely because their party attachments are based on criteria other than environmental policy. Party alignments on the environment (and other New Politics issues) still tend to cut across the traditional Left/Right party lines defined by Old Politics issues.

Previous research also suggests that elite polarization along a policy dimensions tends to be greater than the amount of polarization among voter blocs. Evidence of this pattern comes from voter/elite comparisons in the United States. Figure 11.6 presents the differences between Democratic voters in 1986 and Democratic members of Congress and between Republican voters and Republican members of Congress. Democratic and Republican voters displayed only modest differences on many of their issue opinions, but party elites accentuated these differences. For example, on six of the

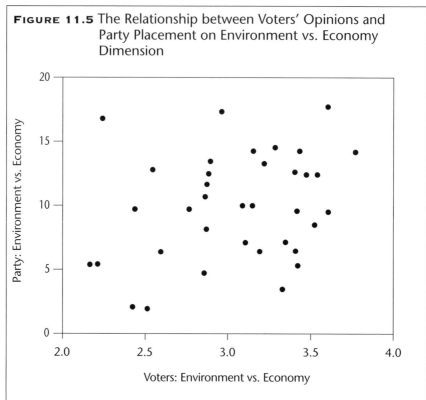

FIGURE 11.5 The Relationship between Voters' Opinions and Party Placement on Environment vs. Economy Dimension

SOURCES: The 30 dyads represent party voters from the 1993 International Social Survey (voter groups from Canada, Spain, Italy, Ireland, New Zealand, the United States, Great Britain, Germany, Japan, and Norway) and party positions from Laver and Hunt (1992).

seven issues in the figure, Democratic elites are more liberal than their voters, while Republican elites are more conservative than their voters on six issues as well. In other words, party elites tended to *overrepresent* the opinions of their constituencies by maintaining more extreme issue positions. Warren Miller (1987, ch. 3) found similar patterns when he compared the American public to delegates to national party conventions in 1980 and 1984; and the same pattern appears in comparing voter/elite dyads in Europe (Dalton 1985). This general tendency explains the greater clarity of party positions at the elite level and the greater intensity of party conflict among elites.

Just as important as the overall level of dyadic correspondence are the factors affecting voter/party agreement. Some parties consistently achieve a close match between the opinions of voters and party elites, while other parties display less correspondence. These variations in party representation determine the efficiency of the party-linkage process.

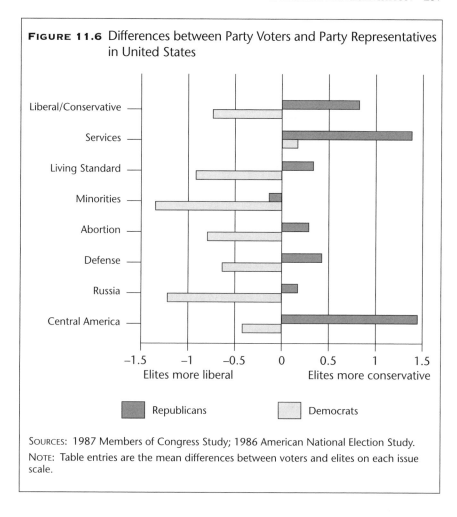

FIGURE 11.6 Differences between Party Voters and Party Representatives in United States

SOURCES: 1987 Members of Congress Study; 1986 American National Election Study.

NOTE: Table entries are the mean differences between voters and elites on each issue scale.

A study of voter/party agreement for forty party groups across nine nations found that the clarity of party positions is an important influence on the representation process (Dalton 1985). Characteristics that clarify party positions make it easier for voters to select a party compatible with their issue beliefs. Centrally organized parties display a strong and consistent tendency to be more representative of their supporters. Centralized parties may be less open to innovation and less inclined toward internal democracy, as critics suggest, but they display greater dyadic correspondence. In addition, voter/party agreement is higher among ideological parties (of either the Left or Right). Apparently these characteristics clarify party positions and make it easier for voters to select a party consistent with their issue beliefs. A centralized party is more likely to project clear party cues, and an ideological image helps voters identify a party's general political orientation.

At the system level, Bernhard Wessels (1999) examined the relationship between institutional structures and voter/party correspondence across several nations. Majoritarian systems, such as the United States and Great Britain, place a greater emphasis on elites representing the modal voter in society, which normally pulls elites toward the center of the political spectrum. In proportional representation systems, in contrast, elites are more closely tied to representing their party's voters. This partisan focus is facilitated by the greater degree of party choice in most PR electoral systems. This systemic distinction reinforces the conclusion drawn from our previous evidence: the style of representation is affected by the institutional structures of the democratic process.

PATTERNS OF POLITICAL REPRESENTATION

It is regrettable that more recent data on the representation process are not available. After all, we have claimed that the representation process is an important measure of the success of modern democracy. Furthermore, the new style of citizen politics that we have described in previous chapters may affect the representation process, though the nature of these effects is uncertain (see Thomassen 1994; Cain, Dalton, and Scarrow 2003). On the one hand, a more sophisticated, issue-oriented public may encourage candidates and parties to be more attentive to public interests. On the other hand, partisan dealignment and candidate-centered politics may weaken representation built upon a system of responsible party government. Still, some broad conclusions about the nature of representation do flow from our findings.

This chapter describes two distinct patterns of representative government among Western democracies. Political representation in the United States is largely dependent on the relationship between individual legislators and their constituencies. Citizens in most other democracies are primarily represented through their choice of political parties at election time. However, some research suggests that this American/European contrast may be lessening. For instance, Warren Miller (1987, ch. 4) discusses the important role that parties play in American representation (also Erikson and Tedin 2001, ch. 11). Our own analyses suggest that the strength of the party government model is weakening in Europe (e.g., chapter 9; Dalton and Wattenberg 2000). Still, the contrasts between the American and European patterns of representation will probably continue to hold.

Both models can provide effective means of citizen/elite linkage, but they emphasize different aspects of representation. The American system of representative government based on individual legislators allows for greater responsiveness to the interests of each legislative district; the political process is more open to new political interests and the representation of minority groups because electoral control at the constituency level is more easily accomplished than control of an entire party. The flexibility of the American style of representation also involves some costs. An entrepreneurial style of representation makes it more difficult for the public to monitor and control the actions of their representatives between elections, and it encourages campaigns to focus on personalities and district service, rather than on policy and ideological orientations. Indeed, studies of congressional elections suggest that personality and constituency service are important influences on voting patterns.

A growing body of empirical research shows that policy outcomes in the United States generally reflect the preferences of the public—although obviously this is, and probably should be, and imperfect linkage. For example, Alan Monroe (1979) found a broad agreement between American policy preferences and policy outcomes in the several hundred specific cases he examined. Benjamin Page and Robert Shapiro (1983) similarly documented a significant correspondence between public preferences for policy change and actual changes in public policy.[8] Sophisticated new empirical analyses are providing new insights into the overall impact of public opinion on the policy process and how this influence interacts with the institutional structure of American politics (Stimson, McKuen, and Erikson 1995; Wlezien 2004).

A party-government model yields a different pattern of political representation. The choice of parties provides the electorate with indirect institutional control over the actions of individual legislators through party discipline. When a party votes as a united bloc, political responsibility is more clearly established. If the public is satisfied (or dissatisfied) with the party's performance, the next election offers the opportunity to act on this evaluation. While the party model strengthens the policy linkage between citizens and elites, it may also produce rigidity and resistance to change. The highly cohesive European parliamentary parties place a necessary premium on party unity and disciplined voting, which hardly provides a fertile ground for experimentation and political change. Parties may be very responsive to their established clientele, but new social groups and internal party minorities may have difficulty gaining representation in the party-government framework.

Research projects working within the party-government framework also find that party choices have meaningful policy consequences. For example, Hans-Dieter Klingemann, Richard Hofferbert, and Ian Budge (1994) analyzed whether the programs that parties offer to the voters are translated into policy after the election. They found that parties are meaningful vehicles for policy control in most democracies. More broadly, recent research demonstrates a general congruence between public policy preferences and government outcomes across a range of nations and across different policy domains (Brooks 1987, 1990; Franklin and Wlezien 1997; Brettschneider 1996). Similarly, after demonstrating that changes in citizen spending preferences are generally translated into shifts in government spending across different policy domains in the United States, Britain, and Canada, Stuart Soroka and Christopher Wlezien (2003) come to a simple conclusion: "democracy works."

Many roadblocks and pitfalls stand in the way of representation, even within a democratic system. In these times of change and political turmoil, the evidence of government failures and party failures is often obvious. Moreover, even close citizen/elite policy agreement is not proof that public opinion is efficiently and effectively represented in modern democracies. A large part of the observed correspondence must be attributed to an interactive process. Voters migrate to the party (candidate) that best represents their views, and the party convinces supporters to adopt these policies. Thus, congruence does not prove that the public can control government. Beyond the general patterns described here, one can think of a host of specific policies on which the impact of public preferences is uncertain. Still, congruence indicates an agreement between public preferences and public policy that is expected under a democratic system. Moreover, it underscores our belief that there is a rationality in public action that elitist theories of democracy doubt exists.

SUGGESTED READINGS

Converse, Philip, and Roy Pierce. *Representation in France*. Cambridge, Mass.: Harvard University Press, 1986.

Erikson, Robert, Michael MacKuen, and James Stimson. *The Macro Polity*. Cambridge: Cambridge University Press, 2002.

Erikson, Robert, Gerald Wright, and John McIver. *State House Democracy: Public Opinion and Public Policy in the American States*. New York: Cambridge University Press, 1994.

Esaiasson, Peter, and Sören Holmberg. *Representative from Above: Members of Parliament and Representative Democracy in Sweden*. Aldershot, Hants and Brookfield, Vt.: Dartmouth Publishing, 1996.

Miller, Warren, et al. *Policy Representation in Western Democracies*. Oxford: Oxford University Press, 1999.

Page, Benjamin, and Robert Shapiro. *The Rational Public: Fifty Years of Trends in Americans' Policy Preferences*. Chicago: University of Chicago Press, 1992.

NOTES

1. The development of two-way cable television, teleconferencing, and other communication advances may lead us to reconsider the physical limits on direct citizen participation in large collectives. Indeed, the technology exists for instantaneous national referendums and national town meetings (Bimber 2003).

2. Previous studies include the following: for the United States, Miller and Jennings (1986) and Warren Miller (1987); for Germany, Hoffmann-Lange (1992) and Herzog and Wessels (1990); for France, Converse and Pierce (1986); for Sweden, Esaiasson and Holmberg (1996); for Australia, McAllister (1991).

3. Previous comparisons of public opinion and opinions of members of Congress in 1978 and 1982 found that the two groups differed by only a few percentage points (Bishop and Frankovic 1981; Erikson and Tedin 2001, 267).

4. In purely statistical terms, almost half of the citizen/elite issue comparisons in these tables yield statistically significant differences (.01 level)—which results, in part,

from the large size of the public opinion samples. See Pierce (1999) for a discussion of alternate measures of assessing citizen/elite correspondence. Because we do not always have access to the original data, we rely on a simpler measure of absolute differences.

5. The median district opinion was based on the difference between the percentages of the presidential vote in the district for the Democratic and the Republican candidates in 1996. The candidate position is an average of opinions on over 200 policy questions. See Ansolabehere, Snyder, and Stewart (2001a).

6. These data were provided by Steve Ansolabehere, and we greatly appreciate this assistance.

7. The power of Philip Converse and Roy Pierce's (1986, ch. 23) analysis was to specify the conditions that strengthen or retard the representation process. These researchers found that citizen/elite congruence varied by policy domain, competitiveness of the district, and the legislator's role conceptions.

8. State-level comparisons provide another opportunity to study the congruence between public opinion and public policy. A recent study by Erikson and his colleagues show a strong policy correspondence (Erikson, Wright, and McIver 1994).

PART FOUR

DEMOCRACY AND THE FUTURE

CHAPTER 12

Citizens and the Democratic Process

We seemingly live in the best of times . . . and the worst of times for the democratic process. In the last decade of the twentieth century, a wave of democratization swept across the globe. The citizens of Eastern Europe, South Africa, and several East Asian nations rose up against their authoritarian governments. The Soviet Empire collapsed, and millions of citizens were enjoying their new democratic freedoms. This led a noted political analyst, Francis Fukuyama (1992), to claim that we were witnessing "the end of history." Humankind's historical evolution was converging on a single form of government—democracy—as the culmination of human development. Even some who had recently proclaimed the end of democracy's international expansion now trumpeted this third wave of democratization.[1]

In the United States, the 1990s also brought unprecedented affluence and economic well-being, as Americans experienced their longest period of sustained economic growth in peacetime. Crime rates dropped, and progress was made on many policy fronts. To a lesser degree, our allies in Western Europe also enjoyed a peace dividend of economic stability and a new era of international security. This was, it seemed, a positive time for Western democracy. The Cold War was over, and we had won.

Despite these signs of progress, there were growing indications that the citizens of these established democracies were becoming more critical of the politicians, political parties, and political institutions that form the basis of the democratic process (Dalton 2004a). The malaise was perhaps most visible and surprising in the United States. Beginning with the crises and political scandals of the 1960s and 1970s—Vietnam, urban unrest, and Watergate—Americans' trust in their politicians sank steadily lower. Jimmy Carter returned from an introspective retreat at Camp David in 1979 to warn Americans that declining public confidence "was a fundamental threat to American democracy." Trust in government partially rebounded during the first Reagan administration, as the president tried to instill a new sense of political purpose and renew the political spirit by evoking uplifting images of a "new morning in America" and America as the "shining city on the hill." By the end of the Reagan–first Bush administrations, however, public skepticism had reasserted itself, fueled by new crises and new scandals. By the mid-1990s, the public's trust in politicians and various political institutions reached historic low points (Nye, Zelikow, and King 1997; Hibbing and Theiss-Morse 1995).

A single example illustrates the transformation in American public opinion: in April 1966, in the midst of the Vietnam War and race riots in Cleveland, Chicago, and Atlanta, the Harris poll found that 66 percent of Americans

---

Internet Resource

Visit the Freedom House web site for information on the extent of
democracy around the globe:

http://www.freedomhouse.org

---

rejected the view that "the people running the country don't really care what
happens to you." In December 1997, however, in the midst of the longest period of peace and prosperity in more than two generations, 57 percent of
Americans *endorsed* that same view. In the opinion of many Americans, it
was the worst of times for our democratic process.

In the wake of the horrific terrorist attacks on September 11, 2001, American images of government shifted dramatically. Expressions of national
pride and patriotism, such as flying the flag, became common. Trust in politicians also improved. But this new mood proved to be fleeting—and limited
to the United States (Dalton 2004a, ch. 2). By mid-decade, sentiments toward
the political system had largely returned to their pre–9/11 levels.

Such problems are not unique to the United States, although they may be
most visible and most hotly debated among Americans. Doubts about democratic politics now seem to be a common theme in advanced industrial societies.
As scandals strained Britons' faith in their democratic institutions in the mid-
1990s, Parliament formed a committee on Standards in Public Life (the Nolan
Committee), before which Ivor Crewe (1995) testified: "There is no doubt that
distrust and alienation has risen to a higher level than ever before. It was always
fairly prevalent; it is now in many regards almost universal." During the 1990s,
Germany achieved a historic ambition: unification as a free and democratic nation. And yet, political trust sank among the German public. President Richard
von Weizsäcker (1992, 164) chastised Germany's political elites, claiming that
politicians and political parties were "power-crazed for electoral victory and
powerless when it comes to understanding the content and ideas required of political leadership." Scandals and growing feelings of political distrust also became more prominent in French politics during the decade.

Admittedly, anxiety about the health of democracy and partisan politics is
a regular feature of political science and political punditry. Over the past
quarter century, a plethora of books, articles, and pamphlets have been published on the topic. There was an important debate about the nation's postwar goals during the Eisenhower administration, and John Kennedy asked
Americans to renew their commitment to state and nation (see Mueller 1999,
ch. 7). Perhaps the most prominent academic study of the period was *The
Crisis of Democracy*, in which Michel Crozier, Samuel Huntington, and Joji
Watanuki (1975) nearly forecast democracy's demise. The introduction to
their book, for example, includes an ominous quote from Willy Brandt, who

supposedly predicted that "Western Europe has only 20 or 30 more years of democracy left in it; after that it will slide, engineless and rudderless, under the surrounding sea of dictatorship" (quoted in Crozier et al. 1975, 2).[2]

Fortunately, the passage of time has shown that the dire predictions of Crozier and his colleagues (as well as Brandt) were wrong, but now it appears that there are new, and real, causes for concern among those who value democracy. A supportive political culture is often considered a requirement for a stable, effective democracy (Almond and Verba 1963). For example, the lack of support for the democratic process was one of the faults that led to the collapse of German democracy in the 1930s. In other cases, the rejection of democratic norms and procedures by political extremists has led to violent attacks on the political system. Even though we see a fundamentally different pattern in current feelings of political malaise, the potential implications for democracy are still significant.

This chapter determines how citizens judge the democratic process today. How is it that as democracy celebrates its success at the dawning of the new millennium, its citizens are apparently expressing increasing doubts about their political systems? In addition, we consider how the new style of citizen politics may contribute to these misgivings, and what the implications are for the future functioning of the democratic process.

THE MEANING OF POLITICAL SUPPORT

"Political support" is a term with many possible meanings. Several political scientists have tried to identify the essential aspects of this concept and link these attitudes to their consequences.

Gabriel Almond and Sidney Verba (1963) referred to attitudes toward politics and the political system as the *political culture* of a nation. Political culture encompasses everything from beliefs about the legitimacy of the system itself to beliefs about the adequacy and appropriateness of political input structures, government policies, and the role of the individual in the political process. The most important of these attitudes is a generalized feeling toward the political system, or *system affect*. Such feelings are presumably socialized early in life (Easton and Dennis 1969), representing a positive attitude toward the political system that is relatively independent of the actions of the current government. Almond and Verba felt that affective feelings toward the political system assure the legitimacy of democratic governments and limit expressions of discontent with the political system.

David Easton (1965, 1975) extended these ideas into a theoretical framework describing the various elements of political support. Easton distinguished between support for three levels of political objects: political authorities, the regime, and the political community:

- *Political authorities* are the incumbents of political office—or, in a broader sense, the pool of political elites from which government leaders are drawn. Support for political authorities focuses on specific individuals or groups of individuals.

- *Regime support* refers to public attitudes toward the institutions and offices of government rather than the present officeholders—such as respect for the office of President of the United States rather than the present chief executive. This level of support also involves public attitudes toward the procedures of government and political institutions, such as the principles of pluralist democracy and support for parliamentary government.

- *Political community support* implies a basic attachment to the nation and political system beyond the present institutions of government. A sense of being "English" (or "Scottish") exemplifies these attachments.

The distinction between these levels of support is essential. Discontent with political authorities normally has limited implications for the overall political process. Citizens often become dissatisfied with political officeholders and act on these feelings by selecting new officials at the next election. Dissatisfaction with authorities, within a democratic system, is not usually a signal for basic political change. Negative attitudes toward political officials often exist with little loss in support for the office itself or the institutional structure encompassing the office.

However, as the object of dissatisfaction becomes more general—shifting to the regime or the political community—the political implications increase. A decline in regime support might provoke a basic challenge to political institutions or calls for reform in the procedures of government. Weakening ties to the political community in a democratic system might foretell eventual revolution, civil war, or the loss of democracy. Therefore, Easton says, "not all expressions of unfavorable orientations have the same degree of gravity for a political system. Some may be consistent with its maintenance; others may lead to fundamental change" (1975, 437).

In addition to the objects of political support, Easton distinguished between two kinds of support: diffuse and specific (also see Muller and Jukam 1977). According to Easton, *diffuse support* is a state of mind—a deep-seated set of attitudes toward politics and the operation of the political system that is relatively impervious to change. For example, the sentiment "America, right or wrong" reflects a commitment to the political system that transcends the actual behavior of the government. In contrast, *specific support* is closely related to the actions and performance of the government or political elites. This kind of support is object-specific in two senses. First, it normally applies to evaluations of political authorities; it is less relevant to support for the regime and political community. Second, specific support is based on the actual policies and governing style of political authorities.

The distinction between diffuse and specific support is important in understanding the significance of public attitudes toward the political process. Democratic political systems must keep the support of their citizens if they are to remain viable. Yet, since all governments occasionally fail to meet public expectations, short-term failures to satisfy public demands must not directly erode generalized support for the regime or political community. In other words, a democratic political system requires a reservoir of diffuse support independent of immediate policy outputs (specific support) if it is to weather periods of public disaffection and dissatisfaction.

The history of German democracy illustrates the significance of diffuse support. The Weimar Republic was built on an unstable foundation. Many Germans felt that the creation of the republic at the end of World War I had contributed to Germany's wartime defeat; from the outset, the regime was stigmatized as a traitor to the nation. Important sectors of the political establishment—the military, the civil service, and the judiciary—as well as many citizens questioned the legitimacy of the new regime and favored the political system of the former German Empire. The fledgling democratic state then faced a series of major crises: postwar economic hardships, attempted right-wing and left-wing coups, explosive inflation in the early 1920s, and French occupation of the Ruhr. Because the political system was never able to build up a pool of diffuse support for the republic, the dissatisfaction created by the Great Depression in the 1930s easily eroded popular support for political authorities and the democratic regime. Communists and Nazis argued that the democratic political system was at fault, and the Weimar Republic succumbed to these attacks.[3]

The democratic transition in the German Democratic Republic also illustrates the importance of cultural and institutional congruence. Surveys of East German youth found a marked decrease in support for the communist principles of the GDR during the 1980s (Friedrich and Griese 1990). These youths led the populist revolution in the East that weakened the regime in the fall of 1989. Moreover, revelations in early 1990 about the communists' abuses of power eroded the regime's popular base still further, and created a race toward unification with the West.

Early cross-national opinion studies provided empirical evidence for the proposition that popular support was a requisite of stable democracy. Almond and Verba (1963) found that system affect in the late 1950s was most widespread in the long-established democracies of the United States and Great Britain. For example, 85 percent of Americans and 46 percent of Britons spontaneously mentioned their political system as a source of national pride. This system affect indicated that diffuse support had developed in these nations over their long democratic histories. Satisfaction with the policy outputs of government was also common in both nations. In contrast, system support was more limited in the newly formed democracies of West Germany and Italy: only 7 percent of West Germans and 3 percent of Italians mentioned their political system as a source of national pride. These findings suggested that diffuse political support was underdeveloped in these systems, raising fears that democracy was still fragile in these two formerly fascist states. The early years of the Federal Republic were closely watched by those who worried that the Bonn Republic would follow the same course as Weimar (Baker, Dalton, and Hildebrandt 1981).

Another cross-national study, by Hadley Cantril (1965), found a similar pattern in public opinion: positive national self-images were more common among the stable, well-run democracies. Ronald Inglehart (1990, ch. 1; 1997, ch. 6) also demonstrated that a democratic political culture is strongly correlated with the stability of democratic institutions. Robert Putnam (1993) similarly found that a supportive political culture was a key factor in making democracy work. Although one can never be certain whether stable government produces popular support, or whether popular support produces stable government, these two phenomena are interrelated.

An authoritarian state may endure without the support of its public, but popular support is essential for a democracy to survive. Therefore, this chapter assesses the breadth and depth of popular support for democratic governance as a crucial element in diagnosing democracy's future.

DECLINING CONFIDENCE IN AUTHORITIES

Public concerns about the democratic process normally begin with questions about the holders of power. Americans might not doubt the institutions of governance, but they were clearly willing to criticize Richard Nixon's actions during Watergate, George H.W. Bush's involvement in the Iran-contra negotiations, and Bill Clinton's personal indiscretions.

Rather than focus on individual incumbents, however, we examine citizen images of political leaders in general. Indeed, a variety of evidence points to Americans' growing skepticism about their leaders. For example, the American National Election Study has measured feelings toward political officials and the government over time (figure 12.1). The early readings described a largely supportive public. Most Americans believed that one can trust the government to do what is right (71 percent), that there are few dishonest people in government (68 percent), and that officials care what people think (71 percent). These positive feelings remained relatively unchanged until the mid-1960s and then declined precipitously. Conflict over civil rights and Vietnam divided Americans and apparently eroded public confidence in their leaders; then Watergate and a seemingly endless stream of political scandals pushed support even lower over the next decade.

Distrust of government officials reached a low point in 1980, after which the upbeat presidency of Ronald Reagan temporarily reversed these trends. As Reagan stressed the positive aspects of American society and politics, opinions rebounded in 1984. However, by the end of the Reagan-Bush era, public trust in government was as low as it had been in 1980. The Clinton administration had a mixed record. By 1994 these indicators had hit historic lows, but steady economic growth and relative international stability then began to shore up public confidence in government. Trust in government grew from 1994 until the end of the decade, according to the ANES surveys. Yet

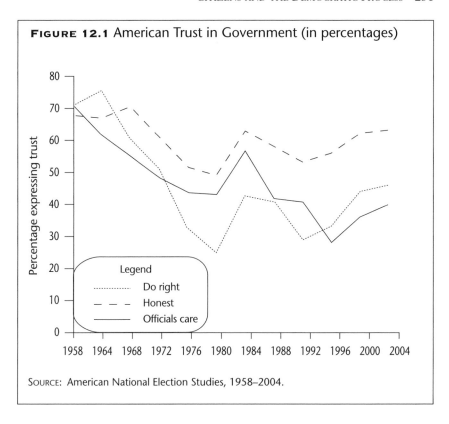

FIGURE 12.1 American Trust in Government (in percentages)

SOURCE: American National Election Studies, 1958–2004.

even with the unprecedented economic growth of the 1990s and the consolidation of democracy around the globe, Americans' trust in government rebounded only to the levels of Reagan's first administration (even while Clinton was being impeached).

Virtually all other long-term public opinion series replicate these downward trends (Nye, Zelikow, and King 1997; Hibbing and Theiss-Morse 2002). For instance, since 1966 the Harris poll has tracked sentiments on two measures of political alienation: "The people running the country don't really care what happens to you," and "Most people with power try to take advantage of people like yourself." Rising levels of assent on both items reflect the public's growing cynicism from the 1960s to the 1990s. Similarly, another series from the General Social Survey asked Americans if they agree with the statement "Most public officials are not really interested in the problems of the average man." The number of cynical Americans increased from 60 percent in 1973 to 76 percent in 1994. The Pew Center for People and the Press (1998a) extended an earlier trend on evaluations of the ethical and moral practices of federal government officials: 34 percent of Americans were critical in 1964, rising to 68 percent in 1997.

Following the terrorist attacks on the World Trade Center and the Pentagon in September 2001, political support spiked upward. Americans expressed more trust in politicians, more confidence in political institutions, and more pride in their nation. But as these events receded in time, opinions began to regress to their pre–9/11 levels. For instance, the *New York Times* poll found that only 31 percent of Americans trusted the government to do what is right in January 2001; this level increased to 55 percent in early October 2001. But by mid-2003, only 36 percent of Americans still trusted the government. As horrific as the terrorist attacks were, they did not reshape Americans' feelings of political support.

When one looks back on this span of American history, it is easy to cite reasons for the public's growing doubts about their leaders. Over any four-year electoral cycle one can identify multiple actions that have diminished the reputations of Congress and the executive branch: Watergate, Iran-contra, the savings and loan scandal, and so on. Candidates promise one thing at election time, but they regularly fail to deliver and may even violate their promises after they are elected (for example, George H.W. Bush's promise "Read my lips, no new taxes"). In addition, some of the most distinguished members of Congress have resigned from office, offering stinging indictments of the institution. As one former Representative said upon leaving office, "May your mother never find out where you work."

While such explanations of decreasing trust focus on the peculiar history of American politics, these same trends are occurring in Great Britain, France, Germany and most other Western democracies as well. Figure 12.2 tracks the decline in citizens' belief that politicians care what people think in our set of our nations.[4] For instance, 53 percent of the French public in 1977 believed politicians cared what they thought; by 1997, only 19 percent shared this opinion. Other trends from these four nations generally display the same pattern of decreasing trust in elected officials (Bromley, Curtice, and Seyd 2002; Kepplinger 1996; Mayer 2000).

Even more significant is the fact that growing public skepticism about politicians and government officials is apparent in virtually all the advanced industrial democracies. In a recent book (Dalton 2004a), I assembled the full inventory of questions that measure support for politicians and government from the national election studies in sixteen Western democracies (also see Norris 1999a; Pharr and Putnam 2000). Typically beginning in the late 1960s or early 1970s, these trends present a stark picture. Overall, *there is a general decline in confidence in politicians in fourteen out of sixteen countries for which systematic long-term data are available.* A common feature of contemporary democracies is the citizenry's increasingly mistrust of elected officials.

ORIENTATIONS TOWARD THE REGIME

Increasing skepticism about political elites appears to be a common development in many advanced industrial democracies, but political scientists dis-

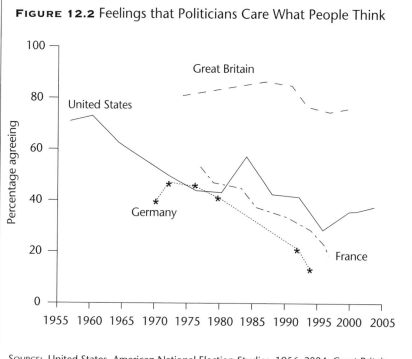

FIGURE 12.2 Feelings that Politicians Care What People Think

SOURCE: United States, American National Election Studies, 1956–2004; Great Britain, 1974 Political Action Survey and British Social Attitudes Surveys, 1987–2000; Germany, German Election Studies, 1969–1994; France, SOFRES Polls, 1977–1997.

agree on whether these opinions reflect doubts about political authorities or more fundamental questions about the regime and democratic process.

The debate was first taken up by Arthur Miller (1974a, 1974b) and Jack Citrin (1974). Miller argued that people were generalizing their dissatisfaction with the repeated policy failures and political scandals of government officials into broader criticism of the political process as a whole. Miller spelled out the potentially grave consequences the loss of regime support could have for the American political process.

Citrin felt that Miller was overstating the problem. He interpreted the declines in political support as a sign of popular disenchantment with the incumbents in government or political authorities in general, not distrust in the system of American government. Citrin (1974, 987) claimed that "political systems, like baseball teams, have slumps and winning seasons. Having recently endured a succession of losing seasons, Americans boo the home team when it takes the field." Citrin maintained that these boos do not show opposition to the process of democratic government, but only to the players in the lineup and their recent performance on the field. Hence, given a few new stars or a few winning streaks, the decline in public confidence would be reversed.

Citrin's cautious optimism seemed warranted in 1974, but now, three decades later, public disenchantment continues. In addition, accumulating evidence suggests that the decline in public confidence has spread to the institutions of democratic government. As table 12.1 shows, the responses to a series of questions designed to tap public confidence in the people running major social, economic, and political organizations indicate that confidence in the leadership of virtually all institutions has tumbled downward over the past three decades. For instance, in 1966 many Americans expressed a great deal of confidence in the executive branch (41 percent) and Congress (42 percent), but these positive evaluations dropped substantially over time. Confidence in the president shot up after the terrorist attacks in September 2001, but it has decreased again since that time (Dalton 2004a, ch. 2). Confidence in business, labor, higher education, organized religion, the press, and the medical profession have undergone similar declines over the past four decades (see below).

Other questions from the American National Election Study examine the perceived responsiveness of government and political institutions. These questions also show a trend of decreasing confidence in parties, elections, and the government in general. Other survey series document increasing public doubts about Congress as a political institution (Hibbing and Theiss-Morse 1995). One observer of these trends has suggested that the contemporary American political creed should read "In God we trust: everyone else pays cash."

TABLE 12.1 Confidence in Leadership of American Institutions (in percentages)

	1966	1971	1973	1976	1980	1984	1988	1993	1998	2000	2002
Medicine	72	61	54	54	52	52	51	39	45	44	37
Higher education	61	37	37	38	30	29	30	22	27	27	25
Military	62	27	32	39	28	37	34	42	37	40	55
Organized religion	41	27	35	31	35	32	20	23	28	29	19
Supreme Court	50	23	32	35	25	35	35	30	33	34	37
Major corporations	55	27	29	22	27	32	25	21	28	29	18
Press	29	18	23	28	22	17	18	11	10	10	10
Executive branch	41	23	29	14	12	19	16	12	14	14	27
Congress	42	19	24	14	9	13	15	7	11	13	13
Organized labor	22	14	16	12	15	9	10	8	12	14	12
Average	48	28	31	29	26	28	25	22	25	25	24

SOURCES: 1966 and 1971, Harris Poll; 1973–2002, NORC General Social Surveys.

NOTE: Table entries are the percentages expressing a "great deal" of confidence in the people running each institution.

Furthermore, the evidence clearly demonstrates that the erosion of public confidence in the institutions of representative democracy is not unique to the United States. Combining the trends available from the advanced industrial democracies shows that trust in the national legislature is decreasing in twelve of sixteen nations for which long-term data are now available—including all four of our core nations (Dalton 2004a, 37–39). For instance, the Gallup poll found that 48 percent of the British public expressed "quite a lot" of confidence in the House of Commons in 1981, compared to only 24 percent in 1996. Germans now speak of the crisis of party government, and the German term *Politikverdrossenheit* (political vexation) has become a common part of the public's political vocabulary.

The 1999–2002 World Values Survey / European Values Survey compared confidence in institutions across our four nations (see table 12.2).[5] The question wording and set of institutions differs from table 12.1, so the results are not directly comparable to that table. Still, the data present a familiar pattern: the public displays little confidence in the institutions of representative democracy. For instance, roughly a third in each nation express "a great deal" or "quite a lot" of confidence in the national legislature. Across the twenty-two advanced industrial democracies included in this survey, majorities express confidence in the legislature in only four nations—a distressing indictment of how citizens view their government. Perceptions of political parties are even more critical (Dalton and Weldon 2004). The 2004 Eurobarometer study found that confidence in political parties averages only 18 percent across the European Union—far below the average confidence levels for a dozen or more other social and political institutions examined. People express more confidence in nonpolitical institutions of government (such as the judicial system or the civil service) than in the institutions of representative democracy.

TABLE 12.2 Cross-National Confidence in Social Institutions (in percentages)

	United States	Great Britain	France	Germany
Education system	—	66	68	73
Judicial systems	—	49	46	62
Civil service	55	46	46	39
Parliament	38	35	41	36
Major companies	54	40	48	36
Labor unions	39	28	35	38
Political parties	23	14	15	17

SOURCES: 1999-2000 World Values Survey / European Values Survey; the party confidence measures for the three European nations are from Eurobarometer 54 (2000).

NOTE: Table entries are the percentages expressing "a great deal" or "quite a lot" of confidence in each institution. Missing data were excluded from the calculation of percentages.

When the signs of growing popular skepticism first appeared in American surveys during the late 1960s and early 1970s, analysts linked these findings to the immediate problems of American politics. American political scientists quickly blamed the "imperial presidency, the structure of Congress, the U.S. pattern of divided government, the new norms of American journalism, and a host of other unique factors in American politics (e.g., Cooper 1999; Hibbing and Theiss-Morse 1995; Craig 1993; Patterson 1993). And yet, the breadth of these trends across other democracies suggests that we are witnessing more than a coincidental slump in politicians' performance. The value of these cross-national comparisons is to see that something more general and more common is affecting the United States and other advanced industrial democracies.

While many factors are at work in producing these trends, we believe that changing public values provide a major source of this political cynicism. Contemporary publics have raised their expectations of government: they are more demanding of politicians and more critical of the processes of representative democracy. Furthermore, an increasingly critical media and more open public discussion of government reinforces public doubts about the political process. Thus, rather than a transient phenomenon, a skeptical public appears to be another feature of the new style of citizen politics.

REGIME NORMS: SUPPORT FOR A DEMOCRATIC REGIME

Many of the survey questions analyzed so far measure support for the incumbents or institutions of the democratic process, or at least they could be interpreted in these terms. One might argue that dissatisfaction with politicians, parties, and even parliaments is a sign of the vitality of democracy—or of an objective reading of contemporary politics by the public. But if dissatisfaction generalizes to the political regime and its values, then it could produce a crisis of democracy.

In earlier historical periods, public dissatisfaction with politicians or political institutions often led to (or arose from) disenchantment with the democratic process itself. This was the case with the democratic challenges of the interwar period (Linz and Stepan 1978). Even during the years immediately following World War II, dissatisfaction with democracy in Europe was often concentrated among antidemocratic extremists on the left or right. If people today are losing faith in the norms and principles of the democratic process, the implications for democracy are fundamental.

To the extent that data on support for democratic norms and procedures are available, however, they suggest that support for political rights and participatory norms have actually grown over the past generation. For instance, the available long-term data suggest that people have become more politically tolerant during the postwar period (Thomassen 1995; McCloskey and Brill 1983). The extension of democratic rights to women, racial and ethnic minorities, and homosexuals has profoundly altered the politics of advanced industrial democracies within the span of a generation (also see chapter 6). At least in principle, there is widespread public endorsement of the political values and norms that underlie the democratic process.

In addition, perceptions of the citizens' role now emphasize a more participatory style and a greater willingness to challenge authority. Inglehart's (1990, 1997) research on postmaterial value change—with its emphasis on participatory values as a measure of postmaterialism—reinforces these points. Inglehart finds growing emphasis on political and social participation as core value priorities. Citizens today expect to participate in the democratic process, and interest in democratic process has increased over time (see chapter 2).

To tap regime values, opinion surveys asked whether democracy is the best form of government. Although there is not a long cross-national time series for this question, the presently high degree of support suggests there has not been a major erosion in these sentiments (table 12.3).[6] On average, about 90 percent of the public in advanced industrial democracies agrees that democracy is better than other forms of government (also see Klingemann 1999; Dalton 2004a, ch. 2). Another question in the WVS/EVS was less evaluative, tapping public support for the idea of democracy. Assent to the statement "The democratic system is good" shows that support is nearly universal within Western democracies. Moreover, in comparison to a Eurobarometer survey of the late 1980s, support for democratic government has increased in most West European nations (Klingemann 1999). Reviewing similar evidence, Dieter Fuchs, Giovanna Guidorossi, and Palle Svensson (1995) conclude that democracy as a principle is positively evaluated by nearly all citizens in Western societies.

In summary, there is a contemporary malaise in the political spirit involving the three key elements of representative democracy: most citizens in the Western democracies are now distrustful of politicians, skeptical about political parties, and significantly less confident in their parliaments. Moreover, these patterns have persisted over several decades and across succeeding government administrations. However, these negative sentiments do not carry over to democratic principles and goals. Commitment to the democratic ideal is nearly universal; if anything, this sentiment has apparently strengthened. Thus, a new style of "dissatisfied democrats" is developing—citizens who are dissatisfied with political institutions but supportive of democratic principles.

COMMUNITY SUPPORT

A final aspect of political support concerns citizen orientations toward the political community and society. System support involves the system affect described by Almond and Verba (1963). A strong emotional attachment to the nation presumably provides a reservoir of diffuse support that can maintain a political system through temporary periods of political stress. One

TABLE 12.3 Support for Democracy (in percentages)

Nation	Democratic system is good	Democracy is better than other governments
Australia	87	87
Austria	96	97
Belgium	89	92
Canada	88	87
Denmark	98	98
Finland	87	91
France	90	93
Germany	95	97
Great Britain	88	78
Greece	98	97
Ireland	90	92
Italy	97	94
Japan	92	92
Netherlands	96	96
New Zealand	91	87
Norway	96	95
Portugal	90	93
Spain	95	93
Sweden	97	94
Switzerland	93	91
United States	89	88

SOURCE: 1999–2002 World Values Survey / European Values Survey.

NOTE: Table entries are the percentages agreeing with each statement. Missing data were excluded from the calculation of percentages.

measure of such feelings involves pride in one's nation. Figure 12.3 displays the percentages of citizens who feel very proud of their nation within the advanced industrial democracies that were included in the first and the fourth wave of the World Values Survey.[7] On the whole, feelings of national pride are relatively high. There are, however, significant national differences in these feelings (Elkins and Sides 2004).

National pride is exceptionally high in the United States: 97 percent of the public in 1981 and 96 percent in 1999 felt "very proud" or "proud" to be an American. Those chants of *USA! USA! USA!* are not limited to Olympic competition; they signify a persistent feeling among Americans.

Most Europeans voice their national pride in more moderate tones. Germans (like the Japanese) are especially hesitant in their expressions of national pride, for the trauma of the Third Reich burned a deep scar in the German psyche in both West and East. Especially among the young, there is a strong feeling that the nationalist excesses of the past must never be repeated. The Federal Republic therefore has avoided many of the emotional national symbols that are common in other industrial nations. There are few political holidays

FIGURE 12.3 Feelings of National Pride

1981–1983		1999–2002
	100	
Australia		Australia/Ireland
United States		**United States**
Ireland		Canada
Canada		Finland
		Denmark
	90	**Great Britain/France**
Great Britain		Italy/Norway
		Sweden
Finland		
France/Italy	80	Netherlands
Belgium		
Norway		
Denmark		Belgium
Sweden		
		Norway
	70	
		Finland
		Germany
Germany (W)		
Japan/Netherlands		
	60	
		Japan

SOURCES: 1981–1983 World Values Survey; 1999–2002 World Values Survey / European Values Survey.

NOTE: Figure entries are the percentages feeling "very proud" and "proud." Missing data were excluded from the calculation of percentages.

or memorials, the national anthem is seldom played, and even the anniversary of the founding of the Federal Republic attracts little public attention. Although most citizens are proud to be German, they refrain from any unquestioning emotional attachment to state and nation (Dalton 1993a, ch. 4).

Beyond these cross-national variations, it is clear that national pride has not eroded over the past two decades. Indeed, the most recent World Values Survey/European Values Survey suggests that national pride is generally growing, which is surprising given the high baseline of opinions in the first survey in the early 1980s. When longer time series are available for specific nations, they too show a pattern or relative stability or growth in national pride over time (e.g., Topf, Mohler, and Heath 1989). As one might expect from affective feelings of community attachment, these sentiments have been relatively impervious to the erosion in political support affecting other orientations toward politics.

DISSATISFIED DEMOCRATS

By some measures, this may be considered the golden age of democracy. At the beginning of the twenty-first century, more nations in the world have become, or strive to be, democracies than at any other point in human history. Furthermore, most of the other political ideologies that once stood as major rivals to democracy, such as fascism and communism, have seemingly lost their legitimacy. Democracy has brought peace, freedom, and prosperity to the advanced industrial societies.

At the same time, citizens have grown more critical of political elites, more negative toward political parties, and less confident of political institutions—and this combination of attitudes points to fundamental changes in the political orientation of democratic publics. The deference to authority that once was common in many of these nations has been partially replaced by public skepticism about elites. Closer scrutiny of government actions by the public and media uncovers political scandals and policy failures that further erode political trust (Pharr 2000; Della Porta 2000). The public's distrust of politicians is based on substantial supporting evidence.

Although feelings of mistrust have gradually broadened to include evaluations of the institutions of representative democracy, public skepticism has not significantly affected support for the democratic regime and political community. As citizens are criticizing the incumbents of government, they are simultaneously expressing strong support for the democratic creed. These mixed sentiments produce a new pattern of "dissatisfied democrats"—a public that is dissatisfied with political institutions but supportive of democratic principles (Klingemann 1999). Rather than the allegiant citizens of the past, these dissatisfied democrats have different expectations about how the democratic process should function and about their roles within that process.

Thus, declining political trust is affecting contemporary politics (Dalton 2004a, ch. 8; Norris 1999c). A more skeptical public tends to question government policies, which probably contributes to the trend toward increased issue voting and growing electoral volatility. In place of the habitual party support of the past, citizens are now more likely to base their voting choices on instrumental criteria. The old refrain, "What have you done for me lately?" is now heard more than ever. And citizens who are skeptical about politicians and parties are less likely to vote—thus contributing to the downward slide in election turnout.

Political distrust also encourages engagement in protest and other forms of unconventional political action (chapter 4). These new forms of activism often strain the democratic process, as demonstrators challenge established political elites and current government structures. The rise of new social movements and citizen interest groups further institutionalizes the changing nature of citizen politics.

A skeptical public is also likely to act differently as citizens (Dalton 2004a; Norris 1999c). Public opinion surveys suggest that people who think their government wastes tax money and is unresponsive to their interests may feel they are justified in fudging a bit on their taxes or taking advantage of government benefit programs. The skeptical citizen may also be hesitant to serve on a jury or perform other public service activities. In short, political support is part of the social contract that enables democracies to act without coercion and with the voluntary compliance of the citizenry—and decreasing support erodes this part of the social contract.

The Democratic Elitist Perspective

One group of scholars has cited these new citizen demands as evidence of a crisis of democracy (Zakaria 2003; Huntington 1981). Supposedly excessive public demands are overloading the ability of governments to perform, they claim. Some conservatives have used the elitist theory of democracy (see chapter 2) to offer a solution to this crisis. In a crude exaggeration of democratic theory, they maintain that if a supportive and quiescent public ensures a smoothly functioning political system, then we must redevelop these traits in contemporary publics. The centrifugal tendencies of democratic politics (and the demands of the public) must be controlled, and political authority must be reestablished. Samuel Huntington (1975, 37–38) assumed the ermine robes as spokesperson for this position:

> The problem of governance in the United States today stems from an "excess of democracy." . . . the effective operation of a democratic political system usually requires some measure of apathy and non-involvement on the part of some individuals and groups. The vulnerability of democratic government in the United States comes . . . from the internal dynamics of democracy itself in a highly educated, mobilized, and participatory society.

More recently, Fareed Zakaria (2003, 248) is even blunter in his critique of American democracy: "What we need in politics today is not more democracy, but less." In short, these analysts maintain that the crisis of democracy has developed because too many people want to apply its creed of egalitarian values to themselves, but democratic systems cannot meet these expectations. They contend that democracy has become overloaded because minorities are no longer apathetic, women are demanding equality, students are no longer docile, and the working class is no longer deferential. If these groups would only leave politics to the politicians—and their expert advisers—"democracy" would again be secure.[8]

Another element of the elitist perspective calls for a reduction in the scale of government. These theorists argue that governments have assumed too large a role in society, which contributes to the overload. This tenet has figured as one of the theoretical underpinnings of Thatcher's, Reagan's, and other neoconservatives' attempts to limit the size of government. But often there seem to be distinct biases in determining which programs the government should no longer support; usually those to be discontinued include social services or environmental programs, rather than programs that benefit conservative constituencies.

Finally, other critiques claim that political support is decreasing because people want to be less involved in government and favor reforms that spare them the burdens of democratic citizenship (Hibbing and Theiss-Morse 2002). This is a provocative argument, but it runs counter to the evidence of their own book and to the empirical evidence presented here. For instance, John Hibbing and Elizabeth Theiss-Morse's survey of American public opinion found that 86 percent favored more initiatives and an expansion of democracy (Hibbing and Theiss-Morse 2002, 75).

Taken together, the cures offered by the elitist theorists are worse than the problem it addresses; democracy's very goals are ignored in its defense. The critics of citizen politics forget that democracy means popular control of elites, not elite control over the populace.

The New Politics Perspective

A contrasting image of the state of democracy comes from Vaclav Havel's address to a joint session of the U.S. Congress in 1990. Havel described the road we are traveling by noting that "democracy in the full sense of the word will always be no more than an ideal; one may approach it as one would a horizon, in ways that may be better or worse, but it can never be fully attained." The New Politics perspective likewise suggests that the current pattern of dissatisfied democrats may represent only another historic step in democracy's progress toward its ideal. Just as earlier periods of dissatisfaction led to the expansion of the mass franchise, the granting of voting rights to women, and populist reforms that strengthened the democratic process, we may be in a new period of democratic reform.

One illustration of the present mix of orientations is seen in the relationship of postmaterial values to political trust and support for the democratic ideal. Figure 12.4 indicates that postmaterialists are distinctly less likely than materialists to express confidence in government. Indeed, the postmaterialists' calls for political reform have partially fueled the public doubts about politicians and political institutions (Dalton 2004a, ch. 5). At the same time, postmaterialists are much more likely to support democratic ideals. For instance, only 39 percent of the most materialist respondents in the 1995–1998 World Values Survey strongly agree that democracy is the best form of government, compared to 67 percent of postmaterialists. Materialists are satisfied with the current government, but they have lower aspirations for democracy. Postmaterialists are less satisfied with current democratic systems, but they have higher expectations. Postmaterialists thus illustrate the creedal passion in support for democracy that Huntington laments—but which offers the potential for democracy to move toward its theoretical ideal, on the horizon.

In short, this New Politics approach offers a different diagnosis of the current situation. One key feature is the changing nature of citizen politics that we have discussed throughout this book. Contemporary publics are better-in-

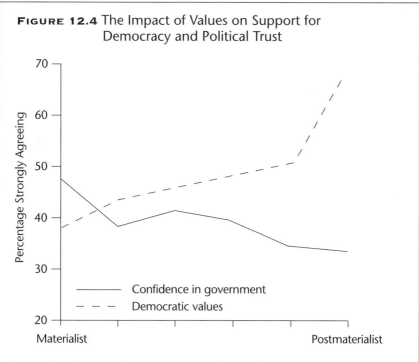

FIGURE 12.4 The Impact of Values on Support for Democracy and Political Trust

Percentage Strongly Agreeing

———— Confidence in government
— — — Democratic values

Materialist   Postmaterialist

SOURCE: Combined data from eight advanced industrial democracies in the 1995–1998 World Values Survey.

NOTE: Figure plots the percentages of those strongly agreeing that democracy is the best form of government and those who are confident in the national government.

formed and better-skilled than previous electorates, and they carry different expectations about how the democratic process should function. People today are also more conscious of their political rights, and more demanding in their individualism. The new style of citizen politics encourages a diversity of political interests (issue publics), instrumental and flexible voting choices, and more direct styles of political action.

In addition, there has been an explosion of citizen interest groups, social movements, and other social groups in recent decades (Meyer and Tarrow 1998; Berry 1999). These groups represent a new style of special interest representation, as citizens can focus their attention and their activity on specific policy concerns—and work through methods of direct action. These interest groups signify a new way of organizing interests and mobilizing public opinion. (One might add the creation of an omnipresent mass media to this change in the pattern of politics). These interest groups also present a challenge to political parties and the established processes of representative government. The structures of representative democracy that were created in the late 1800s often seem ill-suited to deal with this plethora of new interests, articulated in new ways and functioning by new rules.

Democratic governments need to accommodate these changing patterns of citizen politics. For instance, the potential for citizen participation is limited by the traditional system of representative democracy, especially in Western Europe. Opportunities for electoral input are scandalously low for most Europeans; the option to cast only a few votes during a multiyear electoral cycle is not a record of citizen input that should be admired. Moreover, beyond elections, these political systems have offered their citizens few ways to participate in the decisions of government that affect their lives. Indeed, often the governments have shielded themselves from even basic public scrutiny, by such means as Britain's Official Secrets Act. The fundamental structure of contemporary democratic institutions was developed in the nineteenth century—and society has changed a good deal since then.

The emphasis on new forms of citizen access and influence is not simply a call for participation for participation's sake. Expanding citizen participation can open up political systems that have been overcome by the sclerosis of corporatist policymaking and bureaucratized administration. The triumvirate of business-labor-government in many advanced industrial democracies often restricts the political interests of other groups. A system that distorts access to the political process is necessarily inefficient in meeting all of society's needs. One can see elements of these problems in the struggles of contemporary party systems in many of these democracies.

Opening up the political process is also a method to ensure that governments become more responsive to a broader spectrum of political demands. This method does not increase the quantity of political demands—the needs of the environment, women, consumers, and other groups exist—but it ensures that these demands receive fair attention from the government and thereby improves the government's ability to address all societal needs.

Increased political involvement also educates citizens in the democratic process. James Wright (1976, 260) noted a basic irony in the elitists' criticisms of citizen participation. The democratic elitists believe that governments can generate more support by convincing citizens of a lie (a sense of political efficacy that is fictitious) than by encouraging citizens to participate and learn of the necessary limits to their influence. The "big lie" may work for a while, but as soon as someone points out the gap between myth and reality, the political credibility of the system falters. It happened to the East European governments in 1989–1991. Call it co-optation, pragmatism, or Jeffersonian idealism, but involving citizens in the democratic process is one method to increase their identification with the process.

Finally, increasing citizen input ultimately ensures the quality of government decision making. As we noted in chapter 1, Thomas Jefferson viewed the public as the major constraint of the potential excesses of government officials. Citizen participation is not a panacea for all of society's modern ills; even educated, informed, and politically involved citizens will still make errors in judgment. As Benjamin Barber (1984, 151) also noted:

> Democracy does not place endless faith in the capacity of individuals to govern themselves, but it affirms with Machiavelli that the multitude will on the whole be as wise or wiser than princes, and with Theodore Roosevelt that "the majority of plain people will day in and day out make fewer mistakes in governing themselves than another smaller body of men will make in trying to govern them."

Since I presented this evaluation of contemporary democratic politics in the first edition of *Citizen Politics*, there are encouraging signs that politicians and governments are responding to the calls for reform. Calls for political reform have become the new catchphrases of politics.

Even more significant is the fact that institutional reforms are actually restructuring the democratic process (Cain, Dalton, and Scarrow 2003). Many nations are reforming administrative procedures to give citizen groups access to the formerly closed processes of policy administration. In Germany, for example, local citizen action groups have won changes in administrative law to allow for citizen participation in local administrative processes. Similar reforms in the United States offer individual citizens and citizen groups greater access to the political process (Ingram and Smith 1993). Similarly, new Freedom of Information laws and ombudsman offices are making government more transparent and accessible to its citizens (Cain, Fabrinni, and Egan 2003).

Other forms of direct democracy are also increasing. Citizen groups in the United States and Europe are making greater use of referendums to involve the public directly in policymaking (Gallagher und Uleri 1996; Scarrow 2003). The judicialization of politics in another important development: increasingly, citizens are using access to the courts to guarantee their rights of democratic access and influence (Stone Sweet 2000; Cichowski and Stone

Sweet 2003). For instance, environmentalists in many nations have gained legal standing in the courts in order to protect the environment from the actions of municipalities or government agencies.

There also are reforms within the structured system of party government. The formation of new parties is one sign of adaptation, but even the established parties are changing internally to increase the role of the members within the party (Scarrow, Webb, and Farrell 2000). The term-limits movement is another expression of these reformist sentiments. A majority of U.S. states have now enacted some type of term-limits legislation, normally through citizen initiatives.

These institutional changes are difficult to accomplish, they often have unintended consequences, and they proceed at a slow pace, but once implemented, they restructure the whole process of making policy that extends beyond a single issue or a single policy agenda. And when such reforms are taken together, there is evidence that the degree of institutional change during the past three decades rivals the reformist surge of the populist movement of the early 1990s (Cain, Dalton, and Scarrow 2003). The processes of contemporary democracies are being transformed to reflect the new style of citizen politics.

Indeed, these adaptations reflect the very strength of democracy to grow and evolve, for the lack of such adaptivity is what brought about the downfall of communism. As the German sociologist Ralf Dahrendorf (1975, 194) noted during the earlier crisis of democracy debate:

> What we have to do above all is to maintain that flexibility of democratic institutions which is in some ways their greatest virtue: the ability of democratic institutions to implement and effect change without revolution—the ability to react to new problems in new ways—the ability to develop institutions rather than change them all the time—the ability to keep the lines of communication open between leaders and led—and the ability to make individuals count above all.

These changes in the style of representative democracy are accompanied by some risks. There may be some growing pains as the political process adjusts to increasing citizen participation, especially in the more tightly structured European political systems. One potential problem is the possibility of a growing participation gap between sophisticated and unsophisticated citizens (see chapter 3). Because the resources required to lobby government directly or to organize a public interest group are greater than those required to vote, a change in the style of political activity may leave behind those in society who lack the education and other skills and resources needed for direct-action politics.

Democracies must also face the challenge of balancing greater responsiveness to specific interests against the broader interests of the nation (Bok 2001; Dalton 2004a, ch. 9). In "political science speak," there has been a dramatic increase in interest articulation over the past generation but an erosion of interest aggregation within the polity. In other words, citizen interest groups, social movements, individual citizens, and various political groups are now more vocal about their political interests and have greater access to the democratic process. At the same time, the ability of political institutions to balance contending interests—and to make interest groups sensitive to the collective needs of society—has diminished. The collective interest is more than just the sum of individual interests, and one of the pressing needs for contemporary democracies is to find new ways to bring diverse interests together.

Participatory democracy can generate political overkill, but it also contains within it an equilibrium mechanism to encourage political balance. In the United States, the process has generally succeeded in retaining the benefits of new ideas while avoiding the ominously predicted excesses of democracy. We should remember that democratic politics is not designed to maximize government efficiency or to increase the autonomy of political elites. Just the opposite. In fact, efficiency is partially sacrificed to ensure a more important goal: popular control of elites. Expanding participation is not a problem but an opportunity for the advanced industrial democracies to come closer to matching their democratic ideals.

In summary, the current crisis of democracy is another stage in the ongoing history of democracy's development. Democracies need to adapt to present-day politics and to the new style of citizen politics. As Dahrendorf (2000, 311) has recently observed, "Representative government is no longer as compelling a proposition as it once was. Instead, a search for new institutional forms to express conflicts of interest has begun." This process of democratic experimentation and reform may be threatening to some, and it does present a risk—but change is necessary. The challenge to democracies is to discover whether they can continue to evolve, to guarantee political rights, and to increase the ability of citizens to control their lives. Can we move democracy closer to the horizon?

SUGGESTED READINGS

Bok, Derek. *The Trouble with Government*. Cambridge, Mass.: Harvard University Press, 2001.

Dalton, Russell. *Democratic Challenges, Democratic Choices: The Erosion of Political Support in Advanced Industrial Democracies*. Oxford: Oxford University Press, 2004.

Hetherington, Marc. *Why Trust Matters: Declining Political Trust and the Demise of American Liberalism*. Princeton: Princeton University Press, 2005.

Hibbing, John, and Elizabeth Theiss-Morse. *Stealth Democracy: Americans' Beliefs about How Government Should Work*. New York: Cambridge University Press, 2002.

Klingemann, Hans-Dieter, and Dieter Fuchs, eds. *Citizens and the State*. Oxford: Oxford University Press, 1995.

Norris, Pippa, ed. *Critical Citizens: Global Support for Democratic Governance*. Oxford: Oxford University Press, 1999.

Nye, Joseph, Philip Zelikow, and David King. *Why People Don't Trust Government.* Cambridge, Mass.: Harvard University Press, 1997.

Pharr, Susan, and Robert Putnam, eds. *Disaffected Democracies: What's Troubling the Trilateral Countries?* Princeton, N.J.: Princeton University Press, 2000.

Putnam, Robert. *Making Democracy Work.* Princeton, N.J.: Princeton University Press, 1993.

NOTES

1. In the mid-1980s, Samuel Huntington (1984) was explaining why there would be no more democracies in the world, a theme consistent with his elitist view of democracy. By the end of the decade, he was describing democratization as a wave that was transforming the international order (Huntington 1991).

2. There has been some debate over the accuracy of this quotation, since Crozier, Huntington, and Watanuki do not identify a source. Moreover, such a statement by Brandt would be in sharp contrast to his well-known admonition that Germany actually needed to "risk more democracy." Even if Brandt did not make this statement, however, other prominent Europeans certainly echoed these sentiments. For instance, the French political observer Jean-François Revel (1983, 3) declared that "democracy may, after all, turn out to have been a historical accident, a brief parenthesis that is closing before our eyes."

3. The argument is also made that diffuse regime support existed in most other Western democracies in the 1930s. Consequently, dissatisfaction focused on the performance of political elites in these systems. These feelings were channeled within the political process, and the basic structure of democratic government persisted in the United States, Britain, and France.

4. The question wording and coding categories were slightly different in each nation, so one should not directly compare the levels of support across nations in this figure. For such comparisons, see Klingemann (1999) and tables 12.2 and 12.3 in this chapter.

5. See the appendix to this book for the wording of the questions in the World Values Survey. For a more extensive comparison of confidence in institutions, see Dalton (2004a) and Klingemann (1999).

6. The two questions were as follows: "Would you say it is a very good, fairly good, fairly bad, or very bad way of governing this country: Having a democratic political system?" and "Democracy may have problems but it's better than any other form of government. Do you agree or disagree?"

7. The question asked, "How proud are you to be (nationality)?" The responses were: (1) very proud, (2) quite proud, (3) not very proud, and (4) not at all proud. The figure presents the "very proud" and "proud" responses.

8. Huntington's advice on limiting political demands overlooks the possibility of constraining the input of Harvard professors, corporate executives, and the upper class. His focus solely on the participation of average citizens suggests that he has confused the definitions of plutocracy and democracy.

Major Data Sources

I n 1948 researchers at the University of Michigan conducted one of the first national election surveys based on scientific sampling methods. The four scholars who eventually directed the early surveys—Angus Campbell, Philip Converse, Warren Miller, and Donald Stokes—wrote the landmark study of American electoral behavior, *The American Voter*. Since then, the Center for Political Studies (formerly part of the Survey Research Center) has continued this election study series at each biennial national election. The American National Election Studies (ANES) has become a national resource in the social sciences and is used by researchers in hundreds of universities worldwide.

A comparable series of British election studies was begun by David Butler and Donald Stokes with the 1964 election. These scholars continued the series through the 1966 and 1970 elections, and then a team of researchers at the University of Essex, led by Ivor Crewe, continued the series in 1974 and 1979. Between 1983 and 1997, the British Election Studies were conducted by Anthony Heath, Roger Jowell, and John Curtice of Social and Community Planning Research (SCPR) in London. A new research team at the University of Essex directed the 2001 British Election Study.

Academic studies of German elections trace their roots back to the 1961 study conducted by Gerhard Baumert, Erwin Scheuch, and Rudolf Wildenmann from the University of Cologne. The Cologne researchers and their students have established this series through the work of Max Kaase, Hans-Dieter Klingemann, Franz Pappi, and the Forschungsgruppe Wahlen (Manfred Berger, Wolfgang Gibowski, Dieter Roth, Mattias Jung, et al.) in Mannheim. The German Election Study series has continued with a new academic group at the Wissenschaftszentrum Berlin für Sozialforschung (WZB).

France lacks a project of continuous academic monitoring and public dissemination of data on citizen electoral behavior. A number of individual scholars have conducted surveys of specific French elections: Roland Cayrol and his associates, Philip Converse and Roy Pierce, Michael Lewis-Beck, Nonna Mayer, Daniel Boy, and their colleagues. The emerging series of election studies provides an opportunity to track the evolution of French political behavior during the Fifth Republic.

Most of the data analyzed in this volume were drawn from the data sources mentioned above and specifically listed below. Most of these data were acquired from the Inter-university Consortium for Political and Social Research (ICPSR) at the University of Michigan in Ann Arbor. Additional data were made available by the UK Data Archive at the University of Essex, England, and the Zentralarchiv für empirische Sozialforschung (ZA), University of Cologne, Germany. Neither the archives nor the original collectors of the data bear responsibility for the analyses presented here.

American National Election Studies (ANES)

1948	American National Election Study (N = 622). Angus Campbell and Robert Kahn.
1952	American National Election Study (N = 1,899). Angus Campbell, Gerald Gurin, et al.
1956	American National Election Study (N = 1,762). Angus Campbell, Philip Converse, et al.
1960	American National Election Study (N = 1,181). Angus Campbell, Philip Converse, et al.
1964	American National Election Study (N = 1,571). Political Behavior Program.
1968	American National Election Study (N = 1,557). Political Behavior Program.
1972	American National Election Study (N = 2,705). Warren Miller, Arthur Miller, et al.
1976	American National Election Study (N = 2,248). Warren Miller, Arthur Miller, et al.
1980	American National Election Study (N = 1,614). Warren Miller et al.
1984	American National Election Study (N = 2,257). Warren Miller et al.
1988	American National Election Study (N = 2,040). Warren Miller et al.
1992	American National Election Study (N = 2,485). Warren Miller et al.
1996	American National Election Study (N = 1,714). Steven Rosenstone et al.
2000	American National Election Study (N = 1,807). Nancy Burns et al.
2004	American National Election Study (N = 1,212). Nancy Burns et al.

British Election Studies

1964	British Election Study (N = 1,769). David Butler and Donald Stokes.
1966	British Election Study (N = 1,874). David Butler and Donald Stokes.
1970	British Election Study (N = 1,885). David Butler and Donald Stokes.

1974	British Election Study, February (N = 2,462). Ivor Crewe, Bo Saarlvik, and James Alt.
1974	British Election Study, October (N = 2,365). Ivor Crewe, Bo Saarlvik, and James Alt.
1979	British Election Study (N = 1,893). Ivor Crewe, Bo Saarlvik, and David Robertson.
1983	British Election Study (N = 3,955). Anthony Heath, Roger Jowell, and John Curtice.
1987	British Election Study (N = 3,826). Anthony Heath, Roger Jowell, John Curtice, and Sharon Witherspoon.
1992	British Election Study (N = 3,534). Anthony Heath, Roger Jowell, and John Curtice.
1997	British Election Study (N = 3,615). Anthony Heath, Roger Jowell, John Curtice, and Pippa Norris.
2001	British Election Study (N = 3,223). Harold Clarke, David Sanders, Marianne Stewart, and Paul Whiteley.

German Election Studies

1953	The Social Bases of West German Politics (N = 3,246). UNESCO Institute.
1961	West German Election Study (N = 1,679; 1,633; 1,715). Gerhart Baumert, Erwin Scheuch, and Rudolf Wildenmann.
1965	West German Election Study, October (N = 1,305). DIVO Institut.
1965	West German Election Study, September (N = 1,411). Rudolf Wildenmann and Max Kaase.
1969	West German Election Study (N = 1,158). Hans-Dieter Klingemann and Franz Pappi.
1972	West German Election Study (N = 2,052). Manfred Berger, Wolfgang Gibowski, Max Kaase, Dieter Roth, Uwe Schleth, and Rudolf Wildenmann.
1976	West German Election Study (N = 2,076). Forschungsgruppe Wahlen.
1980	West German Election Study (N = 1,620). Forschungsgruppe Wahlen.
1983	West German Election Study (N = 1,622). Forschungsgruppe Wahlen.
1987	West German Election Study (N = 1,954). Forschungsgruppe Wahlen.
1990	German Election Study, November (West = 984; East = 1,095). Forschungsgruppe Wahlen.
1994	German Election Study, September (West = 1,013; East = 1,068). Forschungsgruppe Wahlen.

1998   German Post-election Study (West = 978; East = 1,041). Mannheimer Zentrum für Europäische Sozialforschung (MZES), the Wissenschaftszentrum Berlin für Sozialforschung (WZB), the Zentralarchiv für empirische Sozialforschung, and the Zentrum für Umfragen, Methoden und Analysen (ZUMA), Mannheim.

2002   German Election Study (N = 2,000). Hermann Schmitt, Mannheimer Zentrum für Europäische Sozialforschung (MZES) and Bernhard Wessels, Wissenschaftszentrum Berlin für Sozialforschung (WZB).

French Election Studies

1958   French Election Study (N = 1,650). Georges Dupeux.

1967   French Election Study (N = 2,046). Philip Converse and Roy Pierce.

1968   French Election Study (N = 1,905). Ronald Inglehart.

1978   French Election Study (N = 4,507). Jacques Capdevielle, Elisabeth Dupoirier, Gerard Grunberg, Etienne Schweisguth, and Colette Ysmal.

1988   French Presidential Election Survey (N = 1,013). Roy Pierce.

1995   French National Election Study (N = 4,078). Michael Lewis-Beck, Nonna Mayer, Daniel Boy, et al.

1997   French National Election Study (N = 3,010). Centre d'Etudes de la Vie Politique Française (CEVIPOF), Centre d'Informatisation des Données Socio-Politiques (CIDSP), and Centre de Recherches Administratives, Politiques et Sociales (CRAPS).

2002   French Comparative Study of Electoral Systems (N = 1,000). Thomas Gschwend and Hermann Schmitt, Mannheimer Zentrum für Europäische Sozialforschung (MZES).

Major Cross-National Studies

1959   The Civic Culture Study (USA = 970, Great Britain = 963, West Germany = 955). Gabriel Almond and Sidney Verba.

1970   European Community Surveys / Eurobarometers (an ongoing series of opinion surveys conducted by the Commission of the European Union).

1974   Political Action Study (USA = 1,719; Great Britain = 1,483; West Germany = 2,307). Samuel Barnes, Max Kaase, et al.

1981–1983   World Values Survey (USA = 1,729; Great Britain = 1,231; West Germany = 1,305; France = 1,200). Gallup Research.

1985–	International Social Survey Program (a coordinated series of public opinion surveys conducted by various sociological institutes in the U.S. and Europe).
1990–1991	World Values Survey (USA = 1,839; Great Britain = 1,484; West Germany = 2,101; France = 1,002; East Germany = 1,336). Ronald Inglehart and the European Values Systems Study Group.
1995–1998	World Values Survey (USA = 1,542; Great Britain = 1,093; West Germany = 1,017; East Germany = 1,009). Ronald Inglehart, Hans-Dieter Klingemann, et al.
1999–2002	World Values Survey / European Values Survey (USA = 1,200; Great Britain = 994; France = 1,615; Germany = 2,036).
1996–	Comparative Study of Electoral Systems; Module I (USA = 1,714; Great Britain = 3,615; Germany = 2,021); Module 2 (USA = 1,534; France = 1,000; Germany = 2,000).
2002	European Social Survey (Great Britain = 2,052; Germany = 2,919).

1999–2002 World Values Survey/ European Values Survey Codebook

One of the key sources of public opinion data in this book is the 1999–2002 wave of the World Values Survey/European Values Survey (WVS/EVS). To assist students and instructors in understanding the causes and correlates of public opinion, we have prepared a subset of the data from the WVS/EVS for instructors to use in connection with *Citizen Politics*. These data have been extensively recoded and reformatted for ease of student usage, by such means as merging categories to ensure reasonable group sizes in cross-tabular analyses. Students can use these data for small research exercises designed by the instructor or for larger research projects that explore the themes in this book or other aspects of public opinion.

This appendix includes a brief description of the World Values Survey and an abbreviated codebook that describes the variables included in this subset. Portable files for the *Statistical Package in the Social Sciences* (SPSS) are downloadable from the CQ Press Web site for this book (http://www.cqpress.com/cs/dalton). A file containing data for the four core nations of this book (the United States, Great Britain, Germany, and France) is described in the codebook that follows.

In addition, the Web site includes a supplemental data set drawn from surveys in twenty advanced industrial democracies that were included in the fourth wave of the WVS. These data allow instructors and students to compare our four core nations to other established democracies (including most of the nations in Western Europe, Canada, and Japan).

The World Values Survey/European Values Survey

The World Values Survey and European Values Survey are a unique resource in the social sciences. The first wave of the project was a coordinated survey of twenty-one nations conducted in the early 1980s by the European Values Survey group. The second wave, done in the early 1990s, expanded to forty-two nations, including many of the postcommunist states in Eastern Europe (Inglehart 1997; Abramson and Inglehart 1995). The third wave, in the mid-1990s, included fifty-four nations and expanded the data collection to several nations in the developing world. The fourth wave of the WVS includes representative national surveys examining the basic values and beliefs of publics in more than sixty-five societies on all six inhabited continents, containing almost 80 percent of the world's population (Inglehart and Welzel 2005).

An international network of social scientists, coordinated by an international directorate, carries out this project. Most surveys are funded from national sources and conducted by leading survey research firms. An international board develops the survey questions, which are translated into the national language by each research institute. The data are then assembled in a single data set and made available to the international research community.

An exceptional feature of the 1999–2002 WVS is the range of nations included in the survey. This data supplement includes the four core nations from this book. The full data set includes survey data for virtually all the advanced industrial democracies, Eastern Europe, and a diverse range of developing nations. Additional information about the WVS/EVS can be found on its Web site (www.worldvaluessurvey.org). The full set of surveys is available from the Inter-university Consortium for Political and Social Research at the University of Michigan, the Zentralarchiv für empirische Sozialforschung at the University of Cologne, and other national social science data archives.

Variable List

V001   Country
V002   Weight

Life Domains

V003   How important is family
V004   How important are friends
V005   How important is leisure time
V006   How important is politics
V007   How important is work
V008   How important is religion

Quality of Life

V009   Feeling of happiness
V010   Are you satisfied with your life
V011   How much freedom do you feel

Parents

V012   Respect parents
V013   Parents responsibilities

Group Membership

V014   Belong church organization
V015   Belong labor union
V016   Belong political party

V017   Belong professional association
V018   Member civil society group
V019   Total memberships

Political Interest

V020   Discusses political matters
V021   Interested in politics
V022   How often follow politics

Protest Politics

V023   Political action: Signing a petition
V024   Political action: Joining in boycotts
V025   Political action: Lawful demonstration
V026   Political action: Unofficial strikes
V027   Political action: Occupying buildings
V028   Protest index

Tolerance

V029   Neighbors: People with criminal record
V030   Neighbors: People of different race
V031   Neighbors: Heavy drinkers
V032   Neighbors: Emotionally unstable
V033   Neighbors: Muslims
V034   Neighbors: Immigrants/foreign workers
V035   Neighbors: People with AIDS
V036   Neighbors: Drug addicts
V037   Neighbors: Homosexuals
V038   Neighbors: Jews
V039   Tolerance: Race/ethnicity
V040   Tolerance: Crime & drugs
V041   Tolerance: Homosexuals & AIDS

Social Trust

V042   Most people can be trusted

Environmental Attitudes

V043   Would give income for environment
V044   Increase taxes for environment
V045   Government should reduce pollution

Job Priorities

V046   Men should have priority for job
V047   Nationals should have priority for job

Attitudes toward Work

V048   To develop talents you need a job
V049   Receive money without work
V050   People who don't work turn lazy
V051   Work is a duty towards society
V052   People should not have to work
V053   Work should always come first
V054   One secretary is paid more
V055   Following instructions at work

Abortion Attitudes

V056   Abortion when woman not married
V057   Abortion if don't want more children

Marriage, Gender and Children

V058   Child needs a father and mother
V059   Woman has to have children
V060   Marriage is out-dated institution
V061   Woman as a single parent
V062   A working mother relationship
V063   Being a housewife fulfilling
V064   Gender attitudes index

Postmaterial Values

V065   Postmaterial values index
V066   Traditional/secular rational values
V067   Survival/self-expression values

Political Values

V068   Greater respect for authority
V069   Freedom or equality
V070   Left/right scale

Economic Values

V071   Incomes more equal
V072   Private ownership of business
V073   Government more responsibility
V074   Competition is good
V075   Firms and freedom
V076   Economic liberalism index

Confidence in Institutions

V077   Confidence: Churches
V078   Confidence: Armed forces
V079   Confidence: Education system
V080   Confidence: The press
V081   Confidence: Labor unions
V082   Confidence: The police
V083   Confidence: Parliament
V084   Confidence: The civil services
V085   Confidence: Major companies
V086   Confidence: Justice system
V087   Confidence: The European Union
V088   Confidence: NATO
V089   Confidence: The United Nations

Evaluating Government

V090   Democracy is developing in our country
V091   Rate political system today
V092   Rate previous political system

Support for Democracy

V093   Having a strong leader
V094   Having experts make decisions
V095   Having the army rule
V096   Having a democratic political system
V097   Democratic regime index
V098   Democracies have poor economies
V099   Democracies are indecisive
V100   Democracies don't maintain order
V101   Democracy best system
V102   Democratic process index
V103   Respect for individual human rights

Political Community

V104   How proud of nationality
V105   Be willing to fight for your country

Immigration

V106   Immigrant policy
V107   Immigrant integration

Party Preference

V108   Left/Right party preference
V109A Party: United States
V109B Party: Britain
V109C Party: France
V109D Party: Germany

Religious Values

V110   Belong to religious denomination
V111   Religious denomination
V112   How often attend religious service
V113   Religious person
V114   Good and evil

Religious Beliefs

V115   Believe in God
V116   Believe in life after death
V117   Believe in hell
V118   Believe in heaven

Importance of Religion

V119   How important is God in your life
V120   Comfort and strength from religion
V121   Moments of prayer
V122   Pray to God outside of religious service

Religion and Politics

V123   Non-religious politicians are unfit
V124   Religious should not influence politics
V125   Better if people have strong religion
V126   Religious should not influence government

Justifiable Actions

V127   Justifiable: Claiming government benefit
V128   Justifiable: Avoiding a transit fare
V129   Justifiable: Cheating on taxes
V130   Justifiable: Someone accepting a bribe
V131   Justifiable: Homosexuality
V132   Justifiable: Prostitution
V133   Justifiable: Abortion
V134   Justifiable: Divorce
V135   Justifiable: Euthanasia
V136   Justifiable: Suicide

Demographic Variables

V137   Geographic groups
V138   Ethnic identity
V139   Gender
V140   Age recoded
V141   Marital status
V142   Have you had any children
V143   Highest educational level
V144   Education recoded
V145   Income recoded
V146   Do you live with your parents
V147   Are you employed now
V148   R's profession/job
V149   R's occupation recode
V150   Are you the chief wage earner
V151   Is the chief wage earner employed
V152   Chief wage earner occupation
V153   Chief wage earner occupation recode
V154A Region: USA
V154B Region: Britain
V154C Region: France
V154D Region: Germany
V155   Size of town
V156   Race/ethnic group

Codebook

V001   Country

1.   United States
2.   Britain

3.   France
4.   Germany

V002   Weight

Most nations in the World Values Survey provide a weight variable used to correct your sample to reflect national distributions of key variables or to adjust for different sampling fractions for population groups. For instance, sometimes rural respondents are undersampled and their responses should be weighted to yield a representative national sample. SPSS can use this weight variable to construct a representative sample; the weight should be used for the U.S., British, French, and German studies.

V003   Family important

For each of the following, indicate how important it is in your life. Would you say it is: Family:
1.   Very important
2.   Rather important
3.   Not very important
4.   Not at all important
9.   Don't know

V004   Friends important

(How important are) friends?
[See V003 for response categories]

V005   Leisure time important

(How important is) leisure time?
[See V003 for response categories]

V006   Politics important

(How important is) politics?
[See V003 for response categories]

V007   Work important

(How important is) work?
[See V003 for response categories]

V008   Religion importan

(How important is) religion?
[See V003 for response categories]

V009   Feeling of happiness

Taking all things together, would you say you are:
1.　　Very happy
2.　　Quite happy
3.　　Not very happy
4.　　Not at all happy
9.　　Don't know; not asked in Britain

V010   Satisfaction with life

All things considered, how satisfied are you with your life as a whole these days? Please use this card to help with your answer.
1.　　Very dissatisfied (1–3)
2.　　Dissatisfied (4–5)
3.　　Satisfied (6–7)
4.　　Very satisfied (8–10)
9.　　Don't know

V011   Feeling of freedom

How much freedom do you feel?
1.　　Not at all (1–3)
2.　　(4–5)
3.　　(6–7)
4.　　A great deal (8–10)
9.　　Don't know

V012   Respect parents

With which of these two statements do you tend to agree?
1.　　Regardless of what the qualities and faults of one's parents are, one must always love and respect them
2.　　One does not have the duty to respect and love parents who have not earned it by their behavior and attitudes
9.　　Don't know

V013   Parents responsibilities

Which of the following statements best describes your views about parents' responsibilities to their children?
1.　　Parents' duty is to do their best for their children even at the expense of their own well-being
2.　　Neither
3.　　Parents have a life of their own and should not be asked to sacrifice their own well-being for the sake of their children
9.　　Don't know

V014   Belong church organization

(Belong to) religious or church organizations:
0.   Not member
1.   Belong to group
9.   Missing data

V015   Belong labor union

(Belong to) labor union:
0.   Not member
1.   Belong to group
9.   Missing data

V016   Belong political party

(Belong to) political parties or groups:
0.   Not member
1.   Belong to group
9.   Missing data

V017   Belong professional association

(Belong to) professional associations:
0.   Not member
1.   Belong to group
9.   Missing data

V018   Belong to civil society group

(Belong to) peace movement, environmental group, women's group, or local community group:
0.   Not member
1.   Belong to group
9.   Missing data

V019   Number of group memberships

Number of organizations to which the respondent belongs (a longer list of groups was included in the WVS):
0.   No group
1.   One group
2.   Two groups
3.   Three or more groups
9.   Missing data

V020   How often discusses political matters

When you get together with your friends, would you say you discuss political matters frequently, occasionally, or never?
1.   Frequently
2.   Occasionally
3.   Never
9.   Don't know

V021   Interested in politics

How interested would you say you are in politics?
1.   Very interested
2.   Somewhat interested
3.   Not very interested
4.   Not at all interested
9.   Don't know

V022   How often follow politics

How often do you follow politics in the news on television or on the radio or in the daily papers?
1.   Every day
2.   Several times a week
3.   Once a week
4.   Less often
5.   Never
9.   Don't know

V023   Political action: Signing a petition

Now I'd like you to look at this card. I'm going to read out some different forms of political action that people can take, and I'd like you to tell me, for each one, whether you have actually done any of these things, whether you might do it or would never, under any circumstances, do it. Signing a petition:
1.   Have done
2.   Might do
3.   Would never do
9.   Don't know

V024   Political action: Joining in boycotts

Joining in boycotts:
1.   Have done
2.   Might do
3.   Would never do
9.   Don't know

V025   Political action: Lawful demonstration

Attending lawful demonstrations:
1. Have done
2. Might do
3. Would never do
9. Don't know

V026   Political action: Unofficial strike

Joining unofficial strikes:
1. Have done
2. Might do
3. Would never do
9. Don't know

V027   Political action: Occupy building

Occupying buildings or factories:
1. Have done
2. Might do
3. Would never do
9. Don't know

V028   Protest scale

[This variable is a count of the number of protest activities the respondent has done in V024–V027.]
0. No protest activities
1. One
2. Two
3. Three or more

V029   Neighbors: People with criminal record

On this list are various groups of people. Could you please sort out any that you would not like to have as neighbors: People with a criminal record:
0. Not mentioned
1. Mentioned
9. Don't know

V030   Neighbors: People of different race

On this list are various groups of people. Could you please sort out any that you would not like to have as neighbors. People of a different race:
0. Not mentioned

1.   Mentioned
9.   Don't know

V031   Neighbors: Heavy drinkers

On this list are various groups of people. Could you please sort out any that
you would not like to have as neighbors. Heavy drinkers:
0.   Not mentioned
1.   Mentioned
9.   Don't know

V032   Neighbors: Emotionally unstable

On this list are various groups of people. Could you please sort out any that
you would not like to have as neighbors. Emotionally unstable people:
0.   Not mentioned
1.   Mentioned
9.   Don't know

V033   Neighbors: Muslims

On this list are various groups of people. Could you please sort out any that
you would not like to have as neighbors. Muslims:
0.   Not mentioned
1.   Mentioned
9.   Don't know

V034   Neighbors: Immigrants/foreign workers

On this list are various groups of people. Could you please sort out any that
you would not like to have as neighbors. Immigrants/foreign workers:
0.   Not mentioned
1.   Mentioned
9.   Don't know

V035   Neighbors: People with AIDS

On this list are various groups of people. Could you please sort out any that
you would not like to have as neighbors. People with AIDS:
0.   Not mentioned
1.   Mentioned
9.   Don't know

V036   Neighbors: Drug addicts

On this list are various groups of people. Could you please sort out any that
you would not like to have as neighbors. Drug addicts:
0.   Not mentioned

1. Mentioned
9. Don't know

V037 Neighbors: Homosexuals

On this list are various groups of people. Could you please sort out any that you would not like to have as neighbors. Homosexuals:
0. Not mentioned
1. Mentioned
9. Don't know

V038 Neighbors: Jews

On this list are various groups of people. Could you please sort out any that you would not like to have as neighbors. Jews:
0. Not mentioned
1. Mentioned
9. Don't know

V039 Tolerance: Race/ethnicity

[On the basis of factor analyses we combined respondents who mentioned race or ethnic groups as people they would not like as a neighbor (V30, V33, V34, or V38).]
0. Not mentioned
1. Mentioned one or more of these groups
9. Don't know

V040 Tolerance: Crime & drugs

[On the basis of factor analyses we combined respondents who mentioned criminals or drug addicts as people they would not like as a neighbor (V29 or V36).]
0. Not mentioned
1. Mentioned one or more of these groups
9. Don't know

V041 Tolerance: Homosexuals & AIDS

[On the basis of factor analyses we combined respondents who mentioned homosexuals or people with AIDS as people they would not like as a neighbor (V35 or V37).]
0. Not mentioned
1. Mentioned one or more of these groups
9. Don't know

V042   Most people can be trusted

Generally speaking, would you say that most people can be trusted or that you need to be very careful in dealing with people?
1.   Most people can be trusted
2.   Need to be very careful
9.   Don't know

V043   Would give income for environment

I am now going to read out some statements about the environment. For each one read out, can you tell me whether you agree strongly, agree, disagree, or strongly disagree. I would give part of my income if I were certain that the money would be used to prevent environmental pollution:
1.   Strongly agree
2.   Agree
3.   Disagree
4.   Strongly disagree
9.   Don't know

V044   Increase taxes for environment

I would agree to an increase in taxes if the extra money were used to prevent environmental pollution:
1.   Strongly agree
2.   Agree
3.   Disagree
4.   Strongly disagree
9.   Don't know

V045   Government should reduce pollution

The government should reduce environmental pollution, but it should not cost me any money:
1.   Strongly agree
2.   Agree
3.   Disagree
4.   Strongly disagree
9.   Don't know

V046   Men should have priority for job

Do you agree or disagree with the following statements? When jobs are scarce, men should have more right to a job than women:
1.   Agree
2.   Neither

3.   Disagree
9.   Don't know

V047   Nationals should have priority for job

When jobs are scarce, employers should give priority to [BRITISH] people over immigrants:
1.   Agree
2.   Neither
3.   Disagree
9.   Don't know

V048   Need job to develop talents

Do you agree or disagree with the following statements? To fully develop your talents, you need to have a job:
1.   Strongly agree
2.   Agree
3.   Neither
4.   Disagree
5.   Strongly disagree
9.   Don't know

V049   Receive money without work

It is humiliating to receive money without having to work for it:
[See V048 for response categories]

V050   Without work people are lazy

People who don't work turn lazy:
[See V048 for response categories]

V051   Work is a duty towards society

Work is a duty towards society:
[See V048 for response categories]

V052   People should not have to work

People should not have to work if they don't want to:
[See V048 for response categories]

V053   Work should always come first

Work should always come first, even if it means less spare time:
[See V048 for response categories]

V054   One secretary is paid more

Imagine two secretaries, of the same age, doing practically the same job. One finds out that the other earns considerably more than she does. The better paid secretary, however, is quicker, more efficient, and more reliable at her job. In your opinion, is it fair or not fair that one secretary is paid more than the other?
1.   Fair
2.   Not fair
9.   Don't know

V055   Following instructions at work

People have different ideas about following instructions at work. Some say that one should follow one's superior's instructions even when one does not fully agree with them. Others say that one should follow one's superior's instructions only when one is convinced that they are right. With which of these two opinions do you agree?
1.   Should follow instructions
2.   Depends
3.   Must be convinced first
9.   Don't know

V056   Abortion when woman not married

Do you approve or disapprove of abortion under the following circumstances? Where the woman is not married:
0.   Disapprove
1.   Approve
9.   Missing data; not asked in the United States

V057   Abortion if don't want more children

Do you approve or disapprove of abortion under the following circumstances? Where a married couple does not want to have any more children:
0.   Disapprove
1.   Approve
9.   Missing data; not asked in the United States

V058   Child needs a father and mother

If someone says a child needs a home with both a father and a mother to grow up happily, would you tend to agree or disagree?
1.   Tend to disagree
2.   Tend to agree
9.   Don't know

V059   Woman has to have children

Do you think that a woman has to have children in order to be fulfilled or is this not necessary?
1.   Not necessary
2.   Needs children
9.   Don't know

V060   Marriage is out-dated institution

Do you agree or disagree with the following statement? "Marriage is an out-dated institution":
1.   Disagree
2.   Agree
9.   Don't know

V061   Woman as a single parent

If a woman wants to have a child as a single parent but she doesn't want to have a stable relationship with a man, do you approve or disapprove?
1.   Approve
2.   Depends [if volunteered]
3.   Disapprove
9.   Don't know

V062   A working mother relationship

A working mother can establish just as warm and secure a relationship with her children as a mother who does not work:
1.   Strongly agree
2.   Agree
3.   Disagree
4.   Strongly disagree
9.   Don't know

V063   Being a housewife fulfilling

Being a housewife is just as fulfilling as working for pay:
1.   Strongly agree
2.   Agree
3.   Disagree
4.   Strongly disagree
9.   Don't know

V064   Gender attitudes index

[This variable is a count of the Index of gender attitudes (from V058–V061).]
0.   No response for gender equality
1.
2.
3.
4.   Four responses for gender equality
9.   Don't know

V065   Postmaterial values index

People sometimes talk about what the aims of this country should be for the next ten years. On this card are listed some of the goals which different people would give top priority. Would you please say which one of these you, yourself, consider the most important? And which would be the next most important?
  1.   Maintaining order in the nation,
  2.   Giving people more say in important government decisions,
  3.   Fighting rising prices, and
  4.   Protecting freedom of speech.

[The postmaterial index counts those select items 1 and 3 as materialists, items 2 and 4 as postmaterialists, and those who select one from both listed are scored as mixed values.]
  1.   Materialist
  2.   Mixed
  3.   Postmaterialist
  9.   Missing data; not asked in Britain

V066   Traditional/secular rational values

[This is a constructed index that taps support for traditional religious values versus secular-rational value orientations. The index is described in Inglehart and Welzel (2005).]
1.   Very traditional
2.   Leaning traditional
3.   Leaning secular
4.   Very secular
9.   Missing data; not available for Britain

V067   Survival/self-expression values

[This is a constructed index that taps support for survival values versus self-expressive value orientations. The index is described in Inglehart and Welzel (2005).]

1. Very survival
2. Leaning survival
3. Leaning self-expressive
4. Very self-expressive
9. Missing data; not available for Britain

V068 Greater respect for authority

Here is a list of various changes in our way of life that might take place in the near future. Please tell me for each one, if it were to happen whether you think it would be a good thing, a bad thing, or don't you mind? Greater respect for authority:

1. Good
2. Don't mind
3. Bad
9. Don't know

V069 Freedom or equality (not asked in United States)

Which of these two statements comes closest to your own opinion?

1) I find that both freedom and equality are important. But if I were to choose one or the other, I would consider personal freedom more important, that is, everyone can live in freedom and develop without hindrance.

2) Certainly both freedom and equality are important. But if I were to choose one or the other, I would consider equality more important, that is, that nobody is underprivileged and that social class differences are not so strong.

1. Freedom
2. Neither
3. Equality
9. Don't know; not asked in the United States

V070 Left/Right scale

In political matters, people talk of "the left" and "the right." How would you place your views on this scale, generally speaking?

1. Left (1–3)
2. (Values 4–5)
3. (Values 6–7)
4. Right (8–10)
9. Don't know

V071 Incomes more equal

Now I'd like you to tell me your views on various issues. How would you place your views on this scale? 1 means you agree completely with the statement on the left; 10 means you agree completely with the statement on the right; and if your views fall somewhere in between, you can choose any number in between.

1. Incomes should be made more equal (1–3)
2. (Values 4–5)
3. (Values 6–7)
4. We need larger income differences as incentives for individual effort (8–10)
9. Don't know; not asked in Germany

V072　Private ownership of business

Private ownership of business and industry should be increased vs. government ownership of business and industry should be increased:

1. Private ownership increased (1–3)
2. (Values 4–5)
3. (Values 6–7)
4. Government ownership increased (8–10)
9. Don't know

V073　Government more responsibility

The government should take more responsibility to ensure that everyone is provided for vs. people should take more responsibility to provide for themselves:

1. Government more responsible (1–3)
2. (Values 4–5)
3. (Values 6–7)
4. People more responsible for themselves (8–10)
9 Don't know

V074　Competition is good

Competition is good. It stimulates people to work hard and develop new ideas vs. competition is harmful. It brings out the worst in people:

1. Competition is good (1–3)
2. (Values 4–5)
3. (Values 6–7)
4. Competition is harmful (8–10)
9. Don't know

V075 Firms and freedom

The state should give more freedom to firms vs. the state should control firms more effectively:
1. State gives freedom to firms (1–3)
2. (Values 4–5)
3. (Values 6–7)
4. State controls firms (8–10)
9. Don't know; not asked in the United States

V076 Economic liberalism index

[This variable is a count of liberal responses on four economic policy questions (V071–V074).]
0. No liberal responses
1.
2.
3.
4. Four liberal responses

V077 Confidence: Churches

I am going to name a number of organizations. For each one, could you tell me how much confidence you have in them: is it a great deal of confidence, quite a lot of confidence, not very much confidence or none at all? The churches:
1. Great deal of confidence
2. Quite a lot of confidence
3. Not very much confidence
4. None at all
9. Don't know

V078 Confidence: Armed forces

(Confidence in) the armed forces:
[See V077 for response categories]

V079 Confidence: Education system

(Confidence in) education system
[See V077 for response categories]; not asked in the United States

V080 Confidence: The press

(Confidence in) the press:
[See V077 for response categories]

V081   Confidence: Labor unions

(Confidence in) labor unions:
[See V077 for response categories]

V082   Confidence: The police

(Confidence in) the police:
[See V077 for response categories]

V083   Confidence: Parliament

(Confidence in) parliament:
[See V077 for response categories]

V084   Confidence: The civil services

(Confidence in) the civil service:
[See V077 for response categories]

V085   Confidence: Major companies

(Confidence in) major companies:
[See V077 for response categories]

V086   Confidence: Justice system

(Confidence in) justice system:
[See V077 for response categories]
9.   Don't know; not asked in the United States

V087   Confidence: The European Union

(Confidence in) the European Union:
[See V077 for response categories]
9.   Don't know; not asked in the United States

V088   Confidence: NATO

(Confidence in) NATO (North Atlantic Treaty Organization):
[See V077 for response categories]
9.   Don't know; not asked in France

V089   Confidence: The United Nations

(Confidence in) The United Nations:
[See V077 for response categories]

V090   How is democracy developing

How democracy is developing in our country:
1.   Very satisfied
2.   Rather satisfied
3.   Not very satisfied
4.   Not at all
9.   Don't know

V091   Rate political system today

People have different views about the system for governing this country. Here is a scale for rating how well things are going: 1 means very bad; 10 means very good. Where on this scale would you put the political system as it is today?
1.   Bad (1–3)
2.   (4, 5)
3.   (6, 7)
4.   Very good (8–10)
9.   Don't know; not asked in the United States

V092   Rate political system in past

Rate political system as it was ten years ago:
1.   Bad (1–3)
2.   (4,5)
3.   (6,7)
4.   Very good (8–10)
9.   Don't know

V093   Having a strong leader

I'm going to describe various types of political systems and ask what you think about each as a way of governing this country. For each one, would you say it is a very good, fairly good, fairly bad, or very bad way of governing this country? Having a strong leader who does not have to bother with parliament and elections.
1.   Very good
2.   Fairly good
3.   Bad
4.   Very bad
9.   Don't know

V094   Having experts make decisions

(Do you feel good about) Having experts, not government, make decisions according to what they think is best for the country:

1.   Very good
2.   Fairly good
3.   Bad
4.   Very bad
9.   Don't know

V095   Having the army rule

(Do you feel good about) Having the army rule:
1.   Very good
2.   Fairly good
3.   Bad
4.   Very bad
9.   Don't know

V096   Having a democratic political system

(Do you feel good about) Having a democratic political system:
1.   Very good
2.   Fairly good
3.   Bad
4.   Very bad
9.   Don't know

V097   Democratic regime index

[This variable is a count of the number of pro-democratic/anti-autocratic responses to V093–V096.]
0.   No democratic responses
1.   One
2.   Two
3.   Three
4.   Four democratic responses

V098   Democracies have poor economies

I'm going to read off some things that people sometimes say about a democratic political system. Could you please tell me if you agree strongly, agree, disagree, or disagree strongly, after I read each one of them? In democracy, the economic system runs badly:
1.   Agree strongly
2.   Agree
3.   Disagree
4.   Disagree strongly
9.   Don't know

V099 Democracies are indecisive

(Do you agree/disagree) Democracies are indecisive and have too much quibbling:
1. Agree strongly
2. Agree
3. Disagree
4. Disagree strongly
9. Don't know

V100 Democracies don't maintain order

(Do you agree/disagree) Democracies aren't good at maintaining order:
1. Agree strongly
2. Agree
3. Disagree
4. Disagree strongly
9. Don't know

V101 Democracy is best system

(Do you agree/disagree) Democracy may have problems but it's better than any other form of government:
1. Agree strongly
2. Agree
3. Disagree
4. Disagree strongly
9. Don't know

V102 Democratic process index

[This variable is a count of the number of pro-democratic/anti-autocratic responses to V098–V101.]
0. No democratic responses
1. One
2. Two
3. Three
4. Four democratic responses

V103 Respect for individual human rights

How much respect is there for individual human rights nowadays (in our country)? Do you feel there is:
1. A lot of respect for individual human rights
2. Some respect
3. Not much respect

4.   No respect at all
9.   Don't know

V104   How proud of nationality

How proud are you to be FRENCH? (substitute your own nationality for "French")
1.   Very proud
2.   Quite proud
3.   Not very proud
4.   Not at all proud
9.   Don't know

V105   Be willing to fight in a war

Of course, we all hope that there will not be another war, but if it were to come to that, would you be willing to fight for your country?
0.   No
1.   Yes
9.   Don't know; not asked in Britain

V106   Immigrant policy

How about people from less developed countries coming here to work? Which of the following do you think the government should do?
1.   Let anyone come
2.   As long as jobs are available
3.   Strict limits
4.   Prohibit people from coming
9.   Don't know

V107   Immigrant integration

Which of these statements is the nearest to your opinion?
1   Maintain distinct customs and traditions
2   Take over customs of the country
9   Don't know; not asked in the United States

V108   Left/Right party preference

If there were a national election tomorrow, for which party on this list would you vote? Just call out the number on this card. If DON'T KNOW: Which party appeals to you most?
1.   Left Party
2.   Right Party
9.   Other party; no answer

V109A Party preference—United States

1. Democrats
2. Republicans
9. Other party; no answer; other nations

V109B Party preference—Britain

1. Labour
2. Liberal Democrat
3. Conservative
9. Other party; no answer; other nations

V109C Party preference—France

1. Extreme Left
2. Communist (PC)
3. Socialist
4. Greens
5. RPR
6. UDF
7. National Front
9. Other party; no answer; other nations

V109D Party preference—Germany

1. PDS
2. Greens
3. SPD
4. FDP
5. CDU/CSU
9. Other party; no answer; other nations

V110 Belong to religious denomination

Do you belong to a religious denomination?
1. Yes
2. No
9. Don't know

V111 Religious denomination

(If religious, denomination:) Which one?
0. No, not a member
1. Roman Catholic
2. Protestant
3. Orthodox (Russian/Greek/etc.)

4.   Jews
5.   Other
9.   No answer

V112   How often attend religious services

Apart from weddings, funerals, and christenings, about how often do you attend religious services these days?
1.   Weekly or more often
2.   Once a month
3.   Only on special holy days
4.   Less often
5.   Never, practically never
9.   Don't know

V113   Religious person

Independently of whether you go to church or not, would you say you are . . .(read out)
1.   A religious person
2.   Not a religious person
3.   A convinced atheist
9.   Don't know

V114   Good and evil

Here are two statements which people sometimes make when discussing good and evil. Which one comes closest to your own point of view?
1.   There are absolutely clear guidelines about what is good and evil. These always apply to everyone, whatever the circumstances.
2.   Disagree with both [if volunteered]
3.   There can never be absolutely clear guidelines about what is good and evil. What is good and evil depends entirely upon the circumstances at the time.
9.   Don't know

V115   Believe in God

Which, if any, of the following do you believe in? Do you believe in God?
1.   Yes
2.   No
9.   Don't know

V116 Believe in life after death

Do you believe in life after death?
1. Yes
2. No
9. Don't know

V117 Believe in hell

Do you believe in hell?
1. Yes
2. No
9. Don't know

V118 Believe in heaven

Do you believe in heaven?
1. Yes
2. No
9. Don't know

V119 How important is God in your life

How important is God in your life? Please use this scale to indicate—10 means very important and 1 means not at all important.
1. Not at all (1–3)
2. 4–5
3. 6–7
4. Very important (8–10)
9. Don't know

V120 Comfort and strength from religion

Do you find that you get comfort and strength from religion?
1. Yes
2. No
9. Don't know

V121 Moments of prayer, meditation

Do you take some moments of prayer, meditation or contemplation or something like that?
1. Yes
2. No
9. Don't know

V122 Pray to God outside of religious service

How often do you pray to God outside of religious services? Would you say . . .

1. Daily
2. Weekly
3. Monthly
4. Less often
5. Never
9. Don't know

V123 Politicians who don't believe god unfit

Politicians who don't believe in God unfit:

1. Agree strongly
2. Agree
3. Neither agree/disagree
4. Disagree
5. Disagree strongly
9. Don't know

V124 Religious should not influence politics

Religious leaders should not influence politics:

1. Agree strongly
2. Agree
3. Neither agree/disagree
4. Disagree
5. Disagree strongly
9. Don't know

V125 Better if people have strong religion

Better if more people with strong religion:

1. Agree strongly
2. Agree
3. Neither agree/disagree
4. Disagree
5. Disagree strongly
9. Don't know

V126 Religious should not influence government

Religious leaders should not influence government:

1. Agree strongly
2. Agree

3. Neither agree/disagree
4. Disagree
5. Disagree strongly
9. Don't know

V127 Justifiable: claiming government benefit

Please tell me for each of the following statements whether you think it can always be justified, never be justified, or something in between, using this card. Claiming government benefits to which you are not entitled:
1. Never (1)
2. 2–4
3. 5–7
4. Always justifiable (8–1)
9. Don't know

V128 Justifiable: avoiding transit fare

Avoiding a fare on public transport:
[See V127 for response categories]

V129 Justifiable: Cheating on taxes

Cheating on taxes if you have a chance:
[See V127 for response categories]

V130 Justifiable: Someone accepting a bribe

Someone accepting a bribe in the course of their duties:
[See V127 for response categories]

V131 Justifiable: Homosexuality

Homosexuality:
[See V127 for response categories]

V132 Justifiable: Prostitution

Prostitution:
[See V127 for response categories]
9. Don't know; not asked in France

V133 Justifiable: Abortion

Abortion:
[See V127 for response categories]

V134   Justifiable: Divorce

Divorce:
[See V127 for response categories]

V135   Justifiable: Euthanasia

Euthanasia—ending the life of the incurably sick:
[See V127 for response categories]

V136   Justifiable: Suicide

Suicide:
[See V127 for response categories]

V137   Geographic groups

To which of these geographical groups would you say you belong first of all?
1.   Locality or town where you live
2.   State or region of country where you live
3.   Nation as a whole
4.   Continent [North America/Europe]
5.   The world as a whole
9.   Don't know

V138   Ethnic identity—United States only

Which of the following best describes you? (Also see V156):
1.   I am a Hispanic American
2.   I am a black American
3.   I am a white American
4.   I am an Asian American
5.   I am an American
9.   Don't know; other nation

V139   Gender

Sex of respondent:
1.   Male
2.   Female
9.   Missing data

V140   Age recoded

Can you tell me your year of birth, please? 19__ This means you are __ __
years old.
1.   15–24

2.　　25–34
3.　　35–44
4.　　45–54
5.　　55–64
6.　　65 and older
9.　　Missing data

V141　Marital status

Are you currently . . . (read out and code one only)
1.　　Married/Living together as married
2.　　Divorced
3.　　Separated
4.　　Widowed
5.　　Single
9.　　Missing data

V142　Have you had any children

Have you had any children? IF YES, how many?
0.　　No child
1.　　1 child
2.　　2 children
3.　　3 children
4.　　4 or more children
9.　　No answer

V143　Highest educational level

What is the highest educational level that you have attained? (use functional equivalent of the following, in given society; IF STUDENT, code highest level he/she expects to complete):
1.　　Incomplete primary education or less
2.　　Complete primary education
3.　　Incomplete secondary technical
4.　　Complete secondary technical
5.　　Incomplete secondary—academic track
6.　　Complete secondary—academic track
7.　　Incomplete university
8.　　University with degree
9.　　Missing data

V144　Education recoded

[This is a collapsed version of V143.]
1.　　Primary education or less

2.   Some secondary education
3.   Some college education or post-secondary training
9.   Don't know

V145   Income recoded

Here is a scale of incomes. We would like to know in what group your household is, counting all wages, salaries, pensions, and other incomes that come in. Just give the letter of the group your household falls into, before taxes and other deductions. [This variable was collapsed into comparable income ranges and divided into three groups.]
1.   Lower income
2.   Middle income
3.   Higher income
9.   Don't know

V146   Do you live with your parents

Do you live with your parents?
0.   No
1.   Yes
9.   Missing data

V147   Are you employed now

Are you employed now or not? [IF YES:] About how many hours a week? If more than one job: only for the main job.
1.   Has paid employment full time (30 hours a week or more)
2.   Part time (less than 30 hours a week)
3.   Self employed
4.   Retired/pensioned
5.   Housewife not otherwise employed
6.   Student
7.   Unemployed
8.   Other
9.   Missing data

V148   Profession/job

In which profession/occupation do you or did you work? If more than one job, the main job? What is/was your job there?
1.   Employer/manager of establishment with 10 or more employees
2.   Employer/manager of establishment with less than 10 employees
3.   Professional worker lawyer, accountant, teacher, etc.
4.   Supervisory—office worker: supervises others

5.   Non-manual—office worker: non-supervisory
6.   Foreman and supervisor
7.   Skilled manual worker
8.   Semi-skilled manual worker
9.   Unskilled manual worker
10.   Farmer: has own farm
11.   Agricultural worker
12.   Member of armed forces, security personnel
13.   Never had a job
99.   Missing data

V149   R occupation recode.

[This variable collapses the categories of V148.]
1.   Middle class (codes 1–5)
2.   Working class (codes 6–9)
9.   Other occupations; no answer

V150   Are you the chief wage earner

Are you the chief wage earner in your household?
0.   No
1   Yes
9.   Missing data

V151   Is chief wage earner employed

Is the chief wage earner employed now or not?
0.   No
1.   Yes
9.   Missing data

V152   Chief wage earner occupation

In which profession/occupation does he/she work? (or did work) If more than one job, the main job? What is/was his/her job there? (R's occupation is copied here if R is chief wage earner)
1.   Employer/manager of establishment with 10 or more employees
2.   Employer/manager of establishment with less than 10 employees
3.   Professional worker lawyer, accountant, teacher, etc.
4.   Supervisory non-manual—office worker
5   Non-manual—office worker: non-supervisory
6.   Foreman and supervisor
7.   Skilled manual worker
8.   Semi-skilled manual worker
9.   Unskilled manual worker

10.   Farmer: has own farm
11.   Agricultural worker
12.   Member of armed forces, security personnel
13.   Never had a job
99.   Missing data

V153   Chief occupation recode

[This variable collapses the categories of V152.]
1.   Middle class (codes 1–5)
2.   Working class (codes 6–9)
9.   Other occupations; no answer

V154A Region—United States

USA: Region where the interview was conducted:
1.   New England
2.   Middle Atlantic states
3.   South Atlantic
4.   East South Central
5.   West South Central
6.   East North Central
7.   West North Central
8.   Rocky Mountain states
9.   Northwest
10.   California
99.   Missing data; other nation

V154B Region—Britain

Region where interview was conducted in Britain:
1.   Northeast
2.   Northwest
3.   Yorkshire and Humbs
4.   East Midlands
5.   West Midlands
6.   Eastern
7.   London
8.   Southeast
9.   Southwest
10.   Wales
11.   Scotland
99.   Missing data; other nation

V154C Region—France

Region where interview was conducted in France:
1. Paris Basin
2. Center-East
3. East
4. Ile de France
5. Mediterranean
6. North
7. West
8. South West
99. Missing data; other nation

V154D Region—Germany

Region (Land) in Germany where interview was conducted:
1. Schleswig-Holstein
2. Hamburg
3. Lower Saxony
4. Bremen
5. Northrhine Westphalia
6. Hesse
7. Rhineland Pfalz
8. Baden-Wuerttemberg
9. Bavaria
10. Saarland
11. Berlin
12. Brandenburg
13. Mecklenburg-Vorpommern
14. Saxony
15. Saxony-Anhalt
16. Thueringen
99. Missing data; other nation

V155   Size of town

Size of town:
1. Under 5,000
2. 5–20,000
3. 20–100,000
4. 100,000 and more
9. Missing data

V156   Race/ethnic group

Ethnic group [Asked only in the United States] (Also see V138):
1.   Caucasian white
2.   Negro Black
3.   South Asian Indian, Pakistani, etc.
4.   East Asian Chinese, Japanese, etc.
5.   Arabic, Central Asian
6.   Other
7.   Hispanic
9.   Not included in British, French, or German survey

References

Aarts, Kees, André Blais, and Hermann Schmitt. 2005. *Political Leaders and Democratic Elections*. Oxford: Oxford University Press.

Aberbach, Joel, and Jack Walker. 1970. Political trust and racial ideology. *American Political Science Review* 64:1199–1219.

Abramson, Paul. 1979. Developing party identification. *American Journal of Political Science*. 23:79–96.

Abramson, Paul, John Aldrich, and David Rohde. 2003. *Change and Continuity in the 2000 and 2002 Elections*. Washington, D.C.: CQ Press.

Abramson, Paul, and Ronald Inglehart. 1995. *Value Change in Global Perspective*. Ann Arbor: University of Michigan Press.

Abramson, Paul, and Charles Ostrom. 1991. Macropartisanship: An empirical reassessment. *American Political Science Review*. 85:181–192.

———. 1994. Question wording and partisanship. *Public Opinion Quarterly* 58:21–48.

Alba, Richard, Peter Schmidt, and Martina Wasmer, eds. 2003. *Germans or foreigners? Attitudes toward ethnic minorities in post-reunification Germany*. New York: Palgrave Macmillan.

Aldrich, John, John Sullivan, and E. Bordida. 1989. Foreign affairs and issue voting. *American Political Science Review* 83:123–141.

Almond, Gabriel, Russell Dalton, G. Bingham Powell, and Kaare Strom, eds. 2005. *European Politics Today*. 3rd ed. New York: Longman.

Almond, Gabriel, G. Bingham Powell, and Robert Mundt. 1990. *Comparative Politics*. 2nd ed. New York: HarperCollins.

Almond, Gabriel, G. Bingham Powell, Kaare Strom, and Russell Dalton, eds. 2005. *Comparative Politics Today*. 8th ed. update. New York: Addison Wesley Longman.

Almond, Gabriel, and Sidney Verba. 1963. *The Civic Culture*. Princeton, N.J.: Princeton University Press.

———, eds. 1980. *The Civic Culture Revisited*. Boston: Little, Brown.

Amand, Sowmya, and Jon A. Krosnick. 2003. The impact of attitudes toward foreign policy goals on public preferences among presidential candidates: A study of issue publics and the attentive public in the 2000 U.S. presidential election. *Presidential Studies Quarterly* 33:31–71.

Anderson, Christopher. 1995. *Blaming the Government: Citizens and the Economy in Five European Democracies*. Armonk, N.Y.: M.E. Sharpe.

———. 2000. Economic voting and political context. *Electoral Studies* 19:151–170.

Anderson, Christopher, and Carsten Zelle, eds. 1998. *Stability and Change in German Elections: How Electorates Merge, Converge, or Collide*. Westport, Conn.: Praeger.

Ansell, Christopher, and Steven Fish. 1999. The art of being indispensable: Noncharismatic personalism in contemporary political parties. *Comparative Political Studies* 32:283–312.

Ansolabehere, Stephen, James Snyder, and Charles Stewart. 2001a. The effects of party and preferences on congressional roll-call voting. *Legislative Studies Quarterly* 26:533–572.

———. 2001b. Candidate positioning in the U.S. House elections. *American Journal of Political Science* 45:136–159.

Arnold, Douglas. 1990. *The Logic of Congressional Action*. New Haven, Conn.: Yale University Press.

Ashford, Sheena, and Noel Timms. 1992. *What Europe Thinks: A Study of Western European Values*. Brookfield, Vt.: Dartmouth.

Bagehot, Walter. 1978. *The English Constitution*. Oxford: Oxford University Press.

Baker, Kendall, Russell Dalton, and Kai Hildebrandt. 1981. *Germany Transformed: Political Culture and the New Politics*. Cambridge, Mass.: Harvard University Press.

Barber, Benjamin. 1984. *Strong Democracy*. Berkeley: University of California Press.

Barnes, Samuel. 1977. *Representation in Italy*. Chicago: University of Chicago Press.

Barnes, Samuel, Max Kaase, et al. 1979. *Political Action*. Beverly Hills, Calif.: Sage.

Bartels, Larry. 2000. Partisanship and voting behavior. *American Journal of Political Science* 44:35–50.

Bartolini, Stefano, and Peter Mair. 1990. *Identity, Competition and Electoral Availability*. New York: Cambridge University Press.

Bauer-Kaase, Petra. 1994. German unification. In *German Unification*, ed. Don Hancock and Helga Welsh. Boulder, Colo.: Westview.

Bean, Clive, and Anthony Mughan. 1989. Leadership effects in parliamentary elections in Australia and Britain. *American Political Science Review* 83:1165–1179.

Bean, Clive, and Elim Papadakis. 1994. Polarized priorities or flexible alternatives? *International Journal of Public Opinion Research* 6:264–288.

Beck, Paul Allen, et al. 1992. Patterns and sources of ticket-splitting in subpresidential voting. *American Political Science Review* 86:916–928.

Beedham, Brian. 1993. What next for democracy? *The Economist*, September 11; special supplement: *The Future Surveyed*.

Bell, Daniel. 1960. *The End of Ideology*. New York: Free Press.

———. 1973. *The Coming of Post-industrial Society*. New York: Basic Books.

Bennet, William, and Samuel Nunn. 1998. *A Nation of Spectators*. Washington, D.C.: National Commission on Civic Renewal.

Berelson, Bernard, Paul Lazarsfeld, and William McPhee. 1954. *Voting*. Chicago: University of Chicago Press.

Berglund, Frode, et al. 2005. Partisanship: Causes and consequences. In *The European Voter,* ed. J. Thomassen. Oxford: Oxford University Press.

Berry, Jeffrey. 1999. *The New Liberalism: The Rising Power of Citizen Groups.* Washington, D.C.: Brookings Institution.

Betz, Hans-Georg. 1994. *Radical Right-wing Populism in Europe.* New York: St. Martin's.

Bimber, Bruce. 2003. *Information and American Democracy: Technology in the Evolution of Political Power.* New York: Cambridge University Press.

Bishop, George, and Kathleen Frankovic. 1981. Ideological consensus and constraint among party leaders and followers in the 1978 election. *Micropolitics* 1:87–111.

Blais, André. 2000. *To Vote or Not to Vote: The Merits and Limits of Rational Choice Theory.* Pittsburgh: University of Pittsburgh Press.

Blais, André, and Agnieszka Dobrzynska. 1998. Turnout in electoral democracies. *European Journal of Political Research* 33:239–261.

Bok, Derek. 2001. *The Trouble with Government.* Cambridge, Mass.: Harvard University Press.

Borre, Ole, and Daniel Katz. 1973. Party identification and its motivational base in a multiparty system. *Scandinavian Political Studies* 8:69–111.

Borre, Ole, and Elinor Scarbrough, eds. 1995. *The Scope of Government.* Oxford: Oxford University Press.

Bowler, Shaun. 2000. Party cohesion. In *Parties without Partisans,* ed. R. Dalton and M. Wattenberg. Oxford: Oxford University Press.

Bowler, Shaun, David Farrell, and Richard Katz, eds. 1999. *Party Discipline and Parliamentary Government.* Columbus: Ohio State University Press.

Boy, Daniel, and Nonna Mayer, eds. 1993. *The French Voter Decides.* Ann Arbor: University of Michigan Press.

Brady, Henry, Sidney Verba, and Kay Schlozman. 1995. Beyond SES: A resource model of political participation. *American Political Science Review* 89:271–294.

Braithwaite, V., T. Makkai, and Y. Pittelkow. 1996. Inglehart's materialism-postmaterialism concept: Clarifying the dimensionality debate through Rokeach's model of social values. *Journal of Applied Social Psychology* 26:1536–1555.

Brettschneider, Frank. 1996. Public opinion and parliamentary action: Responsiveness of the German Bundestag in comparative perspective. *International Journal of Public Opinion Research* 8:292–311.

Brody, Richard. 1978. The puzzle of political participation in America. In *The New American Political System,* ed. A. King. Washington, D.C.: American Enterprise Institute.

Brody, Richard, et al. 1994. Accounting for divided government. In *Elections at Home and Abroad,* ed. M. Kent Jennings and T. Mann. Ann Arbor: University of Michigan Press.

Bromley, Catherine, and John Curtice. 2003. Where have all the voters gone? In Alison Park, et al. *British Social Attitudes, 19th Report*. Newbury Park, Calif.: Sage.

Bromley, Catherine, John Curtice, and Ben Seyd. 2002. Confidence in government. In *British Social Attitude Survey*, ed. Roger Jowell et al. Brookfield, Vt.: Dartmouth Publishing.

Brooks, John. 1987. The opinion-policy nexus in France—Do institutions and ideology make a difference? *Journal of Politics* 49:465–480.

———. 1990. The opinion-policy nexus in Germany. *Public Opinion Quarterly* 54:508–529.

Bryce, James. 1921. *Modern Democracies*. Vol. 1. New York: Macmillan.

Budge, Ian. 1999. Party policy and ideology: Reversing the 1950s. In *Critical Elections*, ed. G. Evans and P. Norris. Newbury Park, Calif.: Sage.

Budge, Ian, Ivor Crewe, and David Farlie, eds. 1976. *Party Identification and Beyond*. New York: Wiley.

Budge, Ian, David Robertson, and D. Hearl. 1987. *Ideology, Strategy and Party Change*. Cambridge: Cambridge University Press.

Bürklin, Wilhelm, et al. 1997. *Eliten in Deutschland: Rekrutierung und Integration*. Leverkusen: Leske + Budrich.

Burns, Nancy, Kay L. Schlozman, and Sidney Verba. 2001. *The Private Roots of Public Action*, Cambridge, Mass.: Harvard University Press.

Butler, David, and Austin Ranney, eds. 1994. *Referendums around the World: The Growing Use of Democracy?* Washington, D.C.: American Enterprise Institute.

Butler, David, and Donald Stokes. 1969. *Political Change in Britain*. New York: St. Martin's.

———. 1974. *Political Change in Britain*. 2nd ed. New York: St. Martin's.

Cain, Bruce, Russell Dalton, and Susan Scarrow, eds. 2003. *Democracy Transformed? Expanding Political Access in Advanced Industrial Democracies*. Oxford: Oxford University Press.

Cain, Bruce, Sergio Fabrinni, and Patrick Egan. 2003. Toward more open democracies: The expansion of Freedom of Information laws. In *Democracy Transformed?* ed. B. Cain, R. Dalton, and S. Scarrow. Oxford: Oxford University Press.

Campbell, Angus, et al. 1960. *The American Voter*. New York: Wiley.

———. 1966. *Elections and the Political Order*. New York: Wiley.

Campbell, Angus, Philip Converse, and Willard Rodgers. 1979. *The Quality of American Life*. New York: Russell Sage Foundation.

Campbell, Angus, Gerald Gurin, and Warren Miller. 1954. *The Voter Decides*. Evanston, Ill.: Row, Peterson.

Cantril, Hadley. 1965. *The Patterns of Human Concern*. New Brunswick, N.J.: Rutgers University Press.

Carmines, Edward, and James Stimson. 1980. The two faces of issue voting. *American Political Science Review* 74:78–91.

———. 1989. *Issue Evolution: Race and the Transformation of American Politics*. Princeton, N.J.: Princeton University Press.

Carty, Kenneth. 2002. Canada's nineteenth-century cadre parties at the millennium. In *Political Parties in Advanced Industrial Democracies*, ed. P. Webb, D. Farrell, and I. Holliday. Oxford: Oxford University Press.

Caul, Miki, and Mark Gray. 2000. From platform declarations to policy outcomes. In *Parties without Partisans*, ed. R. Dalton and M. Wattenberg. Oxford: Oxford University Press.

Central Intelligence Agency. 2004. *World Fact Book*. http://www.odci.gov/cia/publications/factbook/index.html.

Cichowski, Rachel, and Alec Stone Sweet. 2003. Participation, representative democracy, and the courts. In *Democracy Transformed?* ed. B. Cain, R. Dalton, and S. Scarrow. Oxford: Oxford University Press.

Citrin, Jack. 1974. Comment. *American Political Science Review* 68:973–988.

Clark, Terry Nichols, and Vincent Hoffmann-Martinot, eds. 1998. *The New Political Culture*. Boulder, Colo.: Westview.

Clark, Terry Nichols, and Seymour Martin Lipset, eds. 2001.*The Breakdown of Class Politics: A Debate on Post-industrial Stratification*. Baltimore: Johns Hopkins University Press.

Clark, Terry Nichols, Seymour Martin Lipset, and Michael Rempel. 1993. The declining political significance of social class. *International Sociology* 8:293–316.

Clarke, Harold, and Nitish Dutt. 1991. Measuring value change in western industrialized societies. *American Political Science Review* 85:905–920.

Clarke, Harold, Allan Kornberg, and Peter Wearing. 2000. *A Polity on the Edge: Canada and the Politics of Fragmentation*. Toronto: Broadview.

Clarke, Harold, and Marianne Stewart. 1998. The decline of parties in the minds of citizens. *Annual Review of Political Science* 1:357–378.

Clarke, Harold, et al. 1999. The effect of economic priorities on the measurement of value change: New experimental evidence. *American Political Science Review* 93:637–647.

———. 2004. *Political Choice in Britain*. Oxford: Oxford University Press.

Conover, Pamela, and Stanley Feldman. 1984. How people organize the political world. *American Journal of Political Science* 28:95–126.

Conradt, David. 2004. *The German Polity*. 7th ed. New York: Longman.

Converse, Philip. 1964. The nature of belief systems in mass publics. In *Ideology and Discontent*, ed. D. Apter. New York: Free Press.

———. 1966. The normal vote. In Angus Campbell, et al. *Elections and the Political Order*. New York: Wiley.

———. 1969. Of time and partisan stability. *Comparative Political Studies* 2:139–171.

———. 1970. Attitudes and nonattitudes. In *The Quantitative Analysis of Social Problems*, ed. E. Tufte. Reading, Mass.: Addison-Wesley.

———. 1972. Change in the American electorate. In *The Human Meaning of Social Change*, ed. A. Campbell and P. Converse. New York: Russell Sage Foundation.

———. 1975. Public opinion and voting behavior. In vol. 4 of *Handbook of Political Science*, ed. F. Greenstein and N. Polsby. Reading, Mass.: Addison-Wesley.

———. 1976. *The Dynamics of Party Support*. Beverly Hills, Calif.: Sage.

———. 1990. Popular representation and the distribution of information. In *Information and Democratic Processes*, ed. J. Ferejohn and J. Kuklinski. Urbana: University of Illinois Press.

Converse, Philip, and Georges Dupeux. 1962. Politicization of the electorate in France and the United States. *Public Opinion Quarterly* 26:1–23.

Converse, Philip, and Greg Markus. 1979. Plus ça change . . . The new CPS election study panel. *American Political Science Review* 73:32–49.

Converse, Philip, and Roy Pierce. 1986. *Representation in France*. Cambridge, Mass.: Harvard University Press.

Conway, Mary Margaret. 2000. *Political Participation in the United States*. 3rd ed. Washington, D.C.: CQ Press.

Cooper, Joseph, ed. 1999. *Congress and the Decline of Public Trust*. Boulder, Colo.: Westview.

Craig, Stephen. 1993. *The Malevolent Leaders: Popular Discontent in America*. Boulder, Colo.: Westview.

Crepaz, Markus. 1990. The impact of party polarization and postmaterialism on voter turnout. *European Journal of Political Research* 18:183–205.

Crewe, Ivor. 1981. Electoral participation. In *Democracy at the Polls*, ed. D. Butler, et al. Washington, D.C.: American Enterprise Institute.

———. 1995. Oral evidence in 'Standards in Public Life: First Report of the Committee on Standards in Public Life.' In vol. 2 of *Transcripts of Evidence*, CM 2850-II. London: HMSO.

Crewe, Ivor, and J. Denver, eds. 1985. *Electoral Change*. Oxford: Oxford University Press.

Crewe, Ivor, and Donald Searing. 1988. Mrs. Thatcher's crusade: Conservatism in Britain, 1972–1986. In *The Resurgence of Conservatism in the Anglo-American Countries*, ed. B. Booper et al. Durham, N.C.: Duke University Press.

Cronin, Thomas. 1989. *Direct Democracy: The Politics of Initiative, Referendum and Recall*. Cambridge, Mass.: Harvard University Press.

Crozier, Michel. 1964. *The Bureaucratic Personality*. Chicago: University of Chicago Press.

———. 1982. *Strategies for Change*. Cambridge, Mass.: MIT Press.

Crozier, Michel, Samuel Huntington, and Joji Watanuki. 1975. *The Crisis of Democracy*. New York: New York University Press.

Curtice, John, and Roger Jowell. 1997. Trust in the political system. In *British Social Attitudes—the 14th Report*, ed. R. Jowell et al. Brookfield, Vt.: Dartmouth Publishing.

Curtice, John, and Ben Seyd. 2002. Is there a crisis of political participation? In *British Social Attitudes: Public Policy, Social Ties*, ed. Alison Park et al. Newbury Park, Calif.: Sage.

Cyert, Richard, and James March. 1963. *A Behavioral Theory of the Firm*. Englewood Cliffs, N.J.: Prentice-Hall.

Dahl, Robert. 1971. *Polyarchy*. New Haven: Yale University Press.

———. 1984. *A Preface to Economic Democracy*. Berkeley: University of California Press.

———. 1989. *Democracy and its Critics*. New Haven, Conn.: Yale University Press.

Dahrendorf, Ralf. 1975. Excerpts from remarks on the ungovernability study. In *The Crisis of Democracy*, ed. M. Crozier et al. New York: New York University Press.

———. 2000. Afterword. In *Disaffected Democracies,* ed. S. Pharr and R. Putnam. Princeton, N.J.: Princeton University Press.

Dalton, Russell. 1977. Was there a revolution? *Comparative Political Studies* 9:459–473.

———. 1984. Cognitive mobilization and partisan dealignment in advanced industrial democracies. *Journal of Politics* 46:264–284.

———. 1985. Political parties and political representation. *Comparative Political Studies* 17:267–299.

———. 1993a. *Politics in Germany*. New York: HarperCollins.

———, ed. 1993b. *The New Germany Votes: Unification and the Creation of the New German Party System*. Oxford: Berg Publishers.

———. 1994a. *The Green Rainbow: Environmental Groups in Western Europe*. New Haven, Conn.: Yale University Press.

———. 1994b. Communists and democrats: Democratic attitudes in the two Germanies. *British Journal of Political Science* 24:469–493.

———. 1996. *Citizen Politics: Public Opinion and Political Parties in Western Democracies*. 2nd ed. Chatham, N.J.: Chatham House.

———. 1999. Political support in advanced industrial democracies. In *Critical Citizens*, ed. P. Norris. Oxford: Oxford University Press.

———. 2000a. The decline of party identification. In *Parties without Partisans*, ed. R. Dalton and M. Wattenberg. Oxford: Oxford University Press.

———. 2000b. Value change and democracy. In *Disaffected Democracies,* ed. S. Pharr and R. Putnam. Princeton, N.J.: Princeton University Press.

———. 2003. Voter choice and electoral politics. In Gordon Smith, et al. *Developments in German Politics*. London: Macmillan.

———. 2004a. *Democratic Challenges, Democratic Choices: The Erosion of Political Support in Advanced Industrial Democracies*. Oxford: Oxford University Press.

———. 2004b. Partisan mobilization, cognitive mobilization and the changing American electorate. Research monograph series, Center for the Study of Democracy, University of California, Irvine. http://repositories.cdlib.org/csd/04-11.

———. 2005a. Politics in Germany. In *European Politics Today*, ed. G. Almond, R. Dalton, G. Powell, and K. Strom. New York: Addison Wesley Longman.

———. 2005b. The social transformation of trust in government, *International Journal of Sociology* 15 (March): 129–145.

Dalton, Russell, and Wilhelm Bürklin. 1996. The social bases of the vote. In *Germans Divided*, ed. R. Dalton. New York and Oxford: Berg Publishers.

———. 2003. Wähler als Wandervögel: Dealignment and the German voter. *German Politics and Society* 21 (spring): 57–75.

Dalton, Russell, Scott Flanagan, and Paul Beck, eds. 1984. *Electoral Change in Advanced Industrial Democracies*. Princeton, N.J.: Princeton University Press.

Dalton, Russell, and Mark Gray. 2003. Expanding the electoral marketplace. In *Democracy Transformed?* ed. B. Cain, R. Dalton, and S. Scarrow. Oxford: Oxford University Press.

Dalton, Russell, and Robert Rohrschneider. 1998. The greening of Europe: Environmental values and environmental behavior. In *British—and European—Social Attitudes: The 15th Report.*, ed. Jowell, et al. Brookfield, Vt.: Ashgate Publishing.

Dalton, Russell, and Martin Wattenberg. 1993. The not so simple act of voting. In *The State of the Discipline*, ed. A. Finifter. Washington, D.C.: American Political Science Association.

———, eds. 2000. *Parties without Partisans: Political Change in Advanced Industrial Democracies*. Oxford: Oxford University Press.

Dalton, Russell, and Steve Weldon. 2004. Public images of political parties: A necessary evil? *Rivista italiana di scienza politica* (December) 34: 381-404.

Della Porta, Donatella. 2000. Social capital, beliefs in government and political corruption. In *Disaffected Democracies*, ed. S. Pharr and R. Putnam. Princeton, N.J.: Princeton University Press.

Delli Carpini, Michael, and Scott Keeter. 1996. *What Americans Know about Politics and Why It Matters*. New Haven, Conn.: Yale University Press.

Delli Carpini, Michael, and Lee Sigelman. 1986. Do yuppies matter? Competing explanations of their political distinctiveness. *Public Opinion Quarterly* 50:502–518.

Dimock, Michael. 1998. Political knowledge and the political environment: Reassessing trends in partisanship, 1960–1966. Paper presented at the annual meeting of the American Political Science Association, Boston.

Downs, Anthony. 1957. *An Economic Theory of Democracy*. New York: Wiley.

Duch, Raymond, and Michael Taylor. 1993. Postmaterialism and the economic condition. *American Journal of Political Science* 37:747–779.

———. 1994. A reply to Abramson and Inglehart's "Education, security and postmaterialism." *American Journal of Political Science* 38:815–824.

Dunlap, Riley, George Gallup, and Alec Gallup. 1993. *Health of the Planet*. Princeton, N.J.: Gallup International Institute.

Dye, Thomas, and Harmon Ziegler. 1970. *The Irony of Democracy.* Belmont, Calif.: Duxbury.

Easton, David. 1965. *A Systems Analysis of Political Life.* New York: Wiley.

———. 1975. A reassessment of the concept of political support. *British Journal of Political Science* 5:435–457.

Easton, David, and Jack Dennis. 1969. *Children in the Political System.* New York: McGraw-Hill.

Eckstein, Harry. 1984. Civic inclusion and its discontents. *Daedalus* 113:107–146.

Ehrmann, Henry, and Martin Schain. 1992. *Politics in France.* 5th ed. New York: HarperCollins.

Elkins, Zachary, and John Sides. 2004. In search of the unified nation-state: National attachment among distinctive citizens. Paper presented at the annual meeting of the Midwest Political Science Association, Chicago.

Erikson, Robert. 1978. Constituency opinion and congressional behavior. *American Journal of Political Science* 22:511–535.

Erikson, Robert, Michael MacKuen, and James Stimson. 2002. *The Macro Polity.* Cambridge: Cambridge University Press.

Erikson, Robert, and Kent Tedin. 2001. *American Public Opinion.* 6th ed. New York: Allyn & Bacon.

Erikson, Robert, and Gerald Wright. 1980. Policy representation of constituency interests. *Political Behavior* 2:91–106.

Erikson, Robert, Gerald Wright, and John McIver. 1994. *State House Democracy: Public Opinion and Public Policy in the American States.* New York: Cambridge University Press.

Esaiasson, Peter, and Sören Holmberg. 1996. *Representative from Above: Members of Parliament and Representative Democracy in Sweden.* Aldershot, Hants., and Brookfield, Vt.: Dartmouth Publishing.

Evans, Geoffrey, ed. 1999. *The End of Class Politics? Class Voting in Comparative Context.* New York: Oxford University Press.

———. 2000. The continued significance of class voting. *Annual Review of Political Science* 3:401–417.

Evans, Geoffrey, and Pippa Norris, eds. 1999. *Critical Elections: British Parties and Voters in Long-Term Perspective.* Newbury Park, Calif.: Sage.

Farah, Barbara. 1980. *Political representation in West Germany.* PhD diss., University of Michigan.

Feldman, Stanley. 1989. Reliability and stability of policy positions. *Political Analysis* 1: 25–60.

Ferejohn, John, and James Kuklinski, eds. 1990. *Information and Democratic Processes.* Urbana: University of Illinois Press.

Fiorina, Morris. 1981. *Retrospective Voting in American National Elections.* New Haven, Conn.: Yale University Press.

———. 1990. Information and rationality in elections. In *Information and Democratic Processes,* ed. J. Ferejohn and J. Kuklinski. Urbana: University of Illinois Press.

———. 1992. *Divided Government.* New York: Macmillan.

———. 2002. Parties and partisanship: A forty year retrospective. *Political Behavior* 24:93–115.

———. 2005. *Culture War? The Myth of a Polarized America.* New York: Pearson Longman.

Flanagan, Scott. 1982. Changing values in advanced industrial society. *Comparative Political Studies* 14:403–444.

———. 1987. Value change in industrial society. *American Political Science Review* 81:1303–1319.

Flanagan, Scott, and Aie-Rie Lee. 2003. The new politics, culture wars, and the authoritarian-libertarian value change in advanced industrial democracies. *Comparative Political Studies* 36:235–270.

Fleury, Christopher, and Michael Lewis-Beck. 1993. Anchoring the French voter: Ideology vs. party. *Journal of Politics* 55:1100–1109.

Franklin, Mark. 1985. *The Decline of Class Voting in Britain.* Oxford: Oxford University Press.

———. 1996. Political participation. In *Comparing Democracies,* ed. L. LeDuc, et al. Thousand Oaks, Calif.: Sage.

———. 2004. *Voter Turnout and the Dynamics of Electoral Competition in Established Democracies since 1945.* New York: Cambridge University Press.

Franklin, Mark, Tom Mackie, and Henry Valen, eds. 1992. *Electoral Change.* New York: Cambridge University Press.

Franklin, Mark, and Christopher Wlezien. 1997. The responsive public: Issue salience, policy change, and preferences for European unification. *Journal of Theoretical Politics* 9:247–263.

———, eds. 2002. *The Future of Election Studies.* Amsterdam: Elsevier.

Friedrich, Walter, and Hartmut Griese. 1990. *Jugend und Jugendforschung in der DDR.* Opladen: Westdeutscher Verlag.

Fuchs, Dieter, Giovanna Guidorossi, and Palle Svensson. 1995. Support for the democratic system. In *Citizens and the State,* ed. H. Klingemann and D. Fuchs. Oxford: Oxford University Press.

Fuchs, Dieter, and Hans-Dieter Klingemann. 1989. The Left-Right schema. In *Continuities in Political Action,* ed. M. K. Jennings and J. van Deth. Berlin: deGruyter.

———. 1995. Citizens and the state. In *Citizens and the State,* ed. H. Klingemann and D. Fuchs. Oxford: Oxford University Press.

Fuchs, Dieter, and Robert Rohrschneider. 1998. Postmaterialism and electoral choice before and after German unification. *West European Politics* 21:95–116.

Fukuyama, Francis. 1992. *The End of History and the Last Man.* New York: Free Press.

———. 1999. *The Great Disruption: Human Nature and the Reconstitution of Social Order.* New York: Free Press.

Gabel, Matthew. 1998. *Interests and Integration: Market liberalization, public opinion, and European Union.* Ann Arbor: University of Michigan Press.

Gallagher, Michael, and Pier Vincenzo Uleri, eds. 1996. *The Referendum Experience in Europe.* Basingstoke, Hants.: Macmillan.

Gallup, George. 1976a. *International Public Opinion Polls: Britain.* New York: Random House.

———. 1976b. *International Public Opinion Polls: France.* New York: Random House.

Geer, John. 2005. *Public Opinion and Polling around the World.* 2 vols. Santa Barbara, Calif.: ABC-CLIO.

Gershkoff, Amy. 2005. Not "non-attitudes" but rather "non-measurement." Paper presented at the annual meeting of the Southern Political Science Association, New Orleans.

Glass, David. 1985. Evaluating presidential candidates: Who focuses on their personal attributes? *Public Opinion Quarterly* 49:517–534.

Goldthorpe, John. 1987. *Social Mobility and Class Structure in Modern Britain.* Oxford: Clarendon Press.

Gordon, Stacy, and Gary Segura. 1997. Cross-national variation in the political sophistication of individuals: Capability or choice? *Journal of Politics* 59:126–147.

Graber, Doris. 1988. *Processing the News: How People Tame the Information Tide.* 2nd ed. New York: Longman.

———. 1993. *Mass Media and American Politics.* 4th ed. Washington, D.C.: CQ Press.

Gray, Mark, and Miki Caul. 2000. Declining voter turnout in advanced industrial democracies 1950–1997. *Comparative Political Studies* 33:1091–1122.

Green, Donald, Bradley Palmquist, and Eric Schickler. 2002. *Partisan Hearts and Minds: Political Parties and the Social Identities of Voters.* New Haven, Conn.: Yale University Press.

Green, Mark, et al. 1984. *Who Runs Congress?* 4th ed. New York: Dell.

Gurr, T. Robert. 1970. *Why Men Rebel.* Princeton, N.J.: Princeton University Press.

Haegel, Florence. 1993. Partisan ties. In *The French Voter Decides,* ed. D. Boy and N. Mayer. Ann Arbor: University of Michigan Press.

Hall, Peter. 2002. Social capital in Britain. In *Democracies in Flux,* ed. R. Putnam. Oxford: Oxford University Press.

Hampton, Mary, and Christian Soe, eds. 1999. *Between Bonn and Berlin: German Politics Adrift?* Lanham, Md.: Rowman & Littlefield.

Harding, Steve. 1986. *Contrasting Values in Western Europe.* London: Macmillan.

Harrison, Lawrence, and Samuel Huntington, eds. 2000. *Culture Matters: How Values Shape Human Progress.* New York: Basic Books.

Hastings, Elizabeth, and Philip Hastings, eds. 1989. *Index to International Public Opinion, 1987–88.* Westport, Conn.: Greenwood.

Heath, Anthony, Roger Jowell, and John Curtice. 1991. *Understanding Political Change: The British Voter 1964–1987.* New York: Pergamon.

———. 1994. *Labour's Last Chance: The 1992 Election and Beyond.* Brookfield, Vt.: Dartmouth Publishing.

Heath, Anthony, and Dorren McMahon. 1992. Changes in values. In R. Jowell, et al. *British Social Attitudes: The 9th Report.* Brookfield, Vt.: Dartmouth Publishing.

Heath, Anthony, and Roy Pierce. 1992. It was party identification all along. *Electoral Studies* 11:93–105.

Heidenheimer, Arnold, and Peter Flora, eds. 1981. *The Development of the Welfare State.* New Brunswick, N.J.: Transaction.

Held, David. 1987. *Models of Democracy.* Stanford, Calif.: Stanford University Press.

Herrera, Cheryl Lyn, Richard Herrera, and Eric R. A. N. Smith. 1992. Public opinion and congressional representation. *Public Opinion Quarterly* 56:185–205.

Herzog, Dietrich, and Bernhard Wessels, eds. 1990. *Abgeordnete und Bürger.* Opladen: Westdeutscher Verlag.

Hess, Robert, and Judith Torney. 1967. *The Development of Political Attitudes in Children.* Chicago: Aldine.

Hetherington, Marc. *Why Trust Matters: Declining Political Trust and the Demise of American Liberalism.* Princeton: Princeton University Press, 2005.

Hibbing, John, and Elizabeth Theiss-Morse. 1995. *Congress as Public Enemy: Public Attitudes toward American Political Institutions.* New York: Cambridge University Press.

———, eds. 2001. *What Is It about Government that Americans Dislike?* New York: Cambridge University Press.

———. 2002. *Stealth Democracy: Americans' Beliefs about How Government Should Work.* New York: Cambridge University Press.

Higley, John, et al. 1979. *Elites in Australia.* London: Routledge & Kegan Paul.

Himmelweit, Hilde, et al. 1981. *How Voters Decide.* London: Academic Press.

Hoffmann-Lange, Ursula. 1992. *Eliten, Macht und Konflikt in der Bundesrepublik.* Opladen: Leske + Budrich.

Hollifield, James. 1993. *Immigrants, Markets and States.* Cambridge, Mass.: Harvard University Press, 1993.

Holmberg, Sören. 1989. Political representation in Sweden. *Scandinavian Political Studies* 12:1–36

———. 1994. Party identification compared across the Atlantic. In *Elections at Home and Abroad,* ed. M. K. Jennings and T. Mann. Ann Arbor: University of Michigan Press.

———. 1999. Down and down we go: Political trust in Sweden. In *Critical Citizens,* ed. P. Norris. Oxford: Oxford University Press.

Hout, Michael, Clem Brooks, and Jeff Manza. 1993. The persistence of classes in postindustrial society. *International Sociology* 8:259–277.

Hout, Michael, et al. 1995. The democratic class struggle in the United States, 1948–1992. *American Sociological Review* 60:805–828.

Humphreys, Peter. 1996. *Mass Media and Media Policy in Western Europe.* Manchester: University of Manchester Press.

Huntington, Samuel. 1974. Postindustrial politics: How benign will it be? *Comparative Politics* 6:147–177.

———. 1975. The democratic distemper. *Public Interest* 41:9–38.

———. 1981. *American Politics: The Promise of Disharmony.* Cambridge, Mass.: Harvard University Press.

———. 1984. Will more countries become democratic? *Political Science Quarterly* 99:193–218.

———. 1991. *The Third Wave.* Norman: University of Oklahoma Press.

———. 2004. *Who Are We? The Challenges to America's National Identity.* New York: Simon & Schuster.

Hurwitz, Jon, and Mark Peffley. 1987. How are foreign policy attitudes structured? *American Political Science Review* 81:1099–1120.

Hutchings, Vincent. 2003. *Public Opinion and Democratic Accountability.* Princeton, N.J.: Princeton University Press.

Ignazi, Piero. 2003. *Extreme Right Parties in Western Europe.* Oxford: Oxford University Press.

Inglehart, Ronald. 1977. *The Silent Revolution.* Princeton, N.J.: Princeton University Press.

———. 1979. Political action. In *Political Action,* ed. S. Barnes, M. Kaase, et al. Beverly Hills, Calif.: Sage.

———. 1981. Post-materialism in an environment of insecurity. *American Political Science Review* 75:880–900.

———. 1984. Changing cleavage alignments in Western democracies. In *Electoral Change in Advanced Industrial Democracies,* ed. R. Dalton, S. Flanagan, and P. Beck. Princeton, N.J.: Princeton University Press.

———. 1990. *Culture Shift in Advanced Industrial Society.* Princeton, N.J.: Princeton University Press.

———. 1995. Political support for environmental protection. *PS—Political Science and Politics* 28:57–72.

———. 1997. *Modernization and Postmodernization: Cultural, Economic and Political Change in 43 Nations.* Princeton, N.J.: Princeton University Press.

Inglehart, Ronald, and W. Baker. 2000. *Modernization, cultural change, and the persistence of traditional values.* American Sociological Review 65:19–51.

Inglehart, Ronald, and Pippa Norris. 2003. *A Rising Tide: Gender Equality and Cultural Change around the World.* New York: Cambridge University Press.

Inglehart, Ronald, and Christian Welzel. 2005. *Modernization, Cultural Change and Democracy: The Human Development Sequence.* New York: Cambridge University Press.

Ingram, Helen, and Steven Smith, eds. 1993. *Public Policy for Democracy.* Washington, D.C.: Brookings Institution.

Inkeles, Alex, and David Smith. 1974. *Becoming Modern: Individual Change in Six Developing Countries.* Cambridge, Mass.: Harvard University Press.

Jackman, Robert. 1972. Political elites, mass publics and support for democratic principles. *Journal of Politics* 34:753–773.

———. 1987. Political institutions and voter turnout in the industrialized democracies. *American Political Science Review* 81:405–424.

Jacoby, William. 1991. Ideological identification and issue attitudes. *American Journal of Political Science* 35:178–205.

Jelen, Ted, Sue Thomas, and Clyde Wilcox. 1994. The gender gap in comparative perspective. *European Journal of Political Research* 25:171–186.

Jennings, M. Kent. 1987. Residues of a movement: The aging of the American protest generation. *American Political Science Review* 81:367–382.

———. 1992. Ideological thinking among mass publics and political elites. *Public Opinion Quarterly* 56:419–441.

Jennings, M. Kent, and Thomas Mann, eds. 1994. *Elections at Home and Abroad.* Ann Arbor: University of Michigan Press.

Jennings, M. Kent, and Greg Markus. 1984. Partisan orientations over the long haul. *American Political Science Review* 78:1000–1018.

Jennings, M. Kent, and Richard Niemi. 1973. *The Character of Political Adolescence.* Princeton, N.J.: Princeton University Press.

———. 1981. *Generations and Politics.* Princeton, N.J.: Princeton University Press.

Jennings, M. Kent, and Jan van Deth, eds. 1989. *Continuities in Political Action.* Berlin: deGruyter.

Jennings, M. Kent, et al. 1979. Generations and families. In *Political Action,* ed. S. Barnes, M. Kaase et al. Beverly Hills, Calif.: Sage.

Jowell, Roger, et al., eds. 1998. *British—and European—Social Attitudes: The 15th Report.* Brookfield, Vt.: Ashgate Publishing.

Judis, John, and Ruy Teixeira. 2002. *The Emerging Democratic Majority.* New York: Scribner.

Kaase, Max. 1982. Partizipative Revolution: Ende der Parteien? In *Büurger und Parteien,* ed. J. Raschke. Opladen: Westdeutscher Verlag.

Kaase, Max, and Hans-Dieter Klingemann. 1994. The cumbersome way to partisan orientations in a "new" democracy. In *Elections at Home and Abroad,* ed. M. K. Jennings and T. Mann. Ann Arbor: University of Michigan Press.

Kaase, Max, and Kenneth Newton. 1998. Commitment to the welfare state. In *British—and European—Social Attitudes: The 15th Report.* ed. Roger Jowell, et al. Brookfield, Vt.: Ashgate Publishing.

Karp, Jeffrey, and Susan A. Banducci. 2005. Electoral systems, efficacy and voter participation. In *The Comparative Study of Electoral Systems,* ed. Hans-Dieter Klingemann. Oxford: Oxford University Press.

Katz, Richard, and Peter Mair, eds. 1994. *How Parties Organize: Change and Adaptation in Party Organizations in Western Democracies.* Thousand Oaks, Calif.: Sage.

Keith, Bruce, et al., 1992. *The Myth of the Independent Voter.* Berkeley: University of California Press.

Kepplinger, Hans Mathias. 1996. Skandale und Politikverdrossenheit—ein Langzeitvergleich. In *Medien und Politische Prozeß.*, ed. O. Jarren et al. Opladen: Westdeutscher Verlag.

Key, V. O. 1966. *The Responsible Electorate.* Cambridge, Mass.: Belknap Press.

Kinder, Donald. 1983. Diversity and complexity in American public opinion. In *Political Science: The State of the Discipline,* ed. A. Finifter. Washington, D.C.: American Political Science Association.

———. 1986. Presidential character revisited. In *Political Cognitions,* ed. R. Lau and D. Sears. Hillsdale, N.J.: Lawrence Erlbaum.

Kinder, Donald, and D. R. Kiewiet. 1981. Sociotropic politics. *British Journal of Political Science* 11:129–161.

Kinder, Donald, and David Sears. 1985. Public opinion and political action. In vol. 2 of *The Handbook of Social Psychology,* ed. E. Aronson and G. Lindzey. Reading, Mass.: Addison-Wesley.

Kinder, Donald, et al. 1980. Presidential prototypes. *Political Behavior* 2:315–337.

Klein, Markus, et al., eds. 2000. *50 Jahre empirische Wahlforschung in Deutschland: Entwicklung, Befunde, Perspektiven, Daten.* Opladen: Westdeutscher Verlag.

Klingemann, Hans-Dieter. 1979. Measuring ideological conceptualizations. In *Political Action,* ed. S. Barnes, M. Kaase et al. Beverly Hills, Calif.: Sage.

———. 1999. Mapping political support in the 1990s. In *Critical Citizens,* ed. P. Norris. Oxford: Oxford University Press.

———, ed. 2005. *The Comparative Study of Electoral Systems.* Oxford: Oxford University Press.

Klingemann, Hans-Dieter, and Dieter Fuchs, eds. 1995. *Citizens and the State.* Oxford: Oxford University Press.

Klingemann, Hans-Dieter, Richard Hofferbert, and Ian Budge. 1994. *Parties, Policy and Democracy.* Boulder, Colo.: Westview.

Knutsen, Oddbjorn. 1995a. Left-Right materialist value orientations. In *The Impact of Values,* ed. J. van Deth and E. Scarbrough. New York: Oxford University Press.

———. 1995b. Party choice. In *The Impact of Values,* ed. J. van Deth and E. Scarbrough. New York: Oxford University Press.

Knutsen, Oddbjorn, and Elinor Scarbrough. 1995. Cleavage politics. In *The Impact of Values,* ed. J. van Deth and E. Scarbrough. New York: Oxford University Press.

Koch, Achim, Martina Wasmer, and Peter Schmidt, eds. 2001. *Politische Partizipation in der Bundesrepublik Deutschland: Empirische Befunde und theoretische Erklärungen.* Opladen: Leske + Budrich.

Kohut, Andrew, et al. 2000. *The Diminishing Divide: Religion's Changing Role in American Politics.* Washington, D.C.: Brookings Institution.

Kornhauser, William. 1959. *The Politics of Mass Society.* New York: Free Press.

Krosnick, Jon. 1990. Government policy and citizen passion: A study of issue publics in contemporary America. *Political Behavior* 12:59–92.

Krosnick, Jon, Matthew Berent, and David Boniger. 1994. Pockets of responsibility in the American electorate: Findings of a research program on attitude importance. *Political Communication* 11:391–411.

Kuklinski, James. 1978. Representativeness and elections. *American Political Science Review* 72:165–177.

Kuklinski, James, Robert Luskin, and John Bolland. 1991. Where is the schema? *American Political Science Review* 85:1341–1357.

Lane, Jan-Erik, and Svante Errson. 1991. *Politics and Society in Western Europe.* 2nd ed. Newbury Park, Calif.: Sage.

Lane, Robert. 1962. *Political Ideology.* New York: Free Press.

———. 1973. Patterns of political belief. In *Handbook of Political Psychology,* ed. J. Knutson. San Francisco: Jossey-Bass.

Laver, Michael, and W. Ben Hunt. 1992. *Policy and Party Competition.* New York: Routledge.

Layman, Geoffrey. 2001. *The Great Divide.* New York: Columbia University Press.

Lazarsfeld, Paul, Bernard Berelson, and Hazel Gaudet. 1948. *The People's Choice.* New York: Columbia University Press.

LeDuc, Lawrence. 1981. The dynamic properties of party identification. *European Journal of Political Research* 9:257–268.

LeDuc, Lawrence, Richard Niemi, and Pippa Norris, eds. 2002. *Comparing Democracies: New Challenges in the Study of Elections and Voting.* 2nd ed. Newbury Park, Calif.: Sage.

Leege, David, Lyman Kellstedt, et al. 1993. *Rediscovering the Religious Factor in American Politics.* Armonk, N.Y.: M.E. Sharpe.

Leege, David, et al. 2002. *The Politics of Cultural Differences: Social Change and Voter Mobilization Strategies in the Post-New Deal Period.* Princeton, N.J.: Princeton University Press.

Leighley, Jan. 1995. Attitudes, opportunities and incentives. *Political Research Quarterly* 48:181–209.

Lewis-Beck, Michael. 1984. France: The stalled electorate. In *Electoral Change in Advanced Industrial Democracies,* ed. R. Dalton, S. Flanagan, and P. Beck. Princeton, N.J.: Princeton University Press.

———. 1988. *Economics and Elections.* Ann Arbor: University of Michigan Press.

———, ed. 1999. *How France Votes.* New York: Chatham House.

Lewis-Beck, Michael, and Martin Paldam, eds. 2000. *Electoral Studies* 19, special issue, *Economics and Elections.*

Lewis-Beck, Michael, and Andrew Skalaban. 1992. France. In *Electoral Change,* ed. M. Franklin, T. Mackie, and H. Valen. New York: Cambridge University Press.

Lijphart, Arend. 1999. *Patterns of Democracy: Government Forms and Performance in Thirty-six Countries.* New Haven, Conn.: Yale University Press.

Linz, Juan, and Alfred Stepan, eds. 1978. *The Breakdown of Democratic Regimes.* Baltimore: Johns Hopkins University Press.

Lippmann, Walter. 1922. *Public Opinion.* New York: Harcourt, Brace.

Lipset, Seymour Martin. 1981a. *Political Man: The Social Bases of Politics.* Baltimore: Johns Hopkins University Press.

———. 1981b. The revolt against modernity. In *Mobilization, Center-Periphery Structures and Nation-building,* ed. P. Torsvik. Bergen: Universitetsforlaget.

Lipset, Seymour Martin, and Everett Ladd. 1980. Public opinion and public policy. In *The United States in the 1980s,* ed. P. Duignan and A. Rabushka. Stanford, Calif.: Hoover Press.

Lipset, Seymour Martin, and Stein Rokkan, eds. 1967. *Party Systems and Voter Alignments.* New York: Free Press.

Lipset, Seymour Martin, and William Schneider. 1983. *The Confidence Gap.* New York: Free Press.

———. 1987. The confidence gap during the Reagan years, 1981–1987. *Political Science Quarterly* 102:1–23.

Listhaug, Ola, Bernt Aardal, and Ingunn Opheim Ellis. 2005. Institutional variation and political support: An analysis of CSES data from 29 countries. In *The Comparative Study of Electoral Systems,* ed. Hans-Dieter Klingemann. Oxford: Oxford University Press.

Listhaug, Ola, and Matti Wiberg. 1995. Confidence in political and private institutions. In *Citizens and the State,* ed. H. Klingemann and D. Fuchs. Oxford: Oxford University Press.

Lovenduski, Joni, and Pippa Norris, eds. 1996. *Women in Politics.* New York: Oxford University Press.

Lupia, Arthur. 1994. Shortcuts versus encyclopedias. *American Political Science Review* 88:63–76.

Lupia, Arthur, and Mathew McCubbins. 1998. *The Democratic Dilemma: Can Citizens Learn What They Need to Know?* Cambridge: Cambridge University Press.

Lupia, Arthur, Mathew McCubbins, and Samuel Popkin, eds. 2000. *Elements of Reason: Cognitions, Choice and the Bounds of Rationality.* New York: Cambridge University Press.

Luskin, Robert. 1987. Measuring political sophistication. *American Journal of Political Science* 18:361–382.

Luther, Richard, and Ferdinand Müller-Rommel, eds. 2002. *Party Change in Europe.* Oxford: Oxford University Press.

MacKuen, Michael, Robert Erikson, and James Stimson. 1989. Macropartisanship. *American Political Science Review* 83:1125–1142.

————. 1992. Peasants or Bankers? *American Political Science Review* 86:597–611.

MacRae, Duncan. 1967. *Parliament, Parties, and Society in France, 1946–1958*. New York: St. Martin's.

Mair, Peter. 1993. Myths of electoral change and the survival of traditional parties. *European Journal of Political Research* 24:121–133.

————. 1997. *Party System Change*. Oxford: Clarendon Press.

————. 2000. In the aggregate: Mass electoral behaviour in Western Europe, 1950–2000. In *Comparative Politics*, ed. H. Keman. London: Sage.

Mair, Peter, Wolfgang Müller, and Fritz Plasser, eds. 2004. *Political Parties and Electoral Change: Party Responses to Electoral Markets*. Newbury Park, Calif.: Sage.

Mann, Thomas. 1978. *Unsafe at Any Margin*. Washington, D.C.: American Enterprise Institute.

Marks, Gary, and Marco Steenbergen, eds. 2004. *European Integration and Political Conflict: Citizens, Parties, Groups*. Cambridge: Cambridge University Press.

Markus, Greg, and Philip Converse. 1979. A dynamic simultaneous equation model of electoral choice. *American Political Science Review* 73:1055–1070.

Marsh, Alan. 1974. Explorations in unorthodox political behavior. *European Journal of Political Research* 2:107–131.

————. 1977. *Protest and Political Consciousness*. Beverly Hills, Calif.: Sage.

Maslow, Abraham. 1954. *Motivations and Personality*. New York: Harper & Row.

Matthews, Donald, and Henry Valen. 1999. *Parliamentary Representation: The Case of the Norwegian Storting*. Columbus: Ohio State University Press.

Mayer, Nonna. 2000. The decline of political trust in France. Paper presented at the meetings of the International Political Science Association, Quebec, Canada.

McAllister, Ian. 1991. Party voters, candidates and political attitudes. *Canadian Journal of Political Science* 24:237–268.

————. 1992. *Political Behaviour: Citizens, Parties and Elites in Australia*. Melbourne: Longman Cheshire.

————. 1996. Leadership. In *Comparing Democracies*, ed. L. LeDuc, R. Niemi, and P. Norris. Newbury Park, Calif.: Sage.

McClosky, Herbert. 1964. Consensus and ideology in American politics. *American Political Science Review* 58:361–382.

McClosky, Herbert, and Alida Brill. 1983. *Dimensions of Tolerance: What Americans Think about Civil Liberties*. New York: Russell Sage Foundation.

McClosky, Herbert, et al. 1960. Issue conflict and consensus among party leaders and followers. *American Political Science Review* 54:406–427.

McCrone, David, and Paula Surridge. 1998. National identity and national pride. In *British—and European—Social Attitudes: The 15th Report,* ed. Roger Jowell et al. Brookfield, Vt.: Ashgate Publishing.

Meyer, David, and Sidney Tarrow, eds. 1998. *The Social Movement Society: Contentious Politics for a New Century.* Lanham, Md.: Rowman & Littlefield.

Michelat, Guy. 1993. In search of Left and Right. In *The French Voter Decides,* ed. D. Boy and N. Mayer. Ann Arbor: University of Michigan Press.

Miller, Arthur. 1974a. Political issues and trust in government. *American Political Science Review* 68:951–972.

———. 1974b. Rejoinder. *American Political Science Review* 68:989–1001.

Miller, Arthur, and Stephen Borrelli. 1992. Policy and performance orientations in the United States. *Electoral Studies* 11:106–121.

Miller, Arthur, and Martin Wattenberg. 1985. Throwing the rascals out. *American Political Science Review* 79:359–372.

Miller, Arthur, Martin Wattenberg, and Oksana Malanchuk. 1986. Schematic assessments of presidential candidates. *American Political Science Review* 80:521–540.

Miller, Warren. 1976. The cross-national use of party identification as a stimulus to political inquiry. In *Party Identification and Beyond,* ed. I. Budge, I. Crewe, and D. Farlie. New York: Wiley.

———. 1987. *Without Consent: Mass-Elite Linkages in Presidential Politics.* Lexington: University Press of Kentucky.

———. 1991. Party identification, realignment, and party voting: Back to the basics. *American Political Science Review* 85:557–568.

Miller, Warren, and M. Kent Jennings. 1986. *Parties in Transition: A Longitudinal Study of Party Elites and Party Supporters.* New York: Russell Sage Foundation.

Miller, Warren, and J. Merrill Shanks. 1996. *The New American Voter.* Cambridge, Mass.: Harvard University Press.

Miller, Warren, and Donald Stokes. 1963. Constituency influence in Congress. *American Political Science Review* 57:45–56.

Miller, Warren, et al. 1999. *Policy Representation in Western Democracies.* Oxford: Oxford University Press.

Miller, William. 1990. *Media and Voters: The Audience, Content and Influence of Press and Television at the 1987 General Election.* New York: Oxford University Press.

Miller, William, and Richard Niemi. 2002. Voting: Choice, conditioning and constraint. In *Comparing Democracies,* ed. L. LeDuc, R. Niemi, and P. Norris. 2nd ed. Newbury Park, Calif.: Sage.

Miller, William, et al. 1990. *How Voters Change.* New York: Oxford University Press.

Milner, Henry. 2002. *Civic Literacy: How Informed Citizens Make Democracy Work.* Hanover, N.H.: Tufts University Press.

Monroe, Alan. 1979. Consistency between public preferences and national policy decisions. *American Politics Quarterly* 7:3–21.

Moon, David. 1990. What you use depends on what you have. *American Politics Quarterly* 18:3–24.

Morris, Richard. 1995. What informed public? *Washington Post National Weekly Edition,* April 10–16, 36.

Mueller, John. 1999. *Capitalism, Democracy, and Ralph's Pretty Good Grocery.* Princeton, N.J.: Princeton University Press.

Müller-Rommel, Ferdinand, and Geoffrey Pridham. 1991. *Small Parties in Western Europe.* Newbury Park, Calif.: Sage.

Muller, Edward. 1972. A test of a partial theory of potential for political violence. *American Political Science Review* 66:928–959.

Muller, Edward, and Thomas Jukam. 1977. On the meaning of political support. *American Political Science Review* 71:1561–1595.

Nevitte, Neil. 1996. *The Decline of Deference.* Petersborough, Canada: Broadview.

Nie, Norman, Jane Junn, and Kenneth Stehlik-Barry. 1996. *Education and Democratic Citizenship in America.* Chicago: University of Chicago Press.

Nie, Norman, Sidney Verba, and John Petrocik. 1979. *The Changing American Voter.* Cambridge, Mass.: Harvard University Press.

Niedermayer, Oskar, and Richard Sinnott, eds. 1995. *Public Opinion and International Governance.* New York: Oxford University Press.

Niemi, Richard, and M. Kent Jennings. 1991. Issues and inheritance in the formation of party identification. *American Journal of Political Science* 35:970–988.

Niemi, Richard, John Mueller, and Tom Smith. 1989. *Trends in Public Opinion: A Compendium of Survey Data.* Westport, Conn.: Greenwood.

Niemi, Richard, and Herbert Weisberg, eds. 2001. *Controversies in Voting.* 4th ed. Washington, D.C.: CQ Press.

Nieuwbeerta, Paul. 1995. *The Democratic Class Struggle in Twenty Countries, 1945–90.* Amsterdam: Thesis Publishers.

Nieuwbeerta, Paul, and Nan Dirk de Graaf. 1999. Traditional class voting in 20 postwar societies. In *The End of Class Politics?* ed. G. Evans. New York: Oxford University Press.

Noelle-Neumann, Elisabeth. 1967. *The Germans, 1947–1966.* Allensbach: Institut fuer Demoskopie.

———. 1981. *The Germans, 1967–1980.* Westport, Conn.: Greenwood.

Noelle-Neumann, Elisabeth, and Renate Koecher. 1987. *Die verletzte Nation: über den Versuch der Deutschen, ihren Charakter zu ändern.* Stuttgart: Deutsche Verlags-Anstalt.

Noelle-Neumann, Elisabeth, and Edgar Piel, eds. 1984. *Allensbacher Jahrbuch der Demoskopie, 1978–1983.* Munich: Saur.

Norpoth, Helmut. 1992. *Confidence Regained: Economics, Mrs. Thatcher, and the British Voter.* Ann Arbor: University of Michigan Press.

———. 1996. Economics. In *Comparing Democracies: Elections and Voting in Global Perspective,* ed. L. LeDuc et al. Thousand Oaks, Calif.: Sage.

Norris, Pippa. 1997. *Electoral Change in Britain since 1945*. Cambridge, Mass.: Blackwell.

———. 1999a. A gender-generation gap. In *Critical Elections*, ed. G. Evans and P. Norris. London: Sage.

———. 1999b. *Critical Citizens: Global Support for Democratic Governance*. Oxford: Oxford University Press.

———. 1999c. Conclusions: The growth of critical citizens and its consequences. In *Critical Citizens*, ed. P. Norris. Oxford: Oxford University Press.

———. 1999d. New politicians? Changes in party competition at Westminster. In *Critical Elections*, ed. G. Evans and P. Norris. London: Sage.

———. 2000. *Virtuous Circle: Political Communications in Postindustrial Societies*. Cambridge: Cambridge University Press.

———, ed. 2001. *Britain Votes 2001*. Oxford: Oxford University Press.

———. 2002. *Democratic Phoenix: Reinventing Political Activism*. Cambridge: Cambridge University Press.

———. 2004. *Electoral Engineering: Voting Rules and Political Behavior*. New York: Cambridge University Press.

Norris, Pippa, and Ronald Inglehart. 2004. *Sacred and Secular: Religion and Politics Worldwide*. New York: Cambridge University Press.

Norris, Pippa, and Joni Lovenduski. 1995. *Political Recruitment: Gender, Race, and Class in the British Parliament*. Cambridge: Cambridge University Press.

Norris, Pippa, et al. 1999. *On Message: Communicating the Campaign*. London: Sage.

Norton, Philip. 2000. *The British Polity*. 4th ed. New York: Longman.

Nye, Joseph, Philip Zelikow, and David King, eds. 1997. *Why People Don't Trust Government*. Cambridge, Mass.: Harvard University Press.

Offe, Claus. 2002. Social capital in Germany. In *Democracies in Flux*, ed. R. Putnam. Oxford: Oxford University Press.

Ohr, Dieter. 2000. Wird das Wählerverhalten zunehmend personalisierter, or ist jede Wahl anders? In *50 Jahre empirische Wahlforschung in Deutschland*, ed. M. Klein et al. Opladen: Westdeutscher Verlag.

Page, Benjamin. 1978. *Choices and Echoes in Presidential Elections*. Chicago: University of Chicago Press.

Page, Benjamin, and Charles Jones. 1979. Reciprocal effects of policy preferences, party loyalties and the vote. *American Political Science Review* 73:1071–1089.

Page, Benjamin, and Robert Shapiro. 1983. Effects of public opinion on public policy. *American Political Science Review* 77:175–190.

———. 1992. *The Rational Public: Fifty Years of Trends in Americans' Policy Preferences*. Chicago: University of Chicago Press.

Palmer, Harvey. 1995. Effects of authoritarian and libertarian values on Conservative and Labour party support. *European Journal of Political Research* 27:273–292.

Parry, Geraint, George Moyser, and Neil Day. 1992. *Political Participation and Democracy in Britain.* Cambridge: Cambridge University Press.

Patterson, Thomas. 1993. *Out of Order.* New York: Knopf.

———. 2003. *The Vanishing Voter: Public Involvement in an Age of Uncertainty.* New York: Vintage.

Pattie, Charles, Patrick Seyd, and Paul Whiteley. 2004. *Citizenship in Britain: Values, Participation and Democracy.* New York: Cambridge University Press.

Peffley, Mark, and Jon Hurwitz. 1985. A hierarchical model of attitude constraint. *American Journal of Political Science* 29:871–890.

Petrocik, John. 1996. Issue ownership in presidential elections, with a 1980 case study. *American Journal of Political Science* (August) 40: 825-850.

Pew Center for People and the Press. 1998a. *Deconstructing Distrust: How Americans View Government.* http://people-press.org/reports/.

———. 1998b. *Public Appetite For Government Misjudged: Washington Leaders Wary of Public Opinion.* http://people-press.org/reports/.

———. 1999. *Retro-Politics: The Political Typology.* http://people-press.org/reports/.

———. 2002. *What the World Thinks in 2002.* http://people-press.org/pgap/.

———. 2003. *Views of a Changing World 2003.* http://people-press.org/pgap/.

Pharr, Susan. 2000. Officials' misconduct and political distrust. In *Disaffected Democracies,* ed. S. Pharr and R. Putnam. Princeton, N.J.: Princeton University Press.

Pharr, Susan, and Robert Putnam, eds. 2000. *Disaffected Democracies: What's Troubling the Trilateral Countries?* Princeton, N.J.: Princeton University Press.

Pierce, John, et al. 1992. *Citizens, Political Communication and Interest Groups.* New York: Praeger.

Pierce, Roy. 1999. Mass-elite issue linkages and the responsible party model of representation. In *Policy Representation in Western Democracies,* ed. W. Miller et al. Oxford: Oxford University Press.

Piven, Frances Fox, and Richard Cloward. 2000. *Why Americans Don't Vote: And Why Politicians Want It That Way.* Rev. ed. Boston: Beacon Press.

Poguntke, Thomas. 1993. *Alternative Politics.* Edinburgh: University of Edinburgh Press.

Pomper, Gerald. 1975. *Voter's Choice.* New York: Dodd Mead.

———, ed. 2001. *The Election of 2000.* New York: Chatham House.

Popkin, Samuel. 1991. *The Reasoning Voter.* Chicago: University of Chicago Press.

Powell, G. Bingham. 1982. *Contemporary Democracies.* Cambridge, Mass.: Harvard University Press.

———. 1986. American voting turnout in comparative perspective. *American Political Science Review* 80:17–44.

———. 2000. *Elections as Instruments of Democracy: Majoritarian and Proportional Visions.* New Haven, Conn.: Yale University Press.

Price, Vincent, and John Zaller. 1993. Who gets the news? Alternative measures of news reception and their implications for research. *Public Opinion Quarterly* 57:133–164.

Prothro, James, and Charles Grigg. 1960. Fundamental principles of democracy. *Journal of Politics* 22:276–294.

Putnam, Robert. 1993. *Making Democracy Work.* Princeton, N.J.: Princeton University Press.

———. 1995. Bowling alone. *Journal of Democracy* 6:65–78.

———. 2000. *Bowling Alone: The Collapse and Renewal of American Community.* New York: Simon & Schuster.

———, ed. 2002. *Democracies in Flux: The Evolution of Social Capital in Contemporary Society.* Oxford: Oxford University Press.

Rahn, Wendy M., et al. 1990. A social-cognitive model of candidate appraisal. In *Information and Democratic Processes,* ed. J. Ferejohn and J. Kuklinski. Urbana: University of Illinois Press.

Reif, Karlheinz, and Ronald Inglehart, eds. 1991. *Eurobarometer: The Dynamic of European Public Opinion.* London: Macmillan.

RePass, David. 1971. Issue saliency and party choice. *American Political Science Review* 65:389–400.

Revel, Jean-François. 1983. *How Democracies Perish.* New York: Harper & Row.

Richardson, Dick, and Chris Rootes, eds. 1995. *The Green Challenge: The Development of Green Parties in Europe.* London and New York: Routledge.

Rieger, Gerhard. 1994. "Parteienverdrossenheit" und "Parteienkritik" in der Bundesrepublik Deutschland. *Zeitschrift für Parlamentsfragen* 25:458–470.

Riesman, David, et al. 1950. *The Lonely Crowd.* New Haven, Conn.: Yale University Press.

Robertson, David. 1976. *A Theory of Party Competition.* New York: Wiley.

Rochon, Thomas. 1998. *Culture Moves: Ideas, Activism, and Changing Values.* Princeton, N.J.: Princeton University Press.

Rohrschneider, Robert. 1993a. Environmental belief systems in Western Europe. *Comparative Political Studies* 26:3–29.

———. 1993b. New party versus old left realignments. *Journal of Politics* 55:682–701.

Rohrschneider, Robert, and Russell Dalton, eds. 2003. Judgment day and beyond: The 2002 Bundestagswahl. Special issue, *German Politics and Society,* summer.

Rokeach, M. 1973. *The Nature of Human Values.* New York: Free Press.

Roller, Edeltraud. 1995. Political agendas and beliefs about the scope of government. In *The Scope of Government,* ed. O. Borre and E. Scarbrough. Oxford: Oxford University Press.

Rootes, Christopher, ed. 1999. *Environmental Politics* 8, special issue: *Environmental Movements: Local, National and Global.*

Rose, Richard, ed. 1969. *Electoral Behavior.* New York: Free Press.

———. 1982. *The Territorial Dimension in Politics.* Chatham, N.J.: Chatham House.

———. 1984. *Do Parties Make a Difference?* Chatham, N.J.: Chatham House.

Rose, Richard, and Ian McAllister. 1986. *Voters Begin to Choose: From Closed-class to Open Elections in Britain.* Beverly Hills, Calif.: Sage.

———. 1990. *The Loyalties of Voters: A Lifetime Learning Model.* Newbury Park, Calif.: Sage.

Rose, Richard, William Mishler, and Christian Haerpfer. 1998. *Democracy and its Alternatives: Understanding Post-communist Societies.* Cambridge: Polity Press.

Rose, Richard, and Derek Urwin. 1969. Social cohesion, political parties and strains in regimes. *Comparative Political Studies* 2:7–67.

Rosenstone, Steven, and John Hansen. 1993. *Mobilization, Participation and Democracy in America.* New York: Macmillan.

Rucht, Dieter. 1998. The structure and culture of collective protest in West Germany since 1950. In *The Social Movement Society,* ed. D. Meyer and S. Tarrow. Boulder, Colo.: Rowman & Littlefield.

Safran, William. 2002. *The French Polity.* 6th ed. New York: Longman.

Saggar, Shamit, and Anthony Heath. 1999. Race: Towards a multicultural electorate? In *Critical Elections,* ed. G. Evans and P. Norris. Thousand Oaks, Calif.: Sage.

Sartori, Giovanni. 1968. Representational systems. *International Encyclopedia of the Social Sciences* 13:470–475.

———. 1976. *Parties and Party Systems.* New York: Cambridge University Press.

Scarrow, Susan. 2000. Parties without members? In *Parties without Partisans,* ed. R. Dalton and M. Wattenberg. Oxford: Oxford University Press.

———. 2001. Direct democracy and institutional design: A comparative investigation. *Comparative Political Studies* 34:651–665.

———. 2003. Making elections more direct. In *Democracy Transformed?* ed. B. Cain, R. Dalton, and S. Scarrow. Oxford: Oxford University Press.

Scarrow, Susan, Paul Webb, and David Farrell. 2000. From social integration to electoral contestation. In *Parties without Partisans,* ed. R. Dalton and M. Wattenberg. Oxford: Oxford University Press.

Schattschneider, E. E. 1942. *Party Government.* New York: Rinehart.

Schickler, Eric, and Donald Green. 1997. The stability of party identification in Western democracies. *Comparative Political Studies* 30:450–483.

Schlozman, Kay, Nancy Burns, and Sidney Verba. 1994. Gender and the pathways to participation. *Journal of Politics* 56:963–990.

Schoen, Harald. 2000. Stimmensplitting be Bundestagswahlen. In *50 Jahre empirische Wahlforschung in Deutschland.* ed. M. Klein et al. Wiesbaden: Westdeutscher Verlag.

Schuman, Howard, and Stanley Presser. 1981. *Questions and Answers in Attitudinal Surveys.* New York: Academic Press.

Schuman, Howard, et al. 1997. *Racial Attitudes in America: Trends and Interpretations*. Rev. ed. Cambridge, Mass.: Harvard University Press.

Schumpeter, Joseph. 1943. *Capitalism, Socialism and Democracy*. London: Allen & Unwin.

Scott, Jacqueline, Michael Braun, and Duane Alwin. 1998. Partner, parent, worker: Family and gender roles. In *British—and European—Social Attitudes: The 15th Report*, ed. R. Jowell et al. Brookfield, Vt.: Ashgate Publishing.

Semetko, Holli, et al. 1991. *The Formation of Campaign Agendas*. Hillsdale, N.J.: Lawrence Erlbaum.

Semetko, Holli, and Klaus Schoenbach. 1994. *Germany's Unity Election*. Cresskill, N.J.: Hampton Press.

Sennet, R. 1978. *The Fall of Public Man: On the Social Psychology of Capitalism*. New York: Vintage Books.

Shanks, Merrill, and Warren Miller. 1990. Policy direction and performance evaluations. *British Journal of Political Science* 20:143–235.

———. 1991. Partisanship, policy and performance. *British Journal of Political Science* 21:129–197.

Shapiro, Robert, and Lawrence Jacobs. 1989. The relationship between public opinion and public policy. In *Political Behavior Annual*, ed. S. Long. Boulder, Colo.: Westview.

Shively, W. Phillips. 1979. The development of party identification among adults. *American Political Science Review* 73:1039–1054.

Skocpol, Theda. 2003. *Diminished Democracy: From Membership to Management in American Civil Life*. Norman: University of Oklahoma Press.

Skocpol, Theda, and Morris Fiorina, eds. 1999. *Civic Engagement in American Democracy*. Washington, D.C.: Brookings Institution.

Skocpol, Theda, M. Ganz, and Z. Munson. 2000. A nation of organizers: The institutional origins of civic voluntarism in the United States. *American Political Science Review* 94:527–546.

Smith, Tom, and Paul Sheatsley. 1984. American attitudes toward race relations. *Public Opinion* 7:14ff.

Sniderman, Paul, Richard Brody, and James Kuklinski. 1984. Policy reasoning and political values. *American Journal of Political Science* 28:74–94.

Sniderman, Paul, Richard Brody, and Philip Tetlock. 1991. *Reasoning and Choice*. New York: Cambridge University Press.

Sniderman, Paul, Louk Hagendoorn, and Markus Prior. 2004. Predisposing factors and situational triggers: Exclusionary reactions to immigrant minorities. *American Political Science Review* 98:35–49.

Sniderman, Paul, and Thomas Piazza. 1993. *The Scar of Race*. Cambridge, Mass.: Harvard University Press.

Sniderman, Paul, et al. 1991. The fallacy of democratic elitism. *British Journal of Political Science* 21:349–370.

———. 2000. *The Outsider: Prejudice and Politics in Italy*. Princeton, N.J.: Princeton University Press.

Soroka, Stuart, and Christopher Wlezien. 2003. Degrees of democracy: Public preferences and policy in comparative perspective. Paper presented at the annual meeting of the American Political Science Association, Philadelphia, August.

Stanley, Harold, and Richard Niemi. 2000. *Vital Statistics of American Politics*. 7th ed. Washington, D.C.: CQ Press.

Stimson, James. 1999. *Public Opinion in America: Moods, Cycles, and Swings*. 2nd ed. Boulder, Colo.: Westview.

Stimson, James, Michael McKuen, and Robert Erikson. 1995. Dynamic representation. *American Political Science Review* 89:543–565.

Stokes, Donald. 1963. Spatial models of party competition. *American Political Science Review* 57:368–377.

Stokes, Donald, and Warren Miller. 1962. Party government and the saliency of Congress. *Public Opinion Quarterly* 26:531–546.

Stone Sweet, Alec. 2000. *Governing with Judges*. Oxford: Oxford University Press.

Stouffer, Samuel. 1955. *Communism, Conformity and Civil Liberties*. New York: Doubleday.

Studlar, D., Ian McAllister, and B. Hayes. 1998. Explaining the gender gap in voting: A cross-national analysis. *Social Science Quarterly* 79:779–798.

Sullivan, Dennis, and Roger Masters. 1988. Happy warriors: Leaders' facial displays, viewers' emotions and political support. *American Journal of Political Science* 32:345–368.

Swanson, David, and Paolo Mancini, eds. 1996. *Politics, Media, and Modern Democracy*. Westport, Conn.: Praeger.

Taagepera, Rein, and Matthew Shugart. 1989. *Seats and Votes: The Effects and Determinants of Electoral Systems*. New Haven, Conn.: Yale University Press.

Tate, Katherine. 1993. *From Protest to Politics: The New Black Voters in American Elections*. Cambridge, Mass.: Harvard University Press.

———. 2001. *Black Faces in the Mirror*. Princeton, N.J.: Princeton University Press.

Taylor-Gooby, Peter. 1998. Commitment to the welfare state. In *British—and European—Social Attitudes: The 15th Report*, ed. Roger Jowell et al. Brookfield, Vt.: Ashgate Publishing.

Teixeira, Ruy. 1992. *The Disappearing American Voter*. Washington, D.C.: Brookings Institution.

Thomassen, Jacques. 1994. Empirical research into political representation. In *Elections at Home and Abroad*, ed. M. K. Jennings and T. Mann. Ann Arbor: University of Michigan Press.

———. 1995. Support for democratic values. In *Citizens and the State*, ed. H. Klingemann and D. Fuchs. Oxford: Oxford University Press.

———, ed. 2005. *The European Voter*. Oxford: Oxford University Press.

Thomassen, Jacques, and Hermann Schmitt. 1997. Policy representation. *European Journal of Political Research* 32:165–184.

Tilly, Charles, et al. 1975. *The Rebellious Century.* Cambridge, Mass.: Harvard University Press.

Times/Mirror Center for the People and the Press. 1991. *The Pulse of Europe: A Survey of Political and Social Values and Attitudes.* Washington, D.C.: Times/Mirror Center.

Tocqueville, Alexis de. 1966. *Democracy in America.* New York: Knopf.

Toffler, Alvin. 1980. *The Third Wave.* New York: Morrow.

Topf, Richard. 1995. Electoral participation. In *Citizens and the State,* ed. H. Klingemann and D. Fuchs. Oxford: Oxford University Press.

Topf, Richard, Peter Mohler, and Anthony Heath. 1989. Pride in one's country: Britain and West Germany. In *British Social Attitudes: Special International Report,,* ed. R. Jowell, S. Witherspoon, and L. Brook: Brookfield, Vt.: Gower.

Uhlaner, Carole. 1989. Rational turnout. *American Journal of Political Science* 33:390–422.

Ühlinger, Hans-Martin. 1989. *Politische Partizipation in der Bundesrepublik.* Opladen: Westdeutscher Verlag.

Uslaner, Eric, and Ronald Weber. 1983. Policy congruence and American state elites. *Journal of Politics* 45:186–193.

van Deth, Jan. 2001. Soziale und politische Beteiligung: Alternativen, Ergänzungen oder Zwillinge? In *Politische Partizipation in der Bundesrepublik Deutschland,* ed. Achim Koch, Martina Wasmer, and Peter Schmidt. Opladen: Leske + Budrich.

van Deth, Jan, and Martin Elff. 2004. Politicisation, economic development and political interest in Europe. *European Journal of Political Research* 43:477–508.

van Deth, Jan, and Elinor Scarbrough, eds. 1995. *The Impact of Values.* New York: Oxford University Press.

van Deth, Jan, et al., eds. 1999. *Social Capital and European Democracy.* New York: Routledge.

Verba, Sidney, and Norman Nie. 1972. *Participation in America.* New York: Harper & Row.

Verba, Sidney, Norman Nie, and J. O. Kim. 1971. *The Modes of Democratic Participation.* Beverly Hills, Calif.: Sage Professional Papers in Comparative Politics.

———. 1978. *Participation and Political Equality.* New York: Cambridge University Press.

Verba, Sidney, and Gary Orren. 1985. *Equality in America.* Cambridge, Mass.: Harvard University Press.

Verba, Sidney, Kay Schlozman, and Henry Brady. 1995. *Voice and Equality: Civic Voluntarism in American Politics.* Cambridge, Mass.: Harvard University Press.

von Weizsäcker, Richard. 1992. *Richard von Weizsäcker im Gespräch mit Gunter Hofmann und Werner Perger.* Frankfurt: Eichborn.

Wald, Kenneth. 1983. *Crosses on the Ballot.* Princeton, N.J.: Princeton University Press.

———. 2003. *Religion and Politics in the United States*. 4th ed. New York: Rowman & Littlefield.

Wallas, Graham. 1908. *Human Nature and Politics*. London: Constable.

Wattenberg, Martin. 1991. *The Rise of Candidate-centered Politics*. Cambridge, Mass.: Harvard University Press.

———. 1998. *The Decline of American Political Parties, 1952–1996*. Cambridge, Mass.: Harvard University Press.

———. 2002. *Where Have All the Voters Gone?* Cambridge, Mass.: Harvard University Press.

Watts, Meredith. 2001. Aggressive political behavior: Predisposition and protest behavior. In *Politische Partizipation in der Bundesrepublik Deutschland*, ed. Achim Koch, Martina Wasmer, and Peter Schmidt. Opladen: Leske + Budrich.

Webb, Paul. 2002. Conclusion: Political parties and democratic control in advanced industrial societies. In *Political Parties in Advanced Industrial Democracies*, ed. P. Webb, D. Farrell, and I. Holliday. Oxford: Oxford University Press.

Webb, Paul, David Farrell, and Ian Holliday, eds. 2002. *Political Parties in Advanced Industrial Democracies*. Oxford: Oxford University Press.

Weisberg, Herbert, and Janet Box-Steffensmeier, eds. 1999. *Reelection 1996: How Americans Voted*. New York: Chatham House.

Weisberg, Herbert, and Steve Greene. 2003. The political psychology of party identification. In *Electoral Democracy*, ed. M. MacKuen and G. Rabinowitz. Ann Arbor: University of Michigan Press.

Weisberg, Herbert, Jon Krosnick, and Bruce Bowen. 1996. *An Introduction to Survey Research, Polling, and Data Analysis*. 3rd ed. Thousand Oaks, Calif.: Sage.

Weisberg, Herbert, and Jerold Rusk. 1970. Dimensions of candidate evaluation. *American Political Science Review* 64:1167–1185.

Weissberg, Robert. 1978. Collective versus dyadic representation in Congress. *American Political Science Review* 72:535–547.

Wessels, Bernhard. 1993. Politische Repräsentation als Prozeß gesellschaftlich-parlamentarischer Kommunikation. In D. Herzog et al., *Parlament und Gesellschaft*. Opladen: Westdeutscher Verlag.

———. 1994. Gruppenbindung und rationale Faktoren als Determinaten der Wahlentscheidung in Ost- und West Deutschland. In *Wahlen und Wähler*, ed. H. Klingemann and M. Kaase. Opladen: Westdeutscher Verlag.

———. 1997. Organizing capacity of societies and modernity. In *Private Groups and Public Life*, ed. J. van Deth. London: Routledge.

———. 1999. System characteristics matter: Empirical evidence from ten representation studies. In *Policy Representation in Western Democracies*, ed. W. Miller et al. Oxford: Oxford University Press.

Westholm, Anders, and Richard Niemi. 1992. Political institutions and political socialization. *Comparative Political Studies* 25:25–41.

Westle, Bettina. 1992. Politische Partizipation. In *Die EG-Staaten im Vergleich*, ed. O. Gabriel. Opladen: Westdeutscher Verlag.

———. 1999. *Kollektive Identität im vereinten Deutschland: Nation und Demokratie in der Wahrnehmung der Deutschen*. Opladen: Leske + Budrich.

Whitten, Guy, and Harvey Palmer. 1999. Cross-national analyses of economic voting. *Electoral Studies* 18:49–67.

Wilcox, Clyde. 1991. Support for gender equality in West Europe. *European Journal for Political Research* 20:127–147.

Wlezien, Christopher. 2004. Patterns of representation: Dynamics of public preferences and policy. *Journal of Politics* 66:1–24.

Wolf, Michael. 2002. Cognitive mobilization. PhD diss., Indiana University.

Wolfinger, Raymond, and Steven Rosenstone. 1980. *Who Votes?* New Haven, Conn.: Yale University Press.

World Bank. 2000. *World Development Report 2000*. Washington, D.C.: World Bank.

Wright, Erik. 1997. *Class Counts: Comparative Studies in Class Analysis*. Cambridge: Cambridge University Press.

Wright, James. 1976. *The Dissent of the Governed*. New York: Academic Press.

Young, Ken. 1992. Class, race and opportunity. In *British Social Attitudes: The 9th Report*, ed. R. Jowell et al. Brookfield, Vt.: Dartmouth Publishing.

Zakaria, Fareed. 2003. *The Future of Freedom: Illiberal Democracy at Home and Abroad*. New York: Norton.

Zaller, John. 1992. *The Nature and Origins of Mass Opinion*. New York: Cambridge University Press.

Zaller, John, and Stanley Feldman. 1992. A simple theory of survey response: Answering questions versus revealing preferences. *American Journal of Political Science* 36:579–616.

Zelle, Carsten. 1995. Social dealignment vs. political frustration. *European Journal for Political Research* 27:319–345.

Ziegler, Harmon. 1993. *Political Parties in Industrial Democracy*. Itasca, Ill.: F.E. Peacock.

Zimmerman, Michael. 1990. Newspaper editors and the creation-evolution controversy. *Skeptical Inquirer* 14:182–195.

———. 1991. A survey of pseudoscientific sentiments of elected officials: A comparison of federal and state legislators. *Creation / Evolution* 29:26–45.

Zuckerman, Alan. 1982. New approaches to political cleavage. *Comparative Politics* 15:131–144.

Index